HAWK'S NEST
SCHENCK'S CP.
McCOOK'S CP.
CAMP McNEIL
BOYER'S FERRY.
TOWNSEND'S FERRY.
MILLERS FERRY.
FAYETTEVILLE
WARNER'S
UNION SCHL.
DICKERSON
NOV. 12th
FLOYD'S CAMP
Laurel Cr.
HAWKIN'S
NOV. 14th
CROGHAN. KP
CASSIDY'S M.
NUGENT'S
NOV. 14th
McCOY'S M.
Big Loup Cr.
LIGHT'S M.
TO PAINT CR.
BLAKE'S OR KETON'S
SETTLE'S
KINCAIDS'
Loup Creek
TAYLOR'S
CAMP 12th.
TO PAINT CR
rmstrong Cr.

Best Regards
David L Phillips

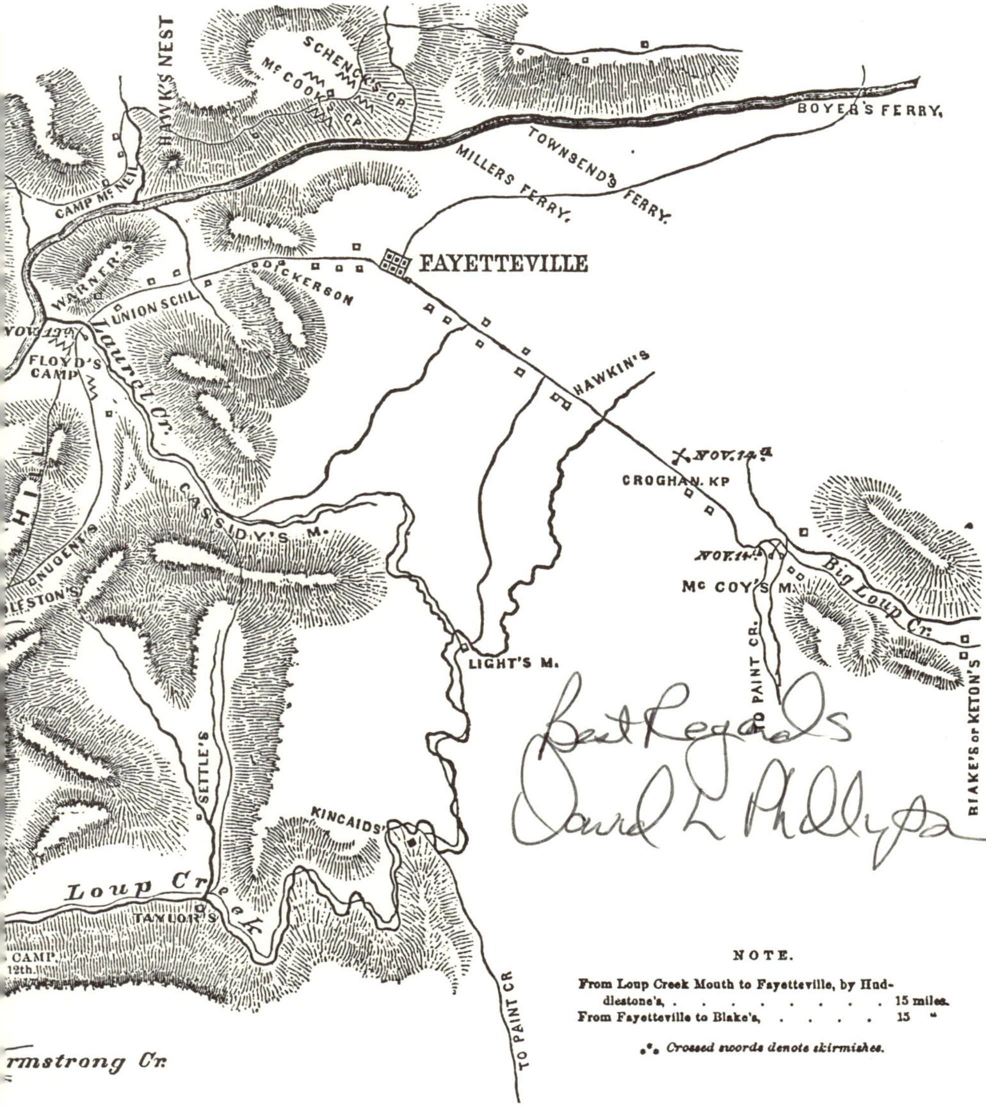

NOTE.

From Loup Creek Mouth to Fayetteville, by Huddlestone's, ... 15 miles.
From Fayetteville to Blake's, ... 15 "

*** Crossed swords denote skirmishes.

War Stories:

Civil War in West Virginia

Edited by

David L. Phillips

and

Rebecca L. Hill, Chief Researcher

Leesburg, Virginia

1991

Published in Leesburg, Virginia, by Gauley Mount Press, 313 Lounsbury Court, NE, Leesburg, Virginia 22075.

LIBRARY OF CONGRESS
CATALOG CARD NO. 91-74045

ISBN: 0 - 9628218-1-0

Printed in the United States of America

The purpose of this book has been to acquaint the reader with first-hand accounts of events that transpired long ago in West Virginia. Many of these events happened prior to the actual creation of the new state from Virginia's western counties and some of the authors were actively involved in either creating the new state or were just as active in attempting to prevent the severing of Virginia into two smaller states.

Civil War history should be of special interest to West Virginians, but there has been far too little of it in the histories which have been published in recent years. Unionists from the new state called her "The Child of the Storm" since the Mountain State was created as a direct result of the political maneuvering of the Federal government as Lincoln's government tried to control the Confederate rebellion. Splitting the strongest state in the Confederacy and admitting a new Northern state into the Union was both a political and military victory for the Federal government at a time when it was hard pressed by Lee's armies.

Unfortunately, very little information on the actual role of West Virginians during the Civil War has made its' way into modern histories. Legend and misinterpretation of facts leave most with a very simplified view of the history of the state and people are left with the impression that "West Virginia seceeded from Virginia in order to help President Lincoln free the slaves." Soldiers drawn from Virginia's western counties have been thought to have served primarily as Union "Home Guards" or as Confederate "bushwhackers -- both of whom changed uniforms to match those of the most recent local victors.

This is far from the truth! Men from Virginia's Trans-Allegheny counties served in at least fifteen Federal regiments, frequently with distinction. They fought throughout the South for the entire war. Federal regiments raised from Virginia's western counties fought under a local commander at the first land battle of the Civil War and others fought in nearly every other major campaign during the war. Three West Virginia cavalry regiments were formed into a single brigade and were assigned to Custer's Division in which they served with distinction. They earned thirteen Medals of Honor during the last week of the war as the Confederates retreated from Richmond and Petersburg.

There were a large number of western Virginians who served the Confederate cause with equal intensity. They often fought to ensure that their "Native State" remained intact among their southern sister states. An unknown number of West Virginians served in the Confederate military in "Virginia" regiments where their area of origin was never recognized by modern historians. At least ten infantry companies serving in the "Stonewall Brigade" were composed of West Virginians -- as was their illustrious commander. Four additional entire regiments of Confederate soldiers were raised in West Virginia and most of these men served through the war, unable to return to their homes in Federally-controlled territory. They were never accorded the recognition given to the Confederate Kentuckians, who under the same circumstances, became the "Orphan Brigade" in history.

The purpose of this book is to simply let readers review the thoughts of the participants in the combat of the war -- on both sides -- from *their* writings. Hopefuly, readers will be stimulated to use these as references as they begin their own historical research projects into the Civil War history of the "Child of the Storm", West Virginia.

Beuhring Jones should have a special place in our memories. He was a gentleman-officer who sincerely cared for the men under his command and wrote:

"...when at the close of the war, they, with streaming eyes and aching hearts, turned away from the 'Conquered Banner'.... In that sad hour, not more than a dozen of the original Dixie Rifles answered at roll-call.

David L. Phillips
Leesburg, Virginia

Acknowledgements

Special thanks must go to several people who were involved in the preparation of the manuscript. Liz Donnelly of the Central Intelligence Agency provided the translation of the "song" from A.B. Roler's diary; Harry Pugh provided illustrations; Becky Hill did most of the research; Susan Corbin produced a beautiful dust jacket; and Sue Phillips helped "translate" handwriting from the 1860's -- a very difficult task. Wick Walker provided the photograph of Nicholas Ramsey's grave which is reproduced on page 187 and my formatting errors left a page for it. Thanks to all for their assistance.

Dave Phillips

Contents

West Virginia was to see early combat in the Civil War as Virginia sought to stabilize her western counties lying adjacent to the Union states of Ohio and Pennsylvania. The inhabitants of these western counties were from a completely different social and political environment than those of their eastern cousins. There had been serious political problems between the two sections of the state of Virginia in the past and the new Confederate state government in Richmond was fully aware that active steps would have to be taken early in the war, if the western counties were to be retained in the Confederacy.

They quickly began to send military officers into the region to begin recruiting among the small farmers and townspeople living in the villages and hamlets in the mountain valleys. Initially, the turnout was relatively good, but the traditional animosity between the two sections combined with many interests in common with the western states began to have an effect.

It is an interesting story and is best understood if the campaign is explained by the participants. This book is a series of diaries, letters, and stories which were written by the men who fought in the Union and Confederate armies as they attempted to gain control of the Kanawha Valley and the remainder of western Virginia for their side.

Henry Howe published The Times Of the Rebellion in the West: A Collection of Miscellanies *in 1867. He explained the campaigns which were fought in the western states and his section on West Virginia is an excellent overview of the mountain-top war which was fought in the newly emerging state. It was published by Howe's Subscription Book Concern in Cincinnati.*

THE TIMES
THE REBELLION
WEST VIRGINIA

West Virginia early became a theater of military operations. These were on a comparatively small scale, owing to the difficulties of providing and sustaining large armies. The country as a whole may be defined as a collection of lofty mountains, with deep narrow valleys that seem to exist merely to define the mountains. Along these valleys are a primitive people, simple in their wants, dressing in homespun, and living a varied life of hunting and agriculture. They are scattered in cabins often miles apart, the mountains encroaching upon them as to leave but mere threads of arable land. The roads for want of room are much of the way in the beds of streams, which are swollen by every heavy shower to raging, impassable torrents. Bridges do not exist excepting at a few points. Military operations are very difficult; transportation at times being impossible.

The best part is in the Northwest, along the valley of the Ohio and its tributaries. In this section runs the Baltimore & Ohio Railroad, which forks at Grafton about 100 miles from the Ohio, one branch terminating at Parkersburg and the other at Wheeling. The secessionists at the beginning made strenuous exertions to hold this country, and suppress its union sentiment: also to possess the fertile valley of the Kanawha, so valuable to them for its abundant crops of grain and inexhaustible supplies of salt.

The first event of the war in West Virginia was the surprise by two union regiments under Cols. Kelly and Lander, on the morning of the 3rd of June, 1861, of some 1500 secession troops under Col. Porterfield, at Philippi, a small village on the Monongahela about 20 miles south of Grafton. None of the unionists were killed; and the loss of the secessionists trifling. The surprise occurred at daybreak; but it so happened that the secessionists mostly made good their escape. Their flight is amusingly described by one present. Said he "Did you ever drive a stake into an ant hill, and watch the movements of the panic stricken inhabitants? It was nothing to this flight. They didn't stop to put on their clothes, much less their shoes; grabbing the first thing they could reach, and dressing as they ran, each turned his face toward Beverly. One fellow had cased one leg in his unwhisperables, when the cannister came whizzing about him -- 'Delay was death,' and with his shirt streaming behind, and the unfilled leg of his pants flopping and trailing behind him, he presented a most comical figure. Some, half-naked, mounted horses unbridled, and grasping the mane, urged them into a sharp run by their cries and vigorous heel-punches. Many took to the thickets on the hills and among these unfortunates the Indianians, after the melee was over, ignorant of their presence, discharged their minie rifles, for the purpose of clearing their guns, and with fatal effect."

Gen. McClellan, in command of the department of the Ohio, for political reasons, refrained from crossing into Western Virginia until after the 27th of May, after the ordinance of secession had been voted upon in a state election. Then the western troops crossed over and took a position at Grafton. On the 11th of July, occurred the battle of Rich Mountain. At that period the secession forces under Gen. Garnett, numbering several thousand men, occupied near Beverly two entrenched camps -- Rich Mountain and Laurel Hill, a few miles apart. Garnett remained at the last named, leaving Rich Mountain under the immediate command of Col. Pegram. Rosecrans was sent with three regiments of Indiana and Ohio troops to make an attack on Pegram. Passing around the mountain, through miles of impenetrable thickets, Rosecrans, assisted by Col. Lander, made a spirited attack upon the upper intrenchment of the enemy, who were routed and fled. McClellan was preparing to attack Garnett, but he fled also. On the 13th Col. Pegram, who had been wandering in the hills for two days without food, surrendered unconditionally. When Pegram advanced to hand his sword to Major Laurence Williams, each instantly recognized the other, and both were moved to tears, and turned away unable to speak for a few moments. They had been classmates at West Point, and had met thus for the first time in many years. The number captured amounted to about 600. Pegram was killed late in the war, at the battle of Hatcher's Run, before Richmond, Feb. 1865.

The same day, Gen. Garnett, with the main body, on his retreat, was overtaken some thirty miles north at Carrick's Ford on Shafer's Fork of Cheat River, by the advance of Gen. Morris. He attempted to make a stand to cover his retreat: his men became panic stricken and fled before half their number. Here Garnett was killed by a sharpshooter. Not a Virginian was at his side when he fell: a young lad from Georgia alone stood by him bravely to the last, and when Garnett fell, he fell too. Garnett was about 40 years of age, a brother-in-law of Gov. Wise, and in the Mexican War aid to Gen. Taylor. He was a roommate at West Point of Major Love, of Gen. Morris' staff.

"But an hour or two before, the major had been talking about his former acquaintance and friendship with Garnett, and had remarked that he would be glad if Garnett could only be taken prisoner, that he might be able to see him again, and talk with him about the government which had educated and honored him. When the major reached the field, a short time after the flight of the rebels, he was led to the bank of the river, where the body of his old roommate lay stretched upon the stones! Who shall blame him for the manly tears he shed kneeling by that traitor corpse? The brave boy who fell by, was taken to the hill above the headquarters and buried by our troops. At his head they placed a board, with the inscription: "Name unknown. A brave fellow who shared his general's fate, and fell fighting by his side, while his companions fled."

The appearance of the battle field is thus described by an eyewitness.

"Returning from the bank where Garnett lay, I went up

to the bluff on which the enemy had been posted. Around was a sickening sight. Along the brink of the bluff lay the dead, stiffening in their own gore, in every contortion which their death anguish had produced. Others were gasping in their last agonies, and still others were writhing with horrible but not mortal wounds, surrounded by the soldiers whom they really believed to be about to plunge the bayonet to their hearts. Never before had I so gastly a realization of the horrid nature of this fratricidal struggle. These men were all Americans -- men whom we had once been proud to claim as countrymen -- some of them natives of our own northern states. One poor fellow was shot through the bowels. The ground was soaked with his blood. I stooped and asked him if anything could be done to make him more comfortable; he only whispered, "***I'm so cold!***" He lingered for nearly an hour, in terrible agony. Another -- young and just developing into vigorous manhood -- had been shot through the head by a large minie ball. The skull was shockingly fractured; his brains were protruding from the bullet hole and lay spread on the grass by his head. And he was still living! I knelt by his side and moistened his lips with water from my canteen, and an officer who came up a moment afterward poured a few drops of brandy from his pocket flask into his mouth. God help us! what more could we do? A surgeon rapidly examined the wound, sadly shook his head, saying it would be better if he were dead already, and passed on to the next. And there that poor Georgian lay, gasping in the untold and unimaginable agonies of that fearful death, for more than an hour!

Near him lay a Virginian, shot through the mouth, and already stiffening. He appeared to have been stooping when he was shot; the ball struck the tip of his nose, cutting that off, cut his upper lip, knocked out his teeth, passed through the head and came out the back of the neck. The expression of his gastly face was awful beyond description. And near him lay another, with a ball through the right eye, which had passed out through the back of the head. The glassy eyes were all open; some seemed still gasping with opened mouths; all were smeared in their own blood, and cold and clammy with the dews of death upon them.

But why dwell on the sickening details? May I never see another field like that! All around the field lay men with wounds in the leg, or arm, or face, groaning with pain, and trembling lest the barbarous foes they expected to find in our troops, should commence mangling and torturing them at once. Words can hardly express their astonishment when our men gently removed them to a little knoll, laid them all together, and formed a circle of bayonets around them, to keep off the curious crowd, till they were removed to the hospital, and cared for by our surgeons.

There was a terrible moral in that group on the knoll, the dead, the dying, the wounded, protected by the very men that had been fighting and who were as ready then as they had ever been to defend by their strong arms every right these self-made enemies of theirs had ever enjoyed. Every attention was shown the enemy's wounded, by our surgeons. Limbs were amputated, wounds were dressed with the same care with which our own brave volunteers were treated. The wound on the battle field removed all differences -- in the hospital all were alike, the objects of a common humanity that left none beyond its limits.

Among the enemy's wounded was a young *Massachusetts boy*, who had received a severe wound in the leg. He had been visiting in the South, and had been impressed into the ranks. As soon as the battle began, he broke from the rebel ranks and attempted to run down the hill, and cross over to our side. His own lieutenant saw him in the act, and shot him with a revolver! Listen to a tale such as that, as I did, by the side of the sad young sufferer, and tell me if your blood does not boil warmer than ever before, as you think, not of the poor deluded followers, but of the leaders, who, for personal ambition and personal spite, began this infernal rebellion."

Some amusing anecdotes were related in this battle.

Previous to the fight, before any shells had been thrown, a Georgian, who was behind a tree some distance from one of our men, called out to him, "What troops are you?" One soldier, squinting around his tree, and seeing that there was no chance for a shot at his questioner, replied: "Ohio and Indiana volunteers." "Volunteers! ______," exclaimed the Georgian, "you needn't tell me volunteers stand fire that way!" The day's skirmish presented some instances of extraordinary daring. Perhaps the most astounding was that of a fellow who undertook to furnish the news to the rebels. One of ***Milroy's Swamp Devils,*** (as the boys of the Ninth Indiana were called,) took a paper and deliberately walked up the road at the foot of the hill, on which the enemy were placed, till he got within convenient talking distance. Then asking them if they wouldn't like to have the news, and they answered in the affirmative, he unfolded his paper and began, "Great battle at Manassas Gap; rebels completely routed; one thousand killed, ten thousand wounded, and nearly all the rest taken prisoners; all traitors to be hung and their property confiscated!" By this time the bullets began to rain down upon him rather thickly, and he beat a rapid retreat to a convenient tree, carefully folding up his paper as he went, and shouting back that if they would come over to camp, he would give them the balance of the news!"

Another incident worth preserving is as follows:

In one of the Indiana regiments was a Methodist preacher, said to be one of the very best shots in his regiment. During the battle, he was particularily conspicuous for the zeal with which he kept up a constant fire. The 14th Ohio Regiment, in the thick of the fight, fired an average of eleven rounds to every man, but this parson managed to get in a great deal more than that average. He fired carefully, with perfect coolness, and always after a steady aim, and the boys declare that every time, as he took down his gun, after firing he added, "And may the Lord have mercy on your soul."

The loss in killed and wounded was slight. In the

result, the enemy were for the time being driven from Northwestern Virginia. The whole affair was a mere skirmish compared to a hundred later battles of the war, too inconsequential to be described in history. But it was the first decided union victory, and gave great eclat to Gen. McClellan, who, in the enthusiasm of the time, was in consequence transferred to the command of the army of the Potomac. A second Napoleon was supposed to have been found in the person of an ex-captain of the U.S. engineers.

The next engagement of importance was the battle of Carnifex Ferry, which took place on the 10th of September between the forces under Gen. Rosecrans and the rebels under Gen. Floyd, ex-secretary of war. Floyd's position was a high intrenched camp on the summit of a mountain in the forest, on Gauley river, opposite the precise point where the Meadow river falls into it. The intrenchments extended about a mile and a half in his front, each end resting on the bank of the river, which here by its curving formed a kind of a bow, while the intrenched line answered for the string. In the center of Floyd's line was an extensive earthen mound, supporting his main battery. The rest of his works were of fallen timber exclusively. The position could not well be flanked, and the only resource was to attack him in front. Floyd had six regiments and 16 pieces of artillery.

On the last day of August, Gen. Rosecrans, moved from Clarksburg, to put himself at the head of his army, and resume active operations. His plan was to engage Floyd in the region of the Kanawha line. After much delay, the army moved from Birch river toward Summerville on the 9th. On the 10th he marched eighteen miles, to near the intrenched position of the enemy, in front of Carnifex Ferry. At three o'clock in the afternoon he began the strong reconnoissance, termed the battle of Carnifex Ferry. This lasted until night came on, when the troops being exhausted, he drew them out of the woods and posted them in line of battle, intending to storm the works in the morning. In the night Floyd having become alarmed at the strength of the attack upon him, silently fled, crossed the Gauley and destroyed the bridge after him. Rosecrans took possession of the camp, captured a few prisoners, and some arms and some stores. The union loss was 114; among the killed was the brave Col. Lowe.

At the time Rosecrans was operating against Floyd, Gen. J.J. Reynolds of Indiana, was stationed with his brigade at the two fortified camps on Cheat Mountain, one called Cheat Summit, and the other Elkwater, seven miles apart by a bridle path. The rebel General R.E. Lee, desired to get into their rear into Tygart Valley, and once there with a large force he would have advanced against Grafton and Clarksburg, the principal military depots in Northwestern Virginia. On the 12th inst. he marched up the Staunton pike, with about 9000 men and from 8 to 12 pieces of artillery. He made attempts for several successive days to take these works; and was finally repulsed on the 15th. Among the rebels killed was Col. John A. Washington, proprietor of Mt. Vernon. He was shot by a small scouting party while reconnoitering, and at the moment he and his escort had turned to flee, the latter galloping off leaving their commander wounded and dying by the road side.

"The party ran up to the wounded man, and found him partially raised upon one hand, attempting to grasp his pistol. As they approached, the dying man smiled faintly, and said "*How are you boys? Give me some water.*" One of the party placed his canteen to the soldier's lips, but they were already cold in death. A litter was made, and the body carried to headquarters, when an examination of the person was made. Judge, if you can, of the surprise excited, when upon his clothing was found the name of *John A. Washington*! Four balls had passed through his body, two entering either lung and any one inflicting a mortal wound. A flag of truce was sent the next morning to the rebels, offering to return the body, and all the colonel's effects. It was met by Lieut. Col. Stark, of Louisana, who was coming to our camp to demand the body. When told that Colonel Washington was dead, Col. Stark was deeply affected, and for some moments was unable to speak at all.

He finally said, "Col. Washington's temerity killed him; he was advised not to go where he did, but was on his first expedition, and extremely anxious to distinguish himself." Col. Washington was attached to the staff of General Lee, as engineer, from which it is judged Gen. Lee in person commands the forces in our front. What a sad commentary Col. Washington's death affords us. His illustrious uncle, the founder of our liberties, the great leader in the war for our independence! The degenerate nephew, taken in arms, fighting against the government his progenitor has called into being; losing his life in attempting to undo what that noble man had done! To be shot in the back was a proper termination to the career of a relative who in selling at an exorbitant price the Mount Vernon estate to a patriotic association of ladies, had speculated upon the bones of George Washington."

Guyandotte, a town of about 600 inhabitants, situated on the Virginia bank of the Ohio, at the mouth of the Guyandotte, twelve or fourteen miles above the Kentucky line, was the scene of tragic events on Sunday night and on Monday, November 10th and 11th. The people were nearly all bitter secessionists. Col. Whaley was forming there the Ninth Virginia (union) regiment, and had with him on Sunday about 120 of his own men, and 35 of Zeigler's 5th Virginia Cavalry. A little after sundown this small body was surprised by a force of several hundred cavalry under the notorious guerrilla chief Jenkins. The attack was entirely unexpected, and Whaley's men were "taking it easy," some at church, some sauntering about, some asleep in their quarters, and only a camp guard out and no pickets. The men rallied and gathered in squads, sheltering themselves behind buildings and making the best fight possible, in which the gathering darkness increased their chances for escape. The rebels pursued the squads, charging upon them around the corners, running down individuals, killing some, wounding others, and taking prisoners. After the fight was over, they hunted many from places of concealment. As our men fought from sheltering positions, and the enemy were in the open streets, the loss was supposed to be nearly equal in killed and wounded, -- from 40 to 50 each. The enemy captured some seventy prisoners. The attack was accompanied by acts of savage barbarity. Some of the fleeing soldiers in attempting to cross the bridge over the Guyandotte, were shot,and those only wounded, while begging for their lives were thrown into the river to be drowned. Others were dragged from their hiding places and murdered. Some poor fellows who had taken to the river were killed as they were swimming, or when they had crawled out on the other bank. One John S. Garnett, who hid on that side was busy at this bloody business. A witness testified that he heard them shout across "John! Ho! John Garnett, shoot them _____ devils coming out of the water there," and two guns went off. "There is another just behind the tree." "Oh! I have that _____ Yankee." Soon another shot and a yell, "I've got one of the ___dad's scalps and a first rate Enfield rifle."

Early the next morning, the rebels fearing a pursuit, left the town, carrying off with them as prisoners some of the union citizens, having first taken and destroyed their goods. When they left, Twenty-one secession women, all with their secession aprons on, paraded and cheered the visitors. Col. Zeigler with a few union troops immediately landed from a steamer, arrested ten of the leading citizens as prisoners. As the people had fired on the troops from their dwellings, the soldiers set fire to the houses of the rebels, which communicating to the others, from one half to two-thirds of all the buildings in the place were burnt.

The guerrilla war in West Virginia was marked with many horrible atrocities and thrilling adventures. There was scarcely a county which did not contain more or less secessionists who degenerated into assassins. They shot down in cold blood their neighbors in open day, and at night stealthily burnt their dwellings. Hundreds of these villains were arrested, but for want of positive evidence discharged on taking the oath of allegiance: when they again renewed their acts of savage barbarity. So little was this sacred obligation observed, so venomous did they remain, that it had its proper illustration in the popular anecdote of the time, told of a union soldier who had caught a rattlesnake; and asked his companion "what should he do with him?" "*Swear him and let him go,*" was the instant response. A writer of the time well illustrates the fiend-like spirit that was rife in these paragraphs.

"A thrilling incident of the war occurred today, within two mile of Parkersburg. There lives in that vicinity a farmer named Smotherton. He is of the *genus* termed "white trash" by the contrabands; a renting farmer, who lives from hand to mouth, ignorant, quarrelsome and reckless. He has quite a family. Smotherton is a secessionist, a very bitter one, and he has imbued the idea and its spirit into all his family, from his wife down to his youngest child. The success of the federal arms has only served to embitter and enrage him, and time and again he has threatened to poison the water which supplies the camp at this place, to destroy by fire the property of his union neighbors, kill their cattle and mutilate their horses.

For several months he has done little else than make threats of this character. His wife was as bad with her tongue as he was, and even his children have been taught to hate and curse those who were for the union. Smotherton being informed he would be driven from the neighborhood if he did not improve his conduct, replied that he would not leave until he had destroyed the property and shed the blood of some of the union men. "They can't hurt me for it," he continued, "kase the war's commenced, an' there haint no law." That seemed to be his firm belief.

To-day two sons of Smotherton, the oldest not yet thirteen years of age, was out in the woods with a rifle. They came across another lad, named King, about the same age, whose family is for the union, and reside in the same neighborhood. The young Smothertons, following the example of their father, immediately called him to account. Young King stood up for the union, which so enraged the other two boys they threatened to shoot him. Young King then boldly straightened himself up and shouted, "Hurrah for the union." The oldest of the Smotherton boys -- not yet thirteen years old, remember -- deliberately raised his rifle, fired, and gave young King a mortal wound. To-night it is said he can not survive until morning.

As soon as the affair became known, a file of soldiers were dispatched from town to Smotherton's hut, which they surrounded, and, without resistance, took the old man, his sons, and two or three other prisoners. I need not say that the soldiers were disappointed in not meeting resistance, for they did not want to bring in any prisoners. The party was marched to town surrounded by bayonets, and committed to prison, to await examination, before the military authorities to-morrow. An indignant crowd followed them, and many voluntarily stepped forward as witnesses. An intelligent country girl said that she heard the boy Smotherton declare, several days ago, that he would shoot the boy King if he did not stop hurrahing for the union, for he (Smotherton) was a seccessionist, and he wasn't agoing to stand it.

Just such people you will find all over Western Virginia, and as their cause sinks they become more desperate, and endeavor to support it by blood and crime. Until they are treated and dealt with as traitors, the war in Western Virginia, will not approximate a close. Our troops curse the policy that has heretofore governed the military authorities, and now they take no prisoners whenever they can avoid it.

Retaliation, as stated above, at last became the common rule. The union scouts learned to take no prisoners. One of the best pictures which gives the lights and shadows of this border war, is drawn by a writer in the first year of the struggle, a union soldier from the New England settlement of Ceredo. He says:

In February, 1861, nine others and myself were threatened with expulsion from the "sacred soil" of the Old Dominion for voting for Lincoln: all residents of Ceredo. In May the war against us raged fiercer, and some of the marked ones left for fear of violence. Some of my neighbors could not leave if they would, and my courageous wife agreed with me that it was better to stay, for we might by that course do more good for the cause than in any other way.

In June and July the excitement was all the time increasing, and by the middle of the latter month it was publicly stated that the "Lincolnites" of Ceredo *must* leave, and notices to that effect were sent to us. We sent back word to them to "come on," we were prepared for them (but we were not though), and defied them.

For several weeks in the middle of summer we watched every night for the coming of the indignant secessionists. They looked for us to submit and take the oath of allegience to the Southern Confederacy, or leave. It was during this time of fearful peril -- for we had sworn to stand by each other and resist to the death if necessary -- that everything else was forgotten. All business was abandoned. The farmers who had been influenced by our position and action, left their crops and joined us in consultation and watch. They were made to understand that they were risking all their property and their lives, and perhaps the lives of their families, by joining us. But they pledged themselves willing to make the sacrifice, if need be, for the sake of the union. Our fears were reasonably increased by the treatment of union men in the adjoining counties, and we did not hope for mercy. The enemy outnumbered us who would *fight* more than three to one; yet our bold stand and defiant declarations kept them back. For many nights my wife did not retire to rest with any certainty that she would not be aroused before morning by the torch and bullets of rebel guerrillas, now organized in three different places in our own county, and in large numbers in the next and nearest county above us. A little band of twenty-five, and sometimes thirty or more, when our country neighbors came in, stood on guard through many summer nights, with such arms as we could pick up, waiting to resist the attack of three hundred or more; but I have no doubt we should have made a desperate resistance.

We had become so exasperated by the infamous threats of the rebels, and so incensed at their conduct toward the union men up the country, that we all felt that it was our solemn duty to resist.

Then began the organization of a regiment. One of the old residents was urged to take a lead in this; we New Englanders pledged ourselves to sustain him. It was a fearful undertaking, but we had the right kind of man to lead off, and it was successful. The rebels were of course indignant that we should attempt to have a military force in the "abolition" village of Ceredo.

It has been one continued whirl of bustle, and excitement and panic. It seems as though years ought to embrace the crowded events of the past few months. In fact, it does seem years since last June. I remember a few scenes, a few days, and the balance is one confused jumble of stirring incidents, panics, fearful and energetic struggles to calm the popular feeling, painful and tedious night watchings, long rides for reconnoitering, anxious consultations, and frequent renewal of pledges. It makes me shudder to think of the danger we escaped. I can hardly realize that we did pass through all and are yet safe, and that the dear ones at home were permitted to remain there, when danger passed so near, -- and particularily since we learned what nefarious plots were concocted for our destruction. While the recruiting was going on we were all the time in danger, and before the regiment was half full we had men out constantly on the scout, either to hunt rebels among the hills, or to guard union men's property away from our camp. While our men were taking prisoners and running the scamps from hill to hiding-place, the union men in Cabell county were rode over rough-shod. Every one who had a shot-gun or rifle, or a grain of powder, was robbed. The robbers also took beef and corn, and the union men in that country said not a word, for fear of faring worse. The few who dared to say anything were driven away or killed. Two others were shot, but recovered, and are now in the union army. One who had always maintained the right of a Virginian, clinging to the old government, was called to his door one morning by some of Jenkins' cowardly crew, and shot dead -- four of the assassins shooting at once. In our county, young men, who were out of the reach of our protection were *forced* into the rebel army. I can not describe with what a high hand many outrages were perpetrated -- how heartless and cruel, and with how little sense of honor, these "chivalrous southrons" committed numerous wrongs upon loyalists, upon their rights, liberty and property. However, every prominent secessionist in our country has been killed or taken prisoner. This is some consolation, though it does not compensate for the suffering of the loyal men.

I entered the army as a private, determined to be useful. I was put where it was thought I could be of most use, and have been constantly and ceaselessly engaged. My duties have not prevented my making some observations of the character and the moral effect of our enterprise.

How curiously -- to me it seems -- has this matter operated. The northerner and the Virginian, it appeared, could never affiliate. They never did. It was plain that a Yankee never would be respected by the Virginian; from the most ignorant to the most cultivated, there was the same inborn prejudice. If common courtesy and studied politeness of the educated man (Virginian) led him into sociableness and cordiality of social intercourse for a time, he would all at once assume a coldness as though he had forgot himself and done wrong. Among the ignorant it was still more unpleasant; but now all is changed. They now seem to think we are one nation -- we are all brothers -- we should all be united -- we should help each other -- we should not remember that one was from a free state, and another was born in a slave state. This is of the union men. The secessionists hate us more, if possible, and hate their neighbors who have joined us still worse. Nothing else, it appears to me could ever have destroyed this prejudice. And to us, who have seen this inveterate prejudice, this appears strange. Is it love of country, or is it the danger?

Who can tell?

I have witnessed many scenes in this brief time which I had never expected to see -- altogether a great deal of the worst of the "horrors of war," and mingled with the soldiers who are roughest and hardest, and heard their talk and their nonsense. Instead of feeling as though I had been hardened, or had become callous to the suffering of man and the cruelty of war, it seems as though the best feelings were sharpened. I know men who never before appeared to have any real and natural love for their families, manifest the best and most encouraging aspects of fraternal affection -- the most delicate and tender love for friends and families -- since this war commenced. Men, unconscious of the best feelings of cultivated natures manifest that tender and affectionate regard for their wives which we expect to see only among the most enlightened and harmonious families. Many of the natives are rough and uncultivated. *The war does them good!* So it seems to me. This is my question: why is it? How would you explain it? How is it possible that civil war, where there is much of awful tragedy, and wherein neighbor will shoot neighbor, to say nothing of the lesser wrongs and outrages, will improve men generally? While they talk so glibly of this one and that one of their acquaintance who are rebels, as deserving to be shot, they seem to be *progressing* in other respects. They become less selfish, more confiding, more generous, more considerate, and better men, I think, altogether. And this while we have not the best discipline in our regiment, and there is none too little whiskey in camp. Is it love for country? Is it that the union is in danger, or that their families are in danger? Would this last produce such an effect? Or is it that the *love for country is such a great and noble virtue that it increases other good qualities in men?* Yes, this is it, it can be nothing else.

The bitter contempt and hate with which the union men were held throughout the south at the outbreak of the rebellion, found full expression in their secession papers of which the following extract published in the Jeffersonian at

Barboursville, West Virginia, in May 1861, is a fair specimen:

Capt. Roger's company of volunteers are making preparations for service. They are a fine body of men, as true as steel, and fighting in the cause of liberty; *every single man of them is equal to a dozen of the base hirelings with whom they have to contend. In the hour of battle, we doubt not but what each man will prove himself a Spartan.*

Should old Lincoln grow so insane as to send 100,000 of his box-ankled Yankees up through this part of Virginia, our mountain boys will give them a warm reception, and *will be sure to save enough Yankee shin bones to make husking pegs with which to husk all our corn for a hundred years.*

A few months of actual experience dispelled some of those pleasant delusions in regard to the cowardice of union men. As the rebels were soon driven by our brave volunteers from their various camps at Philippi, Laurel Hill, Cheat Mountain, Gauley river and other points, they left behind in their panic hurry, bushels of private letters. These revelations of the inner life of the rebellion, are important contributions to the history of the times. They illustrate the ideas that prevailed among the poor whites of the South, their ferocity against the people of the free states; and an ignorance so profound as to show how readily they became the willing instruments in the hands of their aristocracy, to perpetuate and increase their own degradation. The most amusing of these were the love letters of which the camps were full. Some of the tender documents could not be exceeded in ferocity of spirit by the cannibals of Fejee. Mingled with good religious advice to husbands by wives to trust in the Lord and to offer up continued prayers for his guidance, are blended requests to kill every Yankee they met, and bring the scalps home as trophies of the war. Little children also write to their papa's for Union scalps, and tender swains and love stricken maidens all appear to revel in visions of blood. We open with one of this description.

Sewel Mountain October 3rd 1861

Dear Maiss Sarah marrgaret Waup I send you my best love and respects to you. I am well at this present time in hoping these few lines will find you in the same helth and in the Same mind as you was when I gote the last letter. My love is round as a ring that has no end and so is my for you. I waunt you not to foregit mea and pick up eny of the Raleign boys fore I am goun to sleep in youres arms if I live and the dam yankee devels dont kill mea. I still lives in hopes the devels Cant kill mea. I hope that we will Jine handes again. I waunt you to never have enything to Saye to the Raleigh boyes they are all purty mutch unean [union] mean I understand and that is a poore Cuntry I no. I have got youres likness yet and kiss hit evry day hites no ende that howe I lov you. I think of you when I am marced into the battle feal. I waunt you to ware the Seccions war riben a white peas of cloth around your wast; the unean [union] lades wars the black beltes around their wast. **

[The writer indulges in some thorough going profanity in reference to "Linken," and expresses a few uncharitable wishes respecting his future.]

* * mair margaret I would like to see you So we could laff and talk all about old times. My pen bade my ink is no count and I hant have but 8 minets to rite to you and I have to rite hit on my lapt. Pleas exkoose mea I have rote 6 letteres and reserved 3 from you and the hole of them thare was mise rote this you see remember mea if this is not except please exkoose mea and burn hitup

Sarah margaret Waup
JAMES BOLTON

From another letter found in Laurel Hill camp we take two lines.

"i sa agen deer Melindy weer fitin for our libertis to dew gest as we pleas, and we *will* fite fur them as long as GODDLEMITY gives us breth."

Here are two letters from loving maidens. The first

according to her own revelations had been some time "on the market."

Mr. _______, DEAR SIR; I take the pleasure in writing you a few lines to-night. And to answer the kind & excepted note. We are all well at present. I think that good health & company is all that one should wish for. I know that I am contented when I am in your good company, that I love to be in so much. But I hope the kind providence will soon permit us to be to gather soon. I wished that all of *those Yankees' heads was shot off and piled up.* Beck has formed a good opinion of you. But I think I like you the best. She said that she wished that she was married. She says that she wants me to put the holtar on first. There is no man here I care anything about now. I was once 12 years engaged, but am free now. There was a certain person told me to keep myself free from all engagements for him, but did not answer, and that was the last. I dreamt about you last night. I thought I heard you talking to papa. I tell you I was almost under John's control, but it may be for the best yet. If things had went on, I would of been married, some time ago. These are times to try persons faith and feelings. I think everyone should be candid. I know that you love me. That love can be returned. I am in for anything that you say, &c., &c.

Wyths vill VA August 17th 1861

Dear SUR -- it is with grate plesur for me to ancer yore letter I was glad to think that you thougt that much of me amany A time I think of you all and wod like to see you all but I think it will be A longe time be fore I will see you all but I hoape that it will not be so longe you sade that you had that arboviter that me and sue give you and that likeness that miss Sue Pattison had of yores she has got it yet. She sase that she is A goante to kepe it. The times air loancem hear know sence you all lefte hear. Il tell you that campe Jacksom lokes loancem know. I havente northen much to rite to you at this time but I hoape that I will have more to rite to you. The nexte time that you rite if that will ever be but I hoap that you will not forgit to rite. I woante you to excuse me for not hav ritten sooner but I cudent. I hearde this morninge that you all was a goanto leave thair and I thaute that I wod ancer it this eaven. I woante you to tell mr. yomce to rite to me. Ancer this as soon as you git this. I have northen more to sa at the present time but excuse bad riten and spellinge. Dearest frende

Miss MaryD McA

Here is a third maidenly letter found at Carnifex Ferry after Floyd's flight by some of Rosecrans' soldiers. It was in a highly scented white envelope. and was evidently adressed to one of the secession chaplains, that "Genuine itinerant Methodist minister." Miss Becky repels the base charge that she is given to tobacco chewing.

Rev. Wm. H. ______ Dear, in high esteem your very welcom letters arrived in due time, which were pleastant visitant. it was truely gratifying to hear of the abundance of good things you were blessed with in N. Carolina. I recon Egypt will certainly divide with Canaan.

Well Parson I suppose you are in the Dominion state this year among polished characters. I don't know how you can think of the plain people in Fentress Tennessee.

I would just say as it regard my useing tobacco it is altogether a false supposition. I protest the use of tobacco in every shape and form, so enough on that subject. Dear _____ I appreciate you as a genuine Itinerant Methodist minister and will take pleasure in any writen correspondence with you. There have been revivals on this mission since you left.

We expect Parson _____ at his appointment. Well Dearest _____ we are many miles apart Oh! the deep between us roll the rough Hills which intervene between you & I. yet all things are possible in the sight of the Lord. May the good Lord bless thee my dearest I hope you will find friendes that will treat you kindly. Oh! that this may be a glorious conference year. You are still remembered by Rebecca.

Things are going on smoothly.

Mary is primping and fixing herself looking for her beaugh. Dear me! Clear the way, move the chairs, & make room. Well Parson, I must now close by soliciting your prayers in my behalf. Respond to this the first opportunity.

Fare-well this time REBECCA _____

Oh! I remember how you looked
Remember well your silvery Tone
and placid smile of sweetest love
Though Many hours have rapid flown.

Poetical effusions in great quantities were found "to fire the Southern heart." This one is a fair specimen. It was obtained at Camp Gauley, among the official papers of the adjutant of a Virginia regiment:

Come all you brave Virginia boys
With hearts both stout and true
Come let us go down to the Mason line
And whip the Nothern crue

Old lincoln is there president
that evry body knows
And he was elected by the Vote
Of men as black as Crows

A Malgamation is ther theme
And that will never do
Come lets go down to the Battle ground
And Whip the Nothern Crue

Be brave and Bold you Valiant boys
And keep your Armors Bright
For Sothern Boys Wonts nothing else
But just the things that Right

God made the peopl Black and white
he made the red man to
And for to mix up is not Right
lets Whip the negro crue

if honor sease your Soards brave boys
And Muskets not a few
Come lets go down to the battle ground
And Whip the Nothern crue

Fight on Brave Boys with out a doubt
On til you gain the Field
The god of Battle he is stout
He will caus our foas to yeald

Our Wives and sweet hearts
tell us go and fight Just like a man
And keep the nothern negro crue
off of Virginue land

If luckey is our doom Brave Boys
in old Abe lincoln hall
On our next Independent day
We will take a Sothern Ball

and when we come safe home Again
Our wives and sweet harts to We
they will welcom us from Washington
for they have nothing elce to do
August the 14th 1861

The war in West Virginia was confined to small battles, skirmishes, and conflicts with guerrillas. One of the most important battles, in its consequences, in the latter part of the war, was that of Droop Mountain, in the Greenbrier County, Nov.6, 1863. In this action, the rebels were attacked in their works on the summit of the mountain by Gen. Averill, and routed with a loss of 400 men.

The guerrilla leaders, Jenkins and Imboden, were, for a time, active and enterprising, and the union troops were kept busy under Cox, Scammon, Crook, Averill, and other union officers, whose terror inspiring raids, and the hardships endured by those who took part in them, will show how noble a part was played in the great drama of the present age by the union loving sons of West Virginia.

The most noted of all raids was that of Averill in the winter of 1863-4. The object of the expedition, which was planned by Gen. Kelly, was to cut the Virginia and Tennessee railroad, and so sever the communication between Lee, in Virginia, and Longstreet, in Tennessee.

Several feigned movements were made in order to mislead the enemy, which were successful. The command of the real expedition was given to General Averill. On the 8th of December, he started from New Creek, near the Maryland border, with four mounted regiments and a battery, marching almost due south, which brought him almost directly between the confederate armies in Virginia and Tennessee. On the 16th, he struck the line of the railroad at Salem, and begun the work of destruction. The telegraphic wire was cut, three depots, with a large amount of stores, destroyed, and the track tore up, bridges and culverts destroyed for a space of fifteen miles; this was the work of a few hours. The enemy in the meantime had learned of his position and operations, and sent out six separate commands, under their ablest generals, to intercept him on his return. They took possession of every road through the mountains which was thought passable. One road, which crossed the tops of the Alleghanies, and was thought impracticable, remained. By this, Averill made his escape, carrying off all his material, with the exception of four caissons, which were burned in order to increase the teams of the pieces. His entire loss in this raid was 6 men drowned in crossing a river, 4 wounded, and about 90 missing. He captured about 200 prisoners, but released all but 84, on account of their inability to walk. In his report,

General Averill says, "My march was retarded, occasionally, by the tempest in the icy mountains, and the icy slopes. I was obliged to swim my command, and drag my artillery with ropes, across Crog's creek seven times in twenty-four hours. My horses have subsisted entirely upon a very poor country, and the officers and men have suffered cold, hunger, and fatigue with remarkable fortitude. My command has marched, climbed, slid, and swam three hundred and fifty-five miles in fourteen days."

What must have been the sufferings on such a march, from cold, fatigue, and hunger, in the depths of winter, in that dreary, inhospitable, mountain wilderness, surrounded by fierce, deadly enemies, thirsting for blood! Writes one:

The nights were bitter. It rained, snowed, and hailed. Imagine the gathering of clouds, the twilight approaching, the wearied soldier and footsore horse climbing and scraping up the steep mountain roads; then the descending of the storm, the water freezing as it touched the ground, the line winding its way up one side and down another, entering passages that seemed to be the terminus of these mountainous creations, and then emerging upon open lands but to fell the fury of the storm the more severe, and he can form but a mere idea of what was the scene on this trying occasion.

Winter warfare in the mountains of western Virginia was as difficult as any of the terrain where the armies confronted one another during the civil War.

The accounts of the war in this section were selected by people in Ohio after the war was over. The Ohioans were Unionists throughout the entire war and the selections reflect their feelings toward the rebels so soon after the war. It is natural that the stories and letters printed in this chapter of the book made the Southerners appear less educated and uncultured than their Northern counterparts. There were obviously many girls in the North who made spelling errors in their letters to their young men in the

Union army which were not published for an accurate comparison. Additionally, there were no letters or stories printed which were sent by well-educated and refined ladies of the South. These would have not have seemed to have been from a "simple, primitive people" or "white trash" that seems to fit the intentions of the Northern editors of the book.

There were some well-educated people in the South and quite a few lived in western Virginia. A few of the following stories will show that education was not limited only to the North.

Beuhring H. Jones was born in Virginia on May 12, 1823. His father was a farmer who saw that the son was well-educated and instructed in religious principles in a proud family that traced its ancestry to Christopher Jones, the captain of the Mayflower.

Just prior to the outbreak of the Civil War, Jones was practicing law in Palmyra, Missouri. He is reported to have opposed secession in the beginning, but after the call for 75,000 volunteers by President Lincoln, Virginia seceeded from the Union. Jones, like many other loyal Virginians in many areas hurried back to their home state where he raised a company of infantry, the Dixie Rifles, and on June 23, 1861, he and the new company of volunteers entered Confederate service.

He participated in the early fighting in the Kanawha Valley under the feuding generals, Wise and Floyd. He was active in the seven days fight before Richmond, and at Mechanicsville led his regiment in a bayonet assault against a Federal battery. He fought at Cedar Run and commanded his regiment in Loring's invasion of the Kanawha Valley in 1862. Later he was to fight at Cloyd's Mountain and commanded a brigade after McCausland was promoted following the capture and death of the seriously wounded Albert Gallatin Jenkins.

Beuhring Jones' last battle was against the invading forces of General Hunter at the battle of New Hope or Piedmont. He was leading a rearguard force, was captured, and was sent to Johnson's Island to spend the remainder of the war as a prisoner. While a prisoner of war, Jones wrote about his experiences as well as those of some of his fellow prisoners. After his release, he collected his manuscripts and those of other prisoners who were held with him and included them in a book, The Sunny Land, or Prison Prose and Poetry *which was published in 1868. The story of his initial experiences as a Confederate captain in Wise's army during the "retrograde movement" out of the valley was included in the book.*

MY FIRST NINETY DAYS
Or the Blunders of a Confederate Captain

About the middle of June, 1861, I raised a company of infantry in Fayette County, then a part of Virginia, and was elected captain, but certainly not on account of my familiarity with the pages of Scott, Gilham, or Hardee, as the sequel demonstrated, for I "had never set a squadron in the field, nor the division of battle knew more than a spinster."

In the latter part of the same month, the company, glorying in the euphonious and significant appellation of the "Dixie Rifles," was regularily mustered into the service of the Confederate States at the Great Falls of Kanawha, by Brig. Gen. Henry A. Wise, to whose "Legion" it was attached.

I had just returned from Lewisburg, and sported a gray jacket, gotten up by a tailor of that place, who, by way of securing the job, had assured me that he was perfectly "*Au fait*" in all the minutiae pertaining to the decoration of military rank. I was quite proud of my up-buttoned, close-fitting "Jacket of Gray," and felt all the importance of the commander, until I was startled from my dream of consequentiality by being addressed by an old soldier as "Corporal Jones" My "Knight of the Shears," equally ignorant with myself had braided me a corporal. My mortification was excessive, nor did I recover my usual composure until spasmodically I tore off the libelous braid, and cast it disdainfully upon the ground.

In the afternoon of that day it became necessary to draw rations and as our supply was at Gauley Bridge, two miles above our encampment and no transportation at hand, I was under the necessity of marching the men up, so they might carry down their "hard tack and bacon." Ignorant of the command necessary to form two ranks, or even to face them in the direction I wished to move, I took my orderly sergeant aside, communicated my intention to move at once upon the supply depot, and directed him to form the company in single line, with the men facing toward the bridge. He thought the suggestion a happy one, and proceeded to execute the order, by taking each man by the jacket collar and forcibly establishing him in the proper position, always accompanied with the important injunction to "stand right there."

At the command, "forward march," given with all the energy I could summon to the aid of a strong pair of lungs, the "Dixie Rifles" moved off in the most approved style. The interminable lines winding with the frequent curves and angles of the road, which coupled with the iregular and unrestrained swinging to and fro, from right to left, and from left to right, of one hundred and eighty awkward arms, brought forcibly to the mind the spiral and confused locomotion of a mighty centipede. Ever and anon, reaching a commanding point, I would cast backward a glance of pride and satisfaction at the vast proportions of my command. Caesar, Alexander, and Napoleon, at some period in their eventful lives, possibly, felt as well as I did then, but I will never concede that either of them felt any better. There was but one unpleasant drop in my cup of happiness. I knew that the company ought to march in two ranks, but how to get it into that shape was the rub.

I had warned the company on taking the line of march, that "talking" in ranks would not only be highly unmilitary, but could not be tolerated at all; so that not a sound broke the funeral silence of that two mile march, save once when an old soldier, who had seen service in Mexico, ventured to speak in a subdued tone to the man immediately in front of him. I detected this, and jealous of my authority as well as being indignant at so wanton a breach of military propriety and stung by what I suspected was a merited criticism upon the Indian file movement and consequently a reflection upon my military accomplishments, I sternly ordered him to be silent, reminding him that I was captain, and as such not to be trifled with, and that as an old soldier ought to know better.

At length we arrived at Gauley Bridge; the rations were

issued, and the order, "shoulder bacon and hard tack," was about to be given, when as luck would have it, up came a four horse wagon driven by a Nicholas county farmer. Fancy myself, by virtue of my captaincy, vested with extraordinary power, in other words a gentlemen of "high claims and terrifying exactions," I proceeded at once to press into service wagon, team and teamster. The farmer protested, alleging that he had been long from home, and could not reach there until late at night, but all this was unavailing. He had encountered what was afterward known as "military necessity," and as a matter of course had to succumb.

Now another difficulty stared me in the face. My men had fallen in line, facing Gauley Bridge and I wished to move them in the opposite direction but I did not know the command for a counter march. "File right" and "File left" were terms unknown to me, or if known, were utterly meaningless. I reflected a moment, nervously twirling my cane, for sword I had none, my face burning, my heart beating audibly, the men silent and expectant, until finally growing desperate, I cried out in the extremity of my agony, "Men, turn your faces the other way." Some turned to the right and some turned to the left, some made the entire circle and stood as at first, while others with countenances as blank as lamp posts, made no effort whatever to obey the order, while my sharpened hearing caught a half-suppressed sound of malicious laughter in the direction of the "old soldier." Finally with the aid of my orderly I got them all turned right and the interminable line that "Like a wounded snake, dragged its slow length along," returned to camp. Here the wagon of the Nicholas county farmer was speedily unloaded. The farmer then approached me in the most deferential, not to say awe-stricken manner, and stammered something about pay. I was astonished at his ignorance of the license of military authority, and indignant at his want of patriotism, replied with much spirit, "Pay, sir, pay indeed. No pay at all, sir. A mere gratuity that you as a loyal and patriotic citizen should esteem a priviledge to render to your country, sir; the Southern Confederacy, sir." With alarm, wonder, mortification and disappointment all depicted in his countenance, he shrank back, took up the lines, cracked his whip, and was soon out of sight. He should have thrashed me soundly on the spot, although at the time, I honestly believed that I was merely exercising an official perogative for the benefit of my country.

A happy idea now suggested itself. I would solve the vexed problem of forming a company into two ranks by being present when Captain Riggs' company was on parade. His men were formed in line. "Facing by the left flank, in two ranks, form company. Company, right face. March," said Captain Riggs. "Eureka!" I almost audibly ejaculated; then hurridly dodging around the corner of an old house standing close by, I hastly took my memorandum book from a side pocket, and eagerly recorded with pencil the talismanic words. By roll call next morning I had memorized them, and was enabled to accomplish the wonderful evolution of forming a company in two ranks to my own entire satisfaction. As to four ranks, I had never heard of such a thing, and should have been strongly inclined to question the sanity of the man who would have hinted the possibility of such a formation. Bear in mind, I had never mustered with the "melish" nor seen the inside of any work on military tactics. Mine was not an isolated case; it was the experience of nine-tenths of the Confederate officers. We were green, yes all of us succulently green.

The enlisted men drew rations regularly, but when I applied for mine, I was politely informed, much to my mortification, that "rations" were not issued to commissioned officers. "How am I to live, sir?" I anxiously inquired. "Indeed, captain, I am not able to answer your question, though I would be most happy to do so, for it is one in which you are most interested," replied the commissary, who was as ignorant of his duties as I was of mine, though not in half so much danger of starvation.

I had not been long at Gauley Bridge until it came my turn to act as "officer of the day" and I felt both complimented and alarmed. I was wholly ignorant of the duties of my position. Major Bradfute Warwick, who subsequently, as a colonel, fell covered with glory at Cold Harbor, was commandant of the post. He was an eastern man, and unacquainted with the geography of that part of Virginia and of the disposition of the inhabitants, and so fancied we were in constant danger of a surprise. In this he was most energetically seconded and sustained by Captain Buckholtz, an officer of much gallantry who was in command of the artillery. He instructed me to visit the pickets twice during the day and three times during the night. The distance to be travelled in making the rounds was about six miles. The roughness of the route, and the labor and peril to be encountered, can not be conceived by any one that has never experienced such a task. In addition to the regular pickets, men were stationed about seventy yards apart, connecting each post with the main camp. These men being perfectly "green" fancied a live Yankee under every bush, and were ready to fire at the least noise.

I was to start on my rounds at precisely nine o'clock. I gathered my blanket and repaired to the guard house. It had rained almost incessantly for "forty days and nights," consequently the rude floor of the guard house bore a strong resemblance to that of a pig sty. I scraped away the looser particles of mud, however, and spreading my blanket, lay down among the guards, Union prisoners, &c., but I consoled myself in my novel and uncomfortable position by the reflection that I was "serving my country," and that our forefathers had trod the same rugged pathway to glory and independence. Indeed my patriotism so far triumphed over my discomforts as to enable me to discover new beauties in the sentiment "*Dulc et est pro patria mori.*"

At the designated hour I was aroused by the officer of the guard, and then began the toil of the night. Varied and startling were the receptions and experiences of my dreary rounds. Sometimes it was a sharp "Halt! Who comes there?" Again it was a hesitating and nervous "Who's that?" And not infrequently it was the startling "click" of a lock that made each particular hair stand on end as the aroused sentinel made ready to fire. I was under the necessity of specially instructing each sentry. When I got back to the guard house I found it was just midnight, the hour for "Grand Rounds," so accompanied by a sergeant and three privates I started again. My experience was about the same as on the preceding round with one or two ludicrous variations. One sentry called out, "who comes there?" "Grand Rounds" was the reply, and this brought the response, "Come on, Grand Rounds." Another asked, "Who are you?" "Grand Rounds" we replied. "Oh, pshaw!" the sentry returned, "I thought it was them fellers coming to relieve me." With Grand Rounds completed, I found myself at the starting point at 3 A.M. wet, muddy and fatigued. I had made only two rounds and my instructions were to make three. To fail was in my opinion, death, ignominious death. I thought of my family which could be left in such unsettled and troublesome times without a provider or protector, and remembering how ill fitted I was for death, I nerved myself for the third round. Away I trudged all alone, and finished the third round about sunrise; the third round finished me about the same hour. I had travelled about eighteen miles, stubbing my feet against stones, falling over logs, jamming against stumps, splashing into mud holes, and wading a sluice of water no less than three times, thirty yards wide and three feet deep. As there were but three captains at a post, this task devolved upon me every third day. No wonder that my countenance grew haggard and wan, and my body weak and trembly, so that my own wife recognized me with difficulty. An iron man could not have endured such hardships unaffected. Yet I bore all cheerfully, and with martyr-like resignation and from a sense of duty, and because I thought at that time that the authority of a commanding officer was unrestricted, and that as a subordinate I was bound to obey all orders whether reasonable or unreasonable.

When commissioned officers were so verdant, what could have been expected of private soldiers? Passing from my quarters to the creek one morning after sunrise to indulge in my usual ablution, I was suddenly halted by a sentinel, some fifty yards to my right.

"Who comes there?" he fiercely demanded.

"Captain Jones."

"Give the countersign, Captain Jones."

"The countersign is not required at this hour."

"Yes it is. Give me the countersign," he screamed, cocking his long mountain rifle, and bringing it to bear directly between my eyes, so that I fancied I could almost see the bullet that was to finish my mortal career. It would have been imprudent to have shouted the countersign, surrounded as I was by laurel where an enemy might have been concealed, so I assayed to draw a little closer.

"Halt! Give the countersign, I tell you, or I will fire."

"I must get closer for I might be overheard."

"Don't care a darn. That's what the fellow said that came around last night, and I'm not going to fool with you much longer neither, Captain. So just sing her out."

Seeing that further parley or expostulation was not only useless but postively perilous, I yelled out "Jeff Davis."

"That's the truck, Captain. Hurrah for Jeff Davis! You can go now," and he resumed his beat.

So apprehesive of a surprise were the superior officers, all eastern men, that finally I got scared myself. I was called up one night by Sergeant Major Pierce who informed me that the enemy were actually crossing New river just above the mouth of Gauley, in great force using three flat boats for that purpose. I was ordered to awaken my men and get them under arms. The boys sprang eagerly for their guns, all but one poor fellow who was unfortunately at that moment attacked with violent pains in the region of the stomach. I was assigned a position in an oat field. Captain Buckholtz labored with great energy to get his artillery in position; wheels creaking, whips cracking, drivers swearing; there we stood in the field, shivering in the dark morning fog, with guns cocked, heads inclined eagerly forward, and eyes strained, vainly endeavoring to peer into the darkness; but no enemy came.

In the latter part of July we began the famous retreat or as General Wise persisted in calling it, the "retrograde" movement from the Kanawha valley. Cox had been whipped at Scary; but another army acting in concert with his movement, was seeking by way of Sutton, Summersville, and the Wilderness road, to gain our rear and thus not only cut us off from our base but capture our whole force. Such confusion and demoralization as then ensued have seldom been witnessed. One entire company, perhaps two, deliberately filed off and went home. Another scattered like frightened sheep; but the captain marched boldly on alone until becoming thoroughly disgusted, he broke his sword and wore his bars no more. Huge sides of bacon were pitched into the mud and trampled under foot. The heads of whiskey and molasses barrels were knocked in and every man helped himself. The Gauley Bridge that had cost $30,000 was burned although the river was fordable for infantry and cavalry about one hundred yards above. It was said, though I never credited the report, that the famous "Hawks Nest" was examined with an eye for its destruction, but was declared non-combustible, and was thus saved for the admiration of future tourists. Every man went it on his own hook. For the first twelve hours, despite the efforts of the general, orders were disregarded and system was lacking. Quartermasters were oblivious to obligations to furnish transportation. My company baggage had been carried across the ill-fated bridge by the men. I waited for transportation until near nightfall, and the bridge was already in flames, lighting the heavens from horizon to zenith with the lurid glare. The army had gone, its retreating footsteps echoing amid the gorges of Gauley mountain, still no transportation, nor would the last lingering quartermaster answer satisfactorily my inquiries. So I moved off, leaving all behind.

Darkness soon came on, and the rain descended only as it did in the summer and autumn of 1861 in the mountains of West Virginia. We had gone a mile when we met a wagon with a four mule team and a negro driver. I pressed into service the wagon, mules and driver, and sent them back and got my baggage. It was now so dark that we could only with difficulty keep the road. I halted the company, told the men to take care of themselves, and they scattered in every direction seeking shelter under rocks and trees from the pitiless storm. I crept down the hillside, carefully feeling my way, and found a dry spot under a huge rock. I called to one of my lieutenants, who soon joined me, and I told him to go in first; he did as I directed, and so completely occupied the whole of the space that I was compelled to lie all night in the rain. While sleep to me was impossible, I could hear the lieutenant snoring boisterously all the night. I had never before regretted being generous, but I did that night, and I think you will concede I had reason. When morning came, I was wet to the bone, and chilled to the marrow. We started again at daylight. General Wise was standing at the top of Gauley mountain. When we came up, he told me to halt my company. I did so, and he furloughed every man who wished to go by his home. The result was, I entered Lewisburg with ten men out of ninety. I was so emaciated and careworn that my most intimate friends recognized me with difficulty.

Having recruited and reorganized his command, General Wise again advanced toward Gauley, while General Floyd, taking the Sunday road, moved toward Summersville. Wise encountered Cox at Big creek, a few miles beyond Hawks Nest, and, after a brisk skirmish, kept up until evening, owing to the failure of a part of his programme, fell back four miles to Woodville (the early name for Ansted), and went into camp. Floyd, having crossed

Gauley at Carnifax Ferry, and entrenched himself on the cliffs, awaited Rosecrans, who, advancing from Cheat mountain, attacked him with great impetuosity. The Confederates, though though outnumbered at least six to one, resisted successfully every attempt to carry their position, until night-fall, when they withdrew with so much secrecy, that the Federal commander received the information of their retreat about sunrise the next morning, when his troops stormed and carried the undefended entrenchments. Floyd did not lose a single man in this battle but two were slightly wounded, one of them the general himself. Rosecrans must have suffered severely, as his men repeatedly assailed the works with great and persevering gallantry. Having recrossed the Gauley, Floyd fell back to Dogwood Gap, at the junction of Sunday road with the James river and Kanawha turnpike. Here he was rejoined by Wise. Cox and Rosecrans continued to advance with a force of at least 15,000 men, while that of the Confederates did not exceed 3,500. The latter fell back slowly to the top of Big Sewell mountain. Halting here a day or so, Floyd began to fortify, but suddenly changing his mind, he retired toward Meadow river, in Greenbrier county, and ordered Wise to follow, which he positively and indignantly refused to do, avowing his determination to oppose his 1,500 men against the 15,000 men of Rosecrans, and thus make a Thermopylae of Sewell mountain. He accordingly named his position "Camp Defiance," and cooly awaited the advance of the enemy.

It is not necessary to recount how, in a few days, Rosecrans came up and went into camp in an equally favorable position about a mile west of "Camp Defiance;" how General Lee came down from the Cheat mountain region, bringing reinforcements; how he examined Wise's position, approved his course, and ordered Floyd to return; how for three or four weeks the rival hosts surveyed each other from their respective mountain strongholds without coming to an engagement; how, confident of the issue, we, from day to day, prayed for the advance of the Federals;

and how, finally, one bright Sunday morning, when General Lee, as we were assured, had made up his mind to execute on the following Tuesday a great strategic movement that promised to result in the complete discomfiture of the foe, we got up and found he had struck his tents and precipitely retreated. I merely wish, in this connection, to relate one other of my adventures as a Confederate captain.

I was officer of the day. We were expecting Rosecrans to attack us. I wished to see the old officer of the guard. I did not know who had acted in that capacity the day before, and had not been enabled to find out by inquiry. I went to the guard tent and mentioned that I wished to see the old officer of the guard. A drummer suggested that if he were to sound his drum, perhaps the individual wanted would come to the guard tent. I can not understand why I thought beating the drum would produce such a result, or why the drummer thought so. I know, however, I caught at the suggestion, and when the drummer asked me if he should sound the "long roll," I answered affirmatively, adding that I supposed that would do as well as anything else. The fact was I had not heard of the long roll before, and did not know the special significance attached to it. He commenced beating the long roll. There happened to be one or two officers in camp who knew that the long roll was a call to arms to repel an attack, or something of that nature. In other words, it was an alarm. They seized their swords, sprang out and called on their men to fall in, instantly; other officers caught the infection and followed the example. In a moment the entire camp was an uproar, rivaling that of Babel itself. From every tent officers buckling on their swords, and privates with cartridge box in one hand and musket in the other, streamed forth like angry bees from so many hives, while above all other sounds, were heard the excited commands of officers, "Fall in, men, fall in!" "Back on the left!" "Out a little in the center!" "There, steady, front!" "Right dress!" &c, &c.

Had I been capable, at that moment, of remembering

anything at all that I had ever read, it would certainly have been Byron's"Waterloo":

"Ah! then and there was hurrying to and fro,
    And there was mounting in hot haste; the steed,
    The mustering squadron, and the clattering car,
Went pouring forward with impetuous speed,
    And swiftly forming in the ranks of war;
    And the deep thunder peal on peal afar;
    And near the beat of the alarming drum,
Roused up the soldier e'er the morning star;
  While the thronged citizens, with terror dumb,
   Or whispering, with white lips: 'The foe! they come, they come'!"

But cries of "the long roll!" "The long roll!" arising on all sides, assured me that I was the author of the mischief, and in the extremity of my mortification, I was senseless and dumb; and then Colonel Spaulding came rushing from his quarters, calling for his horse, and demanding in an excited manner, "What does all this mean?" If ever man desired "A lodge in some vast wilderness, some boundless contiguity of shade," deep, dark, impenetrable shade, at that one of the Bengal jungle variety -, I was certainly that man.

In reply to his question, I succeeded, by a desperate effort, in stammering out that there was nothing serious the matter; that I had told the drummer to beat for the old officer of the guard, and he had with my sanction, beat the "long roll"- I being ignorant of the peculiar import and the probable effect thereof.

For a moment, anger and a keen sense of the rediculous appeared to struggle for the mastery; but the latter triumphed, and directing his orderly to tell the captains to dismiss their men, with an emphatic smile on his countenance, he invited me to his tent, and there good-humoredly explained to me the mysteries of the "long roll." Brave , accomplished, generous Spaulding! Two weeks later his body, a bloody corpse, was borne in a blanket to camp by four of his men. He had approached too close to the pickets of the enemy, and received two balls through his breast.

A few days after the retreat of the Federals from Sewell, General Lee sent two famous scouts, one of them afterwards Captain William Heffner, who was killed at the battle of Lewisburg, in May, 1862. They were ordered to leave their guns in camp, as the object was information as to the location of the enemy. They found the enemy encamped in a field belonging to Colonel George Alderson. Under cover of the brush the scouts crept up to the fence enclosing the field, and while lying there, General Rosecrans and Cox rode up to within thirty yards, halted, and sat on their horses engaged in conversation for some time. Captain Heffner told me he could have counted the buttons on their coats. Had the scouts carried their guns, the career of the two Federal commanders would have ended that bright October morning. William Heffner and comrade were dead shots, and with their long mountain rifles, at two hundred paces.

Suffice it to say, that I afterwards saw much service, and endured much suffering, for I was in the field from the beginning to the close of the war, excepting from the 5th of June 1864, to June 19, 1865, during which time I was a prisoner of war at Johnson's Island. I was with Lee, in the swamps of South Carolina, on the sand hills of Wilmington, in front of McDowell at Fredericksburg; in the "Seven Days' Battles", on the Chickahominy. With Jackson, at Cedar Mountain; with Loring, in the Kanawha valley; with Ransom, in the southwest; with "Tiger John" McCausland at Piney, Princeton, and the Narrows; with Jenkins, at Cloyd's farm; and William E. Jones, at fatal Piedmont; but during those first "Ninety days" with Wise, in the Kanawha valley and on Sewell mountain, I underwent more real suffering and hardship, than in all after military life.

And the "Dixie Rifles"; where are they now? Alas! some are sleeping beneath the magnolias of the south; some on the hills of Fredericksburg; some at Mechanicsville, Cold Harbor, and Frazier's farm; some at Piney, Princeton and the Narrows; some at Cloyd's farm; some at Piedmont, Winchester, Kernstown, Cedar creek, Fisher's hill, and on the banks of the Opequon; some at the White Sulphur, Richmond, and Lynchburg; some at Camps Morgan and Chase; some at Point Lookout and Elmira; some have gone home with broken constitutions; some maimed and almost helpless for life. With their gallant comrades of the glorious "old 60th," they everywhere bore their full share of suffering, and danger, and death; and, when at the close of the war, they, with streaming eyes and aching hearts, turned away from the "Conquered Banner," which

"through gory,
Yet is wreathed around with glory,
And will live in song and story,
Though its folds are in the dust;
For its fame on brightest pages,
Penned by poets and all sages,
Shall go sounding down through the ages
Furl its fold though now we must."

In that sad hour, not more than a dozen of the original Dixie Rifles answered at roll call.

"On Fame's eternal camping ground,
Their silent tents are spread:
While Glory guards with solemn round
The bivouac of the dead!"

After he was released from the prison camp at the end of the war, Beuhring Jones was not allowed to practice his chosen profession, law. He returned to Lewisburg in poor health and rejoined his wife. He turned to newspaper work as an assistant editor of the Greenbrier Independent.

At the time of his death on April 28, 1872, he was the Assistant Secretary of the West Virginia Constitutional Convention which was meeting in Charleston. The assembly passed a resolution of sympathy which stated :

"In the death of Col. Jones, this Convention has lost

an efficient officer, the state a patriotic citizen, society an esteemed member, the bar an upright attorney, and the church an exemplary Christian."

The entire Convention attended his funeral.

Levi Welch was a member of the Kanawha Riflemen, a company of volunteers from the vicinity of Charleston, West Virginia, who served as infantry under the command of General Henry A. Wise. Welch participated in the 1861 Kanawha Valley campaigns, Wise's "retrograde movement" out of the valley, and was sent to Richmond as a guard for a group of prisoners. He became ill during the retreat from Cotton Hill in November, 1861, and was discharged because of poor health.

Welch recovered, was appointed a cadet at the Virginia Military Institute and was in charge of one of the cadet guns during the battle of New Market when the VMI cadets won fame and glory for their institution.

Welch was requested to write an article for the West Virginia Historical and Antiquarian Society by the society president, John P. Hale, also an early member of the Twenty-second Virginia Volunteer Infantry Regiment, then called the First Kanawha Volunteer Infantry. Hale was the artillery commander at the battle of Scary Creek, but had been trained as a physician prior to the war. He formed the society in which he served as president in 1890.

Welch sent Hale a letter on his recollections of the battle of Scary Creek and this was published in the West Virginia Historical Magazine Quarterly *in January, 1901. This was Vol.1, No.1 of this publication and a single copy cost $.25.*

Battle of Scary

Dr. J.P. Hale, Editor West Virginia Historical Magazine, Charleston, W.Va.:

Dear Sir: In compliance with your request, I herewith send you some of my recollections of the fight at Scary Creek, in this county, one of the first fights of the late Civil War.

The "Kanawha Riflemen," on July 17, 1861, were ordered from Camp Tompkins, near Coal's Mouth, to meet the advance of General Cox's Federal forces. Being a private in that company, my observations were confined, most of the time to a small field of vision.

The riflemen were deployed as skirmishers, in advance of the other troops, in front of Hale's Battery extending up the ravine along a brush fence. I was the last file on the left. With considerable interest, not unmixed with anxiety, I saw a glittering line of steel extend through the thin woods and cover our front. I saw, I think, the first puff of powder smoke and a bullet hit the stump on which I sat. A large beech tree was opportunely near me, and I immediately sought the protection of its trunk. As the puffs of smoke increased the beech tree seemed to wonderfully decrease in size. But for personal reasons I stuck to it. Captain Albert G. Jenkins, afterwards a Brigadier-General, came up the line of skirmishers, with his hat off, and the blood streaming down his hair and neck, and called for someone to go and get his horse, tied to a stake behind Hale's Battery. He did not, like King Richard, promise a kingdom for his horse, but I was thinking of the kingdom to come, and a chance to dodge it. So I left the beech tree, and ran through the brush, over a hill and mounted the horse. I rode up to the battery and saw a dismounted cannon being propped up for service by a lot of determined men. I asked one of them, "Where is my brother?" "Who is your brother?" "Lieutenant Welch of this battery." "There he lies. He has done his duty." Then I looked where the soldier pointed, and saw my brother upon the ground lying where he fell, with his head almost severed by a flying piece of iron from the cannon that he was aiming when it was struck and dismounted by a cannon ball. As he lay with both arms extended in the shape of a cross, he reminded me of Christ crucified. One died for all mankind, the other for his native state, with the same willingness.

I rode the horse to where I left Captain Jenkins, and when I tried to dismount, I could not get my foot loose from the stirrup, and he could not mount. I was very much afraid that the tangle would be undone by bullets, but solved the riddle by pulling out my camp knife and cutting the stirrup leather in two. I then repaired rapidly to my friend, the beech tree, and Captain Jenkins went his way in the fight, while I got the stirrup off my foot.

About this time a lot of our men rushed in on our left with blue trimmings on their uniforms. One of them fired at me, and I yelled to my next file on the right, that we were being outflanked by the Yankees. My gun, at this time, was unloaded. He turned, and taking the same view of the situation as I did, with a sudden aim, he shot one of the supposed Yankees through and through. I do not remember how the mistake was rectified, but it was, before the poor boy died. The artillery of the enemy for some time had been making the most noise, but suddenly we heard a new sound. It came from the "Peacemaker," (a gun cast by Mr. Job Thayer at his foundry in Malden) the new sound was caused by the miscellaneous missles it blew at the houses across the creek, behind which the enemy were fighting. Trace chains, mashed horseshoes and other kinds of scrap iron made the boards and shingles fly and the Yankees also.

The order passed to the skirmishers to rally on the center, which we did, and Lieutenant Nicholas Fitzhugh led us across the creek, and while we were burning some buildings to prevent their giving shelter again to the enemy, in case they should return, a lot of Federal officers rode up, supposing that we belonged to their army, on account of our incendiary occupation. One of them asked us where the rebels were. We closed in around the lot, and gave them the information sought. They were Colonel DeVilliers, Col. Neff and others. They consented after some parley to visit Richmond. I then got permission from Lieutenant Fitzhugh to go across the hills to the Upper Falls of Coal river, where my mother was at that time, and tell her the sad tidings of the death of her son.

Here ended my first lesson in the catachysm that followed.

Very respectfully,

LEVI WELCH

Levi Welch recovered his health, attended VMI, participated in the battle of White Sulphur Springs when he visited his former comrades in the 22nd Virginia during a school break during the late summer of 1863. He served as Colonel George S. Patton's aide-de-camp during that battle. Later he was put in charge of one of the artillery pieces of the Cadet battery at the battle of New Market. He survived the war and lived in Kentucky, then he moved to California, but he returned to Charleston where he wrote this letter late in life.

James D. Sedinger became a member of the "Border Rangers" on December 10, 1860 when the unit was formed as a volunteer company responsible for defending a portion of Virginia's Ohio River border. He fought through many of the early campaigns of the Civil War, and when the "Border Rangers" became Company E, Eighth Virginia Cavalry, Sedinger remained with the company for most of the remainder of the war. He and the "Border Rangers" participated in the raid into Pennsylvania during which Chambersburg was burned to the ground in reprisal for the burnings by Union troops in the Shenandoah Valley.

Sedinger was captured during the battle at Fisher's Hill on September 22, 1864, and he was a prisoner for the rest of the war.

He wrote a unit history which is a valuable study in the personal experiences of ordinary soldiers which is especially fascinating when the initial fighting is explained. Most of the pages have been reproduced, but a few pages were missing from the original manuscript. These missing pages are represented by ....in this reproduction. The original typescript is part of the holdings of the West Virginia Archives in Charleston.

THE BORDER RANGERS

This command was first organized at Guyandotte, Virginia, December 10, 1860, to protect a Virginia flag, that floated from a flag staff erected on the bank of the Ohio River, with Ira P. McGinnis as Captain. We kept the flag afloat until the 20th ofApril, when Albert Gallatin Jenkins came to see us and made us a speech, then we disbanded and went with him to his home at Green Bottom with what arms we could get, principally shot gun, and there we ate our dinners. Each man cut himself a piece of lead pipe off the Captains, for he had plenty. From there we went to the old Green Bottom Baptist Church and met the boys from Mason County, who were armed the same way we were. We then elected Albert Jenkins our Captain and started to the mouth of Coal River to go into camp. For the first time, we felt as if we were soldiers. We camped all night at Buffalo on the Kanawha River, on a gentleman's farm by the name of "Hall." He fed us and our horses and the next morning we started for St. Albans arriving about two o'clock that day. We went into Camp in the Episcopalian parsonage, had to cook our own dinners. There were just one hundred and one (101) of us reported to roll call the next morning. We were all mounted tolerably well. There we drilled cavalry drill and thought we could whip the world. Our commissary department was looked after by the ladies of Cabell and Mason Counties, who kept us well supplied with boiled ham, roasted chicken, baked light bread, biscuit, cake and pies, everything that they could think of to tickle the palate and we enjoyed ourselves better than we ever did afterwards. Our clothing, the same way, whenever a wagon would come into camp, the boys would make a break for it and he would be certain to find something for him from his sweetheart, sister or mother. After three weeks of this kind of life, we were detailed to do picket duty on the Kanawha

River Road, James River and Kanawha Turnpike.

We continued picket and scout duty until the 20th day of May, when we completed the organization by the election of H.C. Evertee, First Lieutenant, killed January 3rd, Jonesville,Virginia; A.H. Samuels, Second Lieutenant, wounded, Green River Bridge; G.W. Holderby, Jr., Second Lieutenant, Captain Company D, 8th Cavalry; Wm. R. Gunn, Orderly Srgt., McCuslands Brigade Cavalry, Major Quartermaster; James Smith, Second Lieutenant, Died 1861; Issac Ong, Third Srgt., died May 16th; James Norman, Fourth Srgt., Promoted Second Lieut.; John Thompson, First Corporal; Jesse Dodson, Second Corporal, afterwards promoted to Second Lieutenant; James D. Sedinger, Third Corporal; James M.Willington, Fourth Corporal, was sworn into Confederate service on the 29th of May, 1861, we continued to scout on starting out in the morning.

DeKalb Hughes, who was armed with a shot gun and an old horse pistol, his horse would not keep in line to count off by fours, struck his animal over the head with the pistol on the re-bound, the fire arm exploded, knocking Hughes off his horse and hurting him badly, but we finally started. During the march,when near Winfield, Putnam County, the advance guard came back with the word that the Yankees were advancing. The company was ordered to prepare for action. One of the young Blankenships, in getting his shot gun unstrung and capping the same, let it go off shooting his brother in the breast with buck shot, but not killing him, as he survived the war, but was never a well man. These, our only accidents, happening to us

....

During our first encampment at Coalmouth on the 11th day of July, we were ordered to Barboursville in Cabell County. We made the march in ten hours. On the morning of the 12th, the Second Kentucky advanced to Barboursville and charged the militia that was posted on the hill in front of the town. The militia, after delivering one fire, broke and left the field. The Company marched off the hill in order, without firing a gun and marched back to Coalmouth without the loss of a man or horse. We took the first of the regiment, but no one was hurt in the company. A Mr. Reynotch was killed by the fire and three others were slightly wounded of the Militia. The loss to the 2nd Kentucky was four killed and twenty wounded. We scouted the road as far down as Teays Valley. On the 14th the scouts discovered the advance of the 2nd Kentucky, taking the Winfield road for the Kanawha river. They reported the fact to headquarters, and the same scouts were ordered to watch the enemy on that road and watch the enemy on the Bill Creek road. On the 17th, John Thompson and another member of the Company on picket duty on the Bill Creek road discovered the Yanks moving by skirmish line through a cornfield, some three hundred yards away. They sat on their horses until the line came within one hundred yards of them, the Yanks opened fire on them. Both succeeded in getting away without getting hurt. Thompson lost his hat and false teeth.

This was at nine o'clock in the morning. The two men fell back on the infantry at the mouth of Scary. One of them was to Camp Tompkins after the rest of the infantry and the Border Rangers at the mouth of Coal. The Company fell in line and started, but were stopped by some young ladies who presented us with a flag. The Ensign was received by Captain Jenkins in a neat speech in which the promise was made that it should never be dishonored. The Capt. fought true to the promise and it was the only flag on the field at Scary and was literally shot to pieces. On that day, it was carried by the Company until the Battle flag was adopted by the Confederacy.

A member of the company brought the flag to this Country and gave it to a young lady to keep until the war was over, which was done, and the young lady, after the member of the old company was married, gave him back his flag. He laid it away to be cherished as a keepsake, but, his wife, who was of a practical turn of mind, one day in wanting some red striping for a rug, tore up the flag for that purpose, twenty years after the war was over.

The enemy drove in our skirmishers at Scary about eleven o'clock in the day and the fight opened in earnest. Our Company took position with our artillery. Capt. Welch was killed while sighting his guns. About this time the right flank was turned and the Yanks were firing at us from the right flank and rear. Capt. Patton ordered the Kanawha Rifles to follow him in a charge and he fell badly wounded. We now received some fresh troops from Coal Mountain who charged the flanking party and drove them back. The charge was successful in turning the left flank of the enemy, who now broke and left their Lieut. Col. Neff on the field and eighteen men killed, who we buried the next day.

Our company mounted their horses and rode over to where the Yankee line of battle was on top of the hill near Mrs. Simms house. While sitting there in line Col. Woodruff, Col. Devillius and their staff rode up to Captain Jenkins and said to him, "Well, you have given the rebels a good thrashing today," when he ordered them to surrender which they did with considerable grumbling. It was twilight and they could not distinguish our uniforms from theirs.

On the next morning some of the boys on going to the river to wash their faces for breakfast, discovered a Yank who had taken refuge in a hollow tree during the fight and pulled him. He was the worst scared man I ever saw. When we found Col. Neff after the fight, he was wounded and had been left on the field. The Capt. asked him who he was and he told him he was Colonel Neff. The Capt. dismounted, took him by the hand, and told him Mrs. Jenkins' words should be made good, that he should be treated gentlemanly and if we remember rightly he was paroled after having his wound dressed. It was in reply to what Col. Neff had told the Captain's wife, that if ever he caught her husband, he intended to hang him, but the tables were turned on the gallant Colonel in this his first fight.

The Colonel had moved his command from Gallipolis down on the Captain's farm, drove off all his stock and nearly everything that was moveable about the house. It was about ten days before the fight at scary that the conversation between the Captain's wife and the gallant Colonel Neff took place.

On the 19th of July the Company fell in and marched to the Ohio River. When we discovered the steamer "Fannie McBrownie"[1] coming up the river, the Company dismounted in a piece of woods and slipped down a ravine and hid themselves in a pawpaw thicket. The Captain walked out and hailed the boat. When she made the bank we charged her. Old Capt Blagg turned to Mr. Holloway, the pilot, and told him to back her out after hiding behind the smokestack of the boat. The pilot told him to come up and take the wheel if he wanted her backed out. We went aboard and searched the boat and took everything we could find that would do a soldier service. A case of swords and four revolvers was all we found on her.

We mounted our horses and rode down to the Captain's house. When we were about one hundred yards, Mrs. Jenkins met us and the Captain proposed three cheers for his little wife. The boys responded right nobly to the call and made the welcome ring. The family was placed in carriages and all the baggage in wagons and we started for the Kanawha Valley.

Upon reaching our old camp, we found that General Wise had ordered a retreat from the valley. We boys felt pretty blue over the matter as we had given the Yankees a thrashing on our side of the river, and Gen. Wise with three times the force we had, leaving without firing a gun, heard Officers proclaiming that West Virginia was sold out, but the old Company stuck to their colors and started up the Kanawha.

At Two Mile Creek below Charleston, the enemy had

---

[1] The actual name of the steamer was the Fannie M. Burns.

possession of the river bank and planted a battery to try to cut us off. We had two steamboats with us, carrying the commissary stores and the infantry, who had to leave their boats and come ashore. After setting them on fire and destroying them, we then ran the gauntlet of the infantry and artillery fire and continued our march up the Kanawha, leaving everything we held dear behind us- in possession of the enemy.

We went into camp at the mouth of Sims Creek and were ordered to act as rear guard from that time on, until we reached the White Sulphur Springs. Then the company was divided and two companies made of it, Capt. Corns was elected Captain of our Company and Joseph Ferguson Captain of the other, Captain Jenkins having resigned. We then formed a regiment and Capt. Jenkins was made Colonel of the Eighth Virginia Cavalry. The old, original Border Rangers were made Company "E" of the 8th and Furgeson's Company was made Company "K".

After remaining at White Sulphur Springs some ten days longer, the Company was ordered to move by forced march to join General Wise near Dogwood Gap on the James River and Kanawha Turnpike. We ran into an ambuscade, but no one was hurt. Colonel Jenkins had his horse killed under him and a number of the boys lost their hats and blankets.

August 25th, we were ordered to make scout on Peter's Creek in Nicholas County where we met the 7th Ohio Infantry. Sedinger was wounded and we fell back on the infantry, under General Floyd. We camped near Cross Lanes. The command formed line of battle and slept on their arms. The morning of the 26th, we moved in the direction of the enemy, who we found cooking their breakfast. The infantry charged the enemy and broke them all up. The Border Rangers then charged down the Peter's Creek road, capturing sixty prisoners, with their arms and accouterments. We then took charge of that road picketing and was left busy catching Yanks for about four days in the mountains on each side of Peter's Creek. On one of these scouts on Panther Mountain, George Rupell was badly wounded in the knee by a party of the enemy whom he met who was trying to get away from us.

On September 1st, General Floyd ordered Captain Corns to report to his company. Upon arriving were formed in line and the General and his men rode down the line and inspected the Company, whom he found armed with new Enfield rifles that we had taken from the 7th Ohio Infantry. He made us a speech, complimenting us on the part we had in the fight and telling us to keep the guns we had captured and never to lay them down until we had driven every Yank out of Virginia.

September 8th, Capt. Corns was ordered to Powells Mt. Upon arriving, we found Capt. Beckley trying to whip Rosencrans' army with the Logan Wild Cats. We under took to help them. When the Yanks sent a brigade of infantry on our flank, it was all we could do to make the run, but we were successful in our escape. Capt. Beckley and infantry started for Summersville and we tried to hold the road ourselves, but we could do nothing with them, as they kept a regiment as advance guard, so we fell back every time they developed enough strength to drive us. It took General Rosencrans twenty-four hours to move us from Fielding McClungs' to Nicholas C.H. We ate our breakfast and mounted our horses, for at this time, the cavalry of the enemy was on the outskirts of the town and we had to go again. We continued our march and rode into the breastworks at Carnifax Ferry with the loss of but two men, Doc Kennedy and James Poindexter, who were taken prisoners by the Rosencrans' cavalry at Summersville.

September 10th, the fight opened at Carnifax Ferry at about one o'clock P.M. by the infantry, led by Gen. Lytle, charging the left center of our line, which was repulsed after the General was wounded and fell from his horse -- the horse coming inside our breastworks. The fight continued until after dark, with all the advantages with us, for we lost only two men killed and six wounded.

After dark, we moved out of the woods and crossed the

Gauley River on our pontoon, bringing everybody and all our goods with us, gun, artillery, not leaving either our dead or wounded comrades with the enemy. The Company, acting as rear guard, the 11th of September, marched to Dogwood Gap again, joined our old Brigade (Wise's). We were then ordered to join our regiment at Fayette C.H. We marched to Loup Creek, the enemy being encamped at the mouth of Gauley River. There was continuous fighting between our outposts for ten days. The Company lost one man, E.C. Bramlette. The enemy finally crossed the river in force and drove Gen. Floyd from Cotton Hill. Driving from Loup Creek, we were thankful to get away, as the last three days we lived on baked pumpkin and parched corn - all that we could find to eat. November fifth, the Regiment was ordered to march to Guyandotte, Virginia. The boys were all happy then, we were going home for the first time since we left in the spring. We arrived November 9th, at 9 o'clock at night, and charged the town. The Border Rangers charged the suspension bridge and took it with orders to hold it. Upon arriving at the bridge, the drummer boy was beating the long roll and never quit until someone shot a hole through his drum. The Yanks were forming in companies on each side of the bridge against the railing. We went through them and dismounted on the west side of the bridge and formed at the end of the pier. About five minutes after forming the enemy concluded to cross and cut out. We waited until they were in fifty feet of us when we opened fire on them. What became of them after that I never knew, but think they jumped over the rail into the river. One swam ashore and came up the bank, and surrendered to us, Mr. James Woods, after staying where he was until all the firing ceased. We crossed the bridge over into town and kissed all the girls in the town. The company lost Al Long, killed, and Jo Collier and John McMahon wounded. Collier died from his wounds, but McMahon soon got well.

We captured all we could of the Yanks, their arms and commissary stores, put out pickets, and stayed all night and left the town the next morning with one hundred and ten (110) prisoners for Dixie. (The picket about the center of the suspension bridge fired his gun and killed Al Long. Someone of the Company shot him. This happened as we charged the bridge. Why he did not throw down and surrender was always a mystery to us. He was a small red headed man - would weigh about one hundred and forty pounds.)

We marched to Taverville C.H. and there received orders to go into winter quarters at the old camp meeting ground in Russell County, Virginia.

December 1st, Lieut. Everett received orders from Gen. Floyd to take his Company down Sandy and arrest Vincent A. Witcher and his command and bring them to his headquarters. We started and on the 6th of the month, found Witcher about two miles below Paintsville, engaged in a fight with some Yanks. We had to help him whip them, which we succeeded in doing after a right stubborn little fight, capturing the whole outfit. The men were paroled and their arms and horns turned over to General Humphry Marshall's command at Prestonsburg, Kentucky. General Marshall, upon ascertaining that Witcher was under arrest, ordered Everett to release him, which was done after the necessary papers were made out. We marched back to Russell Camp meeting ground and rested up a few days, and on on January 1st, 1862, the Captain received orders to report to Col. Junniper.[2]

We were ordered to Jumping Branch to do picket duty on all roads leading to Raleigh C.H.

January 25th, Lieut. Samuels and fifteen men went to Shady Springs on the pike leading to Raleigh C.H., formed ambuscade and waited for the Yanks who came along pretty soon and eight of them were killed or wounded. None of the Company were hurt. At the same time ten of the boys were sent to Richmond Falls on New River to

[2] This is Colonel Jennifer.

capture Wm. Richmond. They succeeded in their enterprise, but on the return trip, after marching all night, all the boys stopped at a house for breakfast, but Arthur Williams and the prisoner, who went on. After going about one mile, Richmond complained of being very tired and asked Arthur to let him ride behind him. Williams complied with his request and had not gone very far, before the first thing Arthur knew, Richmond was trying to cut his throat and came very near doing it, but Arthur succceeded in getting away from him, rolling off the horse on one side and Richmond on the other. Richmond had Arthur's gun which he succeeded in snapping at Williams, and then broke for the timber getting away. The young man was three months getting over his scuffle with Richmond, but he never let another Yankee ride with him - it made no difference how tired he was.

February 8th, the enemy drove us from Jumping Branch to the mouth of Bluestone on the New River, where we found the 45th Virginia Infantry in line, ready to receive our friends, the enemy. After a skirmish, lasting two hours, the boys fell back to Raleigh Court House, where they, leaving us in possession of the field, for which we were thankful to them, as most had fallen in love with some of the girls in the neighborhood and we did not want the Yanks to keep us hemmed up on the wrong side of Bluestone.

There was a little incident that happened while we were in camp there that ought to be preserved. One morning Lieut. Samuels asked one of the boys to go with him on an independent scout. They both started and after riding some time, four miles from camp, Samuels stopped at a farm house and told his friend to get off with him, as this was the end of the scout. When the people opened the door, Capt. Corns and one of his friends had charge of the fort. Samuels and his friend saluted the Capt. who addressed Samuels in this manner "Lieut., I understand you told Capt. James Sheffy that you thought I was a man who thought discretion was the better part of valor. I want to know if you said it." Samuels said to him, "Yes, sir, I made the remark and I believe and will prove it to you right now. You are armed, I see, draw your pistol, for here is mine." The Captain broke for the door, his friend with him, and Samuels hit the door facing with his shot as the gallant Captain beat a precipitate retreat for his horse. Samuels' friend asked him why he did this and his reply was that the Capt. did not show him any courtesy and he had simply given him a chance to get even and he accepted it.

We continued performing scout and picket duty as before, the enemy holding Shady Springs and Princeton and the Company holding the country between Shady Springs and Princeton. March 10th, we received orders to report to Princeton forthwith. Upon arriving at Princeton, we found the town deserted and the enemy just coming in. We fell back from them fighting them as best as we could and whenever an opportunity presented itself until we reached Sedden, the county seat of Bland County, Virginia, where we found the regiment. From Sedden, we marched to Wolf's Creek and went into camp. We received orders to mount and move on to Pearisburg, the county seat of Giles County, Virginia. We found the enemy in possession of the town. The infantry moved on them and a charge was ordered and right gallantly responded to by the men. We drove them to the mouth of East River and fell back to the Narrows of New River which we fortified and the Company was sent up Wolf's Creek to picket all roads that led to Princeton.

While the company was performing this duty, Capt. Corns was elected Col. of the regiment and H.C. Everett, Captain, A.H. Samuels, Ist Lieut., and John Thompson, Jr., 2nd Lieut.

On May 15th the 34th Ohio Infantry crossed the East River Mountain by a bridle path and surprised the company. They succeeded in killing Ed Doyle, capturing John Ong and Thad Flowers - no one else hurt or lost. On the 16th, Lieut. Samuels and twenty men sent to the mouth of East River and the Monroe side of the river and there were deployed as sharp shooters, fighting the 12th Ohio Infantry and a battery of six pieces. We didn't lose a man or horse during the time.

On the morning of the 18th, our forces on the Mercer side of the river moved down the river on the enemy who left in a hurry. The twenty men on the Monroe side under Samuels forced the river and joined the company, who led the advance until within two miles of Princeton where at dark we ran into three piles of knapsacks which belonged to three different regiments. It being dark, we could not tell what to do and waited for the infantry to come up. While waiting, some of the boys, hearing the rumbling of wheels, became demoralized and yelled that the enemy was planting artillery in the road to shell us. We ran away and did not return for three days. General Heath[3] and staff came up and ordered us to fall back. We hated to leave our capture, but some of the boys nailed three or four knapsacks apiece and spent the next day seeing what they could find that would be of benefit to them. There was a good many letters from their sweethearts that afforded the boys considerable amusement. The enemy retreated from Princeton ....

The line of battle charged the enemy with Rowan's Battery - lost all the guns and left the field as we saw it in a disgraceful manner. General Heath ordered a retreat with the loss of one battery and some fifty prisoners. The Company covered the retreat back to Union in Monroe County. The enemy left Lewisburg that night and gave us Greenbrier County, which we soon occupied. Gen. Jenkins was sent to us and took command of the cavalry at this time. We stayed in Monroe and Greenbier Counties until the 20th of August, when we left for the Tygarts Valley. Our command consisted of the 8th Cavalry and Jackson's Battalion.

We struck a scouting party of the Yanks about eight

3 General Henry Heth pronounced his name "Heath."

miles from Beverly with the advance. The General ordered a charge and led the attack. The party all ran but the officer, who undertook to fight all of us. The officer was killed, John Thompson had his horse shot. Gen. Jenkins then flanked to the left with the command and crossed the Rich Mountain.

He ordered Capt. Everett to hold Tygarts Valley with our company until dark and then to follow the command, which we did. We marched all night, reaching the Brigade at daylight next morning. The Company fed and ate breakfast, slept about one hour and started after the command again, about ten miles in the rear. The first cross roads we came to in our march, we found about one hundred citizens had assembled with shot guns and squirrel rifles to dispute our passage. Everett ordered a charge and the citizens broke after firing at us and we had lots of sport catching them. It appeared to me that they were all in uniforms as each and every one of them had red flannel backs in his vest and in his shirt sleeves. All of them we caught, we took their guns away and Everett told them to go home and behave themselves or some of them would get killed.

We had to make three different charges from French Creek to Buchannon that morning all about like the first one. There were none of the Company hurt, but several of them had close calls there. The militia did not fare so well as several of them were hurt pretty bad.

The General and command had captured the town before we caught up with them captured one hundred and thirty (130) prisoners and a great quantity of all kinds of food including sugar, coffee, flour, bacon, clothing of all kinds, five thousand muskets, one piece of artillery. All this stuff was burned up and destroyed. General Jenkins paroled the prisoners and we started on our march to Weston that night in time to reach the town at daylight.

The morning of the 1st of September, it was a foggy morning and the Col. detailed twenty men of the Company to locate the enemy who we were told had concluded to use the foundation of the asylum as breastworks. The twenty men felt their way close to the walls, but found the enemy gone, and sent one of the boys back to the General with the information that the enemy had gone. The twenty men deployed as skirmishers, went across the open field and found the camp of the enemy in possession of a few camp stragglers who they took in, and found that it was the Sixth West Virginia Regiment who had left sometime in the night. They did not know when. Pretty soon, the infantry picket came in and they surendered to us. The Gen. paroled fifty prisoners here and destroyed everything that was left - camp equipage and stores.

We started on our march for Grantsville, but found no enemy there and resumed our march and started for Spencer. On our way, the advance in passing a farm house, an old lady having seen us, came running to the fence - her hair disordered and her homespun dress half fastened, very much excited as she asked us who we were. The boys told her we were Confederate soldiers. She, upon receiving this, commenced yelling for Jeff Davis and singing, "Glory Hallelujah, is my son John with you?" We did not know John, so we had to leave her.

Upon arriving near Spencer, the advance halted and waited for command to come up, as we had learned the fact that Rathbone's Regiment 11th West Virginia Infantry and Capt. John P.Baggs company independent scouts. The General then spread the command out so as to show off as large as possible. We did look as if we were some three thousand strong and we were in plain view of Spencer. The General sent in a flag of arms and run up the white flag. We marched into town and were received by the citizens as their deliverers, as the southern people had been treated badly- especially by Bagg's company. Our Company was detailed to look after the prisoners that night and to pay particular attention to the independent company which we did, and the full compliment of prisoners were there next morning. We had to agree to guard the prisoners to the Ohio River before paroling, as they said they would be killed in making the march without arms to Ripley. The advance spread the report that we were following with the Yanks as prisoners. The whole company turned out to greet us, men, women and children.

In passing through the Parsons neighborhood, one of the ladies pointed out a Yank, who had visited them the day before and mistreated her, to her husband. The husband wanted satisfaction then and there. The officer in command asked the Yank about it. He denied the story, but the lady told him he was the man. The officer asked the Yank if he was willing to fight Parsons. He said, yes, if he had fair play.

The boys formed a ring around them and the southern man had the best of the fight. It was a bare knuckle fight to the finish. The lady told her husband she was proud of him and she reckoned the Yankees would let her alone in the future.

Upon arriving at Ripley, the General decided to go into camp for the night picketing all roads leading to Ripley. Wash Smith who was on vidette on the Ravenswood road caught a quartermaster trying to slip through the woods and get to the Ohio River. The Captain surrendered to Wash, who brought him into camp with his outfit and turned him over to the General. Upon examination it was found that his chest contained seven thousand ($7000) dollars in greenbacks. The money was exchanged with the boys for Confederate money and that money turned into the Quartermaster of our Brigade, and the boys had friends and relatives on the border left the greenbacks with them for their use.

After breakfast, we fell in and resumed our march to the Ohio River at Ravenswood, charged the town and captured several Yanks. Here all prisoners were paroled and told to take care of themselves. There were some Yanks on the Ohio side of the river who kept up a constant fir on us from 9 A.M. until 2 P.M. when the regiment was ordered to fall in, ford the river and capture them, if possible. The moment the command started to ford, the Yanks ceased firing and we could never find any of them.

Upon reaching the road, the General concluded to continue on down the river on the Ohio side to Racine, which we did, capturing that town. There we recrossed the river to the Virginia side without the loss of a man or horse. The boys made several horse trades with the buckeye farmers along the road and generally had the best of it in their trades. We marched from opposite Racine to Buffalo on the Kanawha River. No incidents worth recording occurred during our march.

Ten men in charge of an officer were sent from Buffalo to Mud River Bridge, now Milton, with orders, if anything was wrong in Cabell to report to the General at Green Bottom. The ten men that went to Milton continued down the turnpike to within a half of a mile of Barboursville. There they met two citizens whom they knew who told them to go back for God's sake, as the town was full of Yanks. After inquiring from the citizens, we found that all they knew was that they saw an officer and eight or ten men turn the corner and they supposed they were merely the advance of some regiment coming to take possession of the town. We concluded to ride into the town and take a look at them.

We rode in as far as Thornburg's store on top of the hill where the officer ordered a charge, having seen a blue coat. We found them at Hatfield's Hotel. About half of them went over the river bank and the rest ran in all directions, the boys firing at them as they ran. We caught two of them before they could get out of the hotel. Lieut. Brown, the officer in command of the Yanks, hid in a bake oven in the back yard of Oscar Mather's house. This was the Sabbath Day and church was going on at the time in the Southern Methodist Church. Three or four bullets struck the building and the preacher did not have to dismiss the congregation. The congregation was found getting towards home as fast as they could possibly go, without waiting for the benediction. The boys felt good even over the result of their charge. We went on to Guyandotte and charged the town, found no one but citizens; told them to stay at home and they should not be disturbed. We went around town, shook hands with everyone and felt as if we were at home once more.

We waited for the command to come down to the Ohio from Green Bottom, rejoined the company and went to Barboursville, where a scout from Hurricane came down and reported to the General that Lightburn and all the forces in the Kanawha Valley were retreating by way of the Barboursville road. We left one of the Companies of cavalry to watch them and fell back up the Guyan River and made a forced march through Wayne County up Twelve Pole into Logan County. We went through Wyoming into Coal River -- down Coal River and struck the Kanawha River at Brownstown. From there we went to Charleston and reported to General Loring for duty.

September 27th, the old company was sent to Col. Ferguson of the 16th regiment for duty, too, as his command were all raw recruits. We moved down the Kanawha River to Red House Shoals. The advance of the Company here found the cavalry pickets of the Yanks, charged them, and drove them to the infantry. They fell back and waited for Col. Ferguson to come up. Upon his arrival he wanted to know where the enemy was and rode down to within two hundred yards of where the Yanks were in thick clusters of pawpaw bushes. The Colonel asked if any of the Company would ride down with him to where we thought they were. Three of them responded, rode down and just in front of the thicket. The infantry was in line with guns and gave us a volley at a distance of ten feet. The Colonel saw them. Having been shot through both wrists, Captain Everett lost his hat, A.A. Hanley his pistol and Sedinger his horse killed.

We fell on the infantry stationed in Charleston. General Loring ordered retreat and it was a continuous fight for four days with the advance cavalry of the Yanks. Our last stand was just below Kanawha Falls whether we hurt them or not don't know after we barricaded the road and fired three or four volleys at them we left. We thought we had everyone in line, but found S.N. Keenan missing, but in about one hour Newt turned all right.

We marched to White Sulphur Springs where we were ordered to New River Bridge for winter quarters. We spent the time there in company with what was left of the Louisiana Tigers, and we had our horses in North Carolina all winter.

On the 24th of March, 1863, we broke camp for a march to the Ohio River on foot. By the time we reached Cabell County, half of the boys were barefooted. We reached Hamlin, now Lincoln County, about dark -- put out pickets in all the roads. About daylight the morning of the 29th, the sentinel on the road brought in a man with a two horse team, who had been hauling bacon to the Yanks at Hurricane Bridge, The man thought we were Yanks and told all the news he knew. While the officer was talking to him, Rod Noel of the old Company noticed that he had on a good pair of shoes. Rod was barefooted and said to him, "Could or would you give me, an old Confederate soldier, a good pair of shoes?" That was the first intimation that the man had that we were Rebels. He said to Rod that he would if he had any but those he had on. Rod asked him if he had any ones at home and he told him, yes -- well, Rod said, "You give me them and you can stand it better to ride home barefooted in your wagon than I can to walk." The man pulled off his shoes and gave them to Rod. He was scared so badly he did not know what he was doing. He and his wagon and horses were sent to the General who told him to go home and behave himself.

We marched nearly all night the next night, arriving at Hurricane Bridge about daylight. The General sent in a flag of truce demanding a surrender. The Capt. in command refused and moved into a fort that was near by and held it against us as we had no artillery with us. John Payne of the Company killed. We flanked the fort and moved that day to Buffalo on Kanawha River, captured two flat boats, went aboard and floated down the Kanawha to Point Pleasant, went ashore and charged the town.

The Yanks got possession of the C.H. and we held the jail. Ed Guthrie was badly wounded, Lieut. Samuels and Holderby both taken prisoners. The enemy reinforced from Galliopolis. We left town and fell back up the river to the mouth of Ten Mile, crossed the Kanawha and marched to Howell's Mill in Cabell County, where we went into camp. The infanry and cavalry from Charleston undertook to cut us off, but failed. We then resumed our march back to Dixie, where we found our horses awaiting us in good condition.

The regiment was taken away from Jenkins' Brigade and sent to the marches of Coal to do picket duty for Col. McCausland. While the Company was on picket duty, between Raleigh and Fayette, Capt. Thurman, the Partisan Ranger, ambuscaded two companies of the Second Virginia Cavalry (Yanks) who fled their horses. That night their horses came to the picket post. The videttes halted them, but they would not stop. The boys fired at them and the picket formed across the road and stopped them, capturing some twenty-five horses, saddles and bridles and sabers. The horses of the Yanks were so frightened that they were trembling with fear and it took us an hour to quiet them. The sabers rattling and striking against the saddles came very near demorilizing the picket post as we couldn't see them until we were in two feet of them.

There was another incident connected with our Company while here. One of the boys had a sweetheart who he used to call on pretty often. One day he went out to see her, and the old gentleman had sent his daughter out to the cornfield to straighten up the corn and do what little hoeing was necessary to do, as he had finished ploughing the field, the boys all being in the army. The young man went over to help the young lady, taking the hoe in his hand to do the work himself. He was not doing the work to suit her, so she took her foot to show him where to hoe and he cut her big toe off almost. She discarded him on the spot and made him leave the field. The story got out somehow and John Mitchell never heard the last of it.

July 14th, three companies of the regiment were sent to the mouth of Loup Creek to burn a large wharf boat that was filled with stores for the Yanks. Upon reaching the river just at daylight, we noticed some Yankees lying down asleep, their horses tied up to the bushes that were near them. We charged them, run through them, capturing nearly all of them, excepting a few who hid themselves in the weeds and bushes nearby. We started out with our prisoners and had to run the fire of a full regiment of infantry across the Kanawha River. Hansford Stewart was killed and Walter Kingsolving wounded so badly that he never was able for duty afterwards.

July 20th, an officer sent down the clear fork of Coal River on a scout and up the marsh fork. At Mr. Petree's found some Wyoming Yanks under the command of a Capt. Cook, dismounted, slipped through a cornfield to within ten feet of the enemy, who we found with their guns stacked, charged them and they all ran, leaving their guns. We caught two of them before they got over the fence on the other side of the house. They were waiting for their dinners. Whether we killed any of them or not we don't know - did not stop to see. There were ten men in our party and we captured twenty-five (25) guns. No one hurt on our side. Ate the dinner prepared for the Yanks, and left the camp with our prisoners.

Upon arriving at camp we found the regiment ready to move, having received orders to head off raid of Wytheville. We found the Yanks on Walker's Creek in Bland County, Virginia. After a skirmish with the head of the command, the enemy took to the mountain and we held the road until daylight. In the morning of the 23rd of July, we then moved on their trail through the mountain. We found several of them that we took as prisoners, one in particular, ought to have a name in history. We think his name was Perry.

In Tazwell County, Virginia, one of the 54th Ohio went

to the house, no one at home but the girl. He told her he wanted a horse, she told him there were no horses on the place but her riding horse and he could not have that. He went to the stable to take the animal, the girl following. He went inside to get the horse, setting his gun down by the door. She picked up the firearm, examined it, found it was loaded, then presented to Mr.Yank and told him to throw up his hands or she would shoot. TheYank complied with her request and she marched him out of the stable, made him fasten the door, then made him march to the house and guarded him until we came along and relieved her. Then the girl broke down and Mr. Yank looked to me as if he thought he ought to be hanged. He was completely cured by his experience with a mountain girl of Virginia. She told us afterwards that he did not offer to do her any bodily harm.

We stayed in Tazwell and Mercer Counties, Virginia, until October 7, 1863, when we were ordered to Abdington, Virginia, to report for duty to Gen. Wm. E. Jones. The regiment was sent to Bristol, Tennessee, with orders to do picket and scout on all roads leading to Bristol. This kind of service was kept up until the 1st of November. There was at this time hard service for the boys. One day while moving out with part of the Company under Lieut. Thompson our orderly Sergt., Daniel Ruffner, who had been drinking, struck a citizen with his revolver. The man, who was armed, shot the orderly and killed him. He made his escape and was hid by his friends. We never could find him. Ruffner was a gallant soldier and a perfect gentleman when sober.

On another occasion eight of the boys went on a little scouting expedition of their own into Sullivan County, Tennessee. There was an old gentleman of well known Union sentiments in that part, who had some old apple brandy. The boys slipped by our pickets in round about way and struck the road about one-half mile from the Yankees guard and came up and charged the old man's house about twelve o'clock at night, waking the gentleman and all his family. He, thinking we were Yanks, ordered the whole family to get up and give the best the house could afford. We had a splendid supper and plenty of fun with the girls. He gave us all the brandy we wanted and filled our canteens when we left. He told us to call at anytime we were in that part of the country and each one of us should have one of his daughters, as they should not marry any one but a Union soldier. We thanked the old gentleman, kissed the girls and left, going the way we came, towards the Yankees. I don't think he ever knew any better.

Nov. 6th, was ordered to prepare three days rations and march to Rogersville, Tenn. On the morning of the 8th, the old Company was ordered to the front and told to form by fortys, as we were to charge a house that was full of militia and Company "A" was to support us. We formed with our revolvers in our hands and started ready for action at any time. On topping a little hill, we found ourselves within twenty feet of a company of Yanks. Capt. Everett ordered a charge, and at them we went head foremost. They started to run and it was a horse race for three miles in the mud. We did get them all but the Capt., his horse was too fast for us or we would have gotten him. They were the muddiest set of Yanks we think that was ever captured when we went back to see how many there was of them. No one of the Company hurt. We reformed after the charge, went into Rogersville and gobbled about all of them that was there. Our captures that morning amounted to eight hundred prisoners and one battery of artillery and a large amount of stores. The boys were pretty well clothed and shod when we had finished up for the day. We had plenty to eat for a Confederate soldier - sardines and hard tack. Several of them had their haversacks well filled and the canteen was not forgotten.

We started on our return to Bristol but was stopped upon reaching the line of the Yanks' retreat to Knoxville and received orders to follow them which we did, catching stragglers all day. We kept up for two days. There was no fighting but a continuous run catching Yanks. Upon arriving near Knoxville we were part of the line in the seige. We stayed until the charge was made on Fort Sanders. The loss to the infantry was terrible. The next morning, Dec. 2nd, was ordered to Clinch River near Walkers Ford. Was skirmishing all day. In the morning when we first found the enemy, the company formed in an open field and was sitting on our horses awaiting orders when some one from the woods fired a shot at us, striking A.G. Ricketts. We helped him off his horse and carried him to a little cabin near by, leaving him in charge of his cousin, Joseph Wilson. Went on after the Yanks, drove them across Clinch River at Black Fox Ford. An officer and 30 men were left to hold the ford. The men all dismounted and hid their horses as best they could, built themselves what little fortification they could and got ready for business. A regiment of cavalry on the opposite side moved up, dismounted, formed line, marched down to the bank and opened fire on us. The enemy was armed with heavy rifles and it was a continuous fire for 30 minutes. Then they about faced and started back for their horses, remounted and moved off, leaving us in possession of the Black Fox Ford. The boys on our side of the river keeping up their fire until the Yanks got out of range. The only thing hurt on our side of the Clinch was an old gray horse that belonged to one of the boys - he could not find shelter for him. It was the hottest fire we were ever under for the length of time.

One little incident connected with this ford is worth repeating. One of the colored boys forded the river, caught one of the Yankees and brought him. Gen. Jones and staff were there when the boy came back with his prisoner. General asked him who he was and what command he belonged to, all of which he answered. Then the General started to leave him. The Yank says, "General what are you going to do with me?" The General replied, "You belong to that negro, he can do what he pleases with you!" "Oh, my God, General, don't leave me that way," tears rolling down his cheeks. But the boy held on to his captive and was turned in by him with the other prisoners captured.

We left the ford about dusk, moved up to the little cabin where we left Ricketts. He was still unconscious. The surgeon said he could not get well as it was concussion. We left him in charge of an old gentleman, John Cabbage, who sat by his bedside until the next morning when he died. He was buried by him in his own private burying ground on top of one of the highest mountains in East Tennessee. As gallant a soldier ever wore a spur, he deserved a better fate. His last words were for his mother. "Tell Mother I died a brave soldier." He was never conscious afterwards.

We moved from there to Knoxville, from there to London, where we met Grant's advance to relieve Burnside at Knoxville. There was a fight every day from that on until the 10th of December. At Morristown we had a right stiff fight of three hours duration. Drove them back and captured several prisoners. Sampson Diamonds of the Co. badly wounded Dec. 14th. The enemy tried to drive us from Bears Station. We gave them a right decent thrashing. None of the Co. hurt.

December 16th, Powder Springs Gap, the Yanks attacked at daylight. Skirmish and fight all day. At dark fell back to a piece of woods. The enemy turned our flank. Sims, Wilson and Sedinger wounded. Will Seymington taken prisoner. Broke camp at dark, marched all night. At daylight on the morning of the 3rd, Capt. Everett was ordered to take the old Co. and Companies I, K and D and charge the picket post. The Capt. made the charge and was successful in capturing the entire force on picket. Some 80 men lost. Lieut. Samuels who succeeded in cutting through the Yanks went on and charged the main body and our battery succeeded in driving the enemy away from his guns. Samuels was killed while sabering one of the gunners. Lon Love, Henry Baumgardner, Will Shoemaker and Charles Morris killed at the same time. Uriah Martin,

George Heath, George Burnsides, John Moore and H.H. Sexton all badly wounded. The fight continued from that time until 4 o'clock in the evening when the enemy surrendered to us after an all day fight, in which they lost a good many men. We rested in the Powell Valley for some 4 days then received orders to move to Strawberry Plains. Found the Yanks in possession, charged them and drove them before us, capturing some prisoners. Held our guard and lived off the country by foraging.

Jan. 20th, Sedinger elected Lieut. caused by the death of Samuels. Continuous foraging and fighting.

Feb. 22nd, fight at Wymers Mills, Tennessee, fight opened at daylight by the regiment charging the camp. S.S. Vinson in command of Co. K led the charge. Vinson's horse fell, shot, just as he struck the enemy's line and caught Sam under him. Jess Meeks and Anderville Frazier killed, Jim Shelton wounded in this fight. Col. Davis in command of the enemy attacked an officer of the Co. who exchanged three shots with the Col. at close range, when the Col. tried to get away but the officer caught him after a hundred yard run and found him badly wounded. We captured almost the entire regiment and considerable stores. We found plenty of hard tack, coffee, bacon, and etc. The boys enjoyed their breakfast for we had marched all night without anything to eat.

March 5th found the 3rd Tennessee Cavalry at Panther Spring Gap, charged their camp and they scattered to the mountains. Captured 100 prisoners and about all of their camp equipage. No one hurt of the Co. but Boyed Hensley and he thought he was killed. In making the charge a bullet struck his haversack, knocking the breath out of him. One of the boys after the fight went to him and asked how he was hurt. "Shot through" was his reply. Upon examination it was found that Boyed had two pieces of wheat bread that was baked on a flat shell rock, common to that country. The bread was made up of salt and water, rolled out flat and baked Johnny cake fashion before the fire. The bread was in his haversack and the bullet went through the other, knocking the young man off his horse, but it took three of the boys half an hour to convince Boyed that he was not shot.

March 10th, 1864, the regiment fell in for reinlistment. The entire regiment reinstated, but the Border Rangers refused. Gen. Jones wanted to know what the trouble was. We told him we wanted to leave the brigade and regiment. We gave him our reasons for it and immediately he gave the Co. 60 days furlough. The boys all came home to the border and such a time the boys had. One of eight went through the country to Parkersburg, spent three weeks in that city and on Blennerhassett Island and had a chance to see how the Southern people felt inside the lines. The party finally left Parkersburg about 9 o'clock by walking down to the wharf and shoving a skiff out in the river with two sets of oars in it and starting down the river for Cabell County, and from there through to Dixie. There were many sad partings on that trip for the mothers all felt that it was the last time they would see their boys, and with a good many it proved true, in fact too many.

Upon going back, we found Jones' Brigade in Wythe Co., Virginia. The Co. served the balance of the war without reinstating. The Brigade rode from Wythesville to Staunton,Virginia, fought the advance of Gen. Hunter for one half a day, fell back to Waynesborough, crossed the mountain into Nelson Co., Virginia, from there through Nelson into Amhurst Co., through Amhurst into Campbell Co., passed through Lynchburg to Liberty where we met Hunter's advance, fought the enemy all the way back to Lynchburg where we met Gordon's Division of infantry for we had been fighting Hunter for three days and could not stop him, went on vidette two days and nights. When Hunter retreated we followed him to Salem, Virginia, where we charged him and broke into a park of artillery, capturing a battery, fell back and waited for the infantry to come up. By this time Hunter was across the mountains. We started on the march for Winchester, Virginia. Down the valley found the Federal forces well-fortified and flanked them when they started on retreat. Then it was a race for the Potomac. We captured several prisoners and a goodly amount of war material, crossed the Potomac and marched to Frederick City, Maryland, the regiment leading the advance.

July the 8th, we found the 8th Illinois Cavalry drawn up in line of battle, formed for charge. When the Illinois regiment left the field we followed them, their battery shelling us, our regiment losing 14 men and several horses by the explosion of a shell in our ranks. Among the number was Harvey Wilson, who was a conscientious Christian soldier from our county and as gallant a man as ever drew a saber.

July 9th, McCausland's Brigade of cavalry made an attack on Ricketts' Division of infantry at Monacy Junction. The 16th regiment of cavalry lost a considerable number of men and some gallant officers. Among the number was Capt. Joseph Morris and Lieut. Robert Solderby, who was an old member of the Company, promoted to a Lieutenant for gallant and meritorious conduct on many battle fields.

February[4] 10th the Brigade left Early's command at Monacy Junction and started to burn a bridge across Gunpowder River between Baltimore and Philadelphia, destroyed the bridge and tore up the rail track for miles. On the evening of the 12th of July found us on the outskirts of Baltimore. The streets were barricaded but the enemy was only militia and what a picnic we had driving them before us, going almost into the heart of the city.

One of the incidents of the march, the boys found a dairy filled with ice cream, cake, smear case and everything manufactured of milk about six miles out of the city, for the city market, and such a time as we had with the old German it belonged to. Two of the Border Rangers got hold of a two gallon freezer of cream and one of the cakes.

---

[4] February is an error. The correct month is July.

While riding along on the march eating the cream and cake one of the lieutenants of Company C of the regiment said, "Hello, boys, what have you to eat?" They told him. His reply was that he had the same dirt for his breakfast. The boys tried his can and found it was Dutch cheese. The boys gave him some of theirs. He cleaned his can and the boys divided with him. It was the first cream he had ever tasted, and the first and last the Company ever had during the war.

Flanked Baltimore and marched on Washington Pike and drove a regiment of cavalry before us into Washington. While on this pike we passed a large seminary full of young lady students. The professors and matrons of the institution tried to control the girls but they could not do it. Every southern girl was over the fence and lined up cheering us as we passed and any lucky knight they knew would have to dismount and the whole line would kiss him after an introduction. It made brave men of the boys after witnessing scenes at that school, the devotion of the southern girls to the cause.

After driving the enemy to the forts that protected the city on that side we found them too strong for us, flanked them and found General Early's command near Covington. Early retreated, the Brigade covered the retreat, fighting the cavalry to Poolsville. The regiment was dismounted and deployed as skirmishers and from 10 A.M. until dark held the enemy in check - Charles Shoemaker wounded badly. We mounted and started for the Potomac, was halted and told to lay down with our horses fastened to us to be ready for any emergency. About 11 o'clock the enemy slipped a battery up to within 200 yards of our line and turned loose on us with grape and canister, causing great confusion. It took us 20 minutes at least to find out where we were.

July 20th found us at Winchester, Virginia, fighting the Federal cavalry. We held the field driving the Yanks to Berryville.

July 23rd fought the Federal cavalry at Komston, gave

the enemy a right decent flogging in this fight. While our regiment was in line waiting for orders there was a Yank charged through our line and back again with his saber in his hand. He did not hurt any one, neither was he hurt.

July 24th Winchester, fought Gen. Crook and drove him before us to Potomac. That night was a terrible night. It was a continuous fight from dark until daylight. Next morning burning wagon trains and shells exploding. It was terrible but beautiful. The entire night we captured one hundred prisoners as our part of the night's work.

July 26th, Brigade was ordered to join Gen. McCausland and go with his brigade into Maryland and Pennsylvania. July 29th captured Hagerstown, Md. Levied contribution of $200000. July 30th captured Chambersburg, Pa. The General levied contribution of $300000 on the city, which the mayor and city council refused to pay. The General told the gentlemen he would give them 30 minutes to change their minds. They at the expiration of time still refused when he ordered Dunn's Battalion to burn the town. Then we witnessed to the fullest extent the horrors of war. The ladies and children of that city knew for the first time what war was, as they were frightened so badly that some of them would not leave their homes and had to be carried to places of safety. The mayor and city council had told the General that if he burned the city, Gen. Averill would catch us and hang every one of us. It was then that the General pulled his watch out and made the reply that he would burn the town and whip Gen. Averill when ever he found him.

July 31st, Gen. Averill overtook us at Hancock, Md. After a two hour fight, he fell back and left us in charge of the field. August 1st tried to take Cumberland, Md., but they were too strong for us and we had to go. August 2nd captured blockhouse at Old Tavern, Md. 153 taken prisoner. A train of ironclad cars came up and took part in the fight, captured the cars, artillery and stores. Sedinger wounded. Aug. 4th tried to take New Creek Station. Found the enemy very strongly entrenched and we fell back to Romney. E.C. Rice wounded in hand.

August 7th Moorefield. The command was surprised at daybreak next morning by Gen. Averill's command. The Co. went out on the Winchester road and rallied at the foot of the mountain, fought Witcher's regiment, 3rd W.Va. Cavalry, and held them in check for 30 minutes until flanked by 4 companies of cavalry. We had to go to save ourselves. Louis Woodrum killed, Maurice Pennybaker wounded and rode from Moorefield to Harrisonburg, Va., without having his wound dressed. Sampson Simmonds taken prisoner.

August 15th, fight with Federal cavalry near Strausburg, drove them to the Potomac and across the river. August 17th the Federal cavalry came back at us near Winchester on the Berryville pike. After 4 hours pretty hard fighting by flank movement got them going and drove them back on their infantry outposts. Roddy Noel hurt with shell. August 25th fight with cavalry near Shepherdstown. Had the best of the fight and drove the enemy through the town. August 26 fight with cavalry near Halltown. Drove them through piece of woodland and ran into the infantry and two batteries which turned loose at us with grape and canister. We were too glad to get away from them.

Sept. 19th, the fight at Winchester opened at daybreak in the morning by a New Jersey Brigade of cavalry charging a South Carolina regiment of infantry on their picket post. The Col. of the regiment had his men in a hollow square. At this time our regiment was in line, we charged the cavalry and drove them away from the infantry, capturing a good many prisoners. The Co. lost one man killed, Joseph Shuler, whose horse ran away with him through the cavalry brigade ahead of the regiment into the Federal infantry who killed him. The battle lasted the entire day with about equal advantages until about 5 o'clock when our left flank gave away and almost made a rout of it. Our Brigade of cavalry and Pegram's Brigade of infantry covered the retreat to Kernstown when Pegram's Brigade of infantry took the stone fence to the right of the pike and held it while our brigade held the left and center. On came the Federal cavalry charging by squadron. When we turned loose on them they found a hornet's nest that did not suit them by any means. What the effect was upon them was manifested by those left alive getting away as fast as possible. The road was full of horses and cavalry men dead and wounded. We then resumed our march up the valley to Fisher's Hill where we went into camp unmolested for two days, throwing up breastworks and getting ready for our next fight.

Sept.22nd, the Yanks moved about 2 P.M. and attacked the entire line, but Gen. Crook with the 8th Corps and the entire Federal cavalry struck the left flank and turned it, capturing almost all our artillery and 800 prisoners. Our regiment being up in the woods on the North Mountain, dismounted fighting as infantry. Col. Cook ordered us to charge which we did and struck the rear of Crook's Corps, who faced about and poured a hot fire into us, killing John Beckwith and capturing Sedinger of the old Company. Gus Wolcott, Arthur Williams and four others of the old Company as they fell back into the North Mountains captured 7 Yanks and took them out with them. The comand retreated up the valley to Woodstock, went into camp. The cavalry picketed all roads leading up the valley. This we continued to do until the 10th of October, when we made forward movement down the valley, encountering the Federal cavalry 4 miles from Fisher's Hill, driving them down the road until we struck the infantry at Cedar Creek where they were entrenched. We then fell back on the infantry who were throwing up breastworks, getting ready for trouble. Then it was a kind of give and take warfare until the 19th of October.

Battle commenced at daylight. Wharton's Brigade of the Breckinridge Division charged the breastworks of the 8th Corps, caught the boys asleep and ran over them, driving the 8th Corps back and over the 9th, completely demoralizing both corps. When we found the 6th Corps in line of battle ready to receive us our success was complete until about noon when Sheridan coming turned the tide of battle against us and we lost as much in the evening as we had gained in the morning.

This battle was lost by the boys being too anxious to reap the fruits of victory and get what they needed out of the Yank's camps, as most of us were barefooted, naked for clothing and hungry. The Yanks had everything in plenty and the temptation was too great to resist - the result was defeat. In the evening at least 10 thousand of our men were straggling in their eager desire to better their condition. We succeeded in getting off with what prisoners we had captured, but we lost as many as we had taken from the enemy. We fell back up the valley. We lost Cyrus Emmons taken prisoner. He was comfortably dressed and in good condition for a winter campaign when taken. We fell back up the valley to Harrisonburg and went into camp doing picket duty on all roads down the valley.

Nov. 4th, Rosser's Brigade joined us and a movement was made on Nov. 12th down the valley, Rosser's Brigade taking the back road, our Brigade taking the main pike. Rosser found Custer at Newtown or when our Brigade was at Newtown. The couriers from Rosser's found us ready for business, we struck Custer in flank and saved Rosser. Joseph Stewart of the Company badly wounded.

It was picket duty and skirmishing with the enemy until Nov. 24th when we left the valley and moved on Moorefield, our Brigade and Rosser's. Gen. Rosser in command, with the intention of tearing up the B&O Ry. We met few Yanks until we arrived at New Creek, now called Keyser. We surrounded the picket post we all had on blue overcoats. The picket thought we were Federal cavalry until we were completely around them when we told them who we were and told them the first man that opened his mouth or made any kind of alarm would be killed. That settled the matter for the young men in charge of the picket post. We then rode on to the fort and our Brigade formed in squadrons within one hundred feet of the enemy without their having the least idea that we were anything but brother Yanks, in fact they were talking to us all the time we were forming, asking how many Johnnies we had caught and brought with us, and never for a moment doubted us until Col. Cook gave the order to draw sabers and charge the fort we caught without a gun in their hands or anything to defend themselves with. We captured the entire garrison all but Col. Southam, the commander who hid himself somewhere we could not find him. He was afterwards dismissed from the service for cowardice, when he could not help himself. If Gen. Sheridan himself had been in command the result would have been the same, for the surprise was so complete that it was impossible to stop it.

Part of our Brigade went to Piedmont to destroy the shops there, which they succeeded in doing to a considerable extent. The command destroyed great quantities of stores at New Creek when the detachment came back from Piedmont. We left for Dixie with some 5oo prisoners, horses, artillery and everything that was moveable, leaving the seige guns after spiking them. Upon arriving in the valley we went at our usual duties of scouting and picket duty until Dec. 10th, when the two brigades moved down the valley to Lucy Springs. Our Brigade was in the advance and we turned loose on them, running over them. It was dark and we were all mixed up in a hand to hand fight. We could not tell friend from foe and Gen. Payne issued orders for us to fall back and get out of the scrape the best we could. We found out from the prisoners we had brought out that it was Gen. Custer's division of cavalry. Capt. Everett was captured trying to rally the 8th Vermont Cavalry, Thomas Dodson taken prisoner. Our force fell back to Harrisonburg and Gen. Custer to Winchester. Then moved to Swope's Depot and went into camp.

Jan. 7th we pulled out for Beverly. The roads and weather were terrible. We left with about 800 men, when we arrived at our destination there was not more than 250 of us. It was five o'clock in the morning, we had not found a picket scout, anything that looked like a Yankee. Our little force formed and moved on the camp, where we found everyone asleep except for 8 or 10 camp guards, which we soon disposed of, and from that time the boys had lots of fun pulling the sleepy Yanks out of bed and getting them ready for their trips to Dixie. There were two regiments -- the 8th Ohio Cavalry and the 34th (commonly called the Tourves). We destroyed everything we could find that we did not need for ourselves, and started with our prisoners for the railroad.

It was terrible on the Yanks to make the march on foot as the snow was at least 12 inches deep and the thermometer about zero. The company fared badly too with frozen feet. Preston Baker was told he would have to have his feet amputated by the surgeon, but he said no, he would rather die. He lived to get well and made one of the most respected citizens in our country.

Upon arriving at Swopes, our Brigade received orders to move near Lexington in Rockbridge Co. where we stayed and recruited until the 6th of February, when we received orders to start on the march for Petersburg. Upon arriving we found Custer in our front again on the north side of the James river, where we continued to do picket and scout duty until the evening of the 27th day of March, when we were ordered to cross to the south side of the river, which we did on the 28th, doing duty in the lines south of Petersburg on the 29th, held our same position. On the 30th marched to Five Forks, encountered the enemy's cavalry which we drove back on their reserves. Our Brigadier, Gen. Wm. H. Payne wounded and left in the enemy's lines. 31st of March Pickett's Division of infantry came to our assistance and we gave Sheridan's cavalry a complete thrashing.

1st of April fell back to our old position at Five Forks. At 3 P.M. on the 2nd the enemy with corps of infantry moved on our position and soon crushed our weak line. Drove some 3 or 4 miles. An the 4th continued our retreat, on the 5th received orders to go the Amelia C.H. to protect the wagon train, drove the Yanks back almost to Petersville. April 6th acting rearguard for Longstreet's Corps, found the enemy at High Bridge, drove him off, capturing 780 prisoners. 7th of April still acting as rear guard for Longstreet. The cavalry attacked our wagon train. Our division turned loose on them in front, Rosser struck in the rear, capturing a good many prisoners, including Gen. Gregg. 8th continued our march in rear of same corps without being disturbed by the Yanks. Night of 8th moved to front under orders. 9th at daybreak formed in squadrons supported.

Sedinger's account stopped at this point. April 9, 1865, was Sunday. This was the day that two great generals met in Wilmer McLean's house in the small country town called Appomattox Court House.

It was not clear from the narrative whether Sedinger was an active participant in the last campaigns of the war. He reported that he was captured in the fight with General Crook's 8th Corps at Fisher's Hill on September 22, 1864. He may have been able to escape from the Federals in the confusion they must have encountered in attempting to manage large numbers of Confederate prisoners of war.

Regardless of whether he was an actual participant in the final battles, he had many friends who survived the war who were members of his "Old Company" who would have been able to assist with the reconstruction of events of the last months of the Confederacy.

William Clark Reynolds participated in the 1861 military campaigns in the Kanawha Valley as a Confederate private. He enlisted into the Kanawha Riflemen in Charleston and served through Scary Creek, the evacuation of Charleston, Wise's "Retrograde Movement" out of the valley, and the final retreat of Floyd from the area of Cotton Hill.

Reynolds' notes that were taken during 1861 are very interesting and one can only wish that he was a more prolific recorder of history. He saw a lot of it.

The interesting sections begin in March, 1861, and give the reader an idea of the character of the young man. The unpublished diary is located in the West Virginia Archives.

March, 1861

20. I am out of money, too lazy to work, anxious to marry and no one will have me.

25. To Malden at night and heard the Rev. Sullivan give a revival sermon. The Rev. Johnson prayed "that the time might soon come when the people of Malden would be as noted for their virtues as for their vices."

27. I am reading the "Woman in White" by Wilkie Collins. Put out a trot line and caught thirteen fish and six quanchs.

29. Good Friday. Went snipe shooting and bagged all I saw -- seven in eight shots -- first snipe of the season.

31. Easter Sunday.

April, 1861

8. Attended the musical soire at W. W. Woods and was the last one to leave in the wee small hours so staid and took breakfast, with the M.H. Truslow's of the Virginia house.

9. While walking up the road this morning I fired three or four shots from my revolver at some water fowl and had the misfortune to frighten Dr. Park's horse, which threw him.

15. Made a small ironed back saw in the a.m. and played eucre with the girls in the afternoon.

16. It has rained for nine days.

17. Considerably heavy snow for the season and the largest flakes I ever saw being about 2 sq. inches in size.

18. Fort Sumpter having a hard time and worse to come.

20. It is reported that Virginia has seceeded from the Union, subject to popular retification. Late frost. Lilacs in bloom.

21. Whipporwills began. I am not yet in status quo.

23. The weather is geting hot and sultry and the civil affairs of the whole country are waxing hotter still.

24. Fight 'till the last foe expires,
Fight for your alters and your fires,
For the green graves of your sires,
God and your native land.

May, 1861

1. This day a year ago I gave my sweet a golden ring. I wonder what she thinks of me now.

3. Went to Malden in the morning and to the foundry and saw the cannon.

4. Militia Muster in Malden. Capt. Thayers Company. Drilled for the first time in my life.

6. Political meeting at the Court House. Heard Major Parks, Summers, Patton, Brown, Carrier [Quarrier] and Laidley on secession and war. *Who's afraid!*

7. Light frost and the weather is still cold. This has been one of the most backward springs I have ever known.

8. Went to Charleston. Joined the Kanawha Riflemen, who were mustered into service this day.

9. Obtained a two-day furlough from Captain Patton.
Company went into camp at 2 1/2 o'clock at the old Camp Meeting grounds below Charleston.

10. At home. Mother and sister working faithfully and willingly on my uniform and there must be other subversion of my nature ere that uniform is disgraced.

11. Parted with my friends at 6 a.m. Reported myself at Camp Lee and entered military duties. Detailed as a guard from 8 a.m. tomorrow till 8 Monday morning.

12. Rev. T.L. Smith preached in the camp at 11 a.m.
Received orders at 7 p.m. to put ourselves in marching order. Hot work to be done tomorrow. Enthusiasm abounds.

13. Company broke camp at 2 a.m. and at 5 1/2 left Charleston on Steamer Moffett. Reached Buffalo at 9 a.m. Met with no resistance at the place and took up quarters in the academy, tho warned by friends as well as enemies to retire. We faltered not.

14. An attack threatened at 8 a.m. and again at 2 p.m. but we are not to be intimidated. I had a good snooze at night for the first time since Saturday.

15. Buffalo, Putnam Co. Virginia.
We are now located at this place. The Kanawha Riflemen, the Sharpshooters and the Buffalo Guards all getting along peacefully.

16. Capt. Becket with company arrived and were serenaded by the Kanawha Riflemen. A row between a bloody six and a bully nine -- the latter victorious.

17. Barracks Buffalo Academy. No excitement. A duel between the King of the Bloody Six and Corporal Welsh squashed by the guard.

18. Went over to Eighteen Mile Creek fishing with Bob Cabel and Donnelly. Caught forty-three fish and drank two bottles of native Isabella.

19. Detailed as guard just a few minutes before Guard-mounting and while making preparations for a walk around town with a friend. Ain't it provoking.

22. Brother Charlie came down to see me. He staid all night. The Border Riflemen (Capt. A.R. Barber [Barbee]) arrived this place.

23. Election Day. Stood guard again. Voted for ratification of the ordinance of secession.

25. John Swann's Co. (Charleston Sharpshooters) was mustered into service.

26. On guard again being the third Sunday in succession I have stood guard. Didn't get to hear the sermon to the volunteers by the Rev. T.L. Smith in the Presbyterian Church. McCherry's Company came down at night creating a false alarm.

29. Left Buffalo by orders of Colonel Tompkins and contrary to the wishes of Capt. Patton and his company. Steamers Moffit and Kanawha Valley to Charleston. Quartered in Brooks Hall.

30. Guard at Elk Bridge. The ladies God bless them sent the best dinner I ever sat down to. Had a hard time at night being totally destitute of bed clothing.

June, 1861

1. Charleston Va. Ran around considerably and drank native wine generally.

2. Went up town and loafed all day.

3. To Coalsmouth and quartered in the Tompkins house and christened it Camp Tompkins. Came to this place as did the Border Riflemen in flat boats.

4. Guard again. Police guard duty as it is here enforced is a great bore and I believe a great humbug.

9. Rev. Wade, Methodist preacher on the camp grounds. Heard the sermon but fell asleep while the closing hymn was being sung.

10. Walked up to the steamboat landing with Sergeant Laidly, J.W. Fry. Went in bathing at night.

13. Was picketed 3/4 mile below the camp. Had a very pleasant time visiting the ladies at Bev. Tompkins while off my post.

15. Made a bed stead for C.C. Quarrier and myself.

17. Lt. Jackson and I fired off our rifles and revolvers.

20. Give me death of those
Who for their country die,
And O, be mine like their repose
When cold and low they lie.

28. General H.A. Wise received us and made a speech. I went home for leave of absence on the Moffatt. First time since May 11th.

29. The steamer AID exploded and sunk at Malden.

July, 1861

3. Went through a disagreeable drill under Lieut. Fitzhugh.

4. This day has ceased to be the anniversary of our independence as our liberties have been trampled upon by those who were our brothers and we are now striving for a new independence. On guard.

5. Came off guard and rolled up my blanket and started for Ripley in Jackson County to meet the enemy. Marched thirty miles on foot thro a rough country with hardly anything to eat.

6. After suffering many privations and hardships we reached Ripley. The 1050 Yankees who were here a few days ago have vamoosed towards Ohio. Deserted village.

7. An alarm was sounded just before day which hurried us all to the field but in vain for the foe did not appear. Went bathing in Mill Creek with Capt. Taylor and Lieut. McClintock.

8. Another false alarm about midnight and another at day break. Left Ripley to defend our own firesides on Kanawha. Staid at Sissionville -- 24 miles and slept in the dog fennel -- minus dinner and supper.

11. War and rumors of war.

12. The enemy is said to be advancing on us from different ways. We packed up our kits and prepared to meet them but as the alarms received were not confirmed we rested in place another night.

13. Capt. Corns Co. marched to Barboursville to meet the foe. A skirmish at Mud Bridge between a few companies

of raw militia and a regiment of northern troops. Supposed loss of enemy 40 men -- ours -- none.

14. 1st Battle of Scarey. Our Co. with Barber and Bailey and a detachment of artillery went to Scarey Creek. Barber and the artillery fired on an approaching column of the enemy which retreated instantly. Later another column fled at the sight of our flag.

15. Our company was picketed by platoons on the two roads below Scarey, myself in the second platoon on the river road. Of the foe about fifty killed and 100 wounded. Our loss was 3 killed and 6 wounded. We captured 3 colonels, 1 lieut. colonel and 2 captains and buried 12 of their forsaken dead. Our noble Capt. Geo. S. Patton was severely wounded.

17. BATTLE OF SCAREY About 1800 U.S. in attack against 600 of our C.S. troops. Action commenced at 1 1/2 p.m. -- lasted about 3 1/2 hours. The U.S. troops were repulsed with the number unknown.

18. Returned from picket after passing a sleepless night and had a scanty coffee-less breakfast being the first morsel of food we've had an opportunity of eating in 26 hours. Returned to Camp Tompkins.

19. Left Camp Tompkins by steamers Valley and Moffett after all night at Coalmouth.

20. Stopped at Chandler's Landing where we stayed nearly all day and night. We were forced to fall back before the superior numbers of our enemy -- the latter number 4500 in camp at Poca.

22. Heard good news from Manassas. Beaureguard repulses Scott with great slaughter.

23. Left the steamer and marched down to Hunter's Stretch where we worked hard all day throwing up breast-works and slept in the trenches at night. Over the mountain and obstructed a road in the afternoon.

24. Worked in the trenches again in the morning, deployed as skirmishers in the afternoon but the enemy not coming nearer than three miles we vacated our post according to orders. Went aboard Steamer Moffett and were beautifully entrapped by the Federals but escaped by a miracle and retreated to Brownstown.

25. Arose at early dawn and continued the retreat until reaching Clifton at 2 p.m. where we remained until 1 at night. We don't fear the foe we are retreating from but are falling back to aid General Lee.

26. Took up line of march at 1 a.m. and went to Gauley and were comfortably quartered at the Fall's House. Our camp equipment was lost when we burned the Moffett and for two days we have had little to eat except the little pick up among friends.

27. The whole of the Wise Legion staid at Gauley all day, wasting time.

29. Marched 12 miles. We would travel much faster were it not for the great amount of ammunition and provisions we are necessarily burdened with. Staid at Anderson's, 35 miles from Lewisburg.

30. Staid at Sugar Grove 22 miles from Lewisburg and slept in wet blankets.

31. Gen. H.A. Wise announced the joyful news that we would be paid and uniformed immediately on reaching Lewisburg.

August, 1861

1. Reached Lewisburg in a soaking rain and was quartered in the fair grounds.

2. Lewisburg, Greenbrier County, Virginia.
Our quarters are very disagreeable having no convenience of wood or water and nothing but stalls, recently occupied by horses, to sleep in.

3. Left Lewisburg in the morning, resting an hour or so at Greenbrier Bridge and reached the White Sulphur Springs early in the afternoon. Quartered in the Carolina Row. I have walked the whole distance -- 113 miles.

4. White Sulphur Springs, went bathing in Howard's creek in the a.m. with Capt. Taylor, having met under the same circumstance four weeks ago.

5. Commenced drilling again. Performed the disagreeable task of washing my own clothes.

6. General J.B. Floyd arrived at noon with about a thousand troops.

8. Salt Sulphur Springs, Virginia. This place is about 28 miles from the "White". Mr. Erskine, proprietor. Found this to be a very pleasant place with about 30 guests. Walked about the grounds in the a.m. and rolled my first ball at ten-pins.

9. Rolled at ten-pins all day with A.P. Fry, W.A. Bradford, H.D. Ruffner, Tom Thornburg, George Lee Brent and Mr. Herbert. Sat up until late bed time with the girls who were tipsy from drinking sherry sanagree.

10. Rolled ten-pins all day. Fixed my rifle which had been loaded ever since the Battle of Scarey. They keep a good table here and a soldier knows how to appreciate such

blessings.

12. Left the "Salt" in the morning on horseback, took dinner with old Mr. Dickerson and had my horse fed for the whole which I was charged but ten cents. Reached the "White" at sunset.

13. The daily routine of drilling. Length of Hotel -- 400 ft. Ball room -- 50 ft. long by 90 ft. wide. Dining room 300 ft. by 60. Parlor 50 by 90 ft.

17. Went up on the hill and ate a few huckleberries.

18. Heard our Chaplain Thompson L. Smith in the afternoon. It is really refreshing to hear a sermon after being so long debarred that pleasure. All because of the misfortune of war.

19. Received marching orders but will not leave until tomorrow. Got on a "bust" at the Big hotel with Col. Reid and Lieut. Laidley and Archie. Took supper with them and slipped into quarters after taps.

20. Ours, 22nd and 36th Regiments left White Sulphur Springs at 10 1/2 a.m., lunched at Lewisburg and staid at night at Bunger's Mill, doing a hot and disagreeable march of 13 miles. Had the pleasure of using tents for the first time.

21. On to Kanawha!
Pulled up stakes and marched thirteen miles further towards Kanawha. Camped in a grove on each side of the road. Got as many blackberries as I could.

22. Rained all day. Pitched our tents this evening in a meadow below the road at the eastern foot of Big Sewell Mt.

23. Pushed forward, crossing Big Sewell Mt. and pitched our tents at Locust Lane.

24. At Carnifax Ferry.

26. THE BATTLE OF CROSS LANES.

Marched out at daybreak under Floyd's command and we drove Col. Tyler from his position, scattered his forces, captured 108 and killed and wounded 75 more. We lost 3 and 20 wounded.

27. Our wagons with the tents and provisions came up to us and we moved our quarters from the brush to the breast-works. I was detailed among the 30 to guard the prisoners. No sleeping allowed.

29. We are still in Gen. John B. Floyd's company (Camp Gauley) on top of the mountain on the north side of Gauley River, 20 miles from its mouth.

30. Prisoners still coming in from Tyler's last defeat.

31. We were mustered and inspected by Col. Tompkins. Commenced reading "What will he do with it" by Buliver.

September, 1861

2. Beautiful day. I put on a clean shirt.

3. Wise attacked the Federals at the Hawks Nest and after a connonade of a few hours without any great consequences, retired without a loss.

4. Dress parade.

5. Laid quiet in our tents and kept up a good fire as the weather is cool for September.

6. The 22nd regiment left Camp Gauley, reached the river

and took the Saturday road to Hopping's and down the turnpike to Tyree's and camped near an orchard.

8. Walked down to the Wise Legion which is encamped a mile below us. Arranged order with Col. Davis and returned. Heard the firing of our cannon at Dogwood Gap.

9. Broke up camp and started back to Floyd's. Staid in a meadow near Reynolds.

10. BATTLE OF CARNIFAX.

Reached Floyd's at 2 o'clock and just in time. Rosecrans attacked us with 6 or 8 thousand men at 3 o'clock p.m. and kept up the fire tho repulsed several times until after night when he withdrew, losing 2000 killed and wounded. Our loss none killed and 7 wounded.

11. Made a glorious retreat in the face of an overwhelming force of the enemy, daylight finding us safely across the river. Took the Sunday road to the Pike and went down to Dogwood Gap. Camped there.

12. In camp. In a flurry of excitement all day in consequence of false rumors of all kinds; that is, the enemy advancing on them, Lee had whipped Rosecrans, then he hadn't.

13. Struck tents at 8 1/2 o'clock and continued to fall back. We have had but one meal since Thursday. Camped on the top of Big Sewell.

15. Found it raining this morning. Heard a distant thunder which we thought and vainly hoped was a cannonade in the enemy's rear.

16. A.P. Fry came in from Lewisburg. We struck tents and continued our retreat through the rain. Had a

disagreeable time marching thro the mud at night but fell asleep every time we halted.

17. Took dinner on top of Little Sewell and marched on coming to a full stop at Meadow Bluff. In all sixteen miles. Orders to cook four days provisions and prepare for an expedition march to commence at 3 a.m.

18. Awoke at early dawn and had the pleasure of finding that the orders of last night had been countermanded. Which gives us a chance of receiving the rest and repose we so much require.

19. Our regiment worked on the breast works on the right flank of Meadow River fortifications. Our company had one axe and two butcher knives to work with so some idea may be formed of the efficiency of our defenses.

20. Enemy reported to be falling back.

21. Cloudy with some rain. Was relieved from guard at 8 a.m. General Robt. E. Lee at Meadow Bluff and took command.

24. Was aroused before day and ordered to prepare marching which we did and arrived at Wise's camp just in time to hear a few rounds of cannon. Deployed and laid upon our arms all night expecting a battle. Slept on the cold ground.

25. Built breast works and prepared rapidly for defence. The enemy supposed to be 10,000 strong is in full view on top of Big Sewell 1 1/2 miles from our lines. We wounded two of our sentinels at night being too alert.

27. Still raining and the whole place is covered with water.

October, 1861

1. Heard of the fighting at Lexington, Missouri between Mulligan and Price in which our arms were crowned with victory. Annie, I hope you are safe!

11. Left by Sewell with Floyd command and took a road leading in a southerly direction to New River. Camped in the brush rainy night on Meadow Creek. Saw the tracks of a tornado.

12. I was detailed on a foraging party.

22. Picketed near Montgomery's Ferry. Three others and I sat within gunshot of the enemy for 24 hours.

24. There are nine companies of our regiment here on Cotton Hill. Under command of Col McCausland.

26. Rode Col. Tompkins horse down to our cooking quarters.

27. Dismantled our cannon and commenced carrying them to the river cliffs.

28. A.P. Fry and N.B. Cabell were here and brot me a letter from Sister Kate.

29. Wrote to Sister Kate but had no opportunity to send the letter.

November, 1861

1. We opened on the camp at Gauley with a rifle piece and on the camp at the falls with two smooth six pounders. Sensation created by a body of Yanks on our rear - captured one.

2. Staid with a piece of the Goochland artillery at the foot of the hill. Sergeant Henry A. Bradford was accidentally

shot by Tom Grant.

4. Henry A. Bradford died this morning about 6 o'clock at Mr. Warner's house.

> There is a land of peace for the glorious dead,
> Where war's wild panic can never spread.

5. Henry Bradford's remains were buried with military honors in Col. Dickinson's family buring grounds.

6. Election Day. Jenkins is my man.

7. Man's inhumanity to man
Makes countless thousands to mourn.

20. Heard rumors of another battle going on at Manassas. Our army is falling back to go into winter quarters. Five or six hundred cavalry passed here on the Tazewell Road.

27. I read seven chapters in my Bible. Snow is three inches deep and still snowing. Saw a deer track.

28. The old Governor killed his hogs and scalded them in hot water and hung them up to dry, he did.

December, 1861

1. Read another chapter in my Testament and was a pretty good fellow all day. Killed an owl and a pheasant, shooting off both their heads.

1. Took the clock to pieces, cleaned and oiled it and succeeded in making it run. We amuse ourselves by making pipes of laurel root.

7. Eclipse of the moon.

9. In camp two miles north of Newberne Depot. Went

through a little drilling and dress parade. Had a severe toothache contracted from sleeping on the ground.

11. Our regiment is under command of Col. W.A. Jackson.

14. Went to Dublin Depot on the Virginia and Tennessee R.R. and this is the first time I have ever seen a Southern Railroad.

25. Christmas Day. Staid in camp and read Allison's *History of Europe.* Invested my money in cakes and pies but didn't get my money's worth.

31. Our regiment embarked on the Va. and Tenn R.R. at Dublin and went to Lynchburg 105 miles via Salem and Liberty. Compelled to remain in the cars all night as the hotels were full.

January, 1862

1. New Years Day. In Lynchburg. Took breakfast at the Cabell House, Wm. Wells, clerk. Was put on guard at 9 o'clock which tended greatly to the hindrance of my enjoyment. Was permitted to go out at night when I made the best of my time eating oysters and drinking punches.

2. Left Lynchburg by Orange and Alexandria R.R. at 10 a.m. reaching Charlottesville 70 miles at 6 o'clock. Were switched to the Virginia Central R.R. without staying at C. and started travelling west.

3. Reached Jackson's River about 9 a.m. and forthwith went into camp. Weather cold and sleeting. I went across Jackson's River in a jolly boat to get some straw to sleep on.

7. Started to march over the Alleghanies to White Sulphur Spring.

8. We have been in service 8 months today. There are only 170 sick at this place now tho at one time there was 1600.

11. Read the newspapers at the hotel.

12. Left the White Sulphur and went into winter quarters at Lewisburg.

Reynolds experienced the same campaign that Isaac Smith reported, but didn't feel the impact that Smith reported of the frequent marches between the commands of the two political generals, Wise and Floyd. Reynolds was a private at the time and followed orders while Smith was a senior officer in the same regiment, the 22nd Virginia. Smith was able to see the indecision and ineffectiveness of the two feuding commanders and was caught up in a political problem brought on by the activities of his Unionist father.

Reynolds enlisted with the objective of avoiding any disgrace to the uniform so lovingly sewed by both his mother and sister. He swore to himself that he would never disgrace that uniform and he was true to his oath. Others may have complained, deserted, or tried to find an hororable release from service, but Reynolds never recorded any disappointment in the army he had entered. He did his duty and was recognized for this when he was detached from the regiment for duty in Brigadier General Echols office in June, 1863. He was promoted to ordinance Sergeant in August of that year and was to survive the war, but was to die at an early age in 1870. He died at the age of thirty-three.

Milton W. Humphries was born in Greenbrier County, Virginia, in 1844. He was familar with volunteer military service from an early age as his father served as a lieutenant-colonel of the Greenbrier militia.

Humphries entered Washington College in September, 1860, and was at the head of his class when the war began. The college became a military school and Humphries studied Field Fortifications and Gunnery. He enlisted in the "Monroe Artillery" which was later to become Bryan's Battery and the young soldier served throughout the war with distinction. He is credited with developing the concept of indirect artillery fire, first employed when the Confederates attacked Fayetteville, (West) Virginia, in 1863.

Following the war, he completed his studies at Washington College while Robert E. Lee was the college president and later was to complete advanced degrees in ancient languages and served as a professor of greek or ancient languages at Vanderbilt, the University of Texas, and at the University of Virginia.

He wrote about his Civil War experiences and completed small books on his experiences in Fayette County, West Virginia, and on the Lynchburg, Virginia Campaigns. He kept a diary and later wrote an autobiography -- both of which are held at the University of Virginia.

A Narrative of Military Operations in Fayetteville and Fayette County During the War 1861- 1863

Scene of Strategic Manuevering By Both Forces in the Early Days
TWO ACTIONS AT FAYETTEVILLE

Diary Records and Personal Recollections of Sergt. Humphreys; Bryan's Confederate Battery, Which Shelled Two Union Regiments Out of Fayetteville Forts May 19, '63 First Use of Indirect Firing Floyd-Wise Feud A Little Episode of Hawks Nest McCausland's Raid An Incident of Beckley Cannonade

By
PROF. MILTON WYLIE HUMPHRIES

1861
STRATEGIC MANUEVERING

Facts from Official Records - Federal advance on four lines- Wise's Legion. Col. Tompkin's 22nd Va. McCausland's 36 Va.- Scarey - Wise's retreat from Gauley Bridge - Returns with Floyd- Conflict of authority- Big Creek - Cotton Hill - Carnifex Ferry - Sewell Mountain - Lee arrives at Meadow Bluff - Wise recalled to Richmond- Rosecrans falls back to Gauley Bridge - Cox advances against Floyd on Cotton Hill - Benham on Laurel Creek- Col. Croghan killed at Glen Jean - Floyd retreats to Raleigh- Fayetteville fortified by Federals as important strategic point.

The object of this narrative is to give an account of such military operations of 1861-3 as occurred in Fayette County, with a concise statement of the more general events with which theywere connected. Most of the facts were obtained from "Official Records of the War of the Rebellion," but some statements are based on personal observation. Many unimportant details are omitted. The narrative will not be encumbered with references to the Official Records, as this collection of volumes is provided with a general index and each volume with a special index and anyone wishing to examine into a particular subject will easily find where it is mentioned in the Records. A single record of an event should never be accepted as true until a careful study of all the reports and correspondence relating to the event in question, and even then it will often be difficult, sometimes impossible, to elicit the truth.

West Virginia did not become a state until June 20, 1863, but Federal troops from West Virginia will be called West Virginians from the beginning.

As soon as a state of war was universally recognized as existing, the Federals invaded Virginia on four different lines: From Washington City directly "on to Richmond;" from Harper's Ferry into the Shenandoah Valley; from the northwest on the Staunton and Parkersburg turnpike, and from the west up the Kanawha River, this line receiving troops also by the Weston, Sutton and Summersville road. This narrative deals only with operations in the fourth region named.

Henry A. Wise, who had just been succeeded by John Letcher as Governor of Virginia, was commissioned as brigadier-general, and authorized to raise, in the Kanawha Valley and adjacent region, an independent force of volunteers, comprising all arms of the service, to be known as Wise's Legion. Two other men, Colonel C.Q. Tompkins and Colonel John McCausland, were also commissioned to raise troops independent of, but cooperating with, the Legion. All three suceeded in raising considerable forces, that of Colonel Tompkins afterward becoming the Twenty-second, and that of Colonel McCausland the Thirty-sixth Regiment Virginia Volunteers, respectively commanded by Colonel George S. Patton and Colonel John

McCausland. The Legion was raised to 2800.

On July 17, 1861, at Scarey Creek, twelve miles below Charleston, a force of infantry under Colonel Patton and cavalry under Colonel A.G. Jenkins and two cannons, numbering in all 800, according to Wise, after a doubtful contest succeeded in defeating a force of 1200, with very slight loss. Details do not belong here. After some manoevering and skirmishing, Wise learned of the approach of strong forces, one column moving towards Gauley Bridge, and decided that it was necessary, especially as he was almost out of ammunition, to abandon the Kanawha Valley, which he proceeded to do, burning bridges, including that at Gauley, behind him. His orders from the war department, received during his retreat, were to fall back as far as Covington, but being allowed some discretion, he encamped at the White Sulphur.

While he was there, John B. Floyd, who also had been Governor of Virginia, (1850-53), and United States Secretary of War under President Buchannan, having been appointed brigadier-general, came with a small brigade. (Wise says about 1200 men), which he raised in Southwest Virginia, to the neighborhood of Sweet Springs. He had been assigned to the same general region to which Wise had been assigned. The two generals were under instructions to cooperate in expelling the Federal invaders. This was a fatal mistake. If it is true, as has been said, that one bad general is better than two good ones, nothing could be much worse that two bad ones, though we can hardly assert that Wise can justly be called a bad general.

Floyd's commission antedated that of Wise, and on August 12, he assumed command of the army of the Kanawha and the country adjacent thereto -- another name for the region assigned to Wise -- the Middle Department of the West.

The two forces moved slowly westward, Wise on the James River and Kanawha pike; Floyd on roads leading to Summersville. From the start there was serious trouble between the two commanders, growing partly out of the fact that Floyd was departing radically from a plan of campaign which Wise had submitted to General Lee, who had fully approved it. This trouble became acute on the occasion of the very first fighting that occurred, which was in Fayette County, just west of Big Sewell Mountain, August 25. Wise had posted a strong picket at Piggot's Mill, some distance from his main force. Floyd sent across from his command about 175 cavalrymen under acting-Colonel Jenkins who, by Floyd's order, relieved Wise's picket and occupied the post themselves. A body of Federals surprised and completely routed them, and when Wise's troops came to their rescue, they flatly refused to obey Wise's orders. He made bitter complaint to Floyd on account of the interference.

Later Wise moved to Dogwood Gap and Floyd to Carnifex Ferry, (called also Carnifix and Carnifax) in Nicholas County, and crossed Gauley River. Here he constructed fortifications which Wise redicules in his account of his troubles with Floyd.

Soon afterwards at Cross Lanes, Floyd surprised and completely scattered a regiment of "lubberly Dutchmen" (he calls them) commanded by Colonel E.B. Tyler.

On September 2 and 3, 1861, Wise, moving towards Gauley from Hawks Nest with about 1250 men and two pieces of artillery, attacked and finally drove away an equal force of Federals from their position just west of a hill around which the pike makes a bend after crossing Big Creek westward. He thereby gained control of Miller's Ferry and Liken's Mill. On September 1, Brigadier Generals A.A. Chapman and Alfred Beckley, commanding militia, drove a small Federal force from Cotton Hill, but it had been found that efficient service for any great length of time, could not be expected of the militia, and Wise did not press his advantage, but fell back to his position near Hawks Nest, and the Federals, in larger numbers than before, re-occupied the position from which they had been driven, but Wise's account implies that he still maintained control of Miller's Ferry.

So far the Federals against whom Wise and Floyd had been operating, were under the command of Brigadier-General J.D. Cox; but soon after the events just narrated, W.S. Rosecrans, West Point graduate of 1842, who had been made a brigadier-general in the regular army and had already rendered very efficient service, was found to be approaching from the north by way of Sutton. On September 10, having on that day made more than a usual day's march, he appeared in front of Floyd's position at Carnifex Ferry at 3 p.m., with 10 regiments of infantry and a proportionate supply of artillery. This was no intrusion into the territory of Cox, for Rosecrans had been given charge of a very extensive department, which included the whole of West Virginia. He spent four hours trying to locate Floyd's trenches, which were concealed by dense woods. In doing this the Federals necessarily exposed themselves in places to the Confederate fire. Artillery also was used by both sides. At 7 p.m., the Federals rested on their arms, and during the night Floyd, knowing the superior strength of his assailants, quietly withdrew and crossed the river. Strange to say, Floyd permitted very important papers to fall into Rosecrans' hands, revealing the fact (according to Rosecrans) that Floyd had 5 regiments and 2 batteries, and a battalion of cavalry, and that considerable reinforcements were approaching. The losses were: Federals killed, 17; wounded, 141; Confederate killed 0; wounded 20. Floyd himself was wounded in the right hand.

Such was what is called the "Battle of Carnifex Ferry." It was really more like a battle than anything else that had occurred in that region; but Floyd seems to exaggerate when he reports as follows: "The attack was made with spirit and determination, with small arms, grape and round shot from howitzers and rifled cannon. There was scarcely an intermission in the conflict until night put an end to the firing." Among the private soldiers and the citizens it was asserted that 1500 Federals were killed, and one prominent citizen of Lewisburg wrote to President Davis that it was reported that the killed "amounted to thousands." The affair gave Floyd great prestige, and his attitude towards Wise seemed to the latter no longer endurable, so he wrote to General Lee asking him to separate the two commands completely by sending himself and his Legion east, and replacing them with other troops, and added: "I feel that if we remain together, we will unite in more wars than one."

After Floyd had crossed the Gauley, Rosecrans did not follow him, and Floyd moved his troops to the James River and Kanawha pike, and about September 13 he and Wise fell back with all their forces to the top of Big Sewell Mountain. Floyd encamped on the main top where Smailes' tavern used to be, and Wise moved three or four miles farther east, and occupied what he considered an almost impregnable position.

According to Wise's account, Floyd on the 16th called a council of war which assembled at 5 p.m. After hearing Wise's arguments an favor of occupying the position he held, Floyd decided to make an examination before coming to a final decision, and on the same afternoon within half an hour after the adjournment of the council, Floyd, without further consultation, notified Wise that he had decided to fall back to the most defensible point between Meadow Bluff and Lewisburg, and that he himself would move with his force at once, and Wise was immediately to get ready to follow. On the 18th Floyd inquired by dispatch why Wise had not obeyed his order to move promptly, and Wise replied that he had not been ordered to move, but only to get ready to move. He added a hope that Floyd would not require him to move at all, assigning reasons for the request. Floyd made no immediate reply and Wise remained where he was. On the 19th the Federals were reported advancing on the turnpike. Such was the state of affairs when, on the 21st General Robert E. Lee arrived in person at Meadow Bluff, having come from the Cheat Mountain Region.

General Lee appears not to have assumed immediate command of either Wise's or Floyd's troops, but to have taken general control of both. He and Wise exchanged notes several times, Lee seemingly regarding Wise's position as the stronger, but Floyd's as the safer because it provided for an approach of the Federals through Nicholas County, and Wise maintaining that to his certain knowledge the entire Federal Force was advancing on the turnpike. On the 25th Lee came to Wise's post, bringing four regiments, and skirmishing began at once.

Rosecrans had moved his immediate command to the turnpike and united it with that of Cox who had been operating on this road, and the combined force, 5200 strong, had advanced to the summit of Big Sewell. This force, according to Wise, was soon increased to 6000.

On the 25th the Federals advanced in force to ascertain the probable strength of the Confederates and reconnoitre their position. A strong body of skirmishers, accompanied by Wise himself, advanced and met those of the Federals, and the skirmishing mentioned above commenced, the Confederates all believing that a powerful assault was about to be made upon them. At this juncture, about 4:30 p.m., there was handed to Wise, under fire, the following amazing and strangely delayed letter:

Richmond, Va., Sept. 20, 1861

Sir: You are instructed to turn over all the troops heretofore immediately under your command to General Floyd, and report yourself in person to the Adjutant General in this city, with the least delay. In making the transfer to General Floyd you will include everything under your command.

By Order of the President,
J.P. BENJAMIN
Acting Secretary of War

General H.A. Wise

Wise immediately wrote a note to Lee asking him for advice as to what he ought to do under the unique circumstances, and Lee replied advising him to "obey the President."

No battle was fought. Rosecrans was too able a general to risk an assault on the Confederate entrenchments. The Federals fell back to the main top and encamped for some time and then gradually withdrew and occupied several points along the road including Gauley Bridge.

It seems proper here to make a digression. That letter to Wise was a most unfortunate thing for Floyd. Wise instantly left what he believed to be a battlefield on which he was to win glory and fame, and hastened to Richmond and, as soon as he could, prepared an elaborate account of all that had occurred between himself and Floyd. The result was that the request that he had previously submitted to General Lee, that he and his Legion be sent east, and some other commander and troops be sent to take their place, was virtually granted, and he retained his rank to the end of the war, and was with Lee at Appomatox.

To replace Wise and his Legion, Brigadier-General W.W. Loring was sent with considerable force, and General Lee formed the purpose of driving the Federals from the Kanawha Valley. With this in view, but without explicitly promising cooperation, he sent General Floyd and his command, extimated at 4000 men (8 regiments) and 700 cavalry by Rosecrans, to the south side of New River, intending to send General Loring down the James River and Kanawha pike; but appeals for reinforcements made by the commanders in the Cheat Mountain region, and the Shenandoah Valley were so urgent that he sent Loring there. It is not clear why Lee permitted Floyd to proceed, unsupported on the north side, to carry out or try to carry out his part of the undertaking.

To comprehend fully the ensuing events it is necessary to bear in mind that for several weeks Rosecrans, with good reason, confidently expected Loring, under Lee's supervision, to advance on Gauley Bridge. He had not only other cause for this belief, but it had been reported to him by some one who had been present that Lee, being told that Rosecrans had said he was going to occupy the Kanawha Valley, had added very significantly, "*if he can.*"

About October 15 Rosecrans having heard that there was a force of Virginia militia between Fayetteville and Cotton Hill, sent Colonel R.L. McCook with an adequate force across at Miller's Ferry. He had a skirmish with and dispersed a small body of men, and learning that there was no strong hostile force over there, he recrossed the river, neglecting to leave a guard on the south side. Rosecrans, much displeased, ordered him on October 25 to send a strong guard over, but the attempt to do so was thwarted by sharpshooters, concealed and of unknown number.

About October 27 Rosecrans learned that Floyd was advancing from Raleigh towards Cotton Hill. On the 29th Floyd drove some Federal outposts down near to the mouth of Great Falls Creek, and on November 1 he occupied Cotton Hill. By means of artillery he made it impossible in the day time for ferry boats to run at the mouth of Gauley or wagons to pass along the road. Floyd claims to have destroyed one ferry boat. This state of affairs with constant skirmishing continued for some time, Floyd says three weeks, but his own account makes it not more than ten days. The cause of Rosecrans' failure to dislodge Floyd earlier has been explained, but as soon as he learned that there was no danger of a Confederate advance from the direction of Lewisburg, he took steps to end the situation. Already on November 4 he had posted Brigadier-General H.W. Benham (first honor West Point graduate of 1837) with 3000 men opposite the mouth of lower Loup Creek to prevent Floyd from getting in his rear if he were attacked by Loring. Now that this danger no longer existed, he formed a plan by which he hoped and reasonably expected to capture or disperse Floyd's entire force. Brigadier-General R.C. Schenck was posted with an adequate force far enough up New River for him to get in Floyd's rear, and complete preparations were made for rapidly crossing, while Benham, also well prepared for crossing the Kanawha, was to press the Confederates in front. Fortunately for Floyd, just as this plan was about to be put in operation, New River rose to such a height that it was impossible for Schenck to cross. Those acquainted with that region and the character of that river will readily understand the situation. The plan was then changed, and Benham was to cross the smoother Kanawha and to pass to his right around to the rear of Floyd, and Schenck was to come down, cross at the same place, and press him in front. Benham's operations seem to indicate that he never understood the change in the plan, and although he effeciently did nearly all the important work that was done, Rosecrans severely criticized him and charges to his disobedience of orders the escape of Floyd's army.

The operations that now occurred are beclouded with all sorts of contradictions in the Official Records. The Condederate and Federal reports naturally contradict each other, but some of the Federal reports contradict other Federal reports; so only a vague approximation to what actually happened will be attempted. The result, however, was that Floyd fell back until pursuit ceased entirely. The details will now be briefly stated:

On November 10, under the supervision of General Cox, Colonel C.A. Devilliers and Lieutenant- Colonel D.A. Enyart crossed the river, each with 200 men, and somehow caused the Confederate artillery to withdraw. Floyd makes the Federals fewer and says they were driven away, but he learned on that day that a Federal reenforcement of 5000 men had "landed at the mouth of Loup Creek". He appears to have acted under the belief that this was true in all his movements. He fell back before this small force, which was re-enforced by 6 companies after dark, and skirmishing continued until midnight, the Federals gained possession of the mountain as far as Blake's farm. On the 11th at day break the advance was resumed, the Confederates skirmishing as they retired, but making no determined stand. When the Federals reached the edge of

Cotton Hill proper, Floyd's wagon train was seen moving on the road towards Fayetteville. Cox then caused his troops to halt so as not to show how few they were, as Floyd was evidently under the impression that a large force was advancing upon him. Rosecrans, however, speaks of a Federal repulse, which seems to have been at this place. In the afternoon a body of 150 men under Major B.G. Leiper, followed the Confederates up the Fayetteville turnpike, crossed Cotton Hill, remained till evening, and fell back half a mile.

The Federal loss in all these operations up to this time was 2 killed, 1 wounded and 6 missing - sufficient evidence that the resistance to the Federal advance must have been slight. The 6 missing were seemingly captured when the first attack on the artillery was made.

On the 12th at 3 p.m., Benham arrived with 3 regiments, amounting to 1500 men and some artillery. He had sent three detached forces to as many different points, but instead of passing around on his right to Floyd's rear he had gone up to the Falls and ascended the mountain directly to Cotton Hill. He at once advanced with a total of 1640 men and finding the Confederates strongly posted, at Laurel Creek, he skirmished till dark, losing 1 killed and 4 wounded. Floyd says that the Federals on this occasion, with superior forces, declined battle and "disgracefully retreated." On that night at 2:30 a.m., (13th) Floyd began to fall back, always fearing that those 5000 men from Ohio would get in his rear. Early on the 13th, Benham followed beyond Fayetteville, finding, he says, evidence of a hasty retreat. Now having 2700 men, some of his detached men having arrived, Benham pressed forward, arriving at Hawkins' farm, 5 miles beyond Fayetteville. He claims to have found abandoned tents, wagons, and ammunition along the road. A little less than 10 miles from Fayetteville, he encountered an advanced outpost not far from McCoy's Mill, (Glen Jean) and there followed a sharp skirmish which lasted half an hour. Here Lieutenant-Colonel St. George Croghan, Floyd's cavalry commander, was killed. The Federals lost none.

Floyd occupied the ridge just beyond Loop Creek as one goes to Beckley. This hill he calls "Loop Mountain," a name apparently unknown in that region and makes this remarkable statement: "In my position on Loop Mountain the enemy declined attacking me, but retreated from that to Gauley in a very disorderly manner." He says this position, not having any strategic advantage, he went on to Piney Creek in Raleigh County. Benham, however, says that finding the main Confederate force apparently prepared for a general action, he began an attack in front and used artillery with effect and sent a force of 750 men to attack the Confederates on their left flank, and when this attack was made their whole force retreated precipitately, abandoning blankets, clothing, camp equipage, etc., and that he pursued, after resting his men for a while, but was recalled by General Schenck to whom General Rosecrans had given command over everything south of the river. The two accounts are absolutely irreconcilable. Benham's account cannot be all fiction, as anyone will readily see on a careful perusal.

Floyd's report of operations was evidently unsatisfactory to the authorities at Richmond, and their polite comments really meant that Floyd had shown the Federals the great importance of Cotton Hill, and then had turned it over to them to fortify. He and his army were not very long afterwards called away from West Virginia and General Lee was notified of that fact.

The Federals utilized the lesson taught them by Floyd and in preparation for the next campaign strongly fortified not Cotton Hill proper, but Fayetteville, as being for various reasons a better strategic place. The fortifications were prepared against attack from both directions.

Here a question arises: Can anyone tell when and by what command the fort at Fayetteville was built which is today believed to be a Confederate work?

The Federal soldiers used to sing to the tune of "Jordan" a badly riming parody of that song, of which parody two stanzas, considered libelous by the Confederates, celebrated the two principal events of this campaign:

"Old Gov'nor Floyd became much annoyed
At the cannonballs awhizzing all around him;
So he took a sudden flight in the dark of the night,
And he landed on the other side of Gauley."

"Old Gov'nor Floyd marched his troops on Cotton Hill
For to cannonade the Yankee camp at Gauley;
But Rosecrans and Cox were as cunning as a fox
And sent him a'running back to Raleigh."

1862
ACTION AT FAYETTEVILLE, SEPT. 10.

Loring Commands Confederate Army of 5000 at Giles C.H. Lightburn suceeds Cox as head of Federal forces in Kanawha - Battle of Fayetteville, Sept. 10 - Federals outnumbered, retreat in night through road mysteriously left open for them to to Kanawha - Loring misinterprets orders and leaves Kanawha for Lewisburg - Army ordered to return - Fruits of Confederate Campaign lost - Interesting episode at Hawks Nest Cliff.

At the opening of the campaign of 1862 the Federals occupied Princeton in Mercer County, and when Henry Heth, who had been Floyd's inspector with the rank of Colonel, and had been made brigadier-general, left Lewisburg to help drive the Federals from Princeton (which was done before he got there), Colonel George Crook occupied Lewisburg with 2 regiments, a battery of mountain howitzers, and a small body of cavalry. Heth, returning from Princeton, managed to surprise Crook's force on the morning of May 23, and although his infantry was fully as strong as Crook's and his artillery greatly superior, through a strange blunder he suffered a crushing defeat and lost most of his artillery. This disaster, followed by other evidences of incompetence, made him intensely unpopular. So he was called away (and made a major-general in the Army of Northern Virginia), and Brigadier-General John S. Williams was sent to take his place. Not long afterwards, W.W. Loring, who had been created major-general on February 15, was placed in command of all the forces in the middle region of West Virginia. In the mean time these forces had been increased until they comprised the Twenty-second,Thirty-sixth, Forty-fifth, Fiftieth, Fifty-third and Sixtieth Regiments, and the Twenty-sixth and Thirtieth Battalions Virginia infantry, and Bryans, Chapman's, Lowry's, Otey's and Stamps' Batteries. General A.G. Jenkins' cavalry force of less than 1000 should also be added, but this force did not operate with the main body during the campaign. Bryan had only two pieces, and the men, about 80, who had no guns, served as infantry with the Twenty-sixth Battalion. These forces were organized into brigades, commanded respectively by Brigadier-General John Echols, Brigadier-General J.S. Williams and Colonel G.C. Wharton. What units made up each brigade is not stated in the records, and there seems, at times, to have been a fourth brigade.

Loring had distinguished himself as major in a regiment of mounted riflemen in the Mexican War; had lost his left arm at Chapultepec, and had been promoted for bravery. A man thus distinguished as a major in a war in which Robert E. Lee served as a captain, and Thomas J. Jackson as a lieutenant, naturally enjoyed great prestige, and the army was elated at his assignment to that department. He kept his forces for a considerable time in camp in the neighborhood of Union in Monroe County. This delay he afterwards ascribed to the necessity of making vast preparations for the coming campaign.

On August 29 the Secretary of War wired Loring that Pope's letterbook, captured, revealed the fact that Cox had orders to retain 5000 men in West Virginia, and to send the rest to Pope, and added: "Clear the Valley of the Kanawha and operate northwardly to a junction with our army in the valley." Loring sent Jenkins on a raid through the region lying north of the Kanawha Valley and concentrated the main force or the greater part of it near Giles Court House (Pearisburg) just above the narrows of New River. On September 6 he marched down on the south side of the river with all the infantry except Echol's brigade, and all the artillery, about 16 pieces. He says he marched with 5000 men, but it is not clear whether this number includes Echols' brigade which he says pursued a much longer route.

On the Federal side, no longer Cox, but Colonel J.A.J. Lightburn was in command of the Department of the Kanawha. His forces consisted of 7 regiments of infantry, 1 regiment of cavalry, and 14 pieces of artillery, (8 mountain howitzers, disposed as follows: At Raleigh Court House, the Thirty-fourth and Thirty-seventh Ohio, 4 mountain howitzers, and 2 smooth-bores, Colonel Edward Siber commanding (2 of his companies being at Fayetteville); at Camp Ewing, ten miles from Gauley Bridge towards Lewisburg, the Forty-fourth and Forty-seventh Ohio, 2 companies of the Second West Virginia Cavalry, and some of the artillery, Colonel S.A. Gilbert commanding; and the rest of the forces: the Fourth, Eighth, and Ninth West Virginia, and part of the Second West Virginia Cavalry, distributed at Summersville and several places along the Kanawha River. Headquarters were at Gauley Bridge.

The campaign now beginning was of very great importance since in Virginia and North Carolina the want of salt was acutely felt, many families being entirely without it, as the King Saltworks in southwest Virginia were their only source of supply, and the Confederate Government hoped to take and hold the Kanawha Valley with its vast salt works extending up the river from Charleston.

Colonel Lightburn, on hearing of Loring's advance, seems never for a moment to have thought of uniting his forces for a general battle, but directed his efforts to saving his supplies. This, however, could not be done without some fighting. The supply trains were ordered to go to Charleston and cross Elk River, and he afterwards complained that they did not cross it until his army arrived there. No attempts to save the contents of the magagines are mentioned in the reports; they were simply burned. One might wonder for what purpose they were there.

Colonel Siber, learning of Loring's near approach, withdrew his force from Raleigh Court House to Fayetteville, which place the Federals, taught by Floyd in the previous campaign had strongly fortified with forts and trenches as already stated. On September 9 he learned that a strong secessionist named Tetam, had said he would need his rifle the next morning; so he sent 7 mounted men he had to take Tetam, and just as these men reached the house about 30 Confederate cavalrymen appeared and chased them down Laurel Creek. Thus warned of the approaching attack, at 11 a.m., on the 10th, Siber sent 4 companies of the Thirty-fourth Ohio under Lieutenant-Colonel F.E. Franklin to Cassidy's Mill on Laurel Creek to cover the right flank as a reconnoitering party, and at noon he sent Captain Carl Moritz with 2 companies of the Thirty-seventh Ohio out on the Raleigh road. About two miles out these met the vanguard of Loring's army. Before the Confederates reached this point, Colonel Wharton with the Twenty-second Virginia under Colonel G.S. Patton, the Fifty-first under Lieutenant-Colonel August Forsburg, and the Thirtieth Battalion Virginia Sharpshooters under Lieutenant-Colonel J.L. Clarke, was sent by a road leading to the left in order to pass around and get in the rear of the Federal position. This force was guided by Mr. Benjamin Jones, the father of Beuhring H. Jones, colonel of the Sixtieth Virginia Infantry. The distance around and the obstacles to rapid movement were so great that it was about 2:15 p.m., when Wharton took position near, but not extending across the road to Cotton Hill, and about 1000 yards from the Federal works fronting on that side. While the Confederates were taking position to begin action, the Federals made a vigorous attack upon them with 6 companies of the Thirty-fourth Ohio, 4 of which were led personally by Colonel J.T. Toland and 2 by Captain H.C. Hatfield on the Cotton Hill road on Toland's right. They made three attacks, but were repulsed each time and retired to their works. Similar attacks of the Confederates upon the Federal works were likewise repulsed. In this fight both sides used artillery, the guns of the Confederates being rifled, but how many and of what battery is not stated in the reports. The Federals used 4 mountain howitzers under Lieutenant H.H. Anderson at the main redoubt. At length both sides became inactive.

It had been agreed that the force on the Raleigh road should refrain from a serious attack on the Federal front until Wharton engaged them in the rear. This force, under Williams and accompanied by Loring, as stated above, met Captain Moritz with his two companies about two miles from the stronghold. This small force offered resistance so stubborn that Loring, who omits mention of their number, says that they were contested every step of the way. As soon as the conflict in the rear of the Federals was heard, Williams attacked the front and right flank of the entrenchments and the redoubt on that side of the Federal position. The reports indicate that the infantry and artillery operated together on a low hill 500 or 600 yards from the fort and the distance being found too great (evidently so for musketry but very small for artillery), it was decided to move nearer to another hill, which movement is thus described by Williams: "Edgar's battalion, under Major Davis, cleared the front of sharpshooters and drove them in gallant style, and the whole of the artillery: Otey's, Stamps', Chapman's, Bryan's, and Lowry's batteries dashed in magnificent style over the ridge, down the slope and up to the top of the next hill, where they unlimbered within 300 yards of the enemy's fort, and opened a terrible cannonade upon it." All this artillery was arrayed against two 6 pound smoothbores in the fort, commanded by

Lieutenant William West.

When the Confederates reached this position. Williams discovered that the position was stronger than had been supposed, and adds: "Besides the square redoubt in front, there was one to the left and rear of the court-house, which was at that moment engaged by Colonel Wharton, and to the right and rear another strong fortress upon a high hill, which commanded both the other forts."

To understand fully what follows, it is necessary to go back a little.

When Colonel Lightburn learned that Jenkins had left Union, he caused Colonel Gilbert to send Colonel L.S. Elliot with six companies of the Forty-seventh Ohio to reinforce the troops at Summersville, and sent Colonel J.E. Paxton with 6 companies of the Second West Virginia Cavalry to look after Jenkins; and learning that Fayetteville was being assailed, he sent 3 *companies* of the Fourth West Virginia Infantry to re-inforce Siber! He also sent Lieutenant-Colonel A.C. Parry to Cotton Hill "to meet the retreating force." He says Parry had 5 companies of the Forty-seventh Ohio; but he had caused Gilbert to send 6 companies of this regiment to Summersville. Could it have been a "Company L?"

At Fayetteville the fighting at the front was kept up till some time after sunset, but the Confederates failed to make any progress. When it was still not too dark to see, the 4 companies that had been detached under Lieutenant-Colonel Franklin and also the 3 companies sent as re-enforcements by Lightburn accompanied by 25 cavalrymen, came in by the Cotton Hill road. These 7 companies were mistaken by Loring for 3 regiments. On the next day he sent a dispatch to the Secretary of War stating that 3 regiments of re-enforcements had come, but that Echols had arrived with his brigade and the Federals, learning of this re-enforcement, had withdrawn in the night. They did withdraw and did it unobstructed and almost entirely unmolested. Between 1 and 2 a.m., Siber first sent the 80 wounded and then the most important trains and finally withdrew the men, all unperceived by the Confederates.

The half day's fighting of this small force-- 1 regiment and 6 companies of another with 4 mountain howitzers and two 6-pounder artillery, some of them heavy caliber, constitutes either one of the most brilliant feats of the war or one of the most dismal failures and instances of ineffiency on the part of the Confederates. In any case Colonel Siber merits the highest praise. There was a report current in the Confederate army that Loring ordered Wharton to leave the way open for the Federals to escape, but there is no hint of this in the Official Records. Loring says that there were so many roads leading from Fayetteville that it was not possible with his force to guard all of them; but he left unguarded the very one the Federals were sure to take. Siber speaks of it simply as his line of retreat and ascribes its being left open to the "considerable loss" (which was really very light) that Wharton had sustained in trying to block it. It looks very much as if Loring thought it best to get what he supposed to be 5 regiments out of their stronghold by any means that might offer, and so disposed his forces that the Federals could march out; but whether intentionally or not, *he let them escape.*

It is a remarkable fact that in this campaign the heavy ordinance of the Federals was served by officers and men detailed from the infantry, there being no trained artillery organizations.

The losses here and elsewhere in this campaign were amazingly light on both sides. They will be summed up at the end.

On the morning of the 11th it was discovered that the Federals were gone. General Williams pursued instantly and reports having found the road "strewn with guns, knapsacks, blankets, overcoats, wagons, hospital and sutlers' stores, horses and men." Whether these men, strewn on the road, were dead, wounded or asleep, he does not say. Wharton and Echols immediately followed

Williams. At Cotton Hill Siber made a brief stand. Williams attacked in front, while Wharton and Echols moved to turn the right flank, where upon Siber retreated to the Kanawha River and moved down the left side, burning magazines as he went.

On the 10th at 3 p.m., when Lightburn heard of the battle going on in Fayetteville, he ordered Gilbert to bring his force, stationed on the Lewisburg pike, down to Gauley, which he promptly did, reporting in person to Lightburn near the falls at 8 p.m. On the 11th, when the Confederates pursuing Siber descended the mountain, some sharp fighting took place between them and Gilbert with the river between the opposing forces. Soon Gilbert, having burned such stores as had not been removed and having blown up a large magazine in the mouth of a hollow near the falls, retreated down the pike on the right side of the river. It has been pointed out that Loring's report is ambiguous as to whether the Federals or Confederates blew up this magazine, but the ambiguity is only grammatical, and besides there is no conceivable reason why the Confederates should have destroyed ammunition virtually in their grasp. As to the destruction of the bridge over Gauley River, about which there has been much discussion, it would be useless to add anything to what others have written except perhaps that it may be worth while to give assurance that the Sixtieth Virginia Regiment was certainly with Loring and there was a Sergeant in it named Andrew Summers. Those interested in the discussion will see why this statement is made.

Lightburn had ordered Elliot on the 10th to bring his command from Suumersville to Gauley, but when he came he found Gauley already taken; so had burned his wagons and went through the hills and joined Gilbert at Cannelton.

The pursuit to Charleston with its frequent skirmishes followed. At Charleston September 12 Lightburn made a stand, but after slight resistance crossed Elk River by the suspension bridge, which he then cut down. The Elk is very deep for some distance from its mouth and there were no means of crossing left for Loring. The reports give minute details of the action here, but they are of no interest. Lightburn, unpursued, retreated by a circuitous route to Point Pleasant, and Loring occupied Charleston until October 8.

In Lightburn's behalf it should be noted that he through misinformation believed Jenkins' force to be twice as great as it was, and was always imagining that a large force of hostile cavaslry was hovering in his rear, while in fact Jenkins was making a very distant circuit through the region north of the Kanawha River and even beyond the Kanawha River.

The Confederate losses from September 6 to 16 were 18 killed, 89 wounded. The Federal losses were 25 killed, 95 wounded, 190 missing. These remarkably small figures indicate that no determined assaults could have been made on the Federal works at Fayetteville.

For many days after the occupation of Charleston there was a constant train of wagons hauling salt away from the Kanawha Valley on roads leading eastward. The Federals were too hard pressed to destroy either the salt furnaces or the great accumulation of salt. With the exception of this temporary gain, all the advantages of Loring's conquest were soon to be simply thrown away.

The Secretary of War, as already stated, had instructed Loring to "clear the Valley of the Kanawha and operate northwardly to a junction with our army in the valley," but this was eighteen days before the Battle of Sharpsburg. General Lee had also proposed or suggested that Loring should move northward, destroying the Baltimore and Ohio Railroad, and passing down Cheat River to join forces in Maryland. But neither the Secretary of War nor General Lee intended that the Kanawha Valley, when cleared of Federals, should be left for them, unopposed, to reoccupy. Lee's language is clear as to that; but when he wrote suggesting the route northward, Loring wrote to Lee, suggesting that the route by way of Lewisburg and Monterey would be better, and without awaiting a reply or receiving any instructions, not more than forty-eight hours after he had written, he began to move on the route he had proposed, leaving the Kanawha Valley totally unprotected. His trains were started on the 8th of October.

A small force, including Bryan's Battery, had been posted at Gauley Bridge. Some Federals, 2 officers and 30 men, had recently been captured not far from Sutton and had been brought to Gauley Bridge. The officers, on their word of honor not to leave, enjoyed freedom, but the enlisted men were kept under guard. An order came for those of Bryan's men who were armed with muskets to guard the prisoners and the ordinance train to Lewisburg and there "await the head of the column." This order amazed everybody. On the 10th the ordinance train arrived and on the next day a lieutenant with most of the men took charge of it, while a corporal with a guard of about 12 men was placed in charge of the prisoners, and the train and prisoners, the latter in front, started for Lewisburg on the 11th.

On the march the prisoners got considerably ahead of the train, there being no order to keep them near each other. This led to a little episode which it seems admissible to narrate as it occurred at the best known spot in Fayette County. Early on the morning of the 12th when the prisoners and their escort approached the place where a path leads a short distance out to Hawks Nest, the prisoners begged earnestly to be conducted out to look down from the crest of that famous vertical rock cliff 650 feet high. The corporal in charge very reluctantly granted the request, and the prisoners were required to go in front of the whole guard. When the former reached the crest, the latter were formed into a curved line behind them. When the prisoners were huddled together on the brink and conversing in a low tone, it occurred to the corporal, especially since the prisoners had been so insistent, that they, outnumbering the guard nearly or quite three to one, might have formed a plot to seize the guard suddenly and hurl them over. So to be ready for such an attempt, he very imprudently, in the usual sharp military tone, gave the command: "*Fix bayonets!*" The effect on the prisoners was like an electric shock. Certainly some, possibly all of them for a moment expected instantly to be shoved over. Of course it quickly occurred to most of them that such an act on the part of the guard was out of the question, but action on the first impulse might have precipitated a horrible tragedy, and certainly all, guards and prisoners alike, breathed easier when they got away from that place. Especially was this true of the corporal, who is today the writer of this narrative.

The prisoners arrived at Lewisburg in the afternoon of the 15th. On the 17th about 9 a.m., they were marched out into Main Street and the "head of the column" which they were to await arrived at that moment, and then and there, just one hundred miles from Charleston, it counter-marched and began to retrace its steps to that place. The Adjutant General, S. Cooper, had sent, on the 15th, a dispatch to Loring, ordering him to turn over command to General Echols, and himself to report in person with as little delay as practicable at the Adjutant General's office in Richmond, and at the same time the Secreatry of War, G.W. Randolph, sent a dispatch to Echols, ordering him to take command with General Williams as his second and at once to march the army back to the Kanawha Valley and make its defense his first object. On the next day (16th) the Secretary of War had written to General Lee, who was at the head of the army in the field, informing him of what had been done and asking him if he could give Loring employment. Lee did not yet know even that Loring had left Charleston, and had written to the Secretary of War on the 15th: "Loring must protect the Kanawha Valley. He must take possession of the salt works at Charleston and keep the enemy out of that country, I think it probable the best service your army can perform; but I shall leave this matter to your better judgement." Of course Loring knew nothing of all this when he started from Charleston.

What could have induced Loring to throw away the fruits of the campaign is an unexplained mystery. The current report, seemingly believed by all, was that Loring, being summoned to Richmond, supposed that he was to bring his army; but this story was erroneous; Loring was conducting his army by way of Lewisburg and Monterey to the Shenandoah Valley.

The weary march back to Charleston and the failure to take the place, followed by the retreat up the valley and the march back through Fayette County during the last days of October, need not be narrated in detail. The Kanawha Valley was permanently given up to the Federals, who resumed, under new commanders, the positions they had occupied when the campaign begun.

1863
DIARY RECORDS, FAYETTEVILLE, MAY 18 AND 19

Confederate plan to recover Kanawha Valley abandoned- McCausland makes sham attack with artillery on Fayetteville to protect Imboden's raiders - Diary entries of author, aged 18, sergeant, Bryan's Battery - First instance of employment of "indirect firing," Fayetteville, May, 19- Confederate retreat to Raleigh - End of McCausland's raid- Incident of Beckley cannonade.

One of the most important things for the army and people in Virginia and North Carolina, was to secure and maintain a supply of salt, and one of the most serious injuries that could be inflicted on the Federals would to have been to destroy the Baltimore and Ohio Railroad. Accordingly, even before military operations had begun in 1863, a plan was formed to attain both of these ends through the same operations. A large force was to move into the region through which the railroad passed, destroy it, and move southward to the Kanawha Valley, while a smaller force was to move down New River on the left side and by threatening to occupy Gauley Bridge, force the Federals to draw off troops that might otherwise re-enforce those defending the railroad.

There was much correspondence between the commanders of different forces in regard to the execution of this plan. Without going into details it must suffice to say here that the plan to reconquer the Kanawha Valley was abandoned in the course of the campaign, but General Wm. E. Jones was sent with a force of cavalry and General J.D. Imboden, though a cavalry officer, with a force of infantry, to destroy the railroad and accomplish whatever else might be practicable. The history of the operations of Jones and Imboden (often called"Imboden's Raid," but officially and more correctly "Jones' Raid") does not belong here. The sending of a small force towards Gauley to divert the attention of the Federals was still, under the changed plan, considered desirable. Accordingly Colonel John McCausland with the Thirty-sixth and six companies of the Sixtieth Virginia, and 4 pieces (two 3-inch rifles and two 12 pound howitzers) of Bryan's Battery, and a company of cavalry, marched for Fayetteville from Princeton on the 16th of May.

At that time Brigadier-General E.P. Scammon was in command of all the Federals in that department. Brigade commander Colonel C.B. White was stationed at Fayetteville with the Twelfth Ohio under Colonel J.D. Hines, and 2 companies of the Second West Virginia Cavalry, and 2 sections (4pieces) of McMullin's Battery of six 3-inch rifles. McCausland probably had only vague and uncertain information concerning the Federal strength, but at least a sham attack was to be made in any case. Scammon in his report says that McCausland had 3 regiments, a battalion of cavalry, and even a Confederate writer, has erroneously added theTwenty-second Virginia to the forces enumerated above.

As the writer will have to mention himself more than once, and such testimony is justly considered dubious, it has been thought best to narrate the incidents of the campaign or raid by copying *verbatim* the appropriate part of a diary kept by him solely for his future information. All additions are enclosed in square brackets, and omissions of irrelevant matters are indicated by dots. Occasionally a dash represents a proper name omitted for reasons that will be obvious to the reader.

The writer, aged 18, was sergeant of the second piece, a 12-pound howitzer, of Bryan's Battery and always exercised his right to point (aim) his piece himself. Captain Thomas A. Bryan was under arrest, but accompanied the battery which was comanded by a lieutenant, another lieutenant commanding the third and fourth pieces. The first piece was under Sergeant A.N. Campbell, afterwards well known in West Virginia as Judge Campbell. The diary will now be quoted.

"May 16. We marched fifteen miles and bivouacked at Shady Springs. Skirmishing in front. On the 18th skirmishing with the enemy continued. Next day (19th) there was considerable skirmishing between some of the enemy and a cavalry company attached as scouts to our brigade.... Several Yankees were captured and some killed and wounded. One or two Confederates were wounded. At 1 p.m., we met the cavalry moving to the rear, saying that the Yankees were in line of battle. We marched on about a mile, which brought us to within two miles of the stronghold of Fayetteville. Here we found a small force of Federal cavalry, and a few rounds from our guns made them retire, which they did without replying, as they had no artillery there. My piece, a 12-pound howitzer, fired five shots which were very good except one struck a tree limb near the piece and was deflected. McCausland pronounced them "beautiful shots".... The steel rifle, "Maggie," jumped out of her bronze trunion band at the first round, breaking off the front sight as she went. We then advanced and at 3 o'clock we arrived in front of Fayetteville. The infantry went down into the woods towards the Yankee works. [The road to Raleigh, after running in a straight line nearly three-fourths of a mile from Fayetteville, turns square to the left, and ascends to a small cleared plateau. Just where it turns there is a partly cleared ridge connecting the plateau with a hill on the right. On this ridge were posted Bryan's third and fourth pieces. The second piece (mine) was posted on the plateau at the end of a straight opening which had been cut in the woods and ran directly toward the Federal fort.] My piece opened first and was immediately answered, and my third or fourth round cutting away the Yankee colors, they shelled us so vigorously [and accurately] with several guns that we were compelled to move to a place nearby where we could not be seen for the timber in front of us, and the smoke behind us rising from the woods [beyond the road] which were on fire. [This is believed to be the first instance of the employment of 'indirect fire" now universally used when it is possible.] ... I was in sole command of this piece, the lieutenant having disappeared without explanation. He may have been supervising the repair of "Maggie." [We fired, slowly as ordered, until night.] The skirmishers reported the forts vacant the next morning before day, but at daylight after about ten rounds were fired at them, they replied. These rounds were fired by the other guns, posted behind the crest of a ridge some 300 yards to the left of my piece. During the night a movement, especially of artillery, had been heard in Fayetteville, but it was the *arrival* of a force from Gauley Bridge, said to have been two [really three] regiments and perhaps a battery. The object of our attack was (as we soon learned) to cause this very movement.... We remained in front of Fayetteville until 2 p.m., or later, and withdrew. "Maggie," repaired during the evening and night, resumed firing [on the morning of the 20th] and at the twenty-second round again dismounted herself. I fired only sixty-five rounds, the orders being to fire very slowly. Having retired twelve miles, we bivouacked for the night.

"Early the next morning, as we were resuming the march, the enemy appeared in our rear. A few shells from the bronze rifle caused their van to retire. We then marched all day unmolested till late in the afternoon. We halted at Raleigh C.H. [now Beckley] and Lieutenant _____ having mysteriously disappeared, and Lieutenant Jennings having been wounded, McCausland placed me in command of the battery, though I was in both senses the youngest sergeant, and ordered me to conduct it about three-fourths of a mile father and park it. Sergeant A.N. Campbell was sent on with "Maggie" to convey her to the railroad and have her thoroughly repaired. The infantry soon was there. Presently scouts came and reported the enemy approaching. McCausland took back 3 companies of infantry and our cavalry company, ordering me to send a howitzer along. I took my own piece, putting another sergeant in charge of the rest of the guns. When we reached Raleigh C.H., [then a small hamlet], McCausland posted my piece in front of a hotel in the south-west angle between the main and Logan roads.... [The enemy] planted a battery on a mountain-top a mile away, where they already had a fortification, and opened on us, their first projectile (seemingly a percussion shell) striking and exploding within ten feet of my piece [and mortally wounding a little girl who was playing around a nearby well]. McCausland came galloping and asked me if I could reach them. Being told that I could do so with shells used as solid shot, as my fuses were for only five seconds, he told me to limber up and gallop off, which we did ignominiously, while the enemy threw shells after us with remarkable precision... When we reached the Beckley place the other pieces and the infantry had gone. We waited until McCausland and the small force that had been sent back came up, and then we marched a few miles and found the army at what we called 'Camp Piney.'"

Here the quotation from the diary ceases, and "McCausland's Raid" ends.

General Scammon, on the 19th, sent 3 regiments and some artillery, probably the rest of McMullin's Battery, to re-enforce White. The report of White and Hines indicate that first the Confederates were supposed to have only three pieces of artillery, then it is ascertained that they had four. Their fire is reported as being accurate, but doing little damage. Early on the 20th the fire is reported as being rapid for a while and then becoming slower. Some of these statements result from the fact that the Federals were ignorant of "Maggie's" behavior. Colonel White describes his pursuit as being attended by continued skirmishing, which must have been a considerable distance in the rear at least of the artillery, as no firing was heard by those in front.

There was no infantry fighting in front of Fayetteville and hence scarcely any casualties. White reports 2 killed, 7 wounded, and 9 missing. This evidently refers to the whole "raid." There were 2 wounded in Bryan's Battery. Further information as to Confederate losses was not obtainable.

To make the narrative complete one more incident, though not strictly belonging here, will be narrated. About 2 miles from Raleigh C.H., where the town of Raleigh now stands, the Confederates made trenches for infantry along the base of the bluff, and fortifications for artillery on a hill on the right of the road as one faces Beckley, and redoubts for two single guns on the brow of the bluff at the edge of a small plateau on the left of the road, making a (still extant) road for the guns to get to this position. The part of the command originally left at Princeton had come to Camp Piney, but "Maggie" was still absent. The diary will now be quoted again.

"Early the next day [July 14] we moved toward the enemy and occupied fortifications that had been made, only two or three miles from Raleigh C.H. My piece (No. 2) and No. 4 (iron howitzers), supported by the Sixtieth Regiment under Colonel B.H. Jones, were placed in positions on the bluff on the left of the road, while all the rest were placed with the Thirty-sixth on a kind of peak on the right. At 2 p.m., my piece fired at about three Federal officers who had come to the foot of the bluff opposite us about 300 yards away. The fuse had been cut for a greater distance and the shell passed among or close over them and struck a bank. The men were dazed for an instant, and then ran back up the road out of sight, holding their swords from dangling. These swords showed that they were officers. When they passed in view of the rest of the battery, a shell was thrown at them from No. 5 ("Nannie"). McCausland would not let any small arms be fired, as our whole position was masked... Then Colonel Jones gave me an order as coming from McCausland to throw some "ricochet" shots into the woods on the hill in front of us. This was a place as impossible as I ever saw for a projectile to ricochet on it; so I assumed that shrapnel was meant and threw a considerable number into the woods.... One cut the top off a pine tree that stood near the base of the steep hill. [Several years ago that tree was still preserved as a sort of a monument.] My piece was the only one that did any firing here except the one shot fired by "Nannie."

"At the proper hours the Yankee drum beat for "dress parade," then "evening roll call," then "lights out" (taps)!

"At midnight a call, 'Sergeant Humphries,' almost in a whisper, aroused me. I answered. 'Come here quick,' said the voice of Lieutenant _____. I obeyed the summons and received orders in a whisper to have my piece and No. 4 with the caissons, moved down the road as quickly as possible. Just then Colonel Jones gave me secret information that the Yankees [in greatly superior numbers] were flanking us around the left and had gotten their artillery in position in our front [probably a mistake]. After an hour's hard work we got everything into the road through rain, mud, and total darkness.... We then commenced a retreat and lost some ordinance and quartermaster's stores and the tents of the Sixtieth Regiment."

During that campaign McCausland's command had no further contact with the enemy.

The Official Records mention a skirmish near

Fayetteville on the 5th of June, but no report of it had been found when the records were published.

GUNNERY NOTES
MILTON W. HUMPHRIES
Sergt., Bryan's Battery, King's Artillery, C.S.A.

ARTILLERY PIECES

There are several ways of classifying artillery or cannon, but here only such cannon will be treated as were used in the field by moving armies, which all fall under the technical head of Light Artillery. When one of these is called "heavy," it means of a heavier sort, such as a 24-pound howitzer.

A cannon of what ever sort is often called a "piece," as when we speak of a "6-piece battery."

The cannon used in 1861-5 were divided into guns and howitzers, but this distinction is often ignored and a howitzer spoken of as a "gun." It should be borne in mind that very little of what is said here is applicable to "modern" artillery.

The howitzers were light cannon, that is the tube surrounding the bore was much thinner than in the case of guns of the same calibre, (diameter of bore); but they had, for the charge of powder, a chamber of smaller diameter than that of the bore. They were all smoothbores and were not intended for solid shot. Three sizes were used: 24-pounders, 12-pounders, and mountain howitzers. The number of pounds denotes the weight of a solid shot for a gun of the same caliber as the howitzer, not that a shell for a 24-pounder would weigh 24 pounds. The mountain howitzers, such as the four used by Colonel Siber at Fayetteville, seem sometimes at least to have been af the same calibre as a 12-pounder, but the barrel was only three feet long and the metal so thin that the cannon without its carrage weighed only 220 pounds. They were the least effective of all cannon and soon went into disuse. The regular 12-pound howitzers were made of cast iron or bronze, the only difference being external, the cast iron pieces being thicker. The 24-pounders were very rare and soon disused. Chapman's Battery had one at Fayetteville.

Guns were either smoothbores or rifles. The smoothbores were iron or bronze 6-pounders or bronze 12-pounders called "napoleons." (The iron 12-pounders, which weighed 3000 pounds, were used only in forts or other permanent defenses).

The rifles were of various calibres and of several kinds, but those chiefly in use were 3-inch rifles, 10-pound parrotts and 20-pound parrotts. The 10-pound parrott had a calibre of a little less than three inches, but the projectiles were longer and hence heavier and these pieces were a little more effective than the 3-inch rifles. By far the most effective of field pieces was the 20-pound parrott, but its weight (gun 2000, carriage 1000 pounds) rendered it unfit for rapid marches, manoevers, and battles on rugged ground. All parrotts were made of cast iron with a wrought iron band around the breech.

AMMUNITION

The artillery ammunition consisted of solid shot, shell, shrapnel (case shot), and canister. The shells, made of cast-iron, had a tolerably thick wall or outer part and the cavity was filled with the strongest powder. A shell, lying still on the ground and exploding, was capable of killing people several yards from it. A shrapnel or caseshot had a much thinner outer wall and a large cavity filled with bullets, the interstices being filled with resin or caked sulphur, and into this mass a small cavity was drilled and filled with powder sufficient to burst the projectile and scatter the fragments and bullets with only a moderate force. After the explosion the fragments and bullets moved with the velocity the projectile had before the explosion; hence shells were intended to explode at or in the object fired at, and shrapnel to explode before reaching said object.

Canister was a thin metal cylindrical case like a tin can filled with balls that "chambered" 7 for 12-pounder smoothbores and 3 for smaller pieces. It was used only for distances less than 400 yards.

Grapeshot, formerly used chiefly to destroy the rigging of ships, was probably never used in the field, but it became customary to speak of "grape and canister" when in fact only canister was used.

INDIRECT FIRE

The term "indirect fire" is calculated to mislead and is often misunderstood. So far as the firing itself is concerned there is no diference between direct and indirect fire. Indirect fire is firing upon a point or place A from a point B which is not visible to people at A. A gun thus concealed from those at which it is firing, is said now to be "defiladed," and indirect fire in the Great War was called simply "defilade," which is no clearer than "indirect fire."

It is necessary, of course, that the trajectory or path of the projectile should pass above the top of the "mask" or intervening object. At Fayetteville, May 19 and 20, 1863, the writer used a grove as a mask, but at Winchester, Va., Sept. 19, 1864, he successfuly used a low hill even with a rifled gun, the one called "Maggie," of Bryan's Battery.

Here the writer begs leave to speak in the first person. In the Confederate army there was a famous battery called the "Rockbridge Artillery." When our country entered the Great War, the Rockbridge Artillery was revived and served with great distinction under Captain Greenlee D. Letcher. An officer of this battery, who had been designated to write a history of the battery, including the period of the Confederate War, being under the erroneous impression that I was a member of the original Rockbridge

Artillery, communicated with me, stating that he had been informed by his superior officers that I had invented "indirect fire," asking me to explain exactly what it was, and requesting me to narrate the occasions on which I had used it. This I did, and the matter came to the attention of Captain Letcher, who urged me, in the interest of true history, to publish the facts, as the French have the credit of having invented it many years after I used it. I claim no credit for the Invention: the thing is so obvious. In fact, if I invented it, I did not do it at Fayetteville, but in my daydreams when I was about 8 years old. How you aim your piece, though it is simple, it would require considerable space to explain.

DRIFT AND SHIFT

A projectile fired from a rifled gun drifts away from the direction in which it is started. If the rotation is to the right, as it usually is, the drift is to the right, and *vice versa*. Its cause is still in doubt, and until recent years the attempts to establish a mathematical formula for calculating the drift have been rendered futile by the fact that the "Terrestial shift" (or simply "shift," first pointed out and so named by the writer) was ignored, its existence being unknown to those who were preparing formulae.

While a projectile is moving through the air, the target or object at which it has been fired is shifting its position in consequence to the rotation of the earth. The shift of the earth is to the left, and hence the projectile seems to deflect to the right in the northern hemisphere, and for the analogous reason to the left in the southern. It is greatest at the poles and zero at the equator. It is easy to calculate for the poles by simple arithmetic and for any latitude it is easily obtained by multiplying what it would be at the pole by the trigonmetrical sine of the latitude. For instance at lat. 30 degrees it is one half what it would be at the pole. Logarithms are not needed, as all trigonometrical works have a table of "Natural Sines."

It should be noted that shift and drift are entirely independent of each other and that projectiles from smoothbores suffer shift.

A.B. Roler served in the "University Volunteers", a miiltary company soon to be mustered into Confederate service after leaving the University of Virginia campus on July 4, 1861. These young students left their education behind to enter a difficult campaign in the mountains of western Virginia under rather unqualified commanders. These "University Volunteers" were to be mustered into "Wise's Legion" as Company G, 2nd Regiment, at Lewisburg, and they marched across the mountains to Gauley Bridge. Roler kept a diary during the initial portion of the company's service and he was an eyewitness to the Confederate "retrograde movement" under General Wise out of the Kanawha Valley as the Federal soldiers under General Cox entered from the west. He saw the burning of the strategic bridge over the Gauley River at Gauley Bridge and wrote an excellent description of the scene.

For the "University Volunteers", this would be the only campaign in which they would participate as a military unit. They were disbanded -- probably because of their small size -- on December 7, 1861.

The diary of A.B. Roler is in the manuscript collection of the Virginia Historical Society. Only the portion directly concerned with the manuevering around Gauley Bridge and the adjacent areas are included in this section.

The Diary of A.B. Roler

July 4th, 1861-- 11 P.M.

We left the Un, today 12 o'clock and are now at Jackson's River in Alleghany Co., Va. Our Co., "Un. Vol," numbers at present with us some 43 men. Several are to come on from the Un. in a few days. We have a nice set of fellows, indeed. Nearly all are students from the Un. of Va. of the last session. It is pleasing to see how differently every one seems disposed to act here from what he did in college.

Formalities in the way of introduction are laid aside and every one talks & acts towards his associates as if he was acquainted all his life.

I have never been in this part of Va before. The scenery all along the road this evening was very fine. This portion of Va is much more mountainous than I thought. There does not seem to be much tillable land in any sections through which we passed today.

I am unable to sleep tonight owing somewhat I suppose to not being accustomed to a hard bed. And the noises around me - the sentinel walking backward and forward with creaking shoes - keeps me from sleeping though every one around me seems to be sleeping. We are quartered tonight in a long hall that seems to have been built for dining purposes. The men are spread around the room in every sort of way. Tomorrow we make the rest of our way towards Lewisburg where we will receive arms & be mustered into service.

Several of our Co. were somewhat intoxicated on our trip this evening. G.W.W. was pretty drunk. We have only a couple of this stamp, though, in the main they are clever fellows. I hope they will quit it.

July 6, 1861--

It is now 1 o'clock A.M. and I am on duty for the first time. We are at Dickinson's Hotel, Alleghany Co. Va, at present having traveled on yesterday about 20 miles. We are accompanied by three teams, one a four horse and two two horse teams, transporting our baggage and hauling such of our numbers as prefer their "jolting" to walking. Either course is attended with some physical prostration and its happy effects are manifest in every individual case tonight. Our "packing away" is somewhat worse than last night quarters not so commodious but the sleeping and resting quite different.

All the way from Staunton thus far this country is quite mountainous and but a small share adapted to culture and that doesn't seem to be very fertile. The country is decidedly better on this side of Covington to what it was on the other side in the region through which we passed.

One of our numbers, M.J. Wilson fr. Texas, was left behind at Covington by some means and is not with us to night.

I think he was detained by having a scabbard made for his bowie knife.

Our crowd seems all to be in the very finest spirits. We have a number of splendid fellows in fact *all* are good fellows at heart. There are only two men in our crowd that are disposed in the least to be notorious. They are not as yet boisterous but are drinking more whiskey than they ought and may be instrumental in leading others astray.

Their names are Williams & Wood.

The sentiment for secession & for sustaining our rights against N. agression seems very unanimous & decided in this county -- though, the people don't make so many outward demonstrations of it as at Charlottesville & the Un. Va.

I find this to be a very pleasant way of spending an hour when I am sleepy.

July 8th, 1861--

We arrived in Lewisburg where we now are on Saturday last from Dickinson's where we supped & remained over night but breakfast by 8 o'clock 5 miles this side of Hugh's between the Little Alleghany and Big Alleghany. From Hugh's we had 8 miles to go to the "White Sulphur Springs" where our wagons arrived at about 12 o'clock though a number of our crowd reached it an hour or more before that by hiking ahead. From the White Sulphur to this place we arrived early on Saturday evening. Our wagons stopped for some time at Greenbrier River as we came by and I had a fine bath in the River just above the bridge. Several in our company walked almost the entire way from Jackson's River. A gentleman by the name of Little who has been journeying with us from Jackson's River bearing dispatches and some cartridges to "Wise" walked the entire way.

The fellows are all in fine spirits and are enjoying excellent health. We have been treated very well in Lewisburg thus far the people have been very kind indeed in furnishing us provisions. Almost as soon as we arrived and it was ascertained that we were from the Un of Va the people of the town offered to do our cooking for us, and have not only have been cooking our rations but have been sending us other delicies in the way of pies, honey, &c.

Lewisburg is not a town of much ado. It has some 1500 inhabitants and four churches. There are regular mails from this place *three* times a week and as many *to* it. The people seem to be very intelligent & refined in their manners.

Our company attended preaching at the Presbyterian church on yesterday by invitation of the Rev. Mr. Barr not the stated minister, however, preached and a fine sermon too form the text "Are not his sparrows sold for a farthing &c."

In the evening the Rev. Mr. Junkin of the

Rockbridge Cavalry, which arrived here on yesterday, he is their Chaplain.

July 13, 1861--

Gauley Bridge, Fayette Co, Va

On Monday evening last Col. Croghan arrived in Lewisburg having in his charge several hundred Rifles & Muskets, ammunition, tents, &c on his way to Gen. Wise. He had a number of Mississippi Rifles with which weapon he armed our company on Tuesday morning. He also asked a guard of 20 men to attend him to Gen. Wise's H.Q. Every one of our number wanted to go with him I believe, but only 20 of our 45 could go and I was one of the number. Accordingly, we started on Tuesday about 11 A.M. and by driving late came to Hennegan's 15 miles.

Here was our first experience in Camp fare and not being provided with camp utensils for cooking we fared pretty roughly on half baked cornbread (unserved meal) and bacon and a few eggs and some sea biscuits that we had with us. I eat sparingly in order that I might live and was far from "living to eat" just about that time.

The next day we marched 20 or more miles to Mr. Tiary's at the foot of Big Sewel. We drove late and the team that I was with which was the last one of the train "hung up" at the middle of the road when we were about 2 1/2 miles from our stopping place. I was detained with it until about 11 o'clock when some of my comrades returned and relieved me. H.H. Harris, R.H. Hull were with me.

The Col. returned also and the major got in about 2 o'clock in the night. Our fare at this place was pretty good. Mr. & Mrs. Tiary were very kind.

The next morning (Thursday) the wagons started off pretty early.

But a man by the name of Keeney, a neighbor to Tiary, whose horses the Col. had "pressed" the evening before and who had failed to bring them at the time appointed, I, one among six of our numbers, returned to Keeney's house about 2 1/2 miles back to bring his horses by force if they could not be obtained otherwise. It was 12 o'clock before we left the premises and then only with one of his worst horses. The Col. was very angry at the conduct of Keeney, who by the way seems to be a pretty hard case thief, liar and everything else that is mean. This is the [one word not legible] every one gives of K. and took along with him also his bull and an idiot Dutchman that K. had in his employ without pay. His name is "Billy" and is here with us, though, he is such an idiot that I don't know that he is sincere or knows what he says. Col. C. did very wrong in bringing him along as he did, though every one that saw him and were acquainted with the Keeney's thought we were doing him a great favor by taking him away. He was getting no pay from the K's and was subjected to all sorts of vices to which they are addicted.

That day we reached Col. Tiary's, a brother of the gentleman with whom we stayed the night before, and fared pretty well. The Col. made himself somewhat officious all the way along in prescribing our bill of fare with the housekeepers and limiting it to bread & bacon and coffee for us men and he himself fare on the fat of the land. Since we have been here we have found out all these things and at present the Col. is not a little unpopular in our crowd

The next morning (Thursday) we passed the "Hawk's Nest" a high and precipitous rock or ledge of rocks on the N bank of the New River seven miles from Gauley. On either side of the river the banks or mountains are high and imposing and the river, which seems to have cut its way through these precipitous ridges, and which can be seen for nearly a mile up & down, looks like a silver thread. The sight is a grand one indeed and by some of our company who have seen the Niagra Falls thought it surpassed the falls.

We arrived here about midday and the Col having delivered up his cargo to Gen. Wise who happened to be here, we were discharged and took up "quarters" on the hill near the old church. Our fare has been much rougher than we have been used to though we can live on it in a pinch.

The following is a list of the gentlemen that are with us, Viz

1. Jas. Dinwiddie Lieut. (Presbyterian)
2. Julian Pratt Sgt
3. W.W. Burgess
4. Chilton
5. John C. Dinwiddie (Presbyterian)
6. Paul DeClonet
7. H.E. Gay
8. N.B. Hammer
9. H.H. Harris (Baptist)
10. L.B. Jones
12. J.D. Lewis (Presby)
13. J.W. Lindsay
14. E.P. Major
15. A.B. Roler (Gen. Ref)
16. M.R. Stringfellow
17. T.W. Sparrow
18. C.W. Turner
19. M.J. Wilson (Meth)
20. A.K. Gaucey (Bap.)
21. F.M. Yancey (Meth.)

The following is one of our songs:

1 *Lauriger Horatius*
Quan dixisti verum
Fugit Euro citius
Tempus edax verum
Ubi qunt o'pocula
Dulciora mello
Rixao pax at oscula Rubentis puellae
2 *Quid juvat aeternitas*
Nominus amare
Nisi terrao filias
Licet et potare
Ubi sunt &c

3 *Crescet uva molliter*
Et puella crescit
Sed poeta tiupiter
Citius cauescit
Ubi sunt &c
4 *Late polet amphora*
Hilares, sodales,
*Bacchus, Pallas, Cypria,**
Nobis sunt pinales.
Ubi sunt &c [5]

---

[5] When truth is told
Laurel-crowned Horatius
Disappeared more quickly than the wind
Oh, where are the undying mugs
That can defeat devouring time?
For peace from battle and the kisses
Of a blushing girl
Are sweeter than wine.

What good is honor
Except to let a son of the earth
Drink and love?
Where are they now?

Wine grows soft to the taste
And a girl will ripen
But the poet
Guards against a swift decay.
Where are they now?

Let the powers of Bacchus,
Pallas & Cypria *
Lie hidden in the wine jugs
Oh, happy comrades.
For we are wing-ed.

* Venus

Gauley Bridge, July 16, 1861--

We are still on the hill near the old church, all well except Sparrow who has a slight diarrhea. We have had rain [he deleted the word *almost*] every day since we left Lewisburg except on Sunday last. Our location is high but still from the abundant rains our tents cannot help being wet to some extent and more or less unhealthy. Our fare is somewhat improved having learned the art of cooking a little better.

Eighteen prisoners were brought to this place on yesterday. The most of them are Union men from some of the Western counties -- one is gentleman, Roberts is his name. I understand that he was in the Wheeling Convention. Two of them are Ohio troopers, two are Jew merchants from Charleston who were engaged in giving aid and comfort to the enemy, one is a Meth. preacher, I understand.

It is reported that the enemy are within two days forced march of us; that there was a fight near Charleston the other day; that the enemy had the best of it.

I am not favorably impressed by any means of the efficiency of the soldiery in this part of the Wise brigade. The officers as a general thing seem to me to be mere makeshifts and the companies are not well drilled. I wish that I could entertain hopes of their success. There is a Louisana Co. here that came in the other day-- a large company -- whom I do think valiant and brave men, who will fight to the death of every one of them.

As for the U.V. I have no doubt they will make as noble a stand and acquit themselves as well as could be expected from so young a band. There is not one among our number whom I believe will shrink when the day of trial comes.

Our trust is in God and we pray for his protection and deliverance in our troubles.

Gauley Bridge, Va., July 18, 1861--

The remainder of the U.V. who were left in Lewisburg came in yesterday. We are all encamped on the hill. Col. Croghan whom we have very fitly surnamed "Panic" hurried them away from Lewisburg, under the impression that we had gone to Charleston and that we had certainly come into contact with the enemy, before they were ready. We are but illy provided with cooking utensils that makes against our comfort much more than one not knowing anything about it from experience, would suppose. Lieut. Dinwiddie is going back to Lewisburg on tomorrow, I understand, and will get all the things we need.

Bread, Bacon & coffee & rice are the great staples in our camp and being cooked by ourselves they are not always the most palatable though seldom fail of being eaten. All our fellows are in fine spirits. The picket guard was furnished from our camp on last evening which required 13 men.

We divided off into messes of 10 men today a temporary arrangement until we get more cooking utensils.

Reports from Charleston say that the enemy were repulsed from that place on yesterday with considerable loss. Reports reach us every day from various points but one half of them not worth anything. I am not at all pleased with the military arrangements at this place. They posted a picket guard but allow men to shoot off their guns in camp without saying anything to them about it. I am afraid that the enemy may have the advantage of us in point of generalship in this section of Va. It doesn't seem to me that the mil. chieftains to whom the S. interest has been confided in this portion of Va. act enough in concert to expell the enemy from our borders very soon.

They are mostly men of political aspirations and seem to me to be individualizing their efforts having their own praise and aggrandizment in view more than their country's good into.

It is thundering pretty loudly in the post this evening

and I reckon we will have rain this tonight again. We have had rain almost every day since we have been here. The corn crop looks very well indeed.

Thursday, July 25, 1861--

On Friday night last we were aroused about 2 o'clock in the morning and marched out in battle array.

The alarm was occasioned by a strange kind of light seen at different times during the night on one of the mountain tops about 1 1/2 miles distant. Supposed to be some signal of the enemy. I, for myself didn't see any light more than what was occasioned by a "lightning bug" and don't believe it was anything else.

On Saturday night last I was appointed Q.M. for the U.V. upon the resignation of Mr. C.E. Young. The duties of this office are numerous and fatiguing. Owing to my pressing duties brought on by my new avocation I have but little time for writing.

Sunday was spent in various duties as are peculiar to camp life. No drills but dress parade at 6 o'clock in the evening. Monday was one of the fullest & most unpleasant days I ever experienced. It rained so incessantly that in our unprotected state we were scarcely able to prepare any food for ourselves. Tuesday morning we were all mustered into the service of the Con States for the term of one year.

I should have stated that on Monday morning there was no little excitement in our camp for a litle while owing to some firing up the river which we supposed at first to be the pickets and then a general engagement with some of the Co's near that picket, but shortly after we had thrown aside our coffee and our bread & meat that we had in our fists and fallen into ranks with our guns and cartridge boxes we learned that it was only one of the Co's firing off their guns with the permission ot the Com. officer, Col Richardson [two small words not legible] of the rain.

July 26, 1861 5 o'clock P.M.--

I am in camp. Company gone on an unknown expedition. Just now hear Capt Crane's voice and know that he has returned to camp. General Wise is here and Co's returning as fast as they can from Charleston. We expect to leave tonight or tomorrow. As yet we have no baggage wagons. Been baking bread and cooking bacon all day to have something for our proposed march.

July 27th, 1861--

Rec'd orders about 3 o'clock yesterday evening to move camp across the river and accordingly picked up our baggage on our shoulders and we carried it over the bridge. The companies were all in motion and there is a great deal more noise & confusion and haste that any occasion for while all this was going on several men were employed in tarring the side walls of the bridge and arranging the lose material in it as to burn with the greatest rapidity. A heavy rain in the meantime came up though we kept pretty dry having taken refuge under a ledge of rocks by the road side the most of our tents and other baggage got quite wet and muddy -- not yet having any baggage wagons in which to put them.

All the other companies shared the same or a worse fate with their baggage. The whole road side for half a mile in fact was strewed with tents, frying pans, coffee pots, ham and middlings of meat and a vast etc. of such like soldier accomodations. The disorder could not have been worse if the main body of the enemy had been right at our heels while it was at least six or seven miles or perhaps, more. Only some of a reconnoitreing party were seen this morning by [word not legible] our party who were at the bridge. When all the companies were over the bridge with their luggage and the commissary stores also were removed at about 11o'clock at night Saturday the bridge was set on fire which was a fine structure of the kind consisting of three arches and costing $35000. It burned very fast and the first arch that was fired fell in less than half an hour. The whole length of the bridge was at least 150 yds and ten minutes after the torch was first touched the whole bridge was one sheet of flame and for five or ten minutes afterwards presented one of the most beautiful sights I ever saw. The night was somewhat cloudy and very damp from the recent rains -- though it had stopped raining by this time -- and the smoke rose from above and beneath in heavy spiral columns which lingered a moment over the burning wreck affording time to be lit up in the most gorgeous colors and then passes off into the air. The currents of the wind was S.E. and was right against the side of the bridge which caused the smoke from the flooring of the structure to circle beneath the arches in beautiful curves and to mingle with that of the roofing after it had passed across. Our position was on the windward side. With the smoke thus circling around and before the bridge had burned sufficiently to obscure all the heavy timbers in the side walls it had the appearance of a bridge of gold with frescoed work of the finest skill. The exclamations of all present was what a beautiful sight! I could not but feel for the loss of the property though I admit of its being a military necessity still the sight was such a [small word not legible] and beautiful sight that I did wish its continuance for a longer period.

Immediately after the last arch had fallen in we were called into ranks and with our guns & knapsacks on our backs marched through the dark and mud 2 1/2 miles up hill all the way to Col.Tompkins' residence. Here we passed the remainder of the night sleeping on his porch. It was about 11/2 in the morning when we got there & the most of our Co. had eaten nothing of any consequence since early in the morning before. This was owing to the impracticality for the most of cooking our food. While we were at Col T. this morning two wagons came along which we at once appropriated to our use and a detachment of us went back to the bridge for tents, provisions &c

which we had left behind the night before.

I had made up my mind before going upon this expedition to have to endure a great many trials & hardships but the experiences of the last 24 hours has been decidedly the worst faring that we have had.

When we went back this morning there was still a great deal of property by the road side for which there was no transportation -- a detachment of soldiers were employed in breaking open kegs of powder & throwing them into the river to prevent falling into the hands of the enemy. Quantities of bacon were also piled up by the road side and hundreds of stands of arms which were remaining after we left.

Today (Sunday) we have marched about 10 miles on our way towards Lewisburg. We passed the Hawk's Nest about 3 miles back but was so fatigued that I did not walk off the road to look at it again. I have given a description of it in another place. I have been unable to remember for five minutes at a time all this day that it was Sunday -- so strange and odd and inconsistent with the holy calm of the Sabbath does all of this marching and packing and cooking seem.

July 31st, Lewisburg --

We arrived at this place late yesterday evening so late that after pitching their tents the most of the messes that were without cold provisions concluded to go to bed without supper rather than try to get supper as they had no wood nor candles. We are all very tired having been marching ever since Sunday morning last. We camped at Meadow Bluff last night where we got some provisions-- ours that we brought from Gauley having expired at that place. We are camped about a quarter mile from town.

Yesterday as we were drawing near to Lewisburg I thought I had never in my life beheld so fine a country -- the country is indeed a fine one a few miles W of L. on the Charleston road, but I apprehend that we were in better condition to appreciate a fine country than any of us had ever been -- having been over so rough & mountainous a district as we had passed. I think this district is called the "Big Flat" of Greenbrier.

Sunday, August 4th, 1861--

Rec'd orders this morning to be ready to march to the White Sulphur Springs by 11 o'clock.

It is supposed that Gen. Wise will repeat his Sunday marching. We are likely to remain at the W.S.S. at least a week and I see no necessity in the world for giving marching orders today. I have not been priviledged to enjoy the Sabbath's recreation & calm for nearly a month. A great many of the fellows are grumbling about the orders but it does no good.

I have resolved to take things easy and make the best of every difficulty.

Monday, Aug. 5, 1861, W.S. Springs--

We arrived at this place early yesterday evening being only 9 miles from Lewisburg. We soon made the journey, though. The most of us were very tired and full of dust. The roads were dustier than any we have traveled over since in W.V. We had just provisions enough for supper last evening and this morning I have been all over the Spring grounds looking for the Com. Dep. Have not found it yet but have the promise of a loan of a day's ration from Capt. Pollock's Co. with which we will try & make out until the Q.M. arrives from Lewisburg and are fixed for issueing rations for the soldiers. On some days like this morning my duties are numerous. This is a beautiful place ... [a short paragraph apparently describing the area is not legible].

Sunday Aug. 11th, 1861
White Sulphur Springs, Va. --

Have been in camp all day. We have a right pleasant location for a camp on a hill back of the S. Spring and affording a fine view of the S. grounds.

The location we first occupied was over the creek near the Ten Pin alley. We were moved to this encampment some days since and like it better than the one across the creek.

Spent the day in writing at my journal more than anything else. Am very sorry that I am so disinclined to reading, meditation and prayer. It is astonishing, indeed, how careless and indifferent I am becoming. Am engrossed so much with the cares of my office as Commissary that I have scarcely any time or inclination for anything else.

Wednesday, Aug. 14, 1861--

Rec'd orders this evening to be ready for marching early in the morning. It is reported that the enemy are not far from Meadow Bluff several thousand strong and Gen. Floyd is near Meadow Bluff with his force has requested Gen. Wise to come on without delay. I have but little confidence in the report believe it to be merely a scarecrow. "Panic" (Lt. Col.Croghan) is there and I am not surprised to hear anything that savors of terror and deadly fight.

Croghan by some of his acts of late has made himself quite rediculous and unpopular moreover with every one with whom he had to do.

We belong to Col. Anderson's Reg. and I am glad of it indeed. "Panic" belongs to Col. Davis' Reg. otherwise I should like it very well.

Rec'd a letter this morning from my lady friend correspondent (B.K.T.) saying that my friend John Wynant of Bridgewater was killed in the battle of Rich Mountain. I am exceedingly grieved & sorry that my esteemed friend & brother has met such an untimely end. John was always a favorite of mine and seemed devotedly attached to me.

I also from the same source learned of the death of my friend JnoS. Gibbons who died in Winchester of some disease that she did not know.

From the same source, that Mrs. Diana Kyle was married to Mr. Robt. Eubank. This seems to me a very improper time for forming connubial relations and for my part, even if all arrangements necessary were ready, would think prudent to put by until after this war.

Saturday Evening, Aug. 17, 1861
Top of Big Sewell Mountain
Greenbrier Co. Va.

We left the W.S.S. on Thursday morning last in route for this place where it was reported the enemy had advanced from Gauley. Gen. Floyd was stationed at Bumgart's Mill four miles W. of Lewisburg. The report was brought that the enemy were advancing and he immediately started off with a detachment of his forces for the enemy leaving tents & baggage behind double-quicking it for several miles, I understand, and at the same time sent an earnest appeal to Gen. Wise at the W.S.S. to come immediately. This was on Tuesday night. Accordingly on Wednesday we cooked an extra supply of provisions and early Thursday morning we set out. Col. Richardson's Reg. and baggage in advance and ours (Col. Anderson's) next. We went 24 miles to Meadow Bluff that day. It was some time after night when we got there, but there was moon shine. Just as we were driving into the encampment over the bridge that was built over the creek owing to the unusual weight that was on our wagon -- a five horse team -- which was carrying all our baggage, knapsacks & all -- the bridge was crushed and down went wagon, horses, driver and all -- fortunately both sleepers of the bridge gave way at the same place at the same instant and everything remained on the bridge entangling only the off wheel horse which was soon gotten out. We unloaded the wagon as soon as could be done and pulled it out and encamped for the night such as it was sleeping on the ground without putting up our tents and eating our cold rations for the most part. Friday we came on to the foot of Big Sewel and from about 5 o'clock in the evening I was never so sick in my life. I was sick at the stomach & was vomiting and at the same time had the worst diarhea I ever saw. I was quite sick all night. The boys were all especially kind to me -- put up my tent and ministered to my comfort in every way they could. This morning when I arose I felt much better and made the journey here 6 miles though I rode all the way with a good [word not legible] of case. I am still very weak from the excessive [illegible] and vomiting of yesterday evening. This is a high & commanding position and I was told when we were at Meadow Bluff that Generals Floyd & Cox were racing for this point but it was all a mistake and I reckon that none of the enemy of any account more than a few scouting parties have been any distance this side of Gauley Bridge.

Sunday Morning, Aug. 18 --

Raining. We are encamped in an oats field and it is inclined to be muddy outside the tent's mouth. This sort of weather makes me think of what I used to think of camp meetings when it rained -- that they would be the most unpleasant places in the world, and that I would rather be any where than there. I think if I live and get home again my sentiments & feelings for the proper appreciation of my comforts and my capacity for enduring what may be termed dirty hardships will be considerably improved. I am not at all fond of camp life. I can endure it and mean to endure it patiently too as I can until honorably discharged but no one will rejoice more at an early peace and a final settlement of our nation's difficulties than myself. I sincerely hope that this mean & destructive war will be terminated before the winter sets in.

Sunday Night 8 1/2 o'clock Aug. 18
Top of Big Sewel

Still raining and very unpleasant. I was told today that this was next to the highest point in Va. I was surprised to hear it but when I reflect on all the country this side of L. is a gradual ascent and the road on the top of the mountain is 5 or 6 miles. I think there is strong probability of its truth. There is also a mountain between this and L. which is called Little Sewel but a [two words illegible].

Monday Aug. 19 (Sewel)--

Raining again this evening and very unpleasant indeed. Have no idea how long we may remain in this place nor which way we will go when we leave here.

McOwens was appointed my Ass. Commissary this morning. Am glad of it. He is a good fellow & will aid me very much in my duties which some days have been increasingly onerous.

Have to day been reading a little tract called "Literary Attractions of the Bible" and a very excellent little work it is.

Wednesday Aug 21st (Locust Lane)--

We left Sewel's top on yesterday and have proceeded 10 miles or more towards Gauley. We are lying in camp this morning and I have no idea how long we will remain here. It is reported that the enemy have entrenched themselves at the Hawk's Nest some 16 miles farther on. How true it is I know not neither do I know what steps will be taken to dislodge them in case they are [illegible word]. This place is Locust Lane.

The following is our Regimental Regulations.

Revilee at 5 o'clock A.M.
Inspection of Quarters 5 1/2
Breakfast 7
First Call for Guard Mounting 7 1/2
Guard Mounting 7.40
Drill 9
Dinner 1
Drill 4 P.M.
Retreat Sundown
Dress Parade 6 1/2
Supper 7
Tattoo 8 1/2
Taps 9

Friday Evening Aug. 25 --

We left Locust Lane about 10 A.M. without any thing occurring worthy of note. Came to Mountain Cove some 10 miles or more from Gauley Bridge. Our march Wednesday was over the road where the [a word is missing from the bottom corner of the page -- probably *Yankees*] few days before had been. They were estimated by some of the people along the road at 3000 or more. Locust Lane was the limit of their march E. and it is said that when they heard of Wise's and Floyd's forces returning they started back at night in about the same disorder, confusion & hurry that we left Gauley. One old man (Alderson, I believe, is his name) at the toll gate some 2 miles back told us they pressed his mules as they came by and that he had not seen them since. Knowing too that he had been a rigid secessionist they showed him a great deal of disrespect and finally went their way.

Yesterday (22nd) while we were encamped at Mountain Cove at about 1 A.M. we were called up and ordered to pack knapsacks and strike tents silently and be off. Scouts of the enemy had been seen on some of the neighboring hills the evening before. They were reported to be tolerably strong a little farther on, and had fortifications at the Hawk's nest. It was said that we were only going back to Dog Wood Gap but when we got there we were ordered to go in the direction of Summersville (Sunday Road). The Reg's were on ahead and they as well as ourselves nearly every one were without a thing to eat in the least not being permitted to kindle any fire with us to make breakfast and having nothing left from the previous evening.

This is a rough country indeed in the direction of S. and the road a simple track and a miserable one. On we went as [illegible word] as we could for about 5 miles when it commenced raining on us. Our wagons by this time had stopped from some misunderstanding with the Wagon Master whether to go or not and presently were ordered back and encamped in a meadow -- raining all the time presently the camp came up and we pitched tents and spent the night [illegible word] pleasantly having suceeded in drying our clothes pretty well. [Illegible word] Arrived at Dogwood gap [illegible word].

Sunday Sep. 1st, 1861. Resumed our march to Pontifax's Ferry over the Summersville (Sunday) road at the solicitation of Gen. Floyd who expected an attack from the enemy. but just before we arrived there information was read that our services were not needed and of course had nothing to do but to march back to Dogwood. Just before starting back Gen. Wise called up our Regt in a sq. around him and adressed them briefly something along this in so

"Soldiers of the 2d Reg.,

"This is the second time that you have marched over these hills to meet the enemy but are not permitted to meet him. Tonight we will encamp at the H. Nest and we will see if he cannot be formed [illegible word]." Cheers for Gen. Wise!!

That evening we returned as far as Dogwood and accordingly...

At this point the journal of A.B. Roler came to a halt. Whether the young Commissary officer was called to duty or there was an alert as the 2nd Regiment of Wise's Legion prepared to meet the Ohioans under Lieutenant-Colonel Frizell who were manuevering toward the rebels, we will never know. The 2nd Regiment continued to manuever on Gauley Mountain while General Floyd marched to Carnifex Ferry (Pontifax's Ferry in Roler's journal) and fought the 7th Ohio at Cross Lanes successfully and soon were to engage the Federal main force under General Rosecrans at Camp Gauley. Roler and the rest of Wise's men were to be ordered to march across Sunday road a third time to the aid of General Floyd, but Floyd ordered a retreat across the Gauley at Carnifex Ferry and joined the men of Wise's Legion in a retreat to Sewell Mountain.

The Federal army and the Confederates under Robert E. Lee would skirmish for several days without bringing on a general engagement at Sewell Mountain before Rosecrans was forced to pull out of his fortifications by the loss of the ferry at Gauley Bridge which made it impossible for his troops to be resupplied.

General Wise was relieved and ordered to Richmond while General Floyd moved most of the troops in his brigade and most of the men previously under the command of Wise to Cotton Hill where they fired cannon across New River into the Federal camp at Gauley Bridge for 11 days before the Rebels were forced to retreat again.

Roler and his small company of college students were to remain involved in the campaign until December 7, 1861, when the company was ordered to be disbanded. Probably most of the men were ordered transferred into other units in order to fill them adequately. Many of these companies were ordered to accompany General Wise to North Carolina's Outer Banks where many of them were captured by one of the first Union amphibious assaults of the war.

Dr. Thomas J. Riddle wrote of his service in the Goochland Artillery during the Kanawha Valley campaigns of 1861. His story appeared in the Southern Historical Society Papers *(Volume XI, January-December, 1883) and it was written long after his service as a Confederate private at the age of sixteen. He served in Guy's Battery which joined Floyd's Brigade as it moved into the mountains of western Virginia to attempt to hold the region for the Confederacy. The men of Guy's battery served throughout the battles of Carnifex Ferry, Sewell Mountain, and the retreat from the region by General Floyd as the Federal noose began to tighten.*

They next went to Fort Donelson -- again under the command of John B. Floyd -- where most of them were captured. Their general was quick to escape by boat with most of his other Virginia troops, but the artillerymen were surrendered with the remainder of the garrison to General U.S. Grant.

The western Virginia campaigns, however, were their first fights and the men did their duty. Riddle provided an excellent description of what he saw and experienced.

Reminiscences of Floyd's Operations in West Virginia in 1861
By Dr. Thomas J. Riddle, Private in the Goochland Artillery

As drops compose the mighty ocean, so the aggregation of isolated facts make up correct history for future research. This must be my apology for presenting this paper to public notice. Though a youth of sixteen summers, when the tocsin of war sounded I entered the service of my native State, Virginia. On the 25th of August, 1861, my company, Guy's battery, consisting of upwards of one hundred men and four pieces of artillery, were ordered to join General J. B. Floyd's command in Southwest Virginia as soon as practicable. We took the Central cars (now the Chesapeake and Ohio Railway), and were conveyed to its terminus at Jackson river by the next evening. Here we encamped that night. The next morning we commenced our line of march by Covington, the White Sulphur Springs, Lewisburg, Meadow Bluff, and across the Big Sewell Mountain, thence to Carnifax ferry, where we joined General Floyd's brigade, about the 8th of September, just a few days before the *Battle of Carnifax Ferry.* General Floyd anticipated an engagement with the enemy at an early day. Consequently he wanted reinforcements as soon as possible, and we lost no time in reaching his command.

As my company had never had the priviledge of participating in battle, they were enthusiastic and very eager for the conflict. Upon forming Floyd's brigade, our battery was at once placed in position, and temporary breastworks erected, which occupied a prominent place, commanding an open field for about a mile direct, and half mile probably in width, with woods on both our right and left flanks. To make an attack upon us, the enemy had to come directly through this open field. In a day or two, however, September 10th, about 2 1/2 P.M., our videts were driven in hurriedly, *and the enemy at once made his appearance in full force.* My company had now prepared for action in reality, ready to give the enemy a warm reception. It is proper to state just here, that Floyd's command did not exceed nineteen hundred available men. It consisted of Guy's battery, four pieces, Jackson's battery, two pieces, all six-pounders, a few cavalry, and the remainder of infantry.

The enemy came bravely forward, and the battle raged furiously from 2 1/2 o'clock, P.M., until darkness caused a cessation of hostilities, which was, doubtless, agreeable and acceptable to both parties.

The enemy fought with undaunted courage and bravery, making successive charges on our works.

In the engagement Colonel Lytle (afterwards a Major-General), who commanded an Ohio regiment, led the first charges. (He was killed subsequently in the battle, I think, of Chickamauga, Tenn.) This brave officer was seriously wounded while leading a charge on us. His fine black stud came over our works with part of the Colonel's equipments, with a mortal wound in his chest, which rendered him worthless. During the battle, General Floyd, who was just in the rear of my battery, received a slight flesh wound in one of his arms. The enemy's loss in this engagement was considered heavy. In the charges on our battery their loss must necessarily have been great. Double the quantity of grape and canister were thrown into their ranks with fearful results -- avenues were made through their ranks at times, yet they for awhile continued to close ranks, and forward, to meet shell and shot, until, doubtless, they were convinced that it was a useless sacrifice of life to persist in the assault.

In this battle our loss was comparatively small, which was due, in a great measure, to our respective positions on the field, our position being the most advantageous one of the two. While we had the advantage in position, yet we labored under the disadvantage in numbers. It was estimated that the enemy had upwards of five thousand men on the field under General Rosecrans, while our command did not exceed nineteen hundred men, as above stated. That night, after the battle was over, about 12 o'clock, owing to our small force, and the reported reinforcements of the enemy, General Floyd very wisely ordered a retreat as quietly as possible. Many of us were asleep behind our breastworks when the evacuation was ordered, broken down from fatigue and excitement, and nothing disturbed our slumber save the groans of the wounded, not far from our fortifications, until an officer of the guard awoke us, saying that we had orders to evacuate our position as soon as possible. Orders were obeyed accordingly as with as little difficulty as could be expected under the circumstances.

Fortunately for us a bridge had just been completed across Gauley river that evening, upon which we passed successfully to the opposite side. Carnifax Ferry is about one and a half miles from the battle ground, and to reach that point a very rugged and rough road has to be travelled (and especially in the dark as we did), winding as it does on the mountain, and should you go too far to the right or left as it might be, you would in all probability be precipitated hundreds of feet.

The retreat was considered one of the most remarkable of the war; in coming down this dangerous road to the ferry that dark night, we only lost one caison, besides a great deal of baggage, which went over a precipice. It was conceded by the command that had it not been for "Guy's" battery, Floyd's brigade would have been captured at the battle of Carnifax Ferry; and General Floyd recognized this fact, and expressed himself as grateful to us for his brigade's successful escape on that memorial occasion.

On the next morning just about sunrise the enemy commenced shelling our breastworks actively -- not knowing we had abandoned our position about twelve o'clock that night, and that we were several miles on the other side of the river. After cannonading for several hours, and receiving no response, the works were at once taken possession of, although they did not pursue us further than the river. After marching several miles, we met General H.A. Wise's Legion, on their way to reinforce Floyd's command. So quietly and expeditiously was this retreat conducted that General Wise's command did not seem to know anything about it until that morning. Both commands now took up a line of march for "Dogwood Gap," not many miles distant -- we arrived at this place the next day. After remaining here two days, about twelve o'clock at night, the long roll sounded, and we were ordered to strike tents at once, and prepare to fall back, as it was reported that General Cox, with a large force, was rapidly advancing upon us; we lost no time in executing these orders, and were soon on the march. Floyd's command fell back to "Meadow Bluff," which consumed several days. Here we encamped for about two weeks. General Wise's brigade fell back to Little Sewel Mountain -- the General fortified his position, and said that he "would remain there until that hot place froze over." In a short while General Rosecrans, with his command of Federal troops came up and took their position, on Big Sewel Mountain, only a few miles from General Wise's position, all in sight.

About the 1st of October, General Floyd was ordered to reinforce General Wise at Little Sewel. These orders were executed in a few days. My command encamped at the eastern base of Little Sewel in anticipation daily of an engagement with the enemy. We remained here nearly two weeks. On a bright October orning, while walking down the mountain slope, I met a Confederate officer, who attracted my attention very much by his personal appearance. He was a noble looking soldier, had the eye of an eagle; he was riding a fine gray steed, and there was something about this officer that challenged my admiration and esteem. He rode up and spoke to me, and asked me where was General Wise's brigade. I informed him; he thanked me and rode in the direction I had given him. Upon meeting one of my officers I asked who was that noble looking officer just passed our camp; he replied that it was General Robert E. Lee, who at that time was little known in the Confederacy, but was destined to become one of the greatest captains the world ever saw, and whose name will ever live upon the brightest page of the historian. After remaining at Little Sewel mountain upwards of two weeks, General Lee made preparations to attack General Rosecrans; contrary, doubtless, to General Lee's expectations, on the morning the attack was to be made, General Rosecrans had very quietly evacuated Big Sewel, and only left a few broken down horses and wagons, and a few tents pitched to make it appear that he still occupied his position. This was considered a very ingenious piece of strategy, as General Lee was much disappointed when he found that General Rosecrans had so quietly and adroitly eluded him on the previous night.

In a day or two after this occurrence General Floyd's command was ordered to Cotton Mountain, probably a hundred miles distant. Floyd's command was now reinforced, and consisted of the following troops: Twenty-first[6] Virginia regiment, Thirty-sixth Virginia regiment, Forty-fifth Virginia regiment, Fiftyth Virginia regiment, and Fifty-first Virginia regiment; the Thirteenth Georgia, Georgia battalion of cavalry, Twentieth Mississippi regiment, a company of Louisiana sharpshooters, Captain John H. Guy's artillery company, and Captains Jackson's and Adam's batteries, and a few cavalry companies. From Little Sewel to Cotton Mountain we had to march through a very rugged section of country, and were compelled to take a very circuitous route in order to reach this place. It was with great difficulty that we succeeded in conveying our cannon up and over some of the mountains we had to cross. Our horses being in such a weakened condition, we had to hitch twelve to one piece of cannon and put our shoulders to the wheels. However, we

---

6 Actually, this was the Twenty-Second Virginia.

reached Cotton Mountain after no little trouble, and went into camp near its southern base.

A few days after remaining here it was reported that the enemy would attempt to cross New river on a certain morning. Two pieces of artillery from my battery were placed on a road leading from the ferry, about two hundred yards distant; but the enemy did not attempt to cross; their pickets fired into us, though did no damage. In a day or two General Floyd ordered a piece of cannon from my battery to be placed upon the summit of Cotton Mountain and to shell the enemy in the vicinity of Colonel Tompkins' residence. It was with great difficulty that we succeeded in conveying the cannon to the top of this mountain, which was accomplished by means of ropes, bushes, &c.

After placing our piece in position, we opened fire on the enemy, and a response was soon received. An artillery duel was kept up ten days, with little damage to either side, the distance too great to do much execution, though the enemy was very much interfered with in consequence of transporting supplies down the river at times, when we would give them a few shells from above.

My command remained in this section of country nearly three weeks, the latter part of which time we had cold, rainy weather, being without tents, and nearly out of rations, save raw beef, and flour without salt to season, and only an improvised piece of board to prepare these supplies on for our plates. The Confederacy was not destitute of provisions at this time, but my command was upwards of one hundred miles from any depot, the nearest was Dublin, Va., and the roads were almost impassable; consequently transportation was well nigh impossible -- I mean a sufficient supply for three or four thousand men. Our troops suffered a great deal from sickness, which was due to inadequate diet and exposure. General Floyd, under these unpropitious circumstances, was necessarily compelled to fall back where supplies were more accessible, though possibly he left sooner than he had anticipated, owing to an authentic report that a large force of federal troops were attempting to cut him off and surround him; this was about the middle of November. We began to fall back as rapidly as possible, leaving one evening and marching some ten or twelve miles before stopping.

After passing a mile beyond Nicholas Courthouse[7] we went into camp. At 4 o'clock the next morning we resumed our march, and made fifteen or twenty miles that day, and encamped about one mile this side of McCoy's Mill in an open field. It is believed that if General Floyd's command had been an hour later in leaving Nicholas Courthouse his forces would have been cut off, as the enemy, in full force, soon came in the vicinity of the Courthouse just after Floyd left. It was said that the general commanding the Federal forces was much surprised and disappointed in not capturing Floyd and his command, and was astonished at the successful retreat of his enemy.

We were pursued by the federals slowly; and on leaving our camp near McCoy's Mill on the morning of the third day the enemy arrived within a short distance of us, and opened fire on us with artillery. This was very unexpected by most of us. However, we at once placed a piece of cannon in position and returned the fire. There was considerable excitement and confusion at this particular time. Colonel Chrowe[8], of the Georgia Battalion of Cavalry, had an engagement with the enemy near McCoy's Mill, in a skirt of woods. In this fight the Colonel was killed. This little skirmish only lasted an hour or two, resulting in very small loss on either side.

General Floyd continued his march to Raleigh Courthouse, which consumed some two or three days. It was raining the whole time, and the roads were in a terrible condition. The command suffered severely. A few horses and wagons were lost on the retreat, as it was impossible to

---

7 Riddle is mistaken. This is Fayette Courthouse.

8 This was Lieutenant Colonel St. George Crogan. Many authors had difficulty with his name when they wrote their memoirs.

bring then with us. Of course they were so disabled as render them useless to anyone.

The enemy followed us a short distant from McCoy's Mill. Floyd continued to fall back several miles the other side of Raleigh Courthouse, just beyond a considerable creek which rose in winter to a great extent. Here we rested for a few days, then resumed our line of march to Peterstown, not far from the Gray Sulphur Springs, at which place we expected to go into winter-quarters and recuperate for the spring campaign. We at once begun to erect our quarters, though in a few days orders came for the command to go to Dublin, Pulaski County, Va. They certainly had been for several months in the most rugged and seemingly forsaken section of the country that I ever saw.

We had suffered both for food and rainment; the latter part of November was very bad on us, it rained, snowed and froze most of the time.

About the 5th of December, 1861, my command proceeded to Dublin depot, and reached our destination on the 9th inst. In a short while, however, orders were received for General Floyd and his brigade to report to General Albert Sidney Johnston, whose command was then in the vicinity of Bowling Green, Ky.

On the 26th day of December, my company of artillery left on the Virginia and Tennessee railroad, *en route* for General Johnston's army.

Thus ends a brief history of my experience in the campaign of 1861, in Southwestern Virginia, under General Jno. B. Floyd's command.

Throughout the war, both sides relied on the efforts of spies to collect vital military and political intelligence on the opposition. The Union spy-master was Allan Pinkerton, the Chief of the United States Secret Service, and he wrote of the activities of one of his agents, Price Lewis, who penetrated the Confederate region near Ohio -- the Kanawha Valley -- early in the war. The story occurred in the area of Charleston, West Virginia, and areas in southwestern Virginia.

The story appears in Pinkerton's book, The Spy of the Rebellion *which was published in New York by the G.W. Carleton &Co.*

East and West Virginia Seceding from Secession - My Scouts in Virginia - A Rebel Captain Entertains "My Lord." An Old Justice Dines With Royalty - A Lucky Adventure - A Runaway Horse - A Rescue.

At this time the condition of affairs in the state of Virginia -- the "Old Dominion'" as it was generally denominated -- presented a most perplexing and vexatious problem. The antagonistic position of the two sections of that state demanded early consideration and prompt action on the part of the Federal Government, both in protecting the loyal people in the western section, and of preserving their territory to the Union cause. Within the borders of this commonwealth there existed two elements, directly opposed to each other, and both equally pronounced in the declaration of their political opinions. The lines of demarkation between these diverse communities were the Allegheny Mountains, which extended through the very middle of the state, from north-east to south-west, and divided her territory into two divisions, slightly unequal in size, but evidently different in topographical features and personal characteristics.

From the early nature of its earlier settlement, and by reason of climate, soil and situation, Eastern Virginia remained the region of large plantations, with a heavy slave population, and of profitable agriculture, especially in the production of tobacco. West Virginia, on the contrary, having been first settled by hunters, pioneers, lumbermen and miners, possessed little in common with her more wealthy and aristocratic neighbors beyond the mountains. They made their homes in the wilds of the woods, and among the rocky formations, under which was hidden the wealth they were seeking to develop, and in time this western country became the seat of a busy manufacturing industry, with a diversified agriculture for local consumption, while the east was largely given up to the production of great staples for export. As a natural result, the population and wealth of the eastern portion, which was thus made to stand in the relation of a mere tributary province to her grasping neighbor, who selfishly absorbed the general taxes for local advantage.

The slave aslo entered largely into the creation and continuance of this antagonistic feeling. According to census, which had recently been taken, it was ascertained that Western Virginia held but a few thousands. It was not a matter of surprise, therefore that secessionism should be rampant in the east, and that a Union sentiment should almost universally prevail in the west. As the institution of slavery was more or less the cause of the war, here, as in other parts of the South, secession reared its most formidable front where the slave interest predominated, and treason was more alert in the centers of accumulated wealth and family pride, whose foundations were laid by the suffering and the toil of the African bondsmen. The war had been waged to defend the "Devine Institution," and it was scarcely to be expected that such a cause would be valiantly championed by men whose self-reliance and personal independence had endeared to them the rights of free and honorable manhood.

When the Convention of Virginia met to consider the question of secession, the slave-holding dignitaries were somewhat startled by the logical, but novel, declaration of one of the western members, that "the right of revolution can be exercised as well by a portion of the citizens of a State against their State government, as it can be exercised by the whole people of a State against their Federal Government." This was followed by another, more pointed and revolutionary, "that any change in the relation of Virginia sustains to the Federal Government, against the wishes of even a respectable minority of her people, would be sufficient to justify them in changing their relation to the State government by separating themselves from that section of the State that had thus wantonly disregarded their interests and defied their will."

The convention, however, denying the pertinency of this logic, passed its secret ordinance of secession on the 17th of April, and within a week popular movements were on foot in the various towns and counties of Western Virginia, to effect a division of the State. The people united in a unanimous protest against the efforts of the slave-holding aristocrats to carry them into a cotton confederacy, and a determination to "secede from the secession," was manifested everywhere. The loyal determination was rapidly followed by popular organization, an appeal for assistance was made to the government at Washington, who promised them countenance and support, and on the 13th of May, delegates from twenty-five counties of West Virginia met at Wheeling, to devise such action as would enable them to fully and finally repudiate the treasonable revolt of East Virginia.

Many circumstances favored their position. The state of Ohio, immediately adjoining, was organizing her military force of volunteers, and Western Virginia was, not long after, attached to the department of the Ohio under command of General McClellan. The blockade of Washington, and other events, had operated to keep the Western troops on the Ohio line, and the Unionists of West Virginia found a protecting military force at once in their immediate vicinity, with a commanding officer who was instructed to give them every encouragement and support.

Meanwhile, Governor Letcher, of Virginia, ignoring the attitude of the people of the West, had issued his proclamation calling for the organization of the state militia, and including Western Virginia in the call. Prompted by a spirit of arrogance or over-confidence, he at an early day dispatched officers to that locality to collect and organize the militia of Western Virginia. Owing to the sparsity of the population, and the hilly and mountainous situation of the country, there were but two principal localities or lines of travel, where a concentration of forces could be best effected -- one of these being the line of the

Baltimore and Ohio Railroad, and the other the valley of the Great Kanawha river. In these districts Governor Letcher sent his recruiting agents, but they soon returned reports of a very discouraging character. The rebel emissaries found the feeling very bitter: That Union organizations existed in most of the counties, and that while fragments of rebel companies were here and there springing up, it was very evident that no local force sufficient to hold the country, would respond to the Confederate appeal, while the close proximity of Union forces at several points along the Ohio, pointed to a short tenure of Confederate authority.

This information was not at all cheering to the rebel Governor of the State, and he determined to maintain his authority in the disaffected protion of the State. To accomplish this, he dispatched a few available companies from Staunton to march toward Beverly, from which point they could menace and over-awe the town of Grafton, the junction of the main stem of the Baltimore and Ohio Railroad, with its branches extending to Parkersburg and Wheeling. The inhabitants showed more alacrity, however, to take up arms for the govermnment than for Governor Letcher or General Lee. A Union Western Virginia regiment, under the command of Colonel Kelley, began to gather recruits rapidly at Wheeling, while the rebel camps between Beverly and Grafton were comparatively deserted, and Colonel Porterfield, who had been sent under orders of Governor Letcher, found his efforts at recruiting decidedly unsuccessful.

On the 23rd of May the State voted upon the ordinance of Secession, and East Virginia, under complete military domination, accepted the ordinance, while West Virginia, comparatively free,voted to reject the idea of secession.

Immediately after the result was ascertained, the rebel troops became aggressive, and Colonel Porterfield dispatched several of his companies to burn the bridge on the Baltimore & Ohio Railroad.

The appearance of these troops was quickly brought to the notice of the Federal authorities at Washington. On the 24th of May the Secretary of War and General Scott telegraphed this information to General McClellan, and inquired, "whether its influence could not be counteracted." General McClellan at once replied in the affirmative, and this was the sole order he received from Washington regarding a campaign in Virginia.

On the 26th, the General ordered two regiments to cross the river at Wheeling, and two others at Parkersburg. They were to move forward simultaneously by the branch railroads from each of these points to their junction at Grafton. The burnt bridges were restored in their passage, and after a most brilliant strategic movement, Porterfield was completely surprised, and the rebels were forced to disperse, in utter rout and confusion.

This complete success of the first dash at the enemy had the most inspiring effect upon the Union troops, and also encouraged and fortified the Western Virginia Unionists, in their determination to break away from the East and to form a new State. This movement was successfully accomplished, and early in June they elected two United States senators, who were admitted to, and took part in the national legislature.

Governor Pierpont, who was head of this provisional State government, organized at Wheeling, made a formal application to the United States for aid to suppress the rebellion and protect the people against domestic voilence. General McClellan, in furtherance of this object, ordered additional forces into the state from his department.

In order to act intelligently in the matter, it was necessary that some definite information should be derived respecting the country which was now to be protected, and from which the invading rebels should be driven. For this purpose the General desired that I should dispatch several of my men, who, by assuming various and unsuspicious characters, would be able to travel over the country, obtain a correct idea of its topography, ascertain the exact position and designs of the secessionists.

For this duty I selected a man named Price Lewis, who had just returned from a trip to the South, and whom I had reason to be satisfied was equal to the task. I resolved, therefore, that he should be one of the party to make this journey, together with several others who were delegated for the same purpose. In order to afford variety to the professions of my operatives, and because of his fitness for the character, I decided that Price Lewis should represent himself as an Englishman travelling for pleasure, believing he would escape a close scrutiny or a rigid examination, should he, by any accident, fall into the hands of the rebels.

Procuring a comfortable-looking road-wagon and a pair of strong gray horses, which were both substantial-looking and good roadsters, I stocked the vehicle with such articles of necessity and luxury as would enable them to subsist themselves if necessary, and at the same time give the appearance of truth to such professions as the sight-seeing Englishman might feel authorized to make. I provided him also with a number of English certificates of varous kinds, and I also supplied him with English money which could be readily exchanged for such currency that would best suit his purposes in the several localities he would be required to visit.

Lewis wore a full beard, and this was trimmed in the most approved English fashion, and when fully equipped for his journey he presented the appearance of a thorough well-to-do Englishman, who might even be suspected of having "blue blood" in his veins. In order that he might the more fully sustain the new character he was about to assume, and to give an added dignity to his position, I concluded to send him with a member of my force who would act in the capacity of coachman, groom and body servant, as occasion should demand. The man whom I selected for this role was a jolly, good-natured, and fearless Yankee named Sam Bridgeman, a quick, sharp-witted young man who had been in my employment for some time, and who had on several occasions proved himself worthy of trust and confidence in matters that required tact as well as boldness, and good sense as well as keen wit.

Calling Sam into my office, I explained to him fully the nature of the duties he would be required to perform, and when I had concluded I saw by the merry twinkle in his eyes, and from the readiness with which he caught at my suggestions, that he thoroughly understood and had decided to carry out his part of the programme to the very letter.

In addition to these, I arranged a route for two other men in my force. They were to travel through the valley of the Great Kanawha river, and to observe carefully everything that came under their notice, which might be of importance in perfecting a military campaign, in which the rebels shoud attempt hostile measures, or that General McClellan might find it necessary to promptly clear that portion of Virginia from the presence of the secession troops. These two men were to travel ostensibly as farm laborers, and their verdant appearance was made to fully conform to such avocations.

Everything in readiness, the two parties were started, and we will follow their movements separately, as they were to travel by different routes.

Price Lewis, the pseudo Englishman, and Sam Bridgeman, who made quite a smart-looking valet in his new costume, transferred their horses, wagon and stores on board the trim little steamer,"Cricket," at Cincinnati, intending to travel along the Ohio River, and effect a landing at Guyandotte, in Western Virginia, at point which they were to disembark and pursue their journey overland through the country.

I accompanied Lewis to the wharf , and after everything had been satisfactorily arranged, I bade him good-by, and the little steamer sailed away up the river.

There were a number of miscellaneous passengers upon the boat, and added to these were a number of Union officers, who had been dispatched upon various missions throughout that portion of the State of Ohio. These men left the steamer as their points of destination were reached, and after they had departed, several of the passengers who had hitherto remained silent, became very talkative. They began in a cautious manner to express their opinions, with the view of eliciting some knowledge of the sympathies of their fellow-travellers in the important struggle that was now impending. Lewis had maintained a quiet, dignified reserve, which, while it did not forbid any friendly approaches from his fellow passengers, at the same time rendered them more respectful, and prevented undue familarity. Sam Bridgeman contributed materially to this result; his deference to "my lord" was very natural, and the respect with which he received his commands convinced the passengers at once that the English-looking gentleman was a man of some importance.

The passengers all appeared to be Union men, and while they expressed their regrets that the war had commenced, they regarded their separation from Eastern Virginia, with undisguised satisfaction.

At midnight, on the second evening, the boat landed at Guyandotte, and Samuel, with a great deal of importance, attended to the transfer of his master and the equipage from the boat to the wharf. Here they found a number of men in uniform, who were ascertained to be representatives of the "Home Guard," and in a few minutes Bridgeman had secured the services of two of them, to assist him in safely landing their effects. This being satisfactorily accomplished, he, apparently in a sly manner, treated them to a drop of good whiskey, which formed a part of the stores they had been provided with. Stopping at the hotel over night, they continued their journey on the following morning. They drove leisurely along, and at about ten o'clock they stopped at a farm-house to rest their horses. They remained here until nearly three o'clock in the afternoon, conversing with the old farmer, who seemed to be much pained at the condition of affairs, but who had two sons in the rebel army. They renewed their journey in the afternoon, and in about two hours reached the little village of Colemouth, where there was a rebel encampment. On passing this they were halted by the guard, who inquired their business and destination. Lewis told him he was an Englishman, accompanied only by his servant, and that he was travelling through the country for pleasure. The guard informed them that he could not let them pass, and asked Lewis to go with him the the Captain's headquarters, which was located in a large stone house, a few hundred yards distant. My operative willingly consented, and leaving Sam in charge of his carriage, he accompanied the soldier to the officer's quarters. He was ushered into a large and well-furnished apartment on the second floor, and in a few minutes the Captain came in.

He greeted my operative pleasantly, and informed him that he regretted the necessity of detaining him, but orders had to be obeyed. Lewis related in substance what he had already stated to the guard, which statement the Captain unhesitatingly received, and after a pleasant conversation, he invited the detective to accept the hospitality of the camp. An English gentleman travelling for pleasure was not to be treated with discourtesy, and upon Lewis' accepting of his invitation, a soldier was dispatched to bring the horses and their impatient driver into camp.

Supper was ordered, and in a short time the Captain and his guest were discussing a repast which was far more appetizing than soldier's fare usually is. During the meal Sam stood behind the chair of Lewis, and awaited upon him in the most approved fashion, replying invariably with a deferential,

"Yes, my lord."

After full justice had been done to the repast, Price directed Bridgeman to bring in from the carriage a couple bottles of champagne, and by the time the hour of retiring had arrived the detective had succeeded in impressing his entertainer with a very exalted opinion of his rank and standing when at home.

Lewis, being an Englishman by birth, was very well posted about English affairs, and he entertained his host with several very well invented anecdotes of the Crimea, in which he was supposed to have taken an active part. and his intimacy with Lord Raglan, the commander of the British army, gained for him the unabounded admiration and respect of the doughty Captain.

From this officer Lewis learned that there were a number of troops in Charleston, but a few miles distant, and that General Wise, who was then in command, had arrived there that day.

After a refreshing sleep and a bounteous breakfast, Lewis informed the Captain that he would continue his journey toward Charleston, and endeavor to obtain an interview with General Wise. The Captain cordially recommended him to do so, and furnished him with passports which could carry him without question or delay upon the road. As they were about taking their leave the Captain put into Lewis' hands an unsealed letter, at the same time remarking with great earnestness:

"My lord, I beg of you to accept the inclosed letter of introduction to General Wise; as I am personally acquainted with him, this letter may be of some service to you, and I should be only too happy if it will be so."

"Thank you;" replied Lewis, "but you have been far too kind already, and believe me I shall always recall my entertainment at your hands with pleasure."

The valiant Captain was not aware that he had been furnishing very valuable information to his gentlemanly visitor, and that while he was unsuspectingly answering his well-directed questions, his servant, the quiet Sam Bridgeman, was unobservedly making notes of all that he heard in relation to the situation of affairs and with regard to the probable movements of the rebel troops.

A rather rediculous incident ocurred to our two travelers after leaving the camp. They had proceeded but a short distance upon their way, when one of the horses they were driving cast a shoe, which made it necessary for them to stop at a little village and secure the services of a blacksmith.

Driving up to a hotel, Lewis alighted from the wagon,

while Bridgeman drove to the blacksmith-shop in order to have his horse attended to. As Lewis ascended the steps of the hotel he noticed a tall, rather commanding-looking gentleman seated upon the porch, who was evidently scrutinizing his appearance, very carefully. The stranger was a man about sixty years of age, but remarkably well preserved, and the lines on his face scarcely gave but little indication of his years. There was an air of seeming importance about him which impressed Lewis with the fact that he must be one of the dignitaries of the place, and as he approached him he very politely raised his hat and saluted him.

The old gentleman returned the saluation with an inquiring gaze, and Lewis, in order to pave the way to his acquaintence, invited him to partake of a drink, which was cordially accepted. In a few minutes, under its influence, the two men were conversing with all the freedom of old friends.

Lewis ascertained that his companion was a justice of the peace, an officer of some importance in that locality, and that the old gentleman was disposed to give his judicial position all the dignity which a personal appreciation of his standing demanded. In a quiet manner, Lewis at once gave the justice to understand his appreciating the honor he had received in meeting him, and by way of a few well-administered flatteries, succeeded in winning the kind regards of the old gentleman. Their pleasant conversation was progressing with very favorable success, when Sam Bridgeman drove up with the team, having succeeded in finding a smithy and in having the lost shoe replaced.

With a deferential, semi-military salute, he addressed Lewis:

"We are all ready, my lord." At the mention of the title the old fellow jumped to his feet in blank amazement, and in the most obsequious manner, and with an air of humility, that, compared with his bombastic tone of a few minutes before, was perfectly rediculous. Jerking off his hat and placing it under his left arm, he advanced, and said:

"If my lord would do me the honor to accept my poor hospitality, I would only be too happy to have the pleasure of his company for dinner; my house is only a short distance off, on the road to Charleston, and will detain you no longer than to rest and feed your horses, and partake of a true Southern meal."

Lewis hesitated or a moment, and then remembering that he had represented himself as travelling purely for pleasure, he did not see how he could avoid accepting his kind invitation.

"I have heard, sir, of the hospitable character of the Southern gentleman, and I assure you I shall be most happy to avail myself of your kindness."

The old Justice could not conceal his pleasure at the prospect of entertaining a "live lord" in his own house, and with evident delight he accepted a seat in Lewis' carriage. he directed the way to his dwelling, which stood back from the road, surrounded by a grove of lofty pines, and then invited his guest within; intrusting the care of the team to the care of Sam and one of the servants, they entered the house, and were soon engaged in discussing the situation of affairs, both North and South. Lewis informed the old Justice that his name was Henry Tracy, of Oxford, England, and that his object was to reach Charleston, but that he was not aware that the country was so unsettled, or he would not have ventured on this trip. He then related his adventure of the day before, and commented favorably on the gentlemanly bearing of the Captain, and the manner in which he had been treated. They indulged in pleasant conversation, on various topics, until dinner was announced.

When they had done justice to an excellent repast, they repaired to a shaded porch in the rear of the house, and Lewis instructed Sam to bring out a bottle of champagne and a bottle of brandy. These, as already intimated, had been labeled with foreign wrappers, so that the deception was complete. The brandy was a very ordinary article, and the wine of an inferior quality, but the old gentleman went into ecstasies over it, and under its mellowing influence, he became familar and confidential, and gave to my shrewd operative much invaluable information. Finally the justice grew profusly demonstrative, and leaning across the table, he said:

"My lord, I have never tasted such a brandy as you carry in all my life, I have a couple of warm friends outside whom I have taken the liberty to send for, and whom I know will be delighted to see you, and still more pleased to taste this excellent liquor."

"Certainly," replied Lewis, "bring them in; I shall be happy to meet them."

Lewis supposed, of course, that the two men whom he had referred were planters and neighbors, but imagine his surprise when the justice returned, accompanied by the blacksmith and cobbler of the village.

After being introduced to "my Lord Tracy," Lewis invited them to take a glass with them, and with evident pleasure, yet with visible embarassment, they accepted the invitation and seated themselves at the table.

It was now that the old gentleman became loquacious; he was loud and profuse in his praises of the brandy; he asserted again and again, that it had never been his good fortune to taste such liquor, in which encomiums the blacksmith and cobbler heartily joined. As the afternoon wore away, and the present supply was exhausted, Sam was dispatched for another bottle, and the social meeting continued until evening. Lewis was careful as to the amount he drank, and intensely enjoyed the whole affair. The idea of the blacksmith and cobbler hobnobbing with an English lord, struck him as being so rediculously funny, that he laughed again and again at the absurdity of the situation. Often during the evening he laughed immoderately, at what they supposed their own jokes and wit, when he was really thinking of the rediculous comedy in which he was playing the leading part. When the hour for retiring arrived, the old gentleman begged as a special favor that he would be allowed to keep one of the empty bottles, as a momento of the occasion of his lordship's dining with him, and to remind of the pleasure he had enjoyed of drinking some rare old imported brandy (made in Cincinnati). The blacksmith and cobbler also looked so longingly at the empty bottles before them, that Lewis could scarcely refrain from laughing heartily, as he graciously complied with their request for a souvenir of the occasion. The evident satisfaction with which they appropriated a bottle apiece, as they started for home, and their hearty thanks as they bid him good-night, was heartily echoed by the old justice, who carefully laid his bottle away as a sacred relic of a never-to-be-forgotten event.

While the party were enjoying themselves on the porch, Sam Bridgeman had been using his time well among the servants, and had gleaned much valuable information from them. They remained overnight with the old gentleman, and on the following morning, after bidding him a kind farewell, they started on their journey. Lewis did not forget, however, before leaving, to take a parting glass with his host, who seemed very reluctant to have them depart. They continued on their way towards Charleston, travelling but slowly, as the roads were heavy from the recent rains. About noon they arrived at a farm-house, to which they had been recommended by their host of the night before. Here they stopped for dinner, and after refreshing themselves, they again went on. The afternoon was warm and pleasant, and their journey lay through a beautiful stretch of country. Driving quietly along, they beguiled the time admiring the beautiful scenery before them, and in pleasant converse. Their enjoyment was, however, suddenly interrupted by the sound of loud voices and the clattering of horse's hoofs immediately behind them. Quickly turning around, the cause of this unusual excitement was at once apparent. A fine black horse, covered with foam, was tearing down the turnpike at break-neck speed, and evidently running away. Upon his back was seated a young lady, who bravely held her seat, and who was vainly attempting to restrain the unmanageable animal. Some distance behind were a party of ladies and gentlemen on horseback, all spurring their horses to the utmost, as if with the intention of overtaking the flying steed in front of them. Intense fear was depicted upon the countenances of those in the rear, and not without reason, for the situation of this young lady was dangerous indeed.

Quick as a flash, my operatives realized the situation of affairs, and the necessity for prompt action. Without uttering a word, Sam Bridgeman turned his horses directly across the road, intending by that means to stop the mad course of the fiery charger approaching them. As he did so, Lewis sprang from the wagon, and with the utmost coolness advanced to meet the approaching horse. On came the frightened animal at a speed that threatened every moment to hurl the brave girl from her seat, until he approached nearly to the point at which my operatives had stationed themselves, and then, evidently perceiving the obstructions in his path, he momentarily slackened pace. In that instant Lewis sprang forward, and grasping the bridle with a strong hand, he forced the frightened animal back upon his haunches. The danger was passed. The horse, feeling the iron grip upon the bridle, and recognizing the voice of authority, stood still and trembling in every joint, his reeking sides heaving, and his eyes flashing fire. The young lady, with a sudden revulsion of feeling, fell back in the saddle, and would have fallen but that Sam Bridgeman, hastening to the relief of his companion, was fortunately in time to catch the fainting figure in his arms. Extricating her quickly from the saddle, he set her gently on the ground, and as he did so the fair head fell forward on his shoulder, and she lost consciousness.

By this time Lewis had succeeded in quieting the excited animal, and had fastened him to a tree by the wayside, and as he turned to the assistance of Bridgeman, the companions of the unconscious girl rode up. Hastily dismounting, they rushed to her aid, and in a few minutes, under their ministrations, the dark eyes opened, and the girl gazed wonderingly around.

After being assisted to her feet, she gratefully expressed her thankfulness to the men who had probably saved her life, in which she was warmly joined by the remainder of the party.

Sam Bridgeman received these grateful expressions with an air of modest confusion, which was indeed laughable, and then said:

"It ain't no use thanking me, Miss, it was my lord here, that stopped the animal."

At the words "my lord," a look of curiosity came over the faces of the newcomers, and Lewis stepped gracefully forward and introduced himself.

"I am glad, ladies and gentlemen, to have been of service to this young lady, and permit me to introduce myself as Henry Tracy, of Oxford, England, now travelling in America."

The three gentlemen who were of the riding party grasped the hand of their new made English acquaintence, and in a few words introduced him to the ladies who accompanied them, all of whom were seemingly delighted to make the acquaintence of a gentleman who had been addressed by his servant as "my lord."

This adventure proved to be a most fortunate one for my two operatives. The gentlemen, upon introducing themselves, were discovered to be connected with the rebel army, and to be recruiting officers sent by Governor Letcher to organize such rebel volunteers as were to be gathered in Western Virginia. By them Lewis was cordially invited to join their company to Charleston, which he cordially accepted. Suggesting that as the young lady, who had scarcely recovered from the accident, might not feel able to ride her horse into town, he politely offered her a seat in his carriage, which offer was gratefully accepted, and attaching the runaway horse to the rear of the vehicle, the party proceeded on their way to Charleston, at which point they arrived without further event of accident.

The young lady whom Lewis had so providentially rescued was the only daughter of Judge Beveridge, one of the wealthiest and most influential men in the State, and upon conducting her to her home, the detective was received with the warmest emotions by the overjoyed father. Lewis was pressed to make the house of the Judge his home during his stay, but gratefully declined the invitation, he took up his quarters at the hotel, where he could more readily extend his acquaintence, and where his movements would be more free.

The young officers whom he had met upon the road had their quarters at the hotel at which Lewis had stopped, and under their friendly guidance no one thought of questioning his truthfulness, or impeaching his professions.

By this means he was enabled to acquire a wonderful amount of information, both of value and importance to the cause of the North, all of which was duly reported to me at headquarters, and by me communicated directly to General McClellan.

The Rebels Attempt to Occupy West Virginia - General McClellan Ordered to Drive Them Out - Early Battle The Federals Victorious - West Virginia Freed From Rebel Soldiers.

Recognizing the importance of holding West Virginia, and of preventing the Union forces from penetrating through the mountains in the direction of Staunton, the rebel authorities had sent two new commanders to that region. Ex-Governor Wise was dispatched to the Kanawha Valley, and General Garnett, formerly a Major in the Federal army, was sent to Beverly to attempt to gather up and reorganize the remnants of Colonel Porterfield's scattered command, and to adopt immediate measures to reinforce them.

General Wise having been assigned to the Kanawha

Valley, was expected to arrive at Charleston on the day following the appearance of my operatives, and the city was in a state of subdued excitement in anticipation of his coming.

In the evening, Lewis, in company with the officers whom he had met in the morning, proceeded to the residence of Judge Beveridge, where he was cordially received by that gentleman and his charming daughter, who had now thoroughly recovered from the effects of her dangerous ride. With rare grace she greeted my operative, and her expressions of thankfulness were couched in such delicate language, that the pretended Englishman felt a strange fluttering in his breast, which was as novel to him as it was delicious. He passed a very delightful evening, and by his knowledge of English affairs, and his unqualified approval of the cause of the South, added to the fact that he was believed to be a gentleman of rank and fortune, he succeeeded in materially increasing the high opinion which had previously been entertained regarding him.

The next morning General Wise arrived, and his appearance was hailed with delight by the disunion element of the city, while those whose sympathies were with the North looked with apprehension and disfavor upon the demonstrations that were being made in his honor.

At the first opportune moment, Price Lewis, with the assistance of his newfound friends, the rebel officers, succeeded in obtaining an introduction to the ancient-looking individual whose career had been marked by such exciting events, and who was so prominent a figure in the tragedy that was now being enacted. He was a small, intelligent-looking man, whose age appeared to be nearly seventy years, and whose emaciated appearance gave every token that he had not long to live. His eyes shone with the brilliancy of youth, and the fires of ambition seemed to be burning brightly in his breast. Perhaps no other man in the South had contributed in so great a degree to hasten the folly of secession, and certainly none rejoiced more heartily

Photograph by Wick Walker

The Grave Of Nicholas H. Ramsey.

He was murdered a few days following the battle of Carnifex Ferry as he returned to his home. The young man was "neutral", but was the son of a staunch Unionist in a largely Confederate region of the state. He was buried by a company of Union infantrymen and the grave was surrounded by a low rock wall by his father and older brother after the war. The monument was placed at the grave by Ramsey's son -- seventy-five years after the war.

Henry A. Wise John B. Floyd

Robert S. Garnett John Pegram

Battles and Leaders

Confederate Generals who served in West Virginia. Wise and Floyd served in the Kanawha Valley Theater while Garnet and Pegram fought in the northwestern areas.

at its final realization.

By his eloquence, and the magnetic power of his presence, he had led the ignorant classes of the State to firm belief in the justice of his cause, and by his teachings he had imbued them with a firm conviction that they were acting for their own best interests, and for the furtherance of the Southern supremacy and success.

Stern and determined, he allowed nothing to stand between him and the accomplishment of his purposes. But a few months before, he had ordered the execution of John Brown, who, with a mere handful of men, had attempted to strike a blow in behalf of the slave. This ardent abolitionist attacked and captured Harper's Ferry, a government arsenal, by overpowering the men who were stationed at that place, but the authorities had been called upon and then, yielding to superior numbers, he was compelled to surrender. In this encounter the majority of his men were slain, and John Brown, with six of his associates, was taken prisoner. This occurred on the 16th day of October, 1859, and on the 22nd day of December, after a hurried trial, the prisoners were ordered by Governor Wise to be publicly hanged. The sentence was duly carried into effect, and the action of John Brown was used by the secession advocates to inflame the minds of the Southern people against the North. Now that secession had become an established fact, it was a matter of question whether the leaders of the Southern cause would not, in the end, strike a far more forcible blow in favor of the emancipation of the slave, than did the impetuous old man who gave up his life at the behest of the Southern leaders.

The General had been previously informed of the presence of Lewis in the hotel, and of his adventure on the day previous, consequently, when he was presented to the new commander, he was received with warm cordiality. The general inquired particularily into his history, and his present movements, all of which were replied to by Lewis in a dignified and satisfactory manner. Under the influence of Lewis' good nature the General became social and familar, and invited him to dine with him in his apartments.

Leaving no opportunity that offered, the detective took advantage of every available suggestion, and the result was he became fully posted upon everything that was of importance, and was enabled to render such an account of his labors as was satisfactory in the extreme. Sam Bridgeman, too, had not been idle, but mingling freely with the soldiers, he had succeeded in learning much of the conditions of the country that was of immense advantage in the after events of the campaign in Western Virginia.

They remained in Charleston about eight days, and then, taking leave of the many friends they had made, they made their way safely back to Cincinnati and reported. The other two men whom I had dispatched upon the same mission traveled by rail across the State of Ohio and reached the West Virginia line at Point Pleasant. Here they began their investigations, and passing unquestioned they roamed through the country, passing eastward as far as Lynchburg. Thence, they made a detour to the South, and journeyed as far as Chattanooga and Nashville, in Tennessee, and thence to Louisville, Ky. Through out their entire pilgrimage they were ever on alert to acquire knowledge, and the immense amount of information which they gathered would only prove tedious to both myself and the reader. It is enough to say that they performed their duty in a manner creditable to themselves and valuable to the cause they represented, and I will simply summarize the situation.

General Garnett had posted himself in the pass at Laurel Hill, with an additional force at Beverly, while another detachment, under Col. Pegram, had established himself in the pass at Rich Mountain. Here he had intended to fortify himself and to await a favorable opportunity for breaking the railroad. He found affairs upon his arrival in a miserable condition; the troops were disorganized and without discipline, arms or ammunition, and General Lee immediately sent him re-enforcements.

This was the condition of affairs, when, early in

July, General McClellan resolved to take the offensive and drive the rebels from West Virginia. In this campaign he received material aid and assistance from that brave officer General Rosecrans, who by superhuman exertions penetrated the pathless forest cutting and climbing his way to the very crest of Rich Mountain.

This movement, difficult as it was, to the South of the rebels, was a complete surprise to the enemy, who was expecting their arrival from the North.

They made a gallant resistance, however, but the Union forces had such an advantage that the contest was quickly decided. The rebel forces were driven from their breastworks and were compelled to take refuge in thickets or the mountains. Their confusion was deplorable, and their defeat unmistakable.

This victory placed the enemy in a very precarious position. McClellan was in his front and Rosecrans in secure possession of the road behind him, and Pegram, realizing the danger that threatened him, returned to his camp and, hastily spiking his guns, he abandoned all his stores and equipments, and endeavored to escape by marching northward along the mountain, intending, if possible, to join Garnett at Laurel Hill.

For the time being, he was successful in eluding the Federal commanders, and after a most laborious march of eighteen hours, found himself within three miles of Leedsville. Here he was doomed to disappointment, for he learned that Garnett had also retreated, and that a strong Union column was in close pursuit. Thus he was again caught between two Union armies, and dispairing of effecting his escape, he sent a proposal to General McClellan, offering a total surrender of his command. The Union General accepted the proposition, and on the following day the half-famished rebel fugitives laid down their arms and became prisoners of war, only too glad to receive once more comfortable quarters and hunger-appeasing rations.

The fugitives from the battle of Rich Mountain carried

the news of that disaster to Beverly, and to General Garnett, at Laurel Hill, and an immediate retreat was ordered. But he was closely pressed by the advancing Union armies, and when General Garnett reached Leedsville, he heard that General McClellan was at Beverly, thus cutting off effectually his further passage southward. He now resolved upon the desperate attempt of turning to the North and reaching St. George and West Union by a rough and difficult mountain road, during which his troops naturally became very much scattered and disorganized. Although he was nearly fifteen hours in advance of his pursuers, they gained rapidly upon him, and not withstanding every effort was made by the rebels to impede his progress by felling trees in the narrow mountain defiles, the Union advance overtook the rebel wagon-train at Carrick's Ford, one of the crossings of Cheat River, about twenty-six miles northwest of Laurel Hill. Here Garnett resolved to risk an encounter, and facing about his troops, he took a position on a favorable and precipitious elevation on the river bank, and planting his guns so as to command the ford and the approaching road, he prepared to defend his retreat. A brisk engagement at once ensued, and after a sharp contest the rebel lines broke and fled, abandoning one of their guns.

Retreat and pursuit were once more commenced, and at the next ford, a quarter mile further on, during a desultory skirmish fire between small parties of sharpshooters, General Garnett was killed. Here the Federal pursuit was discontinued, and the rebels left in the hands of the victors their entire baggage train, one gun, two stands of colors and fifty prisoners.

Estimated according to mere numbers, these battles of Rich Mountain and Carrick's Ford appear somewhat insignificant in contrast with the great battles of the rebellion, which occurred during the succeeding three years. Hundreds of engagements of greater magnitude, and attended with much more serious loss of life, followed these encounters, and decided the mighty problem of

Northern success, but this early skirmish with the rebels on Rich Mountain, and this rout of Garnett's rearguard at Carrick's Ford, were speedily followed by great political and military results, which exercised a powerful influence upon the after-conduct of the war. They closed a campaign, dispersed a rebel army, which had for a long time been harassing a State whose sympathies were with the Union, and they permanently pushed back the military frontier to the borders of rebellious territory. Now, is it too much to say that the brilliant success which attended this first agressive movement of General McClellan had a marked effect upon the public mind? That they gave a general impression of his military skill is not to be doubted, and he was from that time the hero of the hour. Certain it is that a train of circumstances started from these achievements which eventually led to his being called to Washington after the reverses at Manassas and Bull Run, and made him, on the first day of November following, the General-in-Chief of all the armies of the United States.

It is not necessary for me to follow the subsequent operations in West Virginia, as my duties were connected with General McClellan and his campaigns in that district ended with the death of General Garnett and the dispersion of his army. About a week afterwards he was called to a new field of duty at Washington city, and it is not my purpose to touch upon events in which I took no part. It is enough to say that, with somewhat fluctuating changes, the rebels were gradually forced back from the Great Kanawha Valley, and the eventual result left West Virginia in possession of Federal troops, her own inherent loyalty having contributed largely in producing this condition. The Union sentiment of the people was everywhere manifest, and the new State government was consolidated and heartily sustained, ending in her ultimate admission as a separate member of the federal Union in June, 1863.

Lewis was a bold and experienced spy who had gained

the confidence of Pinkerton, the spymaster. Pinkerton sent Lewis into rebel territory again in an attempt to locate one of his best agents, Timothy Webster, who had not reported on schedule. This was early spring in 1862. Unfortunately, Lewis and another of Pinkerton's operatives located the missing spy in his Richmond hotel, sick, but were soon arrested by suspicious Confederate authorities. The two were to confirm their guilt when they escaped from the Henrico Jail, but were recaptured in the swamps to the northeast of Richmond. Pinkerton's missions were risky and the penalty for espionage was death.

Michael Egan joined the Union army as a private, but soon after arriving at Clarksburg he volunteered to serve as a military express courier. He delivered messages between Clarksburg and Gauley Bridge, Virginia, at a time when the roads were extremely dangerous to travel. There were Confederate "bushwhackers" to be avoided along the route and a sudden rapid turn in a bend on the road which would suprise a Federal outpost or patrol could be quickly fatal for the courier.

He wrote about his adventures after the war and these were published as The Flying Gray-Haired Yank or The Adventures of a Volunteer. *The book was published in Philadelphia by Hubbard Brothers in 1888.*

Military Express Courier Line established between Clarksburg and Gauley Bridge - Appointed First Courier West Virginia Bushwhackers - Bill Parsons - First Meeting With General Rosecrans - Arrested as a Rebel Spy by Union Troops - Tried by "DrumHead" Court Martial Sentenced to be Shot - Narrow Escape from Ignominious Death

On the 31st of August, 1861, General Rosecrans, with his brigade, moved out of Clarksburg, and took up his line of march in the direction of Gauley Bridge, 133 miles distant. He encamped that night near Jane Lew, fifteen miles west of Clarksburg.

In consequence of the stoppage of the mails it became necessary to establish an express a courier line to his headquarters, to convey to the officers of his column their letters and official documents from the headquarters of the army at Washington. General Rosecrans therefore ordered Captain Charles Leib, Assistant Quartermaster, at Clarksburg, to establish a line of couriers for this purpose.

Captain Leib had, at this time, a large depot of supplies at Clarksburg, and consequently a large number of subordinates; but amongst all his small army of teamsters and other employees he failed to find one volunteer to bear dispatches to the general, not withstanding the fact that Captain Leib tendered them the use of his finest horses, a complete set of small arms, and wages to the amount of forty dollars per month, with rations.

None of his employees were enlisted men, so he could not enforce his orders in this particular. Their reasons for refusing were obvious. A short time before two young men attempted to convey dispatches to Colonel Tyler, of the 7th Regiment, Ohio Volunteers, in the same direction, but they were rather summarily disposed of by the bushwhackers; one, a splendid young fellow, James Flesher by name, ... , was killed outright, and the other, Mifflin

Cutright, was badly wounded; they both resided near Weston.

Captain Leib, in his book, "The Chances for making a Million," thus describes these marauding bandits:

"The bushwhackers are composed of a class of men who are noted for their ignorance, indolence, duplicity and dishonesty; whose vices and passions pecularily fit them for the warfare in which they are engaged, and upon which the civilized world looks with horror. Imagine a stolid, vicious-looking countenance, an ungainly figure, and an awkward, if not ungraceful, spinal curve in the dorsal region, acquired by laziness and indifference to maintaining an erect posture; a garb of the coarsest texture of homespun linen, or 'linsey woolsey.' tattered and torn, and so covered with dirt as not to enable one to guess its original color; a dilapidated, rimless hat, or cap of some wild animal's skin, covering his head, the hair of which had not been combed for months; his feet covered with moccasins, and a rifle by his side, a powder horn and shotpouch slung around his neck, and you will have the beau ideal of the West Virginia bushwhacker.

"Thus equipped he sallies forth with the stealth of the panther, and lies in wait for a straggling soldier, courier, or loyal citizen, to whom the only warning given to his presence is the click of his deadly rifle. He kills for the sake of killing, and plunders for the sake of gain. Parties of these fercious beasts, under the cover of darkness, frequently steal into a neighborhood, burn the residences of loyal citizens, rob stores, tan yards and farm houses of everything they can put to use, especially arms, ammunition, leather, clothing, bedding, and salt.

"They do not stop at pillage, for oft times is their track marked with blood. The leaders of some of these bands have acquired great notoriety by their coldblooded brutality and adroitness at theft; and of these is a man who in days gone by enjoyed to a great degree the confidence of the people of West Virginia. He, together with ex-Governor Wise, did much to make bushwhacking respectable in the estimation of the depraved and ignorant....

"A notorious bushwhacker is Bill Parsons, or 'Devil Bill, as he is called. Bill is filthy in appearance, and, like the rest of his class, has low instincts, and is ferocious as a hyena. It is said he has eleven wives, and it a well known fact that one of them is his own daughter. He resides in Roane county, where he has been guilty of many gross outrages."

The quartermaster's employees had ears for news of this kind, and, naturally enough, none of them were prepared to run the gauntlet. Thomas H. Croghan, a dashing, military-looking fellow, was forage master under Captain Leib; he told the captain that there was a man in town who he thought would do the work. Croghan and myself had both received a military training in the same school in Ireland, and were well-acquainted and good friends. He introduced me, with considerable eulogism, to Captain Leib, who received me very affably, and said he hoped that I would undertake the duty spoken of.

I was fully conscious of the dangers and responsibilities of the position, but after the flattering introduction of my friend,and the apparent confidence reposed in me by the appointing power, I decided to accept. Having done so, I was soon well armed and mounted, and received my dispatches about five o'clock P.M., with orders to deliver them to General Rosecrans, and, if possible, to ride at the rate of eight miles an hour. My horse being a good one I made good time, and arrived in camp, at Jane Lew, some time before seven o'clock P.M.

It was about dusk as I approached camp, and I was promptly challenged at the guard post with:

"Who comes there?"

"A friend with the countersign. Call a corporal of the guard and have me conducted to the general's headquarters," I answered.

This was complied with immediately and I rode

along leisurely with the corporal to the general's tent. The soldier entered and announced his message, and the general soon after came out; I saluted him, announced my name and delivered my dispatches. He remarked that my name was not unfamilar to him, and we had quite a friendly chat of a few minutes' duration; he then directed me to put up for the night at the little village of Jane Lew, and return with the dispatches to Clarksburg in the morning.

I was so highly impressed with the general's qualities as a gentleman and a soldier that I was prepared to serve him at all hazards, even had I no higher stimulus.

I returned to Clarksburg as directed and there waited for return dispatches until eight o'clock the next morning, when, well mounted on a horse of high mettle, I proceeded at the regular schedule rate of eight miles an hour and arrived at Weston, a distance of twenty-four miles, at eleven o'clock P.M., September 1st.

On approaching the town I slackened up, expecting to find an outpost of our troops reported to be then stationed at Weston,but found none. I then thought I should encounter one at Coalstone bridge, the eastern boundary of the town, but did not; and reached the centre of the town without being challenged. I learned from a few stragglers whom I met on my way in that there were two or three regiments encamped on, or near, the State Asylum grounds; the main body of the troops having continued on the march and encamped near Bulltown.

My horse had slipped a shoe, and, although a good animal, showed signs of fatigue. I wished to report to the officer in command and either get a fresh horse or have some other proper person proceed with the dispatches. I crossed West Fork bridge, on the northern part of town and in close proximity to the asylum ground, the encampment of the troops, where above all other places there should have been a guard, without being halted by any one; in fact I had entered and passed through the town and up to the headquarters of Colonel Ewing, who was in command of the troops, the 30th and 47th Ohio Regiments, without being challenged.

I reported and showed my dispatches to the colonel, who received me very kindly. Understanding my late and fast ride, he asked me to partake of some refreshments. Captain Smith, his gentlemanly quartermaster, handed me a glass of good liquor, of which I drank moderately. I then said that if I had a fresh horse I would proceed to Bulltown with the dispatches. Colonel Ewing directed me to report to the post quartermaster, Ransom, who would either relieve me of the dispatches or furnish me with the needed animal. Before leaving the colonel asked how I got into the quarters. This was a ticklish question. A straight forward answer would be a serious charge against all the pickets. I therefore told him that when I approached the camp I called for a corporal of the guard to conduct me to his headquarters.

I found Captain Ransom in bed at Bailey's Hotel; he told me he would have the dispatches forwarded early next morning.

Upon coming down from the captain's room I was taken into custody by a guard, and placed in close confinement in a Sibley tent. The officer in charge of this guard had been, for some time previously, stationed at Weston, and therefore he must have known me, but being in command, as I suppose of the pickets on that night, September 1, 1861, and conscious of having been derelict in his duties in allowing them to desert their posts, he was fearful, no doubt, of this fact becoming known through me, knowing, as he did, that such a serious breach of discipline was, according to military law, punishable with death. He had, therefore, in order to save himself, helped to trump up false charges against me; some of which were, I afterwards learned, that I had been prowling about the precincts of the encampment on that evening; that I had been a rebel spy at the battle of Bull Run; and that I must have killed the regular courier, or dispatch bearer, etc.

At this time, however, I was kept in total ignorance of all this, they did not even once intimate to me their reasons for my arrest and the placing over me of an armed guard, which later on they saw fit to double. In answer to my inquiries as to the meaning of it all, the men in whose immediate custody I was either could not or would not tell me.

Some time after midnight I was aroused from a deep reverie by the entrance of a gentleman. That he was a gentleman, brave and intelligent, became deeply impressed upon my mind, because, among all the officers of these two regiments, he was the only one whom I found to possess these desirable qualities; this was Captain Smith, brigade or regimental quartermaster. He was the first and only one to make me aware of the tragic role I was about to play. He told me that they were trying me under"Drumhead" Court Martial, for being a rebel spy. He seemed quite sympathetic and kind, and seemed, personally, to entertain no doubt of my loyalty. He wanted me to take something to eat, but I declined, with thanks. Captain Smith then left, but returned again an hour or so later, and informed me that I had been found guilty and was to be shot at nine o'clock that morning. This would leave me with just five and a half hours to live. The thoughts of my wife, then about twenty years old, who, with our two dear little ones, aged respectively four and two years, was then living nine miles northwest of Weston, and in a delicate state of health, in which a sudden shock or fright might be attended with serious consequences to her, might well have unmanned me during this trying ordeal; but when the dawn of morning came, and after the tap of the martial drum, squad after squad of the troops appeared at my tent, at the entrance of which I stood, and with exulting and taunting remarks called me "d__n rebel spy," their conduct only served to steel me to a bearing of scornful defiance, and I called them cowards and poltroons, whom Russell, of the *London Times*, had published as such, for throwing down their arms at the first battle of Bull Run.

There was one individual, Vixbeck by name, that figured in this little tragedy, who could, I think, be safely called a counterpart in disposition to the atrocious Simon Girty, of Indian notoriety. He was one of the guards placed over me, and he cruelly overstepped his orders in adopting every method he could devise to annoy and intimidate me, or induce me to run from his demonstrative threats, in order that he might have a slight pretext for appeasing his evident thirst for my life. With the eye and grimace of a fiend he would bring his bayonet to the position of "charge bayonets" with the steel scarcely two feet from my breast, the hammer at full cock, and all the time fingering the trigger nervously, urged by many of his comrades of the same gentle stripe to "let it go off, accidentally, into the d__n rebel spy," as they kindly styled me. This creature, if he is alive to peruse this description of himself, may feel I have done him an injustice; but I do not think he is possessed of sufficient courage to ask me to retract it.

My brother, Thomas Egan, two years my senior, together with his family, was living at Weston at the time of my arrest. He was then the proprietor of the Union House, and was himself Union to the core. He was a most kind and affectionate brother. He had heard of my dangerous situation early that morning, and, in a state of distraction, hurried over to the officer's quarters to explain to them their mistake. They did not allow him to approach me, but from the entrance of my tent where I stood I could see a squad of men driving him out of the camp at the point of the bayonet. This treatment of my brother by the troops created considerable indignation among the citizens of the town, where he was very well and favorable known.

In my behalf Colonel Ewing was also waited upon by several of the most prominent and influential men of the place. They assured him, in the strongest terms, of my loyalty, and of the impossibility of my being guilty of the charges made against me; and, in conclusion, stated that unless I was at once released, a full report of the proceedings would be forwarded to General Rosecrans. The colonel, however, remained obdurate, and, as it was now about nine o'clock, the detail of my execution was made. I was led forth, and they loaded in my presence.

At this critical juncture, and after I had given up all hopes of life, a telegram was handed Colonel Ewing, dated Clarksburg, from Captain Leib, demanding, in language he well knew how to employ, my instant release.

The colonel then, for the first time since my arrest, condescended to see me. He ordered his men to set me free, and approaching me in the most afable manner he could assume, said he hoped I would excuse him for the hasty and harsh treatment I had received, adding that "the exigencies of the times, and the necessity for strict discipline, justified rigid measures."

I took occasion to remind him that it was the total absence of discipline that had endangered my life; that the enemy possessed of half his force on this night might have annhilated his entire command before it would have been possible to check the onslaught; that he did not have a picket, or outpost, in any direction surrounding his camp, and concluded: "I was, sir, about to pay the penalty of this very strict discipline you talk of, but I shall lay the circumstances, in proper form, before General Rosecrans." When I had finished I turned and walked away.

We will now revert, briefly, to the cause of my deliverance. When arrested I was divested of everything of value, including my memorandum book and pencil. When Captain Smith visited me the second time to inform me that I was to be shot at nine o'clock the next morning, I asked him for paper and pencil, which he cheerfully furnished me. I there upon indited a telegram to Captain Leib, stating as briefly as possible my critical condition, brought about, I claimed, by the culpability of Colonel Ewing and his command, and requesting that he (Leib) wire Ewing to release me. Captain Smith kindly took this message to the telegraph office, and had it forwarded to Clarksburg. The reader knows the result. To the kindness of Captain Smith therefore, and the efficient working of the telegraph line, which had been in operation only a few days, do I owe my escape from the ignominious death of a spy.

Upon my release my effects were returned to me. on going into town from camp I took out my diary to make some entries, as was my usual custom, when Dr. T.B. Camden, who was accompanying me, wisely reminded me that I was acting imprudently, as this action on my part might be noticed and taken advantage of by the angry and still doubting troops.

When I appeared before my brother and his family at their home, I found them and my wife, who had come into town early that morning, in a state of great distraction, and lamenting me as dead; but

> "*Soon my presence allayed their fears,*
> *While reactive joy smiled through their tears.*"

My wife and brother Tom's family now united in entreating me, in the strongest terms, to discontinue so hazardous and ill-requited a position, the duties of which would now compel me to run the gauntlet of a two-fold enemy -- that of the rebel bushwhackers on one side and this portion of our troops on the other; the latter being fearful of the results of my threatened report, and being anxious, my friends insisted, "to remove me on a very slight pretext." I loved my family as tenderly as could any husband and father; the salary, forty dollars per month, was no great inducement, as for that amount alone I would not make one such trip, and I was under no legal or binding obligation, military or civil, to detain me in the service if I wished to retire, It may therefore appear strange when I state that the only motive I had in remaining was a desire to be of use to the government in my humble though perilous way, a way, too, where few volunteers seemed willing to take a chance. Expert horsemanship also was essential to a military courier's work, and a good many soldiers were lacking there.

A Timid Superintendent - Poor work and Early Dismissal His Successor also a Failure - Capture of Two Couriers Escape of One and His Quick Promotion and Subsequent Official Decapitation - My Appointment as Superintendent

General Rosecrans was now briskly following Floyd and Wise towards Gauley Bridge.

Captain Leib, Assistant Quartermaster, appointed Mr. A.F. Newman Superintendent of the Express Courier line, with instructions to establish stations eight miles apart, prepare a timetable, and order the couriers to push forward as rapidly as possible with the dispatches for General Rosecrans and his command. They were also directed to watch the military telegraph line, and to report to the nearest office when the line was discovered to be out of order.

Newman, on his first trip, when he had penetrated some distance into the enemy's lines, became painfully suspicious of danger; many of the horses of his line were captured also, and others were returned to Clarksburg with sore backs, and lame, and otherwise ill-treated by their riders; the mails became very irregular; the general grumbled; his staff grumbled, and there was a general grumbling time at headquarters, so he was discharged.

Mr. Angus M. Reiger, an itinerant preacher from Clarksburg, was next appointed. He made two or three trips and then resigned, nor could he be induced to make another trip. This is not surprising when it is known that the wild bushwhackers along the line were so unchristian-like as to fire, with deadly intent, upon his reverence.

About this time two stout, intelligent men, named, respectively, Peter Bryson, who served with credit afterwards, and J.L. Merryman, were captured by Captain Imboden, and a squad of rebel infantry, at the house of Mr. James Boggs, a loyal man, on the top of Powell mountain.

The prisoners were taken as far as Meadow Bluffs, where Merryman begged off. He had been a schoolteacher, and was gifted with an easy flow of language and a good address. He was a widower, having several young children dependent on him for support. He dwelt with pathetic earnestness upon this latter circumstance before Captain Imboden, and said that he sympathized with the Southern cause as much as anybody, but the necessity of providing for his motherless children found him in the position of courier, which was but a civil one at most. He was successful in his pleadings and was allowed to return home, while Bryson was taken to Libby prison.

Soon after this, Merryman reported to Captain Leib, at Clarksburg, and recounted to him, in thrilling words, his marvelous exploits in effecting his escape from the "rebs." He stated to the captain, with many additions, that shortly after his capture by the rebels he was escorted by one of their number to a spring to procure water; arrived there, he knocked down the guard and effected his escape, and by the exercise of great bravery and shrewdness he finally got through, after suffering many privations. His plausible story was believed, and, as a reward for his brilliant achievements, he was immediately promoted to the superintendency of the line. I never could understand, except on one hypothesis, how Merryman could be induced to undertake such a perilous position, which he cheerfully did immediately after being paroled by Captain Imboden. He now set about picking up several of his friends for the purpose of giving them the fancy places on the line, discharging or transferring old and good men to do so. He made a requisition on Clarksburg for fresh horses and supplies; and in his personal outfit the inner man was not forgotten.

Being the first courier on the line, my station was eight miles from Clarksburg, but this was a place that he had his eye on for one of his favorites. He showed considerable pomposity when he came out where I was stationed, and soon gave me to understand that he purposed a number of changes on the line, and that he would have to place me about thirty or forty miles farther out. I was aware that I stood well at headquarters; that I could have superintended the line from the start if I had wished to, and that I might disregard with impunity the orders of the new superintendent; but I told him that I was ready to go immediately on any part of the line that he wished, but at the same time suggesting that it might be better to permit me to remain where I was.

He paid little attention to my remonstrance but ordered me to get ready to start. Fully equipped, Merryman and myself proceeded to Jane Lew, our next station, a good Union village, notwithstanding the chief residents were relatives of "Stonewall" Jackson. It had always been a hospitable town for the weary stranger to put up at, and being acquainted there I introduced Mr. Merryman as our new superintendent, and he was received with great cordiality and respect.

Here at Jane Lew was stationed Robert Carruthers, an intelligent Englishman. He was well adapted to the business, being a light weight and a good horseman. He too had to leave in order to make room for another pet.

I wish to remark here, that the appointment of competent citizens on a courier line through an enemy's country was a wise idea, as they were subject to less danger and interruption than a uniformed soldier would have been.

The change of stations proved a bad one for Carruthers. Merryman placed him in about the worst place on the line, in consequence of which he had several narrow escapes, and lost considerable Government property. We now pushed on for Weston, where we made a short stay; next to Crowell's, thence to Jacksonville, where Merryman left me. On my second trip after arriving at Jacksonville I rode to Weston, fifteen miles distant and reported by wire to Captain Leib, at Clarksburg, the circumstances of my transfer. He telegraphed Merryman and myself to return to headquarters immediately. I noticed on our return, that the new superintendent was not quite so merry as when he first started out to make wholesale changes on the line; he was now very affable in his manner toward me and appeared to suspect that he may have made a mistake in ignoring the respectful suggestions I made to him.

Captain Leib had the reputation of being a man of ability and good judgement; he was also a man of few words, and these were usually sharp and to the point. Mr. Merryman and myself soon stood before him in his office. He addressed himself to Merryman, and, in his characteristic style, said:

"Sir, I do not require your services any longer; render up whatever government property you may have in your charge."

During this scene the large, intelligent eyes of the dashing foragemaster of the post, Tom Croghan, were fixed on the short-lived superintendent; there was a short but funny history in the peculiarity of the broad, quizzical grin of the inimitable Irishman as he surveyed the now crest-fallen ex-superintendent.

Captain Leib now turned to me, "Mr. Egan," said he, "if you had so intimated you might have been in charge of the express line from the start; and now, I wish you to take charge of it, and if you do so I am satisfied it will be efficiently worked."

I thanked him for his confidence in me, and said I would strive to not disappoint him in his favorable impression of me. It is apparent from the following paragraph taken from his book, "*The Chances for Making a Million*," that he did not change his opinion of me:

"Michael Egan," says he, "was the only superintendent of the express line who was really efficient. He was the first courier sent forward, and in the discharge of duty stopped at nothing: swam streams swollen by the heavy rains of that country, crossed the mountains when he knew the bushwhacking bloodhounds were on his track, and when warned not to attempt their passage would quietly reply: 'Captain Leib ordered me not to stop until I had reached headquarters, and I must obey.' He is an

Irishman by birth, had received a liberal education, and in his younger days was in the British service. He knew not fear, and finding him competent and meritorious we promoted him."

I now proceeded to make an inventory of all the government property on the line, which occupied some time. Being aware of the existence of many defects in the system, I at once went to work in earnest applying remedies. I made no sudden or ill-advised changes, however, but carefully examined the condition of affairs at each station, particularily the treatment given the horses. As a result of my first trip I became very angry at the manner in which a large number of the poor animals had been treated. I am fond of horses, and am always painstaking in my care of them, but on this inspection I found the majority of them lame, or afflicted with sore backs, or both, or otherwise neglected. I could not understand how a horse used only two hours in the twenty-four could by reasonably fair treatment be used up in such a brutal manner.

I soon shaped things differently at every station, and, as a result, thenceforward there were no complaints, nor causes for complaint, from Headquarters.

The Military Telegraph - Mastering a Vicious Horse - A Reminiscence of Dublin Park - On the "Hog Back" Chased by a Squad of Rebel Cavalry - Saved by My Horse's Noble Qualities - A Long Way Around, But a Safe Way Home - Accomodations for Man and Beast.

In addition to the express mail route, General Rosecrans established a military telegraph line between Clarksburg and Gauley Bridge. This line had suffered from more or less interruption for some time before I was made superintendent. I used it quite often afterwards to transmit to headquarters any information that I thought of benefit to the service. I have frequently, while travelling over the line, dismounted and repaired the wire where broken, having a slight knowledge of "splicing," acquired previously.

I was now almost incessantly in the saddle, not remaining a single day in one place. Swollen rivers and streams sometimes checked general travel, but I was never balked by such impediments, invarably plunging my horse into the streams and swimming them, generally without mishap.

On one of my trips over the mountains, when approaching Summerville, Nicholas county, West Virginia, I was confronted for the first time with something like military order. I was halted and challenged, in accordance with strict military rules, by a soldier well put up, orderly, and clean. I at once thought there must be an officer in command who knew his business. That officer was General George Crook, then colonel of the 36th Ohio Infantry. In winter, when other troops were languishing in idleness, his were healthfully employed in cleaning their accoutrements and in drilling under large sheds, which he had erected for the purpose.

In 1861-62 a number of government horses and a large supply of forage, including hundreds of bales of hay, were kept at Clarksburg as a depot of supplies for our troops, then pushing out into the wilds of West Virginia after Floyd and Wise. Thomas H. Croghan, whom I have several times mentioned, rode a very fine horse, selected by himself from among the choicest in the corral. As superintendent of the express line I was also provided with a good animal, and when in Clarksburg, Croghan and myself almost daily practised jumping our horses over the bales of hay which were piled up in an apple orchard near the quartermaster's headquarters. A great many of the men who were unacquainted with this style of horsemanship looked upon these feats as foolhardy, and anticipated the breaking of our necks sooner or later. But we were used to this sort of equestrian exercise, having acquired, while boys together in Ireland, a considerable proficiency in hurdle and ditch jumping.

The necessities of the express line made the securing of extraordinarily good horses for the couriers very essential, and in my capacity of superintendent I was always on the alert to obtain for them such needed animals. I secured possession of one, by chance, in November, 1861, that served me nobly as my individual saddlehorse on many occasions afterwards, and he once undoubtedly saved my life.

One day about noon, on arriving at Clarksburg after a continuous ride of 133 miles from Gauley Bridge, I saw when opposite Dent's hotel, a dashing and fiery gray horse and his rider both furiously contending for the mastery. The horse, I learned, was government property, and was known as "Hannibal;" the animal was in the habit of going when and where he pleased, and had conquered, since his purchase by the quartermaster, three or four of the clerks who had undertaken to master him. Jimmy Runyon was now astride of him. Jimmy was a son of the master of transportation, and was a plucky lad who seldom failed in doing anything he undertook.

There was quite a crowd collected around the horse, attracted by his rearing and plunging; he had quite a hard mouth, and the boy's tugging at the bridle reins seemed to have little effect upon him. Rushing to the side walls of adjacent houses, and to the sign posts on either side of the street, the vicious animal sought to scratch and bruise his rider's legs. In one of these collisions with a sign post the saddle girth broke, and Jimmy received a hard fall and some severe injuries in consequence. Once again the horse was victorious and confirmed in his sulk. It was, as I said, about noon, and the horse, after throwing his rider, was led over to the corral to be fed. I had my eye on the horse and followed, determined to have him, if possible.

Colonel Runyon was a ruddy and robust man, about five feet-ten inches hight and weighing about 200 pounds. He had a long, flowing, silvery beard, and was quite stern and imperious in his commands, but withal possessed of great kindness of heart beneath his rough exterior. He had learned of the accident to his boy and was at the stables when the gray was led in. He was in a towering rage and angry enough to shoot the offending horse. He opened on Dominick Tierney, the stable boss, and gave him a severe overhauling for permitting his idolized son to have the dangerous horse, knowing him to be such. As the colonel started to leave the stable I spoke up and said:

"Colonel, let me have the horse, please; I need a good one in my courier express business."

He looked at me as if doubting my sanity, and replied: "I do not wish to have a hand in your death, sir. Samuel Selby, 'Chap' Wheeler and others, as well as my son, Jimmy, have tried him, and each trial has been a failure and attended with increasing danger."

I still persisted in my entreaties for the horse. "Egan, you may have him," said the colonel finally; "but he will most certainly kill you."

"I'll try him right now," I rejoined; "and if he does kill me, the bushwhackers will be saved the trouble of doing it."

I went into the horse's stall and proceeded to bridle and saddle the steed. While doing so, Tierney, with whom

I was well acquainted, whispered to me to let him finish eating before attempting to take him out, as to do so would, he thought, be very dangerous. I disregarded this friendly advice, however, and after securing a good riding whip, with a heavy butt, I took out and mounted the gray.

As was to be expected, there were a number of employees and hangers-on waiting to see the exhibition, when they learned that I had asked for and received the horse.

I had a very unfavorable place - an apple orchard with trees, bales of hay, wagons and other obstructions - in which to make the trial of subjugating the beast. The trees, being numerous, were the most dangerous. The animal, failing in his efforts to unseat me by high kicking, plunging, buck jumping, etc., made a direct drive toward the trees before mentioned, seeming to have, in doing so, no more regard for his own safety than he had for mine. But, by one who can use the bridle and roller spurs properly, a horse going at a good rate of speed may be easily turned from an obstruction in his path. In this case I saved the horse and myself from injury, although his mouth and sides showed evident signs of punishment endured from the bit and spurs. He now became quite obedient and passive in my hands, and I rode out of the gate and up and down the pike several times without any further trouble.

This rough riding reminded me of a feat of horsemanship, and about the finest I ever witnessed, which occurred in June, 1845, on the grand parade grounds at Phoenix Park depot, in the city of Dublin, Ireland.

It was just after morning parade, and several squads of constabulary were yet drilling in the park, when an orderly, who was an expert rough rider, mounted on a splendid dark bay horse, which was then being broken for the cavalry, came out of the depot yard and started for the "castle" for orders. When at the entrance to the barracks the horse refused to go out. Then ensued a long and exciting struggle between horse and rider for supremacy, resulting, finally, in the horse coming out victorious.

There now approached from the direction of the stables a gentleman who walked rapidly to the centre of the square, where the excitement was. This officer, for such he proved to be, was about twenty-five years old, and about six feet high; in general build he was a perfect model of perfect manhood; he was fair as a lily, with large, intelligent blue eyes, somewhat piercing in their glance; a healthful, blooming tint suffused his cheeks, and his fine yellow hair was parted behind, in the then prevailing fashion, and kept, like all his person, in the neatest military style. In his right hand he carried a small but cutting riding-whip, and on his heels were two highly burnished roller spurs. This was Head Constable Pilkington, Chief Drill Master of the Cavalry. The horse had just succeeded in throwing and severely bruising his rider as Pilkington approached. Grasping the reins firmly, he made one bound and was in the saddle; and no sooner was he safely seated than he pressed the cruel "rollers" into the wild steed's legs, poising there for a second, and then pitched forward a great distance, tearing up the fine gravel in all directions in his frenzied efforts to throw his rider. Now the officer reversed the whip, bringing the handle, or butt, down with a crashing blow on the brute's head whenever the latter would rear up, at the same time applying, with all the strength of his legs, the "rollers" to the sides of the devilish horse, now stained red with gore.

Among all the numerous spectators to this thrilling scene, the head constable was the most cool. The horse now ceased his plunging and dashed ahead towards the adjutant's office, where his rider turned him, and flew up the square and down in the direction of the city at full speed, and then back again, re-passing the main entrance, where the horse made another feeble attempt to go in, but he was no longer his own master. The horse was now broken, but might relapse into vicious ways again if allowed to fall into incapable hands.

The occurrence here narrated was as vivid in my mind that day, after the lapse of seventeen years, as upon the day when it took place, and it struck me as being not dissimilar to my experience, except, of course, the wide difference in the appearance of the two riders and their surroundings.

"The grand old Phoenix Park that Nature, more than art, adorns;
Perfumed so richly by the giant old hawthorns,
Whose majestic limbs expand to meet their neighboring row,
Filled with blossoms, thick as hops, and fair as falling snow;
Or like soft showers, descending on the emerald sward below.

"There, too, in classic, sculptures art, you'll find on observation,
That rare bird whence the Park derives its appellation;
Methinks the Eagle, emblem of Liberty, would improve the breed
of this mystic fowl, whose unproductive seed
Has lain too long in a land unfree.

"Here, also, the aristocratic child, with attendant maid,
Daily from Dublin City came to sport and promenade,
And breathe the gentle breeze, so bracing, fair and mild,
Imparting rosy tinted cheeks alike to maid and child.
On a fairer, lovlier spot Dame Nature never smiled."

It may not be amiss here to introduce to the reader a few other of the gray horse's peculiarities. The one I found the most difficulty in breaking him of was a propensity for rushing headlong into rivers, creeks, etc., whenever he met with them; and the deeper they were, the better he seemed to enjoy it. He was a pacer, 'loper, and a fair troter. While galloping he moved so smoothly that a good marksman could do some fair shooting from his back. I believe he was a brave animal also, as shooting did not annoy him, or cause him to swerve in the least from his course. As I have before stated, I am very fond of horses, and,in this case, there seemed to be a growing mutual attachment between the horse and his rider. I had him about four weeks when he showed me one of his best and most reliable qualities.

On the night of the 15th of November, 1861, I put up at the house of Mr. Benjamin Skidmore, in the town of

Sutton, Braxton county. The night proved very stormy; a heavy rain accompanied by high winds prevailed for several hours. Next morning on repairing to the stable where our relay horses were kept, I was agreeably surprised to find the gray there and in seeming good condition. I had several horses at my disposal, but I preferred to hold Hannibal in reserve for the most dangerous part of my route.

As I advanced in the direction of Gauley Bridge I noticed havoc done by the late storm. It was about noon when I forded the Little Birch river. This stream is on of the clearest in the state, and is bordered for a long distance on both its banks with spruce pine and evergreen. On approaching the river from the east, the road way had quite a steep descent to the bed of the stream, and when on the other side, it wound around the hill in a zigzag fashion for about half a mile until a level plain on the summit was reached. This strip of road was known as the "hog-back," because of its narrow surface and precipitous sides. It was not at any part more than thirty feet wide, but was level and in fair condition for travel. At its very narrowest part, I discovered a large oak tree lying squarely across the road, one of the results of the previous night's storm. The tree completely blocked the road, its huge limbs and roots holding it about three feet from the ground.

I came to a halt, staggered by the obstruction; how should I proceed? The interlacing of the smaller limbs with the roots of the tree made it impossible to lead the horse under the fallen oak.

The almost perpendicular sides of the "hogback" made any attempt to go around it impracticable and dangerous. The only thing remaining to be done was to jump it. I had not up to this time been checked by the elements, and I did not feel disposed to give up now. The gray had some practice in jumping over the hay bales at Clarksburg for our amusement, but never met anything like that which now confronted him. I walked him up to the tree,which was fully five feet high, and the animal could barely look over it. Turning, I rode back some twenty or twenty-five yards, and, wheeling him right about, faced the tree. The road was level, as I have said, with a fine white sandy surface. Pressing the rollers to the faithful animal's sides, he made a straight shoot for the obstruction, and, when within two yards of it, he rose gallantly in the air and cleared it like a bird.

The scene from this mountain road is fair to look upon. In front one can see for miles away a beautiful and richly cultivated valley, but not the vestige of a house or enclosure; while on both sides of the road rise high and majestic huge rocky, circular-shaped ranges, surmounted by a wide expanse of primeval forest; the whole reminding one of what we read of the Great Wall of China. So we moved along, amidst the friendly solitude, more engrossed in the contemplation of the beauties of nature than on the belligerent spirit of man.

When a half mile from the fallen tree my pleasant meditations were suddenly interrupted by the appearance, as I turned a bend in the road, of a small party of Confederate cavalry. I did not take long in deciding my line of action, but fell back instantly. As I did so, the "Johnnies" raised a yell and dashed towards me at full speed. Several shots were fired at me without effect, and I returned the salute by emptying the chambers of one of my "navies." They then ceased firing, and it became an exciting race, narrowed down to a question of the speed and endurance of our horses. On we go in this way for some time, when, in a hurried, backward glance, I see them coming pell mell and apparently on me. One of their number was far in advance of his comrades, and was mounted on an exceptionally fleet steed. Things were looking "blue" for me when I again approached the fallen tree. I braced up as I neared it, and, checking my noble animal slightly, I raised him at the right moment, and he cleared the obstruction beautifully, coming down firmly on his legs on the other side. I then descended the mountain leisurely, feeling satisfied that my pursuer's game was blocked. The literal interpretation of the old adage, "It's an ill wind that blows nobody good," struck me very forcibly. What was now to be done? Should I proceed, or turn back and once more run the risk of encountering the enemy, who would, no doubt, keep a sharp lookout for me. If it were simply a question of profit, or remuneration for the risk incurred, I would not hesitate a moment to continue on my backward way. Mr. Peter Duffy, an old resident, and one of the best posted men as regarded its dangers on the whole line, told me he would not make the trip over it, in my capacity, for one thousand dollars. Had I been killed, or crippled in this service, neither my family nor myself would receive a cent in compensation for my loss or injury, as I was not at this time an enlisted man.

Determined to finish my journey, I rode down to the Little Birch river, about a half mile from where my pursuers were baulked by the tree, and, turning down the stream to the left, followed its meanderings for some distance, until I came to a favorable place for ascending the mountain. Leading my horse, I scrambled up its steep and rocky sides. At last I found myself upon the road again, after making a toilsome circuit of about three miles, and from there to Big Birch river, five miles away,I kept a sharp watch out for the enemy.

On arriving in the afternoon at the home of Mr. Frame. I found his wife, an estimable lady, in quite a nervous state of mind. She was aware that the rebels were on my trail, and was fearful of my having fallen into their hands, or of my possibly having received injuries. I did not tarry long, but, after a hasty dinner from the good lady, I sped away over Powell mountain, and landed all right in the dusk of that evening at Peter Duffey's, where myself and horse were well cared for.

Loss of Government Property on the Courier Line - Testing the Courage of a New Courier - His Satisfactory Trial Thieving Guerrillas - A Cold-Blooded Murder - Arrest of the Perpetrators - Their Trial and Punishment - First Glimpse of General Crook.

During the seven months that I was in charge of the express line very little government property in that service was lost. Personally, I did not lose a dollar's worth, although there was a sharper lookout for me than any of the couriers. Of these latter, a few who sustained repeated losses were plainly given to understand that their continuance in the government's service would depend, in a great measure, upon the care taken of the property submitted to their charge.

On my second inspection trip I took with me two couriers and two horses required for the western end of the line. The horses were to be exchanged for such as were used up from sore backs and ill treatment and their riders were to replace the men who so abused and neglected the other animals. The couriers, two young Irishmen, were named, respectively, Patrick Power and Patrick McManus. They were heavier than I should have wished for the purpose, but being brave and reliable, they proved more serviceable than would lighter weights not possessing these qualities.

Although, as yet, I had no proper test of it, I did not doubt my judgement in selecting these men for their pluck and intelligence. Before they reached their appointed stations, however, one of them underwent a satisfactory trial.

When nearing the eastern base of Powell mountain, the dusk of evening was closing in on us and a soft, fleecy snow had commenced falling thick and fast, increasing the intensity of the gathering darkness. Travelling over this dreary and solitary mountain, never pleasant, was now doubly lonesome, because of the blinding snowstorm, which made our effort to keep the trail extremely difficult, and further, on account of the uncomfortable knowledge of the immediate presence of the besetting perils in the shape of murderous guerrillas.

Power had occasion to stop and dismount, while McManus and myself rode leisurely ahead. Soon after Power came cantering up, but missing his belt, containing his navy revolvers, he returned to find them. While he was gone we came in sight of a small log-house standing close to the road. It was the only one for miles around, and was owned by a loyal man named Boggs, who had to leave both house and farm, because of the constant warfare made upon him by the guerrillas, who thickly infested this section. I told my companion to keep about eight or ten paces in my rear, and to move as fast as I did until we had safely passed the house, which, although deserted by its owner, was known as a rendexvous for small parties of bushwhackers.

At the very time we were hurrying past the place, these robbers and murders, whose eyes were as sharp as the nocturnal prowlers of the mountain forest, had drawn bead on us, and were only prevented from shooting us by one of their number, Clinton Duffel, who, as we subsequently learned, told them that they might safely secure our horses and other property that night at our intended stopping place, a short distance ahead, without the trouble of killing us. To do Duffel justice, it is fair to state that he preferred to secure his share of Uncle Sam's property without killing anybody.

Arrived at the base of the opposite side of the mountain, we turned to the left and entered a valley of some extent, at the entrance of which was a scattered settlement known as Hookersville. Here "Mac" and myself halted and awaited the approach of Power, who had not yet rejoined us. Owing to the lateness of the night and the heavy falling snow, we could only see only a few feet in our front. So we waited a short distance from the path, determined to surprise and possibly frighten the new courier. Shortly the portly Power came unhurriedly down the hill, and when he was directly opposite to where we stood concealed, in a counterfeit voice I called out sternly, "Halt!" Without drawing rein for a moment, the brave fellow answered in a clear, strong voice, "All right." and at the same moment his revolver came on a line with our heads and we gladly called a truce.

This incident, together with the nerve he displayed on other occasions while on the line, had no small influence in securing his promotion in my company afterwards.

The night was growing darker and travelling was every moment becoming more difficult, as we were compelled to ride slowly in order to avoid pitching into the numerous holes and pitfalls lying beneath the freshly fallen snow. In about an hour after leaving the mountain we arrived at the house of Mr. Craig, which was our next station. The local courier, Carruthers, met us at the gate. He requested me to remove his station a half mile to the west, to the house of Mr. Peter Duffey, where he said he could obtain better accomodations. He had already talked to the Duffeys on the subject and they were satisfied. I agreed to do as he requested and decided to make the change at once. Mrs. Duffey, a kindly and much esteemed middle-aged lady, English by birth and education, and Courier Carruthers, a thorough "John Bull," were delighted at my conceding to the latter's wishes so readily.

It turned out to be a very lucky move for all concerned. On this very night we had four valuable horses, including my gray, at Mr. Duffey's, a prize not likely to be overlooked by the hungry bushwhackers. Carruthers, while stationed at Craig's, had been robbed twice previously to this time, his station being about in the worst place on the whole line for that sort of thing. Bearing these latter facts in mind, I determined to keep watch upon our animals, a precaution I had often taken before, and often took afterwards, when I chanced to be in a questionable locality.

The stable was situated about one hundred yards from the dwelling house and at the foot of a small hill, whither we repaired, and after having done justice to a hearty supper, and gave the horses a thorough cleaning and rubbing down; after which I examined the stable and its surroundings carefully and found it fairly satisfactory as a defensive position in case of attack. The building was a barn and stable combined, of goodly dimensions, constructed of large, hewn logs, the interstices of which could serve admirably for port holes. We returned to the house and passed a pleasant evening until about eleven o'clock, when we again went to the barn and, disposing ourselves under the hay and corn fodder, awaited the arrival of thieves.

We were so placed that we could all command a range of the entrance to the barn. I cautioned the men to remain about ten or twelve feet apart, so as to divert the fire of the bushwhackers, and to waste no ammunition, but to make every shot tell. Our weapons were Colt's navy revolvers, with ten rounds to each man. We kept to our posts until morning, but were happily not disturbed. By mere chance we missed an encounter with horse-thieves that night, as we learned afterwards. A party of ten or twelve men had broken into Mr. Craig's stable in the expectation of finding our horses there; but the change effected by Carruthers' request had averted the trouble, and no doubt saved Uncle Sam the four animals they sought.

Some time later, in November of the same year, I found on reaching Sutton, going west, a part of Captain Rowand's command, Company C, 1st West Virginia Cavalry, quartered in the town, This squad had just succeeded in bringing into camp four prisoners: John Cole, his wife and son, and Samuel W. Windom, all of whom were charged with murder. The wife and mother, a hardened old wretch, and her son subsequently escaped with very light punishment, by giving evidence against the two others that resulted in their execution.

Cole appeared to be about fifty, and Windom about forty years of age. The older man was well known in the locality as a grafter of fruit trees. In appearance he would pass for anything but an Adonis. Windom was a heavy set man, with a large head, heavy eyebrows and coarse, bushy whiskers that almost completely covered his face. The pair looked fully capable of committing the awful crime with which they were afterwards clearly proven to be guilty.

The crime was the murdering in cold blood of a private soldier of the 36th Ohio Infantry Volunteers. He was a young lad, not over nineteen years old, who had foolishly straggled from his command, alone and without arms. In this way he had visited Cole's house, a few miles from town. He talked to Mrs. Cole and her son for a while, and got a drink from the former; he then went to the meadow and stopped for some time, boy-like, looking at the two men, who were mowing.

In the meantime Mrs. Cole called to her husband, who laid down his scythe and went to her. She said to him: "What are you going to do with that Yankee spy?" On his not appearing to understand her meaning, she told him plainly that he ought to kill the soldier. Cole thereupon returned to where his partner was and held a private conversation with him, divulging his fiendish intentions towards the innocent lad, to all of which Windom readily agreed. All of this time the poor "boy in blue" had not the remotest idea that final judgement had been passed upon him; but he was soon awakened to a realization of his danger by Cole and coolly telling him that they were going to kill him, and asking him what he had to say. To this heartless anouncement the frightened lad made no response, but ran away as fast as his legs would carry him. Windom, being a powerful and active man, pursued and shortly overtook and brought back the scared and dejected captive to where old man Cole was awaiting them. Windom held the boy in a firm grip, while his companion deliberately unfastened his scythe blade from the snead, and with one mighty cut of that sharp instrument severed the head from the body of the unfortunate soldier. They then covered the headless trunk with a pile of brush and stones.

Next morning, after seeing the prisoners, I resumed my journey towards Gauley Bridge.

On my return a couple of days later, when about eight miles east of Gauley, I came to a creek that crossed the road and emptied into Gauley river, which at this point flowed parallel with the pike for some distance. The creek was near the farm of Mr. M.F. Morris, and was then much swollen, very turbulent and overflowing its banks from the recent heavy rains.

About the time I reached this stream General Crook, then Colonel of the 36th Ohio, appeared on the other bank, accompanied by a mounted escort. It looked foolhardy to attempt to swim the horses across the rapid current, especially so when, as now appeared to be the case, the animals were not adequate to the undertaking. The colonel, after surveying the situation for a few minutes, wisely took up the left bank of the stream for some distance, until he found a more favorable place for making the effort.

It would certainly be the height of arrogance in me to lay claim to anything like the intrepidity of the noble Crook, but on this occasion I had a long-legged horse, whose qualities as a swimmer I had previously tested, so we took the stream, heading up the current for about ten yards, and after a severe struggle made the riffle; but we had such a narrow escape from being swept into the river, that I would have been very loathe to try it again.

Crook was, at this time, on his way to Charleston, on the Big Kanawha, where, as president of the general court martial which later convened at that place, he tried among other cases that of the murderers referred to in the preceeding paragraph. I chanced to be at Sutton on the day that Cole and Windom were executed. They showed considerable nerve during the trying ordeal. Both confessed to the commission of the crime substantially as I have told the reader, and their act of cruelty illustrated the antipathy many residents in that section then felt to all representatives of the government, and the utter lack of conscientiousness among those evil doers.

Repairing the Telegraph - Preparing for a Night Surprise Another anticipated Night Attack - Names of the Stations on the Express Line - Attitude of the Farmers Along the Route - Their Kindliness to Couriers Poorly Recompensed My Feelings on the Subject - Efforts to Secure a Settlement of Their Claims - The Poor Result - Discontinuance of the Courier Line

Ten days after this unpleasant occurrence at Sutton, when going east on a tour of inspection, I rested at Sommerville, then the headquarters of General Crook. I called at the telegraph office, as was my usual custom, and the operator, a young, smart and brave little fellow, named Smith, told me that all connection east by wire was cut off; that the line was broken and destroyed in several places; that he was going to get a team and a detail of men from the commanding officer and start the following day to rebuild the destroyed portion; and concluded by requesting that, as I was going in that direction, I should remain and accompany his party.

I replied that if I could be of any use I would willingly do so. Early next morning the team, with coils of wire, tools, rations, etc., was in readiness. The detail, consisting of six men and a sergeant, together with the operator, lineman and teamster, eleven in all, made quite a harmonious, though somewhat heterogeneous, crowd of Americans, Dutch and Irish.

It was night when we reached William Frame's house at Big Birch river, after passing over fourteen miles of the line and doing a surprising amount of work. The line had been most injured near where we halted for the night; in fact, it was one of the worst places for the enemy's cavalry raids on the whole route. For such a small party we had considerable government property with us, enough at least to make it worth an effort on the part of one of these hungry bands to raid us during the night. Sure enough, we received information from a friendly source that we were to be swooped down upon that night by a party of rebel guerrillas and our property carried off.

We held a consultation to devise means to protect ourselves and avert the threatened loss. Entirely unsolicited, I was requested by the boys to take command of the little party during the night. I modestly accepted the responsibility, and when time came I disposed of the members of our party as, in my opinion, best suited our purposes. I placed a man at each of the three most important approaches to our camp, and arranged for their relief two hours later by three fresh pickets, and so on until nine of our party should have performed guard duty, by this method giving each of them two hours on and four hours off duty.

The sergeant's duty was to relieve the guards at the proper time; the operator we held in reserve. The sergeant and myself did not sleep any during the night, but continued to visit the pickets occasionally during the long hours until morning. Once or twice the dogs raised a howl, alarmed at some unusual sounds not far distant, but we were not disturbed. Our intended visitors may have received word that we were reasonably well-prepared for them, and decided, no doubt, to defer their contemplated attack for a more favorable opportunity.

After breakfast next morning I took leave of my late comrades-in-arms, and about noon arrived at Sutton, the central station on the line. This place was a small village before the war, but at the time of which I write it had grown still smaller by reason of the frequent raids its inhabitants were subjected to. A result on one of these depredatory visits was the burning of about half of the houses in the town.

When I arrived I found about one-half of Company C, 1st West Virginia Cavalry, quartered in the village, the officer in command had just received information that a force of rebels, more than twice his number, were going to assault him that very night. The result of this announcement was considerable excitement among the troops, a majority of whom were in favor of falling back to their regimental headquarters at Weston. I was made aware of the situation, and was asked what I thought of it. By this time I had become pretty well accustomed to the numerous raids that were always about to, but rarely did, occur; and so I replied that I intended to go to Weston in the morning, and would have to see, or feel, the enemy before starting the other way.

The troops finally concluded to adopt my course, and remain where they were. A guard was kept up during the entire night, however, and I volunteered to assist in the duty. In addition to my two "navies," I was provided with an old sabre, but of course had no occasion to use it. In the morning I laid down my bloodless sword and hied me away to Weston.

There were sixteen stations on the line, as follows:

Clarksburg	Miles Distance from
Basil's	7
Jane Lew	15
Weston	22.5
Crowell's	30
Jacksonville	38
Bulltown	46
McNemer's	55
Sutton	63
Little Birch	71
Big Birch	80
Duffey's	90
Sommerville	98
Brown's	106
Gross'	114
Morris'	123
Gauley Bridge	133

The farmers along this route were in the best of times

poor in circumstances; but at this time they were badly stripped by both armies. Not withstanding this fact, they cheerfully made the greatest efforts to feed and house our men and horses. Neither the commissary nor quartermaster's supplies could be furnished at most of these places, even at a cost three or four times greater than these people charged; their usual price being only twelve and a half cents per meal.

For seven months these farmers bore the maintenance of this line, receiving therefore during all this time but two months pay. I told these people at the time that the United States Government would surely pay them. They seemed to repose confidence in me, but probably had more in the government whose humble servant I was. I am sorry to state that, after the lapse of nearly twenty-seven years, our government has not yet paid this debt.

I have always thought that there rested on me a moral obligation to try to have these poor and honest people paid a debt of such evident justness. With this end in view, immediately upon the discontinuance of the line, which was at my suggestion, I went over the route and secured from the farmers itemized statements of their claims for board and forage, and returning to Clarksburg presented them to Captain Huntington, a newly-appointed assistant quartermaster.

This gentleman was a great stickler for "red tape." He was very pompous in his manner, and evidently had a full appreciation of his own importance. He ignored the claims, and refused, in addition, to pay me two weeks salary then due. Being anxious to get into active service in the field, I dropped all consideration of these claims, and proceeded to organize a company of infantry, which I did in eight days.

After the war I removed with my family from the locality of the line, and later from the State, and for a long time I did not have the means or the encouragement to make another effort in this direction; but in March, 1877, I became troubled with the idea that these people generally might be impressed with the belief that I made personal use of their claims. The possibility of such an imputation so weighed upon me that I started from Allegheny City, Pa., a distance of over four hundred miles, went over the old line, and made a personal visit to all of the claimants, or their heirs, and found that my suspicions had a basis in fact, at least with a majority of them.

From these claimants I procured a new set of claims duly signed and sealed by the clerks of the different county clerks, with certificates attached. These I took to Washington, D.C., and placed in the hands of a claim agent, to whom I agreed to give ten per cent of the amounts for his assistance in adjusting and securing their payment. After sending out three sets of papers, at three different periods, each time causing the claimants the trouble and expense of preparing revised claims, paying clerk fees, etc., and expending quite a sum personally, I have secured as a result the munificent sum of thirty dollars as a partial payment of these claims.

Michael Egan left the civilian service where he served as a courier performing dangerous duty on the route between Clarksburg and Gauley Bridge, Virginia, and formed a company of volunteers for service in the Union army. He remained in the army and left Federal service at Appomattox as Captain, 15th Regiment, West Virginia Infantry Volunteers.

Andrew Barbee studied medicine under his future Father-in-Law, Dr. John J. Thompson, and graduated from the University of Pennsylvania in 1851 with a medical degree. He was later to serve as captain of the "Border Rifles", a volunteer infantry unit that was to become Company A, 22nd Virginia Volunteer Infantry Regiment.

He and his young Brother-in-Law, John Thompson, (the first Confederate soldier to be wounded in the fighting at Carnifex Ferry) served together in the 22nd Virginia and Andrew frequently used his medical skills to care for the frequently wounded John Thompson and other men in the company who needed medical attention.

Andrew Barbee was not to escape the war without injury. He was seriously wounded in the elbow at the battle of Scary Creek and in the battle of White Sulphur Springs, he was wounded in the left arm and struck in the hip with a gun barrel which partially paralyzed his leg. He returned from a period of convalescence to Lewisburg in late 1863 where he assisted with the wounded from the battle of Droop Mountain.

It was during this time in Lewisburg that he found time to write several letters to his family. At least one of the letters was released by the senior Federal officer at Gauley Bridge for delivery to Barbee's family. That officer was Rutherford B. Hayes, a future President of the United States. The letters were preserved and are in the holdings of the National Archives.

Lewisburg, Monday, December 7th, 1863

My Dear Wife,

Your notes bearing dates "Oct 6th" & "Nov. 6th", with letters from Pa & Ma (dates "Oct 7th") were handed me last Friday evening by Captain Thompson, upon my return to this place, after an absence of two months. I was *glad* to learn that you were all in such fine health & getting along so very well. Bro. John rec'd a slight flesh wound about the neck on the late fight on Droop Mountain. The ball entered just above the clavicle, & near the large blood vessel of the neck, on the left side, & inclined to the right oblique upwards, came out on top of shoulder. He has suffered very little from it. Is now on duty on Ct. Mar. Will not be exposed to camp life for months. His old wound in right eye is getting along well. At times when exposed to great fatigue in cold & wind there is considerable discharge of thick matter from the orbit, but a little rest & the use of cold water & syringe to work out the paste & all is well again. Let the Dr. know that this discharge is from orbit & not from disease of lachrymal sack or duct. The free lachrymal discharge from which he was once so much annoyed, has well nigh entirely passed off. He is doing very well & in very fine spirits.

For the information of the families of "Border Riflemen" (Co. A) & "Kanawha Riflemen" (Co. F) 22 Va Reg. I enclose list of casualties in the late fight on Droop Mountain. I also enclose the notes hurriedly taken on death of my Dear Bailey & McClannahan. They were my truest best friends. I loved them much. Sent the obituary on Lieut. Mc to his kinsman Misses Burt that it may be sent to his parents. Col. Patton told me that in my absence he had written the family of Lt. Mc as a gentleman &gallant officer. Tell all who knew my lamented McClannahan that he died as he lived, the true Va gentleman & brave C.S. soldier. Poor me, with *shock*, Morris & Stubbard of our old Co., together with other true friends & gallant soldiers now "*sleep their last sleep*" on Droop Mountain. My loss is great. I mourn sincerely!

All our wounded both C.S. & U.S. near us & under our care are doing well. Every attention is being given them. I am happy to inform you that I have sufficiently recovered from my wounds rec'd at Dry Creek[9] fight August 26 & 27 as to be able again to take command of my Reg.

My wounds have entirely healed. While East a large piece of bone worked out near right elbow joint from which again followed an Erysipelatous inflammation, & gave me much pain. All however is now well. I sometimes suffer pain about my left hip where I was beaten with a gun. Sometimes I fear the heavy blows rec'd on the crest of Ishium will yet bring about caries on that part of the bone. Hope not tho I can not yet bear the pressure of my belt & sword or pistol. My right arm is some stiff about elbow joint, yet whilst I cannot straighten I can *bend* it so as to be able thus early to use my hair & tooth brush, tho I have but little strength in my right arm yet. I think in time I shall very nearly get entire use of the arm & shall soon gain my strength, unless more bones work out which I am not inclined to think will.

I visited while East all our friends & relatives on either side. Was with Capt. K. a good deal. Dr. K. is in bad health. Been suffering for a long time with chronic diarrhea. Mr. Wm T. is better of it & in better health than when I saw him last winter. Your Aunt & Uncle K, Mrs. Dr. M & Miss Maggie very well. I like all of them very much. Did not get to see Dr. M. He is Maj. in 2 Va. Rgt. C.S.A. & with Gen. Lee. Ramsey is still Capt & a splendid gentleman & gallant officer. Has done very hard

---

9 Dry Creek is also called the battle of White Sulphur Springs.

service. I have written Uncle Bob several times, but cannot hear from him. Don't know where he is. I visited J.D.W. Tell Ma. all well. His oldest daughter married Capt. A. Walden, Rapphk. They have one child. J.D.W. has one son in C.S.A. No more old enough. Fannie A. quite well. Sinn S. in Ten. with her sister, Mrs. M. All our friends in Luray well except Dr. Rust he is paralyzed. Mary S. (now Mrs. Wm A. Harris Jr) is still in Luray. Bet and young Broodas are going to be married. Gen. Meem again married. Married the bethrothed of his Bro. who was killed in C.S. Army. Our old parents well but very feeble. All my Bros. Sisters neices & nephews well. Ten thousand messages were sent to you, Ma, Dr., sister Kate & Mol Guess them can't write them. *Love* in abundance & assurance of "kind rememberance" was in the *budget*, I know.

While East on furlow, I took advantage of my wounds &c, &was not idle. I was with *Lee* in his late fights also Stewart - was in fifteen miles of Alxda. I have sold our statue of the "Coquette" only got for it *seven thousand dollars* ($7000.00) I settled with Bros. Wm & Gabe. Took up all bonds & pd. them every dollar I owed them. Settled with father & pd. him for the family of servants bot in /60 also the amt. due him for money loaned me while in Phila. 1857. I also settled up & pd. all I owed in Madison County. Thus you see, my dear, I have not been idle. I have now arranged my business, that should I in any way be lost to you & my children, you will have no difficulty in settling up my estate. I have some money in Dixie together with some very valuable servants (certainly I have neither money or property elsewhere) & if I am killed or should die before we meet again, you will find my papers, Repts. of Accts., Bonds taken up, &c. in a little "record book." You will find record of all debts acts & bonds pd. by me since I entered the army - also a record of all Bonds & debts due me &c, &c. I have not written above to give you pain or uneasiness. It is proper that you should know something of my business, & I trust the Federal Authorities may do you the favor to pass this letter to you. It is proper too that I should acquaint you with the fact that I am not altogether indifferent or unmindful of the uncertainty of a soldier's life. I have of late had a very signal warning & had I been cut off & killed when I so very narrowly escaped we could never have settled my business. Now you will have no difficulty. I think it possible that I may buy property in Dixie after awhile. Our servants far back south are quite well. They are well clothed, fed & are happy. I saw them not long since. They all send *love* & howdy to you & the children & say they want you to come to them.

Mrs. Swindler (whom I called to see yesterday) told me that you were looking very badly. Have you had the Dentist at work in your mouth? *Please* have your teeth filled, & one replaced or put in where you had to have extg since I left you. Mrs. S says you have gotten into Mother's & Sister Ada's old habit. *Please stop it*! You are too delicate & your lungs are too weak to undertake to go through what Mother or sister did. Besides I believe it *killed* sister. You know she is dead. You know your promises to me when with me at Gauley Bridge *Remember*, I beg you!

Mrs. S. says that you told her that you would come to me when I get in winter quarters, If I would *invite* you. Let me say to you my dear wife, that "Winter Quarters" of a soldier is no place for women & children. To have you then within two, five often miles of me, not be able to spend those long, dreary winter evenings in the dear society of you & our children, would give me pain, & I had rather then that you were as now, more than 100 miles distant from me. I *know* now that I cannot see you, & I try to be content whereas were you anear me, I should always be wanting to be with you, & would no doubt sometimes neglect my duty *to be with you* something as yet I have *never done as a soldier.* You know my wife of the trials & difficulties of a refugee in Dixie in winter time. I am not want that you *should.* You know me too well, I trust, to suspect the *longing desire* that I have, to be with you & my children, but there are circumstances over which I have no control, then we must try & be content. I think just now that I know what is best for you then dear one,stay where you are -- you are with a dear poor father. He can do better for you & the children, & you will be more comfortable & happy with him, than I could make you were you anear me. I am *honest*, & write *facts*. It may seem an imposition upon your Pa. He, however, knows properly how to appreciate the whole matter. I shall endeavor to be content & happy as is possible for me under the circumstances to be. I am looking to the future when better, brighter & happier days shall restore me in peace to your arms & security under our own "vine & fig tree" & to your arms, my darling once more. I may yet repay dear Pa & Ma & sister for all they have borne on our account. Be contented & happy as you can,& *doubt* not, *I pray you* my own dear wife, the fidelity, deep devotion & undying love

of your affectionate Husband
Andrew R. Barbee

To "Maggie dear"
P.S. Kiss our darlings Blanche & Kate for me - tell them that "dear pappa *loves them* & is dying to see them. Tell them to write me often. Andr.

Barbee was soon to start a letter to his two children. He began writing them on December 7 and December 10, but was unable to complete the letter until December 24. The 22nd Virginia had been involved in some manuevering in an attempt to "trap... Gen. A. USA"-- a reference to an attempt to cut off Union General Averell following his raid into southwestern Virginia.

My Darlings Blanche & Kate

I will write you a line before I retire upon my"soldier's couch". In letter rec'd from "Ma" dated November 6th I was informed that you had rec'd my letter dated September 28th & 29th & yet, you, having opportunity of writing & sending me an answer did not do it. This, little dears, is almost unpardonable negligence on your part. How glad how truely delighted would "dear pappa" have been to have rec'd letters from you. You do not *know* what joy & exquisite delight your little letters give me, then why not write me more often? Do write me often. Take pains too in writing me, form your letters well & be sure that you never misspell a word. Do not risk asking "Ma" how to spell any word you may be in doubt about, but always have your Dictionary near you & refer to it. Don't forget this. Write both of you & tell me what you are studying -- if geography -- what Geography? How far advanced in arithmetic? How far in grammar? How many pieces of music you play & sing -- the names of every piece you sing & play. Tell me how many hours you study your books & how many hours you practice pr. diem.

Tell me everthing. Who is your teacher? And where do you have to go &c &c?

Thursday December 10th, 1863

I have some sweet music for you and Blanche that I will send you soon. Did you ever rec. a bundle of music from me? you never mentioned it.

The letter was not completed until two weeks later after Barbee wrote this first pages. He and his regiment were involved in the pursuit of General Averell and his Federal troops after they had raided into southwestern Virginia. Barbee explained some of his activities to his children:

Near Lewisburg Dec 24 1863

Some tall marching & countermarching we have done since was written. Gen. A (U.S.A.) wouldn't come in trap we fixed for him, but fought out through Col. Jackson's command. Our late campaign was the most severe we have ever known. The weather was *very* cold, windy, rainy, sleety, &c. We encamped on top of Sweet Spring Mountain the coldest place in Va. We are all back again safe & sound. Your Uncle John is well sends love to you both. He would be proud & delighted to rec. letters from you. He *loves* you dearly. He is the best Uncle I believe you have. He is always kind to your "pappa". Write him often. I love him very much & think he is the best boy I ever saw or knew. Have you learned to knit? If so knit Uncle Jno. & Pappa a pr. of socks. Your Ma tells me that you both learn well & are attentive & good children. Your grand Pa writes me about you. It pleases me well to hear such good reports from my dear little darlings whom I love more than all the world Love Ma Grand parents & all

Yr. affc. Pa
A.R. Barbee

Barbee found the time to include a letter to his Father-in-Law, Dr. John Thompson, the father of John, the boy he thought so highly of and was treating for a missing eye as well as a wound in the neck.

Lewisburg, Greenbrier County, Va.,
Thursday December 10th 1863

Dr. J.J. Thompson:
My dear Sir

I wrote Maggie & the children last Monday. I have not yet sent their letters off -- will send them with this. I have but little to add in way of news since my letters to my wife & children last Monday. I refer you then to those letters for news &c. Also for account of condition of your son John's wounds &c. &c. He continues to do well. Is on duty & in fine spirits. My own health was never better -- my wounds are well & tho I have no strength in my right arm, & it is rather stiff about elbow joint, yet I am on duty

& I have had no return, or even symptom of Rheumatism for some six or eight months. The fear of cardiac disease, has in great degree passed off, & I am by far better content, & happier than I have been since in the army, that is , as regards my health. I intend paying more attention to myself this winter than I have ever heretofore done. While East my sisters gave me a great many warm clothes - such as socks, & flannel undershirts. "Dixie"-made goods. Upon going to camp today I found some friend had sent to my cabin a pair of heavy strong boots for "Col. Barbee" with my Compliments." Did not say who, & I could not recognize the handwriting. In looking around I found two flannel shirts, 2 Hkfs, & many little notions all neatly done up & accompanied with a very kind little note, evidently the hand writing of a lady, but there was no name to it. Bro. rec'd something of the same sort. Don't know who sent his. You see then my dear sir, that we are not altogether forgotten or cared for, even tho separated from the loved ones at home & deprived of many little things they might fix up for our comfort. Tell Maggie not to get uneasy about my recg. "kind notes" with some little indispensables &c. from some of my female friends. She knew that I needed the clothing & with her own hands made it up for me. I think I know who sent the package to John & myself. We feel very grateful. While I think of it tell my wife that John & myself rec'd a letter a short time since from our old friend Dr. Johnson also letters from his daughters Miss Catherine & Mrs. Gillespie. All were well except Mrs. G. oldest child (Mary) who was suffering with "ear ache". The letters were written "Augst 29th" but I did not get them until my return to Reg. The old Dr seems a good deal concerned about John & myself, but I am going to write him & his daughters long letters in a few days & let him know that we are both well of our wounds & on duty. We would love dearly to visit the old gentleman & his family, but cannot get a furlow now.

I never felt less like writing in all my life. I have been thinking of you all the day long. I have been thinking too of Dear Ma, Sisters, My own Maggie & Darlings little Blanche & Kate. It unfits me for letter writing now. I have not seen or heard of "Mcbeth", but will use every effort to find whereabouts.

All Co. A, & Co. F are well -- the wounded will all soon be on duty again. I have *one thousand dollars* ($1000) of poor Wm Hubbard's money -- rather I have it at interest for him & have had it for more than twelve months. He (Wm H.) poor fellow was killed in fight on Droop Mountain 6th ___. Does Mr. Wm H's father still live? If so he is the proper heir, as Wm had no wife & died without a will. I will take care of his means. Poor John Smith left but little money behind. Dick Cartwell who gets wounded every fight is doing well & will again be for duty soon. Lt Wm H. Bailey wounded in leg is doing well & will report for duty soon -- also Paul Dickerson, Sears ________, Pete Bailey, Young Watkins, Lanham, Tucker & others of "Border Riflemen" who have not already returned to duty will in a few days. Pete Bailey & Watkins like myself were both wounded in right elbow &each of us will have stiff joints for a time. I visit our sick & wounded & attend them as regularily as tho I were a Surgeon in the Army. I see that none of the wounded (C.S. or U.S.) are neglected. My own wounds have taught me a good deal about the treatment of gun shot wounds. While I regard cold water the great panacea for gunshot wounds, it has nevertheless been abused. Some surgeons apply it from the *moment* you rec a wound until the wound has healed entirely. In my own case, cold water was applied to my wounds in arm & hip, (2) after I had bled to syncope & (1) stunned & knocked over by shells & before reaction had set in. But for a young lady, a Miss Caldwell, who nursed me, refusing to keep up the application of cold water as directed, after seeing me have severe chills -- cold extremities & *stiff jaws*, I should now been sleeping among the dead. She properly gave me freely of Bourboun Whiskey, Paragoric & Landsnum & all such things as she could command. After drinking a pint & half of whiskey, one tea cup of Paragoric & 2 oz of Landsnum I began to be myself & took two or three grains of morph. & went to sleep. After I awoke cold water to my wounds was grateful & I kept it constantly applied till the inflammation all subsided & supperation fairly estblished & cold water became unpleasant to the senses, then in opposition to every M.D. I discontinued the use of it. I so directed all the nurses in the hospitals. No wounded ever done better than ours have. I have seen very many wounds injured by the long continued application of cold water. I would like to have your medical opinion on many subjects could I see you. I am going to study surgery well this winter. Love to all. Respects to Dr. Stewart & family & Aunt Betsy Mildred & Mrs. Jeff. Hastily & sincerely.

Andrew R. Barbee

Barbee next wrote home a few days before Christmas and wrote at least four letters to his family back in Union-controlled territory. He had just returned to the area where the Confederates were to spend the winter after trying to catch General Averell's raiders.

Near Lewisburg, Va December 23rd, 1863

My Dear Maggie;

December 7th I wrote you a long letter Dec 10 I wrote your Pa & Blanche & Kate. The letters were expected to have been sent through pr. Flag of Truce but demonstrations from the enemy led us to suspect that no Flag of Truce would likely be sent. In a day or two orders were rec'd to "cook 3 days rations &c." Saturday 12th inst. we began march & after the coldest, hardest, & most severe time we have *ever* had returned yesterday. We did not catch Gen. Averell as we ought have done. Had Maj. Gen. S. Jones been a Gen we would have accomplished much. As it was we accomplished nothing at all. "No body hurt" as Abe says. There is hope for change in this Dpt. & a close & steady watch will be kept in all future times for Mr.

Averell. He destroyed a great deal & had only about 160 men & 200 or 300 horse & five ambulances captured. *Shame* for this Dpt. I was as usual in command as now of 22 Reg. I miss Maj. Bailey. Capt. McDonald (Sr. Capt of 22 Reg) succeeds Maj. Bailey. We are again building winter quarters. Soon as we get them done, I am going to apply myself closely to books all winter. I feel like studying & improving the winter months. I would like my dear wife to have you & our darlings with me, or anear me, but I know it would not be well were it even possible. Think of me during the long dreary winter days & nights if not on march you may imagine me sitting in my cabin out in the woods with book in hand studying. I am building a comfortable house -- no one is to occupy it but myself & negro man. If John gets off Ct. Mar.[10] this winter he will come -- if he does not, I shall through choice be all alone.

We have a poor opportunity of writing or of studying at least I have, for I have always been in command. It may not be so this winter all the time. You will see from my letter Dec 7th & 10th to you & Pa that I tried to let you know that I had rcd your letters without letting *others* know that I got letters from you other than pr. flag truce.[11] I rcd the shirt Flannel, buttons, Hkfs, soap, thread, &c. John also rcd his package from Sister Kate. We needed the clothes. I need *drawers* worse than anything else -- can't get them here. I can't wear flannel drawers -- Heavy cotton. Dick Roberts, (dear old fellow) sent me a pr of most excellent heavy double sided high cavalry boots -- he also sent boots & shoes to his Bro. They come in well. Wish some one would send John a pr of boots -- he needs them -- such as mine are cost $200 here. Officers cannot live, feed & clothe themselves on Commission. A Bill

---

10 John Thompson was away serving on a Court Martial panel.

11 Apparently, Barbee sent and received letters in ways other than by a flag of truce arrangement. Scouts were probably sent through Federal lines and with the support of Partisan Ranger units, they were able to penetrate to the vicinity of Charleston -- over 100 miles away.

before Congress now allows rations for officers. If it passes, then we may be able to clothe ourselves. We have nothing to eat but beef & bread, but enjoy it -- are of good cheer -- would rather be reduced to *Bread* nay to *Starvation* than yield one pot or kettle to the enemy. This war may last always but we will never be *subjugated.* It seems sometimes that God Almighty is against us but *he is not* & hope whispers all will yet be well. (I am interrupted every moment -- I am sitting out in the woods without tent or cabin yet, but a most *everlasting* smoky fire. My hands are cold & numbed. Must stop awhile & warm & then write some furloughs.

Every one is hushed for the night. I am setting "tailor fashion" with my "Record Book" in lap before a large log fire writing you. We have no candles in camp. I am compelled to write by firelight if I write you after night. I wish sometimes I could steal away to some comfortable room & there lock myself up alone & write you a whole day & night. I have much I like to write you about, but am always hurried & so often interrupted that it is impossible to remember half I'd like to write you. My letters must certainly be very disconnected & uninteresting. I never read them over after writing them for fear of being so ashamed that I will destroy them. I try to content myself that some letter, or some sort of apology for a letter is better than no letter at all. Then to tell you that John, Tom, & myself with *all* the Border Riflemen are well & good spirits must constitute a larger part of the *interesting* matter of my letter. John is in camp tonight but will return to Lewisburg tomorrow. I am going to town tomorrow evening (Xmas Eve) & if nothing happens, & the Comdg. Genl will consent I shall remain in Lewisburg all night, having consented to drink "egg nog" with a party of ladies Xmas morning. Wonder if they will make as good & nice egg nog as you, Kate & Ma used to make the Dr & myself? *No*, I know they will not. Wish I could be with you all. I know when you drink your egg nog & Ma sets down to her fine Xmas dinner & the Dr begins to carve the old turkey cock that some of you, if not *every* one of you will wish & say "I wish the poor boys -- Andr. & Jno. were here."

I'll promise to remember each one you the first sip & every sip of egg nog I take. I know I could enjoy the egg nog at home most. Maggie, I try to be & may seem to be, happy but --oh! my God -- when I remember you & my dear children cut off from, & how long we have been separated, I feel indeed that I cannot bear up under it. I have never clung to you & our children with half so much affection & devotion as since in the army. When you use to scold at me & quarrel at me, & complain at me, I wondered whether I did love you with that devotion that other men loved their wives -- I wondered what effect these long absence & cruel war would have upon me -- whether I would ever grow more careless of you than I had hitherto been. I only feel now that every day of suffering every additional hardship that I have had to bear -- every privation that has been foist upon me has tended only to strengthen the tie that links us together. Should we meet again & be blessed in peace, oh my wife how happy we shall be. Will we not live out the remnant of days each with affection deep & tender striving to make the other happy? Let's swear that we will.

Some poet wrote "Absence makes the heart grow warmer." It is true, but in times like these, where one accustomed as I have been to indulge in all sort of luxuries, is suddenly deprived of *everything* -- even the necessary comforts of life -- every moment of his life is being spent in anxious care about his bleeding comrades & country, these then are things which makes the heart grow warmer & cling more tenatiously to its first love. But pardon this strain. The fire burns the top of my head & I must soon stop. It is past 12 o'clock. Every one is asleep. I do not feel sleepy. I will however lie down & think on of you & our little pets.

You will see in my letter of the 7th inst. that I mention something about my business affairs. I believe this is the first time in my life that I ever imposed any tax of this kind upon you, but I did not want you to be altogether ignorant of our situation. I may be killed or die, so may John & our "old clothes" left & you know not how. Pardon this. The book upon which I write --"Record Book" & the books of my journal -- will always be left with a friend when I go to the battlefield, so that should anything happen to me you will be written to & the books &c all turned over to you. Try & collect or tell your Pa to collect at least enough of our *firm* to give such amt. of money as you may wish for self & children. I feel no uneasiness about you. Few poor soldiers are so blessed as I, so far as provisions for his family is concerned. I hope to live to reciprocate the kindness of your dear parents & sisters to you & children. John & I are coming home some of these days & then we can manage for &take care of *you all.*

I told John of the opportunity of writing & told him he must write -- he begged me to write. I told him of course I should but he ought to. He asked to be excused. Poor fellow dislikes to write -- Excuse him. He *would* write if he knew I would not, or if I were not here. Send him a pr. of boots & pants -- me two pr of drawers if you can. Jno.'s commission --$130.00 -- & mine --$170--is hardly supporting us, feeding & clothing us. Had I depended only upon my Com. I should now be behind hand, but at my leisure outside the army I have seen chances for making two or five hundred dollars & have always taken advantage of them & after paying all my debts (the sale of "Coquette" but little overpaying the expense &c & amt. of balance interest &c upon her.) I have some several thousand dollars at interest. I shall watch every chance for making money & will *catch* at it. I have more capacity for making & saving money than I ever dreamed I had. Were I not in the army I could make a fortune in a few years now. I do desire to make something *now* for you & our children so that I may not be so hard run when the war is over & we permitted once more to be in peace together. Trust me dear, I am bending every energy & doing the best I can for you. But *here comes the thought & rememberance of what Mrs. Swindler told me. That you smoke!* You told me at

Gauley that you would smoke no more. It makes me unhappy to think my wife should be addicted to such a *filthy* habit. *Please never smoke again.* For you I am making far greater sacrifices. Grant me this last request & write & tell me that you are firm in the resolve to smoke never more. Have your teeth fixed.

Send me your & the children's likeness

Yr affc Andrew

The opportunity for sending letters through the Federal lines continued over Christmas Day and Andrew Barbee took advantage of this and sent a letter to his Father-in-Law, Dr.Thompson.

Dr. John J. Thompson:

My Dear Sir:

I have heard several times of late that there was a good deal of land on Ka Valley for sale -- have heard quite recently that Thos. Markham, Sr. was anxious to sell his land. If you can buy this land do so -- buy land in your own name &give check for me for the payments. I heard that Thomas M. Sr. will sell & come to Dixie -- that will suit -- pay all the Confed money you & Maggie can raise & check on me for balance with *assurance* that all will be met. After having pd. Father for Negroes bot. & for money advanced me to graduate on (which accnts were charged me vs. on his estate book) the two amounting to near three thousand dollars & after having pd. upwards of one thousand dollars in Madison Co. & settling with my Bros. & owing none of them a dollar, I can pay down *now* some *three thousand five hundred* ($3500) dollars & by selling several horses & other trade on hand could in ten days raise some five or six thousand dollars. If you can buy the land for me (in your name to amt. of $10,000 $15,000 & will not draw on me for more than $5000 at a time and let the balance be in annual payments of two or three thousand dollars I will meet them promptly. Of course we have no other currency here but Confed. Try & buy land on above plan.

There is no land for sale in Dixie that I can find besides it is too high. I would rather you would purchase in Ka. Val. for me. Tell me something of the Lewis farm you Bot. whether there is anything said about the payments due on it. Write me freely. I have some money at interest & some in perishable stock -- whilst I have some confidence on Confed. money yet I had greatly prefer having all I could raise of it invested in land. Write me whether you can buy *land* &c. so that I may look else where. I don't want money about me. Confed money is looking up & is cheerfully taken in payment of old debts. If Mr. Lewis *wants* money and will take mine I will advance the amt. you owe him for the farm you bot. before commencement of war.

The trustee Henry Clay Dickinson is in Dixie if you can secure your title to that farm write me & tell me whether if Mr. H.C.D. will rec. the money due, whether you would like me to pay it for you. I need your council, but know not how to get it.

I have not heard of Macbeth yet.

My servants are well & happy -- wish I had Jonas. I was offered $10,000 for Martha & children a few days ago She (Martha) loves Maggie & our children & is a good woman & has a sprightly set of children & I would not sell her for twice or 3 times $10,000. I would not part from her at all. I have them far back in Dixie -- they are well clothed & happy.

John is doing well -- gay & happy -- he never has *blues* or any such thing -- always full of life. He may write home.

Dr. if you or Ma can send John a pr. of heavy double soled boots & a pr of pants do so. Either will cost $100 in Dixie. I try to keep John along on his com. Do not think he wastes his means. He sometimes says he is going to quit the army in the spring & make some money, but again he says he is in for the war. (I do not know what exactly he has for making money). In candor, I regard him as one of the purest best & most honorable & gallant boys I ever saw or knew, & I have no relation in the world to whom I am more devotedly attached. We have been Brothers truly "share each others joys, and wept each others tears" One has never known a sorrow but it was soothed by the other. Feel assured that we care for each other & try to add to the comforts & happiness of each other. And now I will join some Ladies in a drink of egg nog. They will allow me the priviledge of drinking a health to the absent "Loved ones at home". I am sure you & Ma will wish for the "poor Boys today". Would we were with you all, if we could be so in peace & security. Wm. Lanham, who was wounded in head & Dick Cartwell in the foot & Steve Burford in leg & others slightly wounded are doing well -- most returned to duty -- Poor Cartwell (as good a man as brave a soldier as ever raised a musket) I fear will never again be fit for the service. He was wounded in the foot. His wound will not disable him on a farm or may not prevent him doing service in army in the cavalry. John Rippetoe has been sick, but now well. I attended him myself. I attend all our old Co. when they get sick & it is my pleasure. I am *never* idle & always at work for my country, friends or self. I love to be active & useful.

Tell Aunt Betsy I do not know where Jim is -- hear he was at Salem a short time since & was well. I have been with the 36th Reg. recently & all the Buffalo boys were well. Tell Rev. Tom Harmon his boys are well -- good boys & good soldiers. Tell me who is the *Heir of Wm H. Hubbard*, of Co. A, 22nd Reg, who was killed on Droop Mountain. I have in my possession 1000 dollars for him which amt. I *made* him make & then took it from him, to put at interest & save for him. I hope none of the families of "Border Riflemen" are suffering for the necessities of life. Remember me kindly to Dr. Stewart, Col Hoge & families, Jim Bowling & family. Tell Geo Thompson at Coal's Mouth that while in Warrenton I was at Dr.

Chilton's & saw his wife's sister. She was quite well & sent many messages

Love to Ma & sisters -- tell sisters I will write them soon. Enquire how this letter reaches you & send me answers. I know you will write me every opportunity. I make many chances to write home but you never get half the letters I write -- *none* I believe pr. flag of truce. I saw my old friend Pete Carpenter a short time ago. Was satisfied about not getting J. I can not find out where Uncle Bob is. Have written him several times, but suppose he never rec'd my letters. John rec'd letter a few days ago from Cousin Ann Martin -- all well in Valley. I do not think well of Dr. K's chronic diarrhea. He is very fleshy rather big bellied -- tho he does not drink. Ramsey is a most excellent gentleman. I like him very much. Kiss our darlings -- Blanche &Kate.

& think on us kindly. yr affc sons
Andrew & John

P.S.
Send the enclosed letter to Miss Patrick. It is from her Bro. Dr. A.S. Patrick, Ast. Surg. 22 Va Reg. He is a true southern gentleman & a good & valued friend. He sees a great deal of trouble about home. You will have *several* opportunities of sending us letters this winter -- let none escape. Send John & myself each a good strong long bladed *pocket knife* -- can't get any out here. We have plenty shirts. drawers &c. John is scarcer of shirts than I am. We will write again soon every chance we get. Keep letters written for the next two months -- write them at your leisure & when you get an opportunity just have to add P.S. with date & latest news.

Geo. Wright (Mrs. Col. H.'s Bro) is very well -- so also is Wm Summers --both good boys & dear friends. Lt. Tyree (Mrs. Las. Bowling's cousin) who was wounded at Droop Mountain is in a critical condition. He is quite debilitated. Has bled a great deal from wounds. He is 20 miles to the rear of me, yet his poor old Father & Uncle Frank came for me to visit him. I go every chance that I have -- he is upon my pres. & treatment. Hope he may get well -- *think* he will --was wounded nape of neck. He, Lt. Tyree, is a good fellow, brave soldier & strongly attached to me, as is *all* the Tyrees. I often see Capt. Frank Tyree. Hope to hear from you soon.

Hastily & affly. yr. Son
Andrew R. Barbee

Barbee was able to complete the letters to his two Sisters-in-Law, as promised. The letter to Kate explains that the Confederate officer wasn't always a rebel. Both Barbee and his Father-in-Law had hoped that secession wouldn't actually happened, but once Virginia left the Union, the matter was settled for Andrew Barbee. He fought until the war was over -- despite the serious wounds that he received which would have been sufficient reason for many others to have left the service as an invalid.

Lewisburg Va
Christmas Day 1863

Miss Kate Thompson,
My Dear Sister;

Your kind letter after "long delay" had at last been rec'd. I was *so* glad Kate to get it, for indeed, Dear sister, I had thought that both you & Ma had grown altogether careless & indifferent about me. I never *could* flatter myself at any time, that I held a very high place in your affections, but since torn from you, and the "loved ones at home" I have earnestly & so constantly striven to discharge a faithful duty to my country, my family & yourself that I had hope (rather forlornly) to have soon some admiration or "touched some tender chord" in your affections. I know then, as your dear letter would induce me to believe, that you are not altogether unmindful of me, but with a sister's love tenderly sympathizing with us, makes me feel proud indeed & nerves me to still bolder &

more daring deeds. I know dear Kate that even while Pa & myself were clinging to & hanging on with a faint hope to the Union, that you were always "sesech" & that your sympathies have always been with those whose breasts were bared in the face of the enemy for the protection of the South. I have ever admired your sentiments &of late love you the more for them. You are unable dear sister -- to take part in this great drama & struggle for *life & Liberty*, but know & remember ever, that in the *great cause* you have at least two fond & devoted Bros. & many proud, gallant cousins, nobly battling to uphold *your principles.* It may seem strange to you, but indeed those of your kind who have been engaged for 3 years in this "cruel war" have become *indifferent to death & to sorrow* would rather perish on the Battlefield than to entertain the thought for a moment that we could ever be conquered. We may die (that is the smallest consideration but for those who may mourn us) but subjugated we never can or will be. Be then steady in faith, watch, hope & pray -- All will be well. We no longer look for or rely (as *some* have fatally) upon foreign intervention -- upon our own strength & the brave souls of the South have we now only to hope for deliverance. Since it has come to this, &all know & feel it, why *all will be well.* Peace will come someday & with it the glorious independence & recognition of the South. Rest content -- never despair -- hold out faithfully &hopefully till Father & Bros. & all male kindred are killed, then to arms ye women & share fate of father, Bro. & husband. Everything just now looks dark, but the *soldier* of C.S.A. is more desperate & determined than ever to drive back the invader or die. What I fear among the true patriots & the soldiery is that they are becoming too recklessly desperate. But let them take the chances to "sink or swim, live or die, survive or perish".

Cousin Maj K & the whole family are anxious to see you &send you many messages. I like the whole family much better than I did before. You would be proud of your cousins Captain & Col. could you see & know of them in

C.S.A. Ramsey, *every* body speaks well of & *likes.* Cousins Maggie & Ann -- I love very much -- did not either trip East get to see "Cousin Emma" (Mrs. F.). She however was well. All your friends in Shenandoah, Rockingham, Page & Rapph. often spoke of you & sent love &c. &c. Some heard that you & one Mr. P.S. were married. I corrected it of course. But "Katie Darling" how are you & him getting along? Would like to know. It is reported here that P.S. & Jno. S. had gone to Canada to avoid conscription in U.S.A. Is it so? I shall always regret that they did not come out with us. I remember them very kindly & hope they may turn up "right side up".

Write me & tell me all about yourself & every thing that was going on. Remember me kindly to Peter & Miss Sallie -- sorry to hear that Miss S. is in bad health. How is cousin Ellen S's health? My kind regards to her & Uncle Chas' family. Why do none of them ever write me. Dear old Grand Pa never answered any of my many letters neither did cousins Misses Chas. Beale. Remember me to all our many friends. We captured *Col. Palsey* from prison a few days ago. Have you any late music? What name? Do not give up your music, sister, practice all the time you can spare from the kitchen & wash tub &c. *I love you more dearly because you write John & I that you can work* & that you are not too ashamed or too lazy to do it. Let's do the best we can while this war is going on, hoping for better & happier days. Love to all. Tell Mollie to write me. Kiss Blanche & Kate &tell them that it is for "*dear pappa*". Excuse mistakes & I will join the ladies in another drink of egg nog. *Wish we were with you!* Ever your

fond & affc. Bro.
Andrew R. Barbee

Andrew R. Barbee completed his Christmas letters to his family residing in the Kanawha Valley. He had to do the writing for both of the members of the family -- himself and his Brother-in-law, John K. Thompson.

Apparently John was not writing home and was probably depressed about the outcome of the war to this point. He had given much for his state and had little to show for it. His salary of $130.00 each month wouldn't buy him a good pair of boots. He talked of getting out of the army, but also mentioned that he was in for the duration of the war. He remained with the 22nd Virginia until the end of the war and was discharged at Appomattox at the age of twenty-two. He had been wounded in the head at Carnifex Ferry, lost an eye at Lewisburg, was shot in the face at White Sulphur Springs, shot in the neck at Droop Mountain, and was shot in the chest at Cold Harbor. He returned to duty and lead the remnants of the 22nd Virginia from the field after the battle of Winchester in 1864. He and his Brother-in-Law, Andrew Barbee, gave the best they had for the State of Virginia and the Confederacy.

Harper's

Figure 1. Formidable terrain of Virginia's western counties

Harper's

Figure 2. Approach of a Confederate cavalry patrol.

Harper's

Figure 3. Confederate cavalry raiders crossing a stream.

Harper's

Figure 4. Bridges on major transportation routes were major targets and were frequently burned.

Harper's

Figure 5. Confederate sharpshooters such as these ambushed Federal supply trains in the Kanawha Valley.

Harper's

Figure 6. Picket duty during the winter.

Harper's

Figure 7. Federal regiments fording a wilderness stream.

Harper's

Figure 8. Federal pickets engaging approaching Confederates as reinforcements arrive.

Harper's

Figure 9. Federal soldiers in ambush positions.

Harper's

Figure 10. Skirmishing in heavy forest.

Harper's

Figure 11. Mountain retreat in a storm.

Harper's

Figure 12. Winter retreat in the mountains.

There was a great deal of interest in the Civil War during the late 1920's as the veterans of the war began to pass from the scene. Many papers and memoirs on battles were published during this period.

This interest extended into West Virginia as participants and scholars collected first-hand observations from elderly veterans and tried to get the material into print.

The following articles appeared in the Pochontas Times, a small newspaper published in Marlinton, West Virginia. The editor of the paper was Calvin W. Price and the author of the article is not listed, but was probably Andrew Price -- then the president of the West Virginia Historical Society.

Mr. Price provides an excellent record of little known events surrounding the campaigning that occurred along the primary transportation route in the region, the James River and Kanawha Turnpike. The article appeared in the newspaper on Thursday, February 10, 1927.

The Feuding Generals - Floyd and Wise

This is a story of two politicians who stirred up a war and became generals overnight and who were so jealous of each other that they both lost their high standing. It is about John B. Floyd and Henry A. Wise and how they failed to hold the southern half of West Virginia in 1861, commonly referred to as the Kanawha Valley campaign.

West Virginia is divided into two parts by an unbroken divide that has recently been named Bison Range. It runs across the State from the mouth of the Kanawha River to the Allegheny Mountain on the east where the counties of Pocahontas, Pendleton, and Randolph corner. North of that divide lived the people who were for the Union by a vast majority, while south of that divide the people were more than half inclined to accept the order to secede.

Charleston was the big town of the southern part, the county seat of Kanawha County, and Lewisburg was the town second in importance. Charleston had about 2000 population and Lewisburg about 800. The salt works on the Kanawha River made the possession of the region important to both armies, to say nothing of the fight that immediately arose to make a separate state from the western part of Virginia.

Henry A. Wise was given a commission as a brigadier general and sent to West Virginia to organize an army to be known as the Wise Legion. John B. Floyd received his commission some days earlier and had a similar mission in southwest Virginia, and an order came to Henry A. Wise to the effect that if these two armies joined in the campaign in the mountains that Floyd was to be commanding officer on the ground that his commission antedated the commission to Wise.

They both moved about the first part of June, 1861, and while there was war between the north and the south, the bad blood was between Wise and his partisans and Floyd and his army.

They were both about the same age. Floyd was fifty-six and Wise was fifty-five.

Floyd was born in Pulaski County. He was a lawyer by profession. In 1857, he was appointed Secretary of War by Buchannan, and when the troubles of the campaign of 1860 came to the fore, he showed an active partisanship for the South. At or about that time the federal government had established arm factories, and a great drive had been made to convert the enormous number of flint-lock muskets into guns suitable for the percussion cap, an invention that had proved its worth. About that time there came a great demand for arms from the southern states. The war clouds were gathering. Floyd as secretary of war wrote in answer to the demands that these muskets in excess of the proper quota would be furnished by the federal government to the states at the price of $2.50 each. He also traded seasoned musket stocks three years in the dry for green musket stocks to Virginia at Harpers Ferry arsenal. He had issued an order to move 124 cannon from Pittsburg to the far south to a place not fitted to receive them, and about this time the president, who was a Pennsylvanian, woke up and at Christmas time, 1861[12], Floyd resigned. He was accused of being a defaulter probably on account of bills for arms against the seceding states, but was never tried. He became active in Civil War on behalf of Virginia, and in conjunction with the C.S.A. was more or less active until his death in 1863. His greatest battle was when he commanded Fort Donelson in 1862 when he escaped by flight and turned the command over to Pillow. Grant took the fort.

Henry A. Wise was born in Accomac county. He was a lawyer. He served ten years in Congress. He was first elected as a Jackson Democrat but soon joined the opposition and was a partisan of President Tyler who appointed him minister to Brazil. In 1855, he was elected

---

12 The date is in error. Floyd resigned in 1860. By Christmas, 1861, the Civil War had been going for over six months.

governor of Virginia. In 1856, he organized a meeting of southern governors at Raleigh, North Carolina, just before the presidential election, the Fremont campaign. After the election he declared that if Fremont had won that he would have raised an army of twenty thousand men and taken Washington.

Wise was governor at the time of the John Brown raid on Harpers Ferry. He was criticized for his management of that affair on the grounds that he made it a national affair and that his accusation that it had been a conspiracy and plot involving the free states, had the effect of making it such, whereas if it had been left to the civil courts and the usual prosecution it would not have divided the country into sections.

James A. Seddon, a prominent Virginian, who was afterwards Secretary of War for the C.S.A. during most of the war, wrote:

"In short, with his policy of swaggering and bullying, Wise has exploited this whole affair to his own selfish aggrandizement, to aid his vain hopes for the presidency, and to strengthen the fragment of a southern part he heads. And as a result has conjured a devil neither he nor perhaps any other can lay, and, arraying the roused pride and animosities of both sections against each other, has brought on a real crisis of imminent peril to both."[13]

... to vote contrary to their campaign pledges, upon the specious plea that in that direction lay peace, and in this he was ably assisted by the late Roger A. Pryor, who is suspected of having Fort Sumpter fired upon at the crucial moment. The Wise's and Pryor, after the war, did not put on the sack cloth and ashes of defeat, but promptly joined the Republican party, and became the beneficiaries of the victors.

The Democratic party busted up the Federalists by nominating and electing Federalists, and the Republican

---

[13] Hodges, M.S., *West Virginia Legislative Handbook and Official Register*, 1929, pg. 882. This quotation was missing from the copy of the Price article.

party followed that course until it has about ruined the Democratic party, and has done an ocasional injustice to some of its own particular stars.

It was not long however until the southern people who with all their faults are probably the most loveable of all races held up their heads again and the proudest societies in the nation are the Confederates. I was amused at the position of one of my daughters the other day who has never shown any disposition to go in for the societies based on colonial times or the Revolution, but who was delighted at an opportunity to join the Daughters of the Confederacy. It was no trouble to name thirteen soldiers near enough kin to entitle her to the priviledge.

About thirty-five or thirty-six years ago there were some overwhelming demonstrations in New York City glorifying the Southern people. John S. Wise had gone there and I heard then that he had about the same experience as Aaron Burr or Benedict Arnold. So being new to editorial duties I drew a picture of John S. Wise in his lonely garret looking down on the procession of Southerners, and the remorse he must suffer. In a week or two I got about the hottest letter of my troubled career from him. I apologized to the effect that I would never have written it if I had any idea that he would ever read it. The next letter I got was very kind and friendly and invited me to visit him in his home in Accomac. They told me afterwards that instead of living in a garret that he belonged to some of the most luxurious clubs in the big city.

Under the date of June 6, 1861, Henry A. Wise was notified to procede at once to the Kanawha country and rally around him all the Southern men he could, and that if his command and Floyd's operated together Floyd should command.

The strength of the Wise Legion on July 8, 1861 was:

General Staff	12	
First and Second Kanawha Regiments	1483	
Kanawha Batallion	459	
Seven Independent Companies	535	
Three Companies of Mounted Rangers	216	total of 2705

Wise had a fine time until about the 20th of July, 1861. On the 17th, he had a fight with the federals at Scarey Creek and claimed a victory over Gen. Cox. Cox claims to have won something between a defeat and a victory. But Wise's spirits soared immensely and he talked like he could win the war if given a little cooperation. Scarey Creek is west of Charleston. But just at this time the federals scattered the Confederates at Rich Mountain, Laurel Hill, Beverly, and Carick's Ford, and Wise was ordered to fall back to some point near Covington where he would go to work under Floyd, and from that time on there was a war within a war.

It was a mistake from the first to put a couple of politicians in command in the Kanawha campaign. There were two popular and efficient military men in that territory, McCausland and Tompkins. They were scions of the aristocracy, fine gentlemen, able officers, with adequate training. They were colonels of the First and Second Kanawha regiments afterwards the 22nd and 36th Virginia Infantry. If they had been given the duty of recruiting the fighting strength there would have been a different tale to tell.

There is not enough room in one article like this to go into many details but it will be stated here that Wise and Floyd were not willing to work together. Floyd's orders would be ignored, and he complained biterly to the Confederate government. Wise laid his soul bare to R.E. Lee as commander in chief of the Virginia troops.

At this place let us look at some civilian views of the feud between the two politicos.

September 10, 1861, Mason Matthews, member of the legislature from Greenbrier county, wrote to Jefferson Davis, that the success of the campaign was threatened by the unfriendly relations existing between the two generals, Floyd and Wise, and expresses it as his opinion that each would be gratified to see the other annihilated. He recommends that both be deposed and a military general appointed in their stead to take charge of both of the divisions. This letter is endorsed by Samuel Price and M. Arbuckle. Mason Mathews was afterwards governor of West Virginia, and Samuel Price served in the United States Senate. M. Arbuckle was presiding justice of the county court for years. W.H. Syme also wrote from Lewisburg that it was common report that the generals were not acting in harmony ... some time ago when and how the bridge across Gauley River at its mouth was burned. Wise says that after winning the battle at Scarey Creek, July 14, that the federals were reinforced that and he had 4000 men divided as follows: at Gauley, 1000, at Coal River, 1000, at Charleston, 2000, and finding that he would be attacked by 20,000, he retreated from Charleston on July 24, and burned the bridge at Gauley on July 27, 1861. His army reached Bungers Mill, four miles east of Lewisburg by August 1.

Floyd has brought his army to the turnpike. It looks like Wise was trying to retain full control of his army which was known as the Wise Legion but seems to have been mustered into the Confederate army in 1862.[14]

The alarming thing to the war office at Richmond was the fact that a great army was marching south through Webster, Braxton, and Nicholas counties down Gauley River to effect a junction with Cox on the Kanawha. Wise seems to have the idea that it was better to take a stand on the east edge of the wilderness forty miles broad that lay between Ansted on the west and the Greenbrier settlements on the east. A great part of lonely road is still observed by the tourist on the Midland Trail.

He was overruled in this and it is plain to be inferred that Wise managed for about two months to keep his legion between the ignominy of losing its identity with Floyd's command, and running headlong upon the federal troops at Gauley Bridge. It was during this period that Wise was writing R.E. Lee what a poor commander Floyd was, and

---

[14] Wise's Legion was mustered into Confederate service in 1861.

Floyd was complaining to the war office that Wise would not obey orders.

Wise managed to stay on the pike while Floyd went north of the pike up Gauley River to Nicholas county.

At Kesslers Cross Lanes on the morning of August 28, Floyd surprised the Seventh Ohio regiment while it was eating breakfast and dispersed it. This place was five miles from Summersville. It seems to have been the point farthest north for Floyd to reach.

A few days after, Wise had a fight at Hawks Nest and claimed a signal victory. On the strength of this he begged to be allowed to take his legion and part in peace from Floyd. He said; "I feel if we remain together, we will unite in more wars than one." He proposes to let McCausland and the 36th go to Floyd and he will take Tompkins and the 22nd. There is evidence that Tompkins was getting restive under the galling necessity of serving under generals with no previous experience. He threatened to resign.

But there was a real army marching down from the north through the central part of the state. The federal advance had been kept out of Greenbrier Valley and they could not reach the Midland Trail by the Seneca Trail and so they were marching down that road that they now proposed to name Stonewall Jackson Road. Just northeast of Ansted, Gauley River turns to where it can force a passage through Gauley Mountain to join the New River at Kanawha Falls. It is about 18 miles as the crow flies from Ansted to Summersville. Just half way on this line is where Meadow River flows into the Gauley, and at this place all the county roads converge to cross over. This place at the mouth of Meadow River on the Gauley, was called Carnifex Ferry in 1861, and it was the site of one of the most bloody battles of West Virginia.

Floyd determined to stop Rosecrans at Carnifex Ferry. The river was broad and between high cliffs. The wagon roads climbed down to the bottom of the gorge and out again. Floyd used the ferry boat and fortified the north side of the river whereas Wise pointed out if he had stayed on the other side of the river he could have kept the army from passing with a handful of men. Rosecrans came on Floyd about three in the afternoon of September 10, and the big guns roared and the muskets popped for three hours. The Confederates held the trenches and suffered little loss. Rosecrans reported his loss in killed and wounded at 141 and Floyd at 20 men. Men said who heard it that it was a teriffic cannonade that afternoon and a bloody battle. During the night Floyd crosed back to the south side of the river leaving a Confederate flag flying. Rosecrans claimed the victory and showed the captured flag and the fact that he was in possession of the battleground. Floyd claimed the victory and won the verbal war with Wise by the same token.

J.P. Benjamin, Acting Secretary of War, by a letter dated September 20, communicated the congradulations of the President of the C.S.A., and enclosed a pre-emptory order to Wise to turn over all troops to Floyd and to report himself in person with the least delay to Richmond. Everything under your command to Floyd, P.D.Q.

Wise could not accept it. He laid it before R.E. Lee. He said in effect those Richmond people did not know that he was encamped and fortified on Sewell Mountain and firing already begun, and that a severe struggle was on. He was needed and would obey if he had time, and even then, if Lee said so. Lee replied: "Obey the President's order." And there upon Wise faded from the picture so far as the campaign on the western waters was concerned.

Floyd came into full honors and did not like the many thousands of soldiers in blue converging on every side. So obtaining Lee's consent, Floyd took most of his troops over to the other side of New River, the south side, where it was more healthy. He refused to take the Wise Legion because he says it was in such a state of insubordination and so ill disciplined as for the moment rendered it unfit for military purposes.

Floyd marched the army down to Cotton Hill between Fayetteville and New River. It will be remembered that the

New River valley narrows into a canyon just above the mouth of Gauley River. The river flows west at this point. The Midland Trail follows the north side of the river and a road from Kanawha Falls follows the south side which joins the new road across the new bridge at Beckwith. The New Bridge as at or near Miller Ferry, and the ferry at Kanawha Falls was called Montgomery Ferry in 1861. Between the two roads runs the river. These roads are separated by distances ranging from one to two miles. The soldiers in camp could look across the abyss at their enemies. Floyd conceived the bright idea that if he had some long range guns he could fire across the canyon and kill somebody. So he asked for two 12 pounder and two 24 pounder rifled howitzers.

This was as late as October 29th, but long before they could come he found that the vastly superior blue army had crossed the Kanawha down at Loop Creek and Floyd got south of Beckley before they knew he had moved. Benjamin sent him one 12 pounder to practice with but it was never tried.[15]

December 4, Floyd was ordered to Newburn with a few remaining troops, nearly all of his fine regiments having been sent to South Carolina. Wise's Legion was ordered to report to Richmond. It saw service under Col. J. Lucius Davis. December 16, Floyd was ordered to place one regiment at Lewisburg for the winter, and to march the balance of his command to join A.S. Johnston at Bowling Green, Kentucky.

In 1862, Letcher, Governor of Virginia, issued a proclamation to raise 10,000 state troops under Floyd. This enlistment was for one year and was called the Virginia State Line. It was complained about bitterly by the recruiters who had to enlist men for three years or the duration of the war. Floyd died in 1863.

---

[15] Floyd actually brought the Federal camp at Gauley Bridge under fire for approximately 10 days in November, 1861.

February 18, 1862, Wise was joined to his Legion under J.E. Johnston, Department of Northern Virginia.

> "Before Time's breath, like blazing
> flax,
> Man and his marvels pass away;
> And changing empires wane and wax,
> Are founded, flourish, and decay."

Those Knights of old their bones are dust, their swords are rust, their souls are with the Lord, I trust.

Andrew Price contributed a second article to the newspaper in Marlinton, West Virginia, on the fighting that went on near Lewisburg. The article appeared in the Pocahontas Times on Thursday, February 10, 1927.

It contained detailed information about the battle of Lewisburg which was fought between the Federal troops under Colonel George Crook and Confederate Colonel Henry Heth in which many of the men in the Confederate ranks were amazed to see that while they outnumbered the Yanks, they were losing the fight.

Battle of Tuckwiler Hill

They used to call it the James River and Kanawha Turnpike when it was little more than a trail, and when it became a broad highway surfaced and finished like a city avenue, they called it the Midland Trail. But in the Civil War it was in constant use by the contending armies. Most of the time these armies were able to avoid one another ... Lewisburg is located in a long hollow place in the hills, and the road tops an eminence on each side. The people of Lewisburg got used to the presence of soldiers, and they were accustomed to see the grays disappear over the hill to the east, and westward look and the land was blue. Or if the blues went over the western crest the eastern hillside soon was gray.

But once in a while these armies would stand and fight. I have had a most trying time to get the battle of Tuckwiler Hill figured out. A historian in one of the best known histories states that there was such a fight but that it was indecisive, both sides claiming it. I have come to the conclusion that there were at least two fights at Tuckwiler Hill, as well as a fight between that hill and Brushy Ridge that many think was the Tuckwiler battle, so it is not too much to say that there were three battles.

This hill is in the richlands, one of the garden places of the State of west Virginia. The first disturbance was when the Second Volunteer Cavalry West Virginia was ordered to sweep the grays out of Lewisburg. They rode with some other troops, and came in the night time. Col. Edgar of Edgar's Battalion heard of the advance and moved his troops to the top of the hill and disposed of them on the top of that hill and along the rail fences. That was in the evening of May 1, 1862. They waylaid the road nearly all night, and he had given the strictest orders not to fire prematurely, but along about the small hours of the night they heard the blues coming and they approached riding four abreast, talking and laughing and not apprehending any danger. A confederate Irishman could not wait and fired his gun when the federals rode up and warned them. In the fire that followed, twelve federal soldiers were killed and seven wounded. No casualties on the confederate side. The federals retired in disorder, and by the breaking of day, a courier arrived under a flag of truce and asked for truce and it was agreed that a cessation of hostilities was to last from 6 a.m. until 11 a.m. This was the morning of May 2nd. Col. Edgar of the 26th, says in his official report that Col. Paxton, the federal commander took advantage of this truce, granted to take care of the dead and wounded, to extricate his army from danger of capture. He left his surgeon and some men. The federal surgeon reported to Col. Edgar that two men were so badly wounded that they could not be moved had obtained permission to stay at Mr. Tuckwiler's and would Col. Edgar kindly lend him a surgeon to help amputate a leg, all which Col. edgar agreed to do.

Col. Edgar was a very gallant figure in the war. A native of Monroe, and a highly educated man, he went through the war much respected as a commanding officer. He fell badly wounded in the battle of Lewisburg. After the war he was president of a college in Alabama and was offered the presidency of the University of West Virginia.

That there was a battle on Tuckwiler Hill on the morning of the 2nd of May, 1862, is proved beyond all doubt by the report of Col. Edgar printed in the records of the United States after the war. Now harken unto the second fight at a place with in sight of the first fight ten days after that. Bear in mind that we are talking about the eventful May, 1862, when a battle was staged in Lewisburg.

Just ten days after the first battle of Tuckwiler's Hill, the Second West Virginia Cavalry advanced again. This regiment had been divided into battalions. They joined the 47th Ohio Volunteer Infantry at Gauley Bridge, and marched to Meadow Bluffs in Greenbrier county. They attempted the same thing that Col. Paxton had failed to do, and that was to sweep the confederates out of Lewisburg.

Accordingly the cavalry was ordered to proceed during the night of the 11th of May under Major Hoffman and Captain Powell, over the road leading by way of Blue Sulphur Springs and to come into the turnpike at a point west of Lewisburg and between Tuckwiler Hill and that place. Colonel Elliot marched his infantry along the pike. The orders were to join at daylight on the morning of the 12th of May. Edgar's Battalion and White's Cavalry were camped in the fields on the west side of Lewisburg all about the junction of the roads. The two federal forces arrived at the junction of the roads at the same time. During the night they had captured some confederate pickets who had informed of the position of Edgar's troops. Other pickets had escaped and informed Col. Edgar of the approach, and though it was still dark there was no surprise on either side. The federal forces charged the confederate camp and those soldiers scattered and let them through so that no one was hurt in this battle. The confederates retreated east and Captain Powell was ordered to pursue the rebel cavalry, and this was done with such promptness, that about daylight on that morning the people of Lewisburg were treated to a horse race on Main Street, the confederate cavalry fleeing before the federal horsemen. The chase was kept up to within a mile of White Sulphur Springs, and resulted in the capture of a number of prisoners. There was no number mentioned in the accounts that I found.

This was a second battle on the road just west of Lewisburg and there is no doubt about it. The confederates prevailed in the first battle and the federal forces in the second. These operations were leading up to a more serious encounter eleven days later.

After the second bout, the federal forces returned to Meadow Bluffs, and the confederates gravitated back to Lewisburg, where they occupied the west crest, which belonged to them. It will be remembered that the year before that both Wise and Floyd had left the Kanawha Valley to be occupied by federal troops, and that on the breaking up of winter, that the confederate armies were anxious to regain that valley. Salt was manufactured there and it was a prime necessity. And the federal forces by the same token were on their way to the east to whip Virginia back into the Union.

On the 16th day of May, 1862, Col. Crook, the Grey Fox, arrived at Meadow Bluff with other troops and proceeded to organize another brigade, the 3rd Brigade of the Kanawha Division, with three Ohio regiments and one West Virginia regiment. It has been stated that Crook had drilled his men hard during the previous winter and that they were in fine condition. He had moved forward quickly and marched through Lewisburg, the confederates making way for him politely, for Crook had the first hard-boiled army that had yet appeared on either side. They were winter drilled. They were allowed to march straight through the pike until they came to Jackson River, and it was then discovered that there were no confederate armies in that direction to be attacked. The only meat that they got that advance was six Moccasin Ranger captains, and the two officers and twenty-five men captured at Callahan Station. These fell to the federal army as prisoners.

At Jackson River Crook learned that a confederate army under Henry Heth was approaching the Midland Trail at right angles over the road that we now call the Seneca Trail. This was the army that had wintered in Mercer county and they were coming to take over the Midland Trail and the Kanawha Valley. Their line of march lay through Union and Ronceverte, and Crook saw that in marching east over the Allegheny Mountain that he had left the way open for a confederate army to march between his brigade and the rest of his division at Charleston and other points west.

So he fell back quickly to Meadow Bluff passing through Lewisburg before Heth arrived. Close on his heels followed the confederate battalion which took up its place on the eastern ridge overlooking Lewisburg.

At that time Lewisburg had a population of about eight hundred persons and was one of the most important towns west of the Allegheny mountain in Virginia. It had six stores, one newspaper, three churches and one academy. The Supreme Court of Appeals met in regular session there. It had a big brick tavern, and it was much like a city as was to be found on the western waters.

Henry Heth and George Crook, the leading characters in this campaign had been classmates at West Point. Lewisburg was to prove to be the place of trial by combat between the two trained officers, and was destined to see the defeat and ultimate end of Heth's military advancement, while Crook was to commence there a military career second to none that was to continue through the Civil War and down to the year 1889, when he departed this life with the rank of major-general, and fame that is as everlasting as the hills.

I have one document in my possession that indicates Heth had arrived in Lewisburg over a month before in person and had looked over the troops at that place, for it is recorded that a delegation of prominent citizens from Pocahontas county had waited on him there and made complaint that while they were confederates and for the south, that by an act of the legislature of virginia, authorizing the formation of companies of rangers or home guards, that Pocahontas county had been overrun by rangers and that the farmers of that county were being deprived of their horses and other property by their own rangers, and unless the Commonwealth of virginia could call off these dogs of war, they demanded the right to send for their young men then serving in the confederate armies to come home and protect the farm from these depredations.

Heth required them to make the charges in writing which they did, the specifications being dated at Lewisburg, April 4, 1862, and signed by William Skeen, prosecuting attorney of Pocahontas county. he blames the hasty legislature that made the rangers possible, and the force that he complained of was the fameous Tuning company, which was afterwards surrounded and wiped out in Webster county. He charges Tuning with killing three men, Arbogast, Buzzard, and Alderman. With three robberies. Fifteen or twenty horses stolen. Heth forwarded the papers to Richmond.

On the morning of May 23, 1862, Heth marched his army by way of Ronceverte and in the early morning placed his line on the east crest just as Crook and his brigade came to the western brow and deployed to the right and to the left so that he formed a line of his hard-boiled infantry in a line along about where the woman's college buildings stand. Then as now, two principle roads run north and south through Lewisburg. One runs by the courthouse and one by the military school. The one by the military school is about half way up the eastern hill, and at that time it had heavy rail fences on it. Heth has been criticised for not posting his infantry behind these fences. He had them much higher up. There was a great rye field up the hill from these fences and it was a forward season and it was high enough to hide a crouching man, and as they tell it to me, Heth's men tried to take advantage of this cover when it was too late.

There was heavy timber out toward Mr. H. Frazier's country place, and this was the only cover that Heth had, and that did him but little good when they crumpled up his right wing, and defeated him. The confederates had some artillery and they fired many shells into the town. One shell burst in the vestibule of the negro church. Another went down the chimney of the Cary home, and the Cary girls, the belles of the town, went to work while the battle was raging its fiercest, to keep the mansion from burning down.

Crook had built sheds for drilling his soldiers the previous winter and had worked them hard. After the heavy firing began and the shell and minie balls were raining down on his command, he moved the infantry forward and secured the road that leads by the military school, and his men sheltering behind the rail fences poured in a devastating fire on Heth's men at from two to three hundred yards range, and it speedily became so deadly that flesh and blood could not stand it and Heth's men turned and faded away towards Ronceverte, on the road on which they had so recently marched to the battle ground. As Heth so sadly reported to the War Office, that after being allowed to pick his place, and with a vastly superior force, he had been defeated.

When the confederates gave way, then came a spectacular charge. It will be remembered that Main Street lies at right angles and across the hollow that is Lewisburg, and that for an hour or so, Gen. Heth had been rolling cannon balls down that street towards Crook, like a lot of bowling balls, but when the galling fire from the rail fences put him out of that, five hundred blue clad cavalrymen charged the whole length of that street and hung on the flanks of the fleeing confederates. That was the grand finale, and it was a day full of sorrow for Lewisburg, for it was solid for the south.

One of the charging cavalrymen rode too close to the edge of the road, and his horse slipped on a flagstone and fell side ways, rolling the rider over into the front yard of a residence, where he had to be helped up.

I suppose the only living man who saw that battle is Marcellus Zimmerman. He was eleven years old and was out in the center of the battlefield during the whole fight riding a stickhorse and playing that he was a horse soldier.

After the fight was over on that beautiful May morning, the work of gathering up the dead and wounded began. Many were found in the deep rye. Col. Edgar was shot through. His blood-stained sword is still to be seen in Ronceverte. The wounded were cared for by surgeons and the town people. The dead were laid out on the floor of the two churches, the old stone church, and the colored church.

In this short and swift fight lasting not over

thirty minutes, the confederate loss was 80 killed, 100 wounded, 157 prisoners, 4 cannon, 25 horses, and 300 stands of small arms. The federal loss was 13 killed, 50 wounded, and 6 prisoners.

The federal cavalry drove the confederates across the Greenbrier river at Ronceverte. Heth reformed his army at Union and rested there for a month and Crook tried to bring on another battle on June 24th, at Union, but Heth retired over Peters Mountain.

At Lewisburg, the federal troops that charged up the hill were three regiments of Ohio Volunteer Infantry, the 36th, 44th, and 47th.

Among the confederates at Lewisburg was the father of J.H.Buzzard, of Huntersville, who has held many important offices in this county.

Crook remained in Lewisburg for sixty days after the battle and then fell back to his camp at Meadow Bluffs.

Of all the battlefields that I have studied, I know of none quite so dramatic as Lewisburg. Fought in a mountain town, before breakfast, and combining rifle shooting, artillery fire, infantry charges, and cavalry, all in a sleepy little city whose inhabitants awoke to hear the cannons boom and the rifles speak, and who had no time to do anything in the way of escape until it was all over.

I see I did not finish what I started to say about the Tunings, the dreaded outlaws mentioned by Mr. Skeen to Gen. Heth. These were three brothers out of the northwest who ravaged this section of the State for years during the war. There were three brothers, Al, Fred and Jack Tuning. The name was probably Chewning. They had the settlers buffaloed and they would come to a farm with their followers and demand to be kept, and no one was brave or foolhardy enough to deny them. They harried the country for years, but finally they were surrounded by about thirty federal soldiers on leave. The outlaws were in the house of James Dyer, on Gauley River, in Webster county. James Dyer was one of the best citizens. He was the first county superintendent of schools of Webster county. The Tunings attempted to run and Al and Fred were shot and killed. Jack got away and went to Ohio where he landed in the pen. The Tunings were wiped out March 4, 1864.

Now as to the third battle of Tuckwiler Hill. Hu Maxwell says that on April 19, 1863, that the battle of Tuckwiler Hill was fought. You will note this was almost a year after the other battles. The federal dispatches call this the battle of Brushy Ridge, a hill about five miles west of Tuckwiler Hill, and it is probable that it was fought between the two places, for the federals rode into an ambuscade and suffered severely. Gen. E.P. Scammon in command of the Kanawha Division ordered Col. Paxton to reconnoiter Lewisburg, and as he rode with the 2nd West Virginia Cavalry, he encountered Edgar's Battalion and suffered a loss of fourteen men as well as losing a large number of prisoners. Col. Paxton, a gallant officer, on making his report to Gen. Scammon was summarily dismissed from the service by the irate general. Gen. Powell took his place and I have a chapter on that remarkable officer about ready to deliver.

Here is the truth about the Tuckwiler Hill fights. On one side in each one of the three encounters was the 2nd West Virginia Volunteer cavalry, and on the other the noted Edgar's Battalion. This is the reason that they run together in the minds of the careless historian.

Chapter XII of the book, A Famous Command: The Richmond Light Infantry Blues, *which was written by Colonel John A. Cutchins in 1934 and published by Garrett & Massie in Richmond contains a great deal of interesting information on the initial campaign of the unit during the western Virginia campaigns. The Richmond Light Infantry Blues was the pre-eminent militia company in the state at the time of the outbreak of the Civil War and was commanded by the son of the recent governor of the state, Henry A. Wise, who was also the commander of the Confederate expeditionary force which moved into the Kanawha Valley in western Virginia to retain it for the Confederacy.*

Colonel Cutchins made use of the company's records and put together an interesting account of the first Civil War campaign of the Richmond Light Infantry Blues.

Mustered Into Service of the Confederacy- Campaign in Western Virginia - Christmas in Richmond

On Monday, the 17th of June, 1861, the Company by its voluntary vote was regularily mustered into service of the Confederate States of America at Lewisburg, Virginia, for the duration of the war. It was ordered to be ready to march on the next day.

On the morning of the 18th the company took up its march from Lewisburg to Gauley Bridge, covering twenty-two miles that day and, after a day's rest, the remaining twenty-four miles. It remained at Gauley's Bridge until Tuesday, the 25th of June, when it advanced twenty-two miles in one day to the Kanawha River.[16]

In view of the frequent movements of the Company, as well as of the fact that there were no actual battles fought during this period, it seems appropriate to relate the company's activities as they appear in the Record Book:

Wednesday, June 26th. This morning we changed our mode of travel from the march by land to that of steam on the Kanawha River. When we arrived at Malden we found a number of ladies saluting us with flags and the waving of handkerchiefs. We landed and presented arms to the Ladies. They then persuaded Captain Wise to let his company remain and take dinner, which was agreed to, and in a few hours they had a sumptous meal prepared for us, to which we did ample justice, our appetites having been wheted by a long fast. After dinner we bade our

---

16 Cutchings wrote an excellent history, but his distances are slightly inaccurate. Lewisburg is approximately 70 miles from Gauley Bridge and the Kanawha River begins there at the junction of the New and Gauley Rivers. The final twenty-two miles mentioned probably brought the Confederate column to Gauley Bridge.

fair entertainers good bye and steamed away for Charleston, at which place we arrived at 4 P.M. and were stationed at the Court House. There we lodged for the night.

Thursday, June 27th. We walked about town in A.M. and in the evening moved out to Camp Lee one mile from town.

Saturday, June 29th. We received marching orders at 9 o'clock P.M. and were soon on our way. Where? We knew not. We walked nearly all night.

Sunday, June 30th. We were overtaken at daybreak by Captain Brock's Cavalry horses which had been sent for our use. We were soon mounted and on our way to Ripley, 40 miles from Charleston, and arrived about night; but instead of meeting Yankees, we were met by the cheers of the inhabitants. The Yankees had left in the morning. We slept that night in the court house.

Monday, July 1st. We were ordered to mount again this morning and under command of Capt. Patton, the Blues and another company, left for the enemy's camp. We went to Cottage Mills about 3 miles from the Ohio River expecting to find Yankees. When about one mile from the place we expected to find them, we dismounted and formed in line of battle ready for an attack, but no Yankees were to be found. But as we were returning they fired at us from an ambush. We returned the fire; the Yankees fled from our presence. Nobody hurt on our side. At night we returned on foot giving our horses to another company who had come to our relief, and took up the line of march for Ripley.

Tuesday, July 2nd. Remained at Ripley.

July 4th. General Wise and Staff arrived today with reinforcements and the line of march was back again to Ripley, Jackson County. Arrived the 6th in Ripley and at night was called to arms, but it proved to be a false alarm. Remained at Ripley, but was awakened by another false alarm.

Monday[17],July 5th. . It was the intention of our commander to make an attack on the Yankees at Ravenswood[18], 11 miles distant, but then concluded not to do so, and started our own return to Charleston and returned as far as Seissonville, or Sessionville.

Friday, July 9th. Marched to Charleston and encamped at Camp Lee and remained until the 13th.

Before quoting further from the company's records it will be well to review briefly the situation in western Virginia at this time. The importance of that section to the Southern cause was fully realized by the Confederate authorities. Political as well as strategic reasons dictated the necessity of sending a large and efficient force to hold it for the Confederacy. The background of the people of the eastern and western parts of the state was quite different. To this was added the physical barrier interposed by the Alleghany Mountains. The result, naturally was to develop divergent interests and views. In fact, the entire section

---

17 The day of the month seems to be in error.

18 The following extract from a letter written by General George B. McClellan, commanding the Department of the Ohio, dated July 5th, 1861, is of interest:

"Four companies at Ravenswood repulsed O.J. Wise night before last. I hope that he determined to renew the attempt, as in that case he will have been cut off by a column of 1200 men under Col. Morton that were to reach Ripley from Letart's at 2 P.M. yesterday. I shall not be surprised to learn before this letter is closed that he is captured."

The following was written by McClellan on July 6:

"A well concerted movement to catch O.J. Wise, with his 800 men, at Ripley, on the 4th, failed in consequence of the rapidity with which the rebels fled at the first notice of the approach of danger."

The reference to O.J. Wise could have meant his father, Henry A. Wise, the Confederate commander, but O. J. Wise was a sufficient catch at this stage in the war to warrant the special attention given him by the Federal commander.

west of the mountains and in the northern part of the Kanawha Valley was strongly pro-Union in its sympathies. However, both sides quickly realized the strategic value of holding western Virginia. In as much as Ohio had been largely settled by Virginians it was hoped that a vigorous and successful campaign in western Virginia would have large political implications and would deny to the Union forces from the Western States the opportunity of advancing down the valley of the Kanawha against the Confederacy.

The Confederates sought to hold or cut the Baltimore and Ohio Railroad, in the northern portion of Virginia, and the Virginia and Tennessee, in the south central portion. That done, the Union authorities would be compelled to rely almost entirely on the one trunk line, skirting the great lakes, for transportation of troops and supplies from the central and northwestern sections of the United States. Furthermore, the main salt deposits of the Confederacy were located in Western Virginia and protection had to be provided for them. So, it will be seen that the Blues were embarking upon a campaign of utmost importance.

The Confederate strategy was to command the natural means of advance and communication by way of the Kanawha Valley. Accordingly it was planned to mobilize two forces, one near Monterey, commanding the main route to Clarksburg, the other at Lewisburg, commanding the approach to Charleston, both by road and by the Great Kanawha River.

It was largely because of the political aspects of the situation in western Virginia that General Wise, despite his lack of military training and experience, was sent there. Someone in whom the people had confidence had to be dispatched to this section if it was to be held for the Confederacy. Wise appeared to be the most available general officer for this duty. The handicaps, however, were too serious to be overcome by anyone. Important points were in the hands of Union troops before the Confederate forces were organized or equipped. The letter of instructions directing General Wise to procede to the Kanawha Valley contained the following: "You must needs rely upon the arms among the people to supply the requisite armament, and upon their valor and knowledge of the country, as a substitute for organization and discipline." Perhaps it was fortunate that General Wise had not had previous military experience, for unless he had, combined with his natural courage and indomitable will, an extraordinary degree of optimism, he might well have felt that his was an impossible task. In war there is no "substitute for organization or discipline."

Upon arrival he promptly issued an invitation to the inhabitants to come to the aid of the State, and proceeded to organize his command. In view of the difficulties facing him his success in raising his force was remarkable. On the 8th of July he reported 2,700 troops under him. About half the number was utilized to form two regiments. In addition there were seven independent companies of about sixty men each, a battalion of about 400 and three companies of mounted rangers numbering 170. Fortunately he had with him some excellent officers of experience to help in the work of organizing and training his forces. Colonel Christopher Q. Tompkins, A West Pointer, was with Wise in western Virginia while Colonel J. Lucius Davis, another West Pointer attached to his command, remained in Richmond for the purpose of assisting at that place. Colonels Charles F. Henningsen and Frank Anderson, who had distinguished themselves in active service in Nicargua, were also assigned to Wise's Brigade.

At the time of the arrival of the Blues, General Garnett, commanding in the northern theatre of operations, had been defeated by the Union forces under General McClellan at Laurel Hill, on the 9th of August, and forced to retire. Garnett's force was overtaken at Carrick's Ford, on the 13th, and again vigorously attacked. General Garnett, rallying his men, was killed. General Loring then was assigned to command. He subsequently took up a defensive position at Valley Mountain. There after the northern theatre was occupied defensively by the Confederates for the time being, while the force in the southern theatre took the offensive.

General Wise advanced up the Kanawha Valley by way of the Gauley Bridge and threw up entrenchments at Tyler Mountain, about five miles west of Charleston, located at the confluence of the Elk and Kanawha Rivers and the only town of importance in that entire section.

The federal troops selected to invade this region consisted of several Ohio and Kentucky regiments, under the command of General Jacob D. Cox. This force had been concentrated at Galliopolis and Point Pleasant, at the mouth of the Kanawha River, where it empties into the Ohio. On the 11th of July, Cox began his movement up the valley, going by steamers as far as the river was navigable. One regiment had been ordered to proceed from Guyandotte, about seventy miles below the mouth of the Kanawha; another, had been ordered to Ravenwood, about fifty miles above, and was to advance to Ripley. The entire force under Cox numbered between three and four thousand men, well-equipped and organized.

A detachment of the Blues had been sent to reconnoitre Ripley. Similar groups had been sent in various directions, but there was no real skirmishing until the 16th of July, when two mounted companies of Wise's Command, numbering 120 men, under the command of Lieutenant-Colonel John Clarkson, encountered a detachment of 200 of the enemy infantry, along the pike in the neighborhood of the Pocataligo, and drove them to the top of the mountain, killing eight and wounding a considerable number of others. At this time the Confederate forces were posted on both sides of the Kanawha and as high up as the mouth of the Coal River. Wise had stationed his men at those points as well as on the Elk River, and at Gauley Bridge, Sommersville and on the Birch River to circuit the enemy approaching up the Kanawha. The numerous mountain passes and cliffs characterizing this section offered many excellent points for defense. On the other hand,the numerous lateral roads which entered the valley from every direction were most favorable to the enemy for flank atacks. The eastern gateway to the valley was at Gauley Bridge which spanned the Gauley River just above the point of its union with the New River to form the Kanawha. It was necessary to guard this point carefully, as well as the roads leading to the rear,to avoid the possiblilty of being cut off by McClellan who was then operating against Garnett.

On the afternoon of the 17th of July, Major George S. Patton, in command of 500 Confederates, encountered the Federal force at Scarey Creek, below the Coal RIver. The federal troops were commanded by Colonel Norton of the 21st, and Colonel Lowe of the 12th, Ohio Infantry. The hostile forces were separated by a deep ravine. The Confederates were thrown into some confusion in the early part of the action by an attempted flank movement of the enemy, but were quickly rallied. Major Patton was wounded and the command devolved upon Captain Jenkins. While the Federal force was superior in numbers and artillery, it was repulsed after a short engagement, leaving about thirty dead and a number of prisoners. Among the latter were three colonels, a lieutenant-colonel and two captains. The retreating Federals were pressed for some distance, but finally were able to cross to the north side of the Kanawha and camped near the mouth of the Pocataligo River. General Wise, with three troops of cavalry and 650 infantry and artillery, determined to follow up the victory gained at Scarey Creek and to advance that night, but finding three regiments of the enemy strongly entrenched behind the Pocataligo and learning of the overwhelming artillery strength of the enemy, he abandoned the idea of pushing the attack.

The disasterous retreat of General Garnett's command after his defeat put Wise in a perilous position. Cox was in his front and McClellan might attack him in the rear. He would thus be caught between two enemy forces.

Accordingly, Wise fell back from Charleston, on the 24th of July, and, on the 27th, crossed the Gauley Bridge which he burned behind him.

Cox promptly occupied the lower end of the valley, advancing as far as Charleston the day after Wise had retired. On the 29th of July he took possession of Gauley Bridge, about thirty-eight miles distant, where he accumulated supplies in order to stand a seige if necessary.

Wise's retreat from the Kanawha Valley had apparently been made in good order and without serious loss. A half an hour, however, after he had fallen back from Tyler Mountain the enemy took possession and nearly succeeded in cutting off Colonel Tompkins' volunteer regiment of about 700 men at Coal River. This force succeeded in making good its escape, though compelled to abandon and set fire to the steamer in which it was moving up the Kanawha.

From Gauley Bridge, Wise proceeded along the James River Turnpike to White Sulphur Springs. a distance of about seventy miles. It was expected that the enemy would advance by the way of Lewisburg, not far from the White Sulphur Springs, to threaten the Southwestern, or the Virginia Central Railroad. Wise deemed it advisable, therefore, to make a stand in the vicinity of Lewisburg until the junction between his forces and those of Floyd or Loring could be effected.

Furthermore, the condition of the Confederate forces at this time, deficient as they were in supplies of every kind, particularily ammunition and transportation, and without shoes or proper clothing, made this course necessary until they could have the opportunity to refit and reorganize. According to Wise's report to the War Department "it was a secret which neither of us (Colonel Tompkins and himself) dared to tell in the Kanwha Valley, that at no time of the whole sixty days while we were marching and countermarching, posting and counterposting, scouting and fighting, day in and day out, in a valley the hardest to defend and the easiest to be attacked in the topography of the country, could we at any time have fired in any general action ten rounds of ammunition in our joint commands."

The following account of the events from the 13th of July to the middle of August is taken from the Company's Record Book:

Saturday, July 13th. Marched to Tyler's Mountain, 5 miles from town, today. We commenced throwing up breastworks and remained there until Wednesday the 17th[19] when at night we took up our line of march in pursuit of the enemy with about 1000 men under command of Col. McCausland. We went as far as Scarey where a fight had taken place on yesterday but the Yankees had retired to their breastworks and our force under Col. McCausland concluded to return to camp and remained at Tyler Mountain until Wednesday, July 24th.

July 24th. Information was received that the enemy was approaching and orders were given to get ready for action. We packed up and were ordered to our positions, but had been there a short time, when we were informed that the enemy was within a mile of us. We were waiting impatiently for them to appear, when we were ordered to retire, and thus passed through Charleston, leaving it to the fate of Yankee hospitality. We travelled all night, and on Friday, 26th of July, arrived at Gauley Bridge.

Saturday, July 27th. We left Gauley Bridge at 4 P.M.

---

19 The following came from a report of General McClellan's:

Hdqs, Dept. of the Ohio
Camp near Huttonsville, Va.
July 15, 1861.

I have sent by Major Marcey a brief account of the operations which have resulted in the dispersion of the rebels in this portion of Western Virginia, and in driving them completely beyond the mountains. I am in constant expectation of hearing from General Cox that his efforts to drive the Wises out of the Kanawha Valley and occupy Gauley Bridge have been crowned with success. Should there be any delay in that quarter I will take a few regiments and move by Weston, Bulltown, Sutton, &c., on the Gauley Bridge, in order to bring the matter to a speedy conclusion.

in a new Regiment[20] under the command of Lieut. Colonel John H. Richardson, and travelled all night in the rain with knapsacks on our backs.

We arrived at Boyd's Mills 5 miles from Lewisburg, and remained there until August 2nd, when we took up the line of march for the White Sulphur Springs, and reached there on Saturday, August 3rd, resting, recruiting and drilling until Thursday, 15th. By command of Brig. General J.B. Floyd, the "Wise Legion," with the Blues at their head, took the line of march again for the West and went as far as Sewells Mountain, from thence to DogWood Gap 16 miles from Gauley Bridge. Thursday, 25th August.[21] Was ordered to "Carnifax Ferry" to meet the enemy, but as usual they had left.

From the 1st of August to the 20th of the same month, remained principally at "DogWood gap," and about the 1st of September had a slight skirmish near the "Hawks Nest." Went with a "Flag of truce" to the "Hawks Nest" next day.

It is difficult to visualize the conditions existing in western Virginia. The Union forces were attempting, and with considerable success, to ingratiate themselves with the people and to encourage a sentiment favorable to their cause. The Confederates, on the other hand, were poorly supplied and equipped; in fact, scarcely supplied and equipped at all, and were attempting to recruit their forces from the citizens of the counties in which they were operating. At all times they were faced by greatly superior numbers of well equipped troops, with unlimited supplies. In addition to this, friction between Generals Wise and Floyd, both former governors of Virginia, and men of great independence of mind, developed to such an extent as to make any cooperation between them utterly impossible.

General Floyd had been Secretary of War in the cabinet of President Buchanan. He had succeeded

---

20 46th Regiment. The Blues became Company A.

21 Either the day of the week or the month is in error.

Jefferson Davis as head of the War Department. When Davis became President of the Confederate States he wired Floyd, a southwest Virginia politician, asking if he could raise a brigade in his section, the men furnishing their own arms. Floyd accepted the commission and promptly entered into direct negotiations with the other Southern States to furnish him arms. While Secretary of War he was twice under fire and, altogether, was quite a tempestuous person. Why the Confederate authorities, knowing as they must have, the characteristics of the two men, could have expected them to cooperate is a mystery. Furthermore, the continued rains and the impassable roads enforced immobility and contributed to the discord.

The condition of Wise's command is set forth in a letter to General Lee, which also supplements the description of the movement as given in the Company Record Book:

Bunger's Mill, Va.
Four miles west of Lewisburg,
August 1, 1861

General R.E. Lee, Commanding, &c.:

Sir: I am here, falling back to Covington, under orders left to my discretion by General Cooper. My situation in the Kanawha Valley was critical in the extreme. After the Scarey affair the enemy fell back and were re-enforced strongly. They increased to five thousand. At Gauley I had one thousand; at Coal, one thousand; and at Elk, and within two miles thereon about two thousand. Thus divided necessarily the enemy could attack,when he chose, double or quadruple my numbers, with far better arms and supplies. I found they were collecting some fifteen thousand troops at Weston and moving to Summersville, at the same time moving up the Kanawha Valley and jamming me at any point I might select to occupy. I determined a prompt retreat, where my forces could cooperate with Generals Loring or Floyd. In thirty minutes after we fell back from Tyler's Mountain the enemy took possession, and nearly succeeded in cutting off seven hundred of Colonel Tompkins' command at Coal. They escaped, and burned the steamer on which they were moving up the river. Save an accident from the defiant disobedience of orders by the lieutenant of McCullough Rangers, losing some baggage and causing the death of one of my sick and the wounding of several of my men, the retreat has been, upon the whole, creditably in order.

We left Charleston last Wednesday week (July 24) and Gauley last Saturday, destroying the bridges there behind us. This I was obliged to do by the great deficiency of transportation, owing to gross inefficiency of the quartermaster's department of my brigade. I have come on slowly. The men had marched and countermarched very much, and were sore and sadly worn out in shoes and clothing, and suffered for want of tents. We arrived here yesterday, leaving a strong rear guard of four infantry companies, attached to two hundred and fifty cavalry. They are scouting the enemy to their teeth. Last night my scouts reported that they were moving in three divisions, converging from Fayetteville, Gauley, and Summersville to a point on this turnpike a few miles back.

At Weston they have a force of fifteen thousand, and from Huttonsville movements are made to join those from Weston at Summersville, to concentrate some ten thousand troops on this road, directly moving on Lewisburg. We will check them all we can, but a force far larger and better organized than mine is as yet must be sent to do it effectually. From Charleston to this place the state volunteers under my command lost from three to five hundred men by desertion. But no man deserted from the Legion. I respectfully submit that I had better be allowed to organize the whole mass and incorporate the state volunteers with my legion in the Confederate service. I think the enemy will now threaten the Southwestern Railroad at New Berne, and then will make a base line from Gauley to Lewisburg.

The Kanawha valley is wholly disaffected and

traitorous. It was gone from Charleston down to Point Pleasant before I got there. Boone and Cabell are nearly as bad, and the state of things in Braxton, Nicholas, and part of Greenbrier is awful. The militia are nothing for warlike uses here. They are worthless who are true, and there is no telling who is true. You can not persuade these people that Virginia can or will ever reconquer the northwest, and they are submitting, subdued, and debased. I have falled back not a minute too soon. And let me say, we have worked and scouted far and wide and fought well, and marched all the shoes and clothes off our bodies, and find our old arms do not stand service. I implore for some (one thousand) stand of good arms, percussion muskets, sabers, pistols, tents, blankets, shoes, rifles, and powder.

Respectfully,
(signed) Henry A. Wise

On the same day General Floyd wrote to General Lee:

"Wise has fallen back. They will not allow it to be a retreat. I hear the enemy have fallen forward and with such rapidity that they occupied his camp, getting tents and camp equippage in fifteen minutes after our people left them. He is in Lewisburg on his way to Covington."

While at the White Sulphur an epidemic of measles which made great inroads, particularily upon the troops from the rural sections, added still further to the suffering and demoralization of Wise's command. In fact so great were the inroads of this disease that the effective strength was cut about fifty per cent. The report from Lieutenant Colonel J.H. Richardson, commanding the 46th Virginia Regiment, gives some idea of the devastating effect of this malady:

HDQRS. FIRST REGIMENT INFANTRY, WISE'S BRIGADE
Camp Dogwood, Va., August 26, 1861.

General: I have the honor to report that the remnant of

my command will be ready to move tomorrow morning by 9 o'clock. I regret that I have to offer an excuse for my regiment, but really think that it is not advisable to send it off as crippled as it is. If it should be called into action in its present condition the result might not prove satisfactory, and I feel that I should be censurable if I did not report these facts. I wish the command to do itself credit, and do not doubt that it will do so under any circumstances, but think it best just to give it a trial at first in its original strength. I beg leave herewith to submit the actual strength of my regiment, as per report of the company commanders: Company A, 39; Company B, 47; Company C, 29; Company D, 41; Company K, 39, amounting in the aggregate to 371 effective men, a little upwards of one-third of the whole command, the measles daily reducing the ranks at the rate of at least 25 a day. According to the report of the surgeon of the regment, it is owing to exposure and fatigue incident to rapid and forced marches. I have presented these facts as a matter of duty, and offer them for your consideration.

Very respectfully, your obedient servant,
(signed) J.H. Richardson
Lieut. Col. Forty-sixth Reg't., P.A.C., Comdg. First Inf., W.B.
To: Brig. Gen. H. A. Wise.

General Floyd was ordered by General Lee to join General Wise at White Sulphur Springs, on the 5th of August, and being the senior in point of service took command. Floyd promptly determined to move into the Kanawha Valley. This plan was strongly disapproved by Wise, who contended that it was a better policy to draw the enemy to the eastern part of the wild, mountainous country lying this side of Gauley, known as the Fayette Wilderness. This would impose upon the enemy the necessity for them to maintain their line of supplies by wagons over mountain roads. On the other hand, if the Confederates advanced it would be necessary for them to maintain their line of supplies over a considerable stretch of mountain road.

It was most unfortunate that a complete lack of

harmony existed between Generals Floyd and Wise. The latter applied to General Lee to separate his Legion from Floyd's command, representing that it had been originally intended as an independent partisan force. General Lee however declined to do this and again stressed the necessity of united action.

On the 13th of August, General Floyd, who had assumed command of all the forces designated to operate against the Kanawha Valley, ordered Wise to join him with his troops. The latter, however, alleging lack of supplies and transportation and sickness among his troops, did not join Floyd until the 16th. He then marched to Big Sewell Mountain with two of his regiments, leaving a third regiment and a regiment of state volunteers under Colonel Tompkins, to follow as soon as possible.

Floyd ordered Wise, on the 19th, to proceed with his force on the following day along the turnpike from Sewell Mountain in the direction of the Kanawha. Thereupon, Wise advanced his command about fifteen miles in the neighborhood of Sunday Road, leading to Carnifax Ferry, where his scouts reported that they had been fired upon. A detachment of cavalry reported having had a skirmish with the enemy near Piggott's Mill and another in the vicinity of the Hawk's Nest about six miles east of Gauley Bridge. He encountered a considerable force at the latter place and was compelled to retire.

The commands of Floyd and Wise were united at the foot of Gauley Mountain on the evening of the 21st of August. It was decided, after a conference between them, that Wise should proceed at three o'clock the following morning to attack the enemy at Carnifax ferry, on the Gauley River some twenty miles above its union with the New River. In the meantime, Floyd was to hold the front of the turnpike and join Wise at the Ferry after covering the train and artillery which had been left at Dogwood Gap. The move was promptly executed by Wise. After a seventeen mile march in ankle-deep mud he found the enemy had crossed the river, having destroyed and sunk one of the two ferry boats and cut the other adrift over the falls. Floyd was informed during the night that the enemy stationed at the south of the Ferry had marched to the mouth of the Gauley. He, thereupon, without notifying Wise, made a forced march by a shorter route than the one taken by Wise, and overtook him early on the morning of the 22nd, shortly after his arrival at the south of Carnifax Ferry. He had joined his command to a small amount of artillery and a hundred of Wise's cavalry. Floyd crossed the Gauley by means of the sunken ferry boat, and ordered Wise, with the remainder of the latters' command, to take position on the Turnpike to check the enemy.

On the 25th of August Floyd learned that Rosecrans had ordered the 7th Ohio Regiment, under Colonel E.B. Tyler, to approach in the direction of the ferry for the purpose of making an attack. He immediately ordered Wise to send one of his regiments to support him. Wise, although feeling he had an insufficient force for the performance of his own mission, had prepared to re-enforce Floyd on the morning of the 25th, when firing was heard in the direction of Piggot's Mill, near the foot of Saturday Road, leading to Carnifax from the James River Pike. Cavalry patrols reported the advance of the enemy. At this time the enemy force under Cox consisted of two regiments at Gauley Bridge, another along the Kanawha covering steamboat communications, with eight companies thrown forward along the Turnpike between Gauley's Bridge and Hawk's Nest where the roadway passed through a series of narrow defiles. A small body of Floyd's cavalry had advanced into the passes beyond Piggot's Mill and had narrowly escaped capture. Wise immediately started a force of infantry and three artillery pieces on a double-quick march. This force caused the enemy to fall back in the vicinity of the Hawk's Nest. On the morning of the 26th, about sunrise, Floyd with his force, re-enforced by the two volunteer regiments under Tompkins and McCausland, which had been sent him by Wise, fell upon Tyler who had advanced as far as Cross lanes, within two miles of the Confederate camp, and dispersed the Federal regiment, which was completely taken by surprise. The enemy lost some twenty or more killed and about one hundred prisoners.

Floyd, on the north side of the Gauley was now on the Federal line of communications between Rosecrans and Cox. Rosecrans had formed a chain of posts from Weston by way of Suttonsville prepared to unite with Cox at Gauley Bridge. Floyd anticipated an attack on the 31st and wrote Wise directing him to send further re-enforcements. Due to sickness and want of forage for the cavalry the available force under Wise's command had been reduced to barely eighteen hundred effectives. With these he had to guard the Turnpike in front of Cox as well as to watch the approaches from the south side of New River. In view of this he replied to Floyd explaining the situation and asking a re-consideration of the order. However, receiving a second order late in the day stating that the enemy was advancing, Wise moved to Carnifax, leaving only a small guard at Dogwood Gap. When he arrived at the cliffs overlooking the Ferry another communication from General Floyd was delivered to him. This stated that from more recent information it was not considered that a union of their forces was necessary at that time and ordered Wise back to Dogwood Gap, whether he went that afternoon. Although his men were weary from their march, Wise announced his intention of taking the Hawk's Nest on the following day. By doing so he would gain possession of Liken's Mill to grind wheat and corn for his troops as well as secure the approaches to Miller's Ferry leading across New River. This would enable him to communicate with the volunteer troops under General Chapman on the south side of the river.

On the 2nd of September, Wise marched from Dogwood Gap to Hamilton within a half mile of the Hawk's Nest. He then advanced along the Pike and drove the enemy beyond Big Creek, a distance of some thirteen miles. The enemy being re-enforced, Wise fell back to

Hamilton and encamped there and at Westlake's Creek, guarding the ferry. From that time until the 10th of September, when the battle of Carnifax Ferry was fought, the position of Floyd and Wise remained practically unchanged. Floyd was north of the Gauley and Wise, on the Turnpike, in the vicinity of the Hawk's Nest, in front of Cox.

Floyd received reports, on the 9th, of the approach of Rosecrans who was marching with three brigades from Clarksburg, with the mission either of joining Cox at Gauley Bridge or of attacking the Confederate force at Carnifax Ferry. Immediately, Floyd ordered Wise to send troops to his support, and the latter dispatched Colonel Tompkins with his regiment at once, though it had just been returned to him two days before at his urgent request.[22] Floyd furthermore ordered Wise to send him one thousand men from his Legion.

22

CAMP NEAR HAWK'S NEST
September 9, 1861 4 p.m.

GENERAL JOHN B. FLOYD, COMMANDING &c.

SIR: In obedience to your orders of yesterday, received at 8:30 o,clock a.m. today (though dated September 9, 1861, 1 o'clocka.m.) I have passed them to Colonel Tompkins, and he is on his march to join you at Carnifax Ferry. As to sending you one of the regiments of the Legion, I find it impossible to do so without endangering the safety of my command. I am now in front of the enemy, numbering from 2,000 to 3,000 men, and have three regiments, reduced by two companies from each left at Dogwood Gap, necessarliy left there, and by measles, to not more than 300 effective men each, and to a corps of artillery, numbering about 150, making in all, 1050 efficient forces, without a breastwork. It is very hazardous to remain where I am with this force, and ifone-third of it be called to re-enforce you at Carnifax, I shall have to fall back again to Dogwood Gap, lose all I gained by driving the enemy to Big Creek, and beyond all quick intelligence and easy communication with Generals Chapman and Beckley by Miller's Ferry, and all the advantages of a first-class mill to grind the meal and flour for my men, where both are difficult and costly to be obtained.

(signed) Henry A. Wise
Brigadier-General

Floyd furthermore ordered Wise to send him one thousand men from his Legion. This Wise declined to do because his effective infantry had been reduced by sickness and other causes to about 1,200, while six out of eight companies of his cavalry had been sent over New River to Loop Creek and Coal River.

On the 10th, about noon, Wise received a communication from Floyd asking why his orders of the previous day had not been complied with, and peremptorily ordering Wise to send 1,000 infantry and a battery of artillery with all possible speed. To this communication Wise answered from Hamilton:

"Mr. Carr hasjust handed my yours of today at 12:05 P.M. It found me here, called to meet the advance of the enemy, who are reported to 44 threaten my picket at the Hawk's Nest, and all my force of three regiments of infantry, a corps of artillery, and two companies of cavalry are under arms , to prevent, if possible, an obvious attempt to turn our right flank and pass us at the Turnpike, most probably to gain Carnifax Ferry in your rear. Under these circumstances, I shall, upon my legitimate responsibility, exercise a sound discretion whether to obey your peremptory orders of today, or not."

Selecting a position sheltered by woods and undergrowth from the enemy's view, Floyd had thrown up temporary entrenchments near Carnifax. Rosecrans, who had come by way of Summersville and had marched seventeen and a half miles that day, with three brigades of his troops, began a reconnaissance of Floyd's position about three o'clock in the afternoon. A spirited engagement then was begun which lasted until nightfall. The federal forces assaulted vigorously despite the nature of the ground, but were repulsed by Floyd whose troops behaved with much coolness and courage. The Union casualties amounted to seventeen killed and one hundred and forty-one wounded, while the Confederate force suffered only a negligible loss.

Floyd sent Wise an order at eight o'clock on the night of the Carnifax engagement directing that he be re-enforced by all of Wise's troops, save one regiment. The message was received after midnight. On the morning of the 11th Wise advanced toward Carnifax and, when about half way to the Ferry, received verbal orders from Floyd to return to Dogwood Gap. Floyd had determined during the night of the engagement that his position was too precarious in the face of a superior force, and therefore withdrew his command to the south side of the Gauley under cover of darkness.

As a result of a conference held in Floyd's camp between himself and General Wise on the 12th of September it was decided that both commands would fall back to the top of Big Sewell Mountain, about seventeen miles east of Dogwood Gap and thirty-two miles from Gauley Bridge. The commands, with the exception of six companies of Wise's cavalry, numbering 240 men under Colonel J. Lucius Davis, thereupon retreated to Sewell Mountain, reaching Big Sewell on the 14th. Floyd encamped on the summit of the mountain while Wise selected a position on the eastern slope, or what was called Camp Defiance.

On the 15th and 16th of September, Floyd's forces were engaged in throwing up breastworks on Big Sewell. However, General Floyd suddenly determined that his position was not a very satisfactory one because of its exposed character. Acordingly, on the night of the 16th he retreated with 3,000 men to Meadow Bluff, in the direction of Lewisburg. General Wise did not have suitable transportation to move his supplies and he, thereupon, disregarded the order of Floyd to bring up the latter's rear. Wise claims that he was strengthened in his course by the wet weather and the dissatisfaction of the troops at any idea of giving further ground in the face of the enemy. In fact most of the officers of the Legion openly stated that if compelled to fall back any further they would resign. On the 18th, General Wise addressed the troops of the Legion, stating in substance that whenever he had retreated here-to-fore it had been in obedience to superior orders; that he was determined to make a stand; that his force consisted only of 1,700 infantry and artillery against an enemy alleged to be 15,000 strong; that he believed his men must be prepared to fight two or three or several to one; and even if the enemy were in the numbers reported the position admitted of successful defense, and he had determined to defend it to the last. He warned that they would probably be attacked front and rear for successive days, and demanded that any officer or soldier who felt doubtful of the result or unwilling to stand by him step forward. He delivered his speech successively to the three regiments of infantry and to the artillery. It was received with the wildest enthusiasm and not a single individual member of the Legion failed to respond. Whereupon, the provisions and baggage wagons were withdrawn to a safe position and the camp was strengthened on all sides. There the Legion remained until about the 20th when it was re-enforced by the arrival of Captain Romers' artillery company with one gun, and one Virginia, one North Carolina and three Georgia companies which swelled the Legion's strength to over 2,000 men.

On the 21st of September, General Robert E. Lee, having joined Floyd at Meadow Bluff, wrote[23] Wise urging

---

23

CAMP AT MEADOW BLUFF, VIRGINIA
September 21, 1861.

General HENRY A. WISE,
Wise's Legion, Camp on Big Sewell, Virginia.

I have just arrived at this camp, and regret to find the forces not united. I know nothing of the relative advantage of the points occupied by yourself and General Floyd, but as far as I can judge our united forces are not more than one-half of the strength of the enemy. Together they may not be able to withstand his assault. It would be the height of imprudence to submit them separately to his attack. I am told by General Floyd your position is a very strong one. This one I have him to unite his troops with those of General Floyd. In reply, Wise expressed his willingness to unite with Floyd at whatever point might be thought best, but asked General Lee to examine his position at Little Sewell before ordering him back to Meadow Bluff. Wise pointed out, furthermore, that it was improbable that the enemy would advance by the Wilderness Road instead of the Turnpike. He estimated their number at about 7,000 men, and felt that the joint forces of General Floyd and himself were amply able to check this force at Little Sewell. On the following day General Lee rode over to Wise's camp and after inspecting his position directed him to hold it until further orders. The peculiar formation of Little Sewell prevented the possibility of a flank attack and made it necessary for the enemy to make a frontal attack up the narrow gorge between precipitious mountain sides. The surface of Big Sewell, however, was a large flat area exposed on the side.

The enemy appeared, on the afternoon of the 23rd, and began to drive in the Confederate pickets. Wise promptly notified General Lee at Meadow Bluff. The latter at first did not appear to credit the report that the enemy was advincing in full force. On the afternoon of the 24th, General Lee, after the receipt of further information from

---

not examined, but it seems to have the advantage of yours, in commanding the Wilderness road and the approach to Lewisburg, which I think is the aim of General Rosecrans. I beg, therefore, if it is not too late, that the troops be united, and that we conquer or die together. You have spoken to me of want of consultation and concert; let that pass till the enemy is driven back, and than, as far as I can, all shall be arranged. I expect this of your magnaminity. Consult that and the interest of our cause, and all will go well.

With high respect, your obedient servant,
(signed) R.E. Lee
General, Commanding.

General Wise, arrived at Little Sewell with re-enforcements and began driving in the Confederate pickets. Wise promptly notified General Lee at Meadow Bluff[24]. The latter at first did not appear to credit the report that the enemy was advancing in full force. On the afternoon of the 24th, General Lee, after the receipt of further information from General Wise, arrived at Little Sewell with re-enforcements of four regiments.

---

24 CAMP ON SEWELL, VA., September 23, 1861

General R.E. Lee, Commanding Forces, &c.

General: The enemy are in strong force on the Big Sewell, I believe in full force (of at least 3,000 men), and a scout just in from Nichol's Mill says 7,000 are reported there. I saw the masses crossing the top of Big Sewell, with artillery and cavalry. We could see about four regiments, and now count thirty camp fires. Their advance commenced firing at mine about one-half hour or an hour by the sun. I cannot retire my baggage wagons or other present incumbrances...My cavalry has crossed New River to this side, and there are none of the enemy on the Old State road. Every few hours I get reports from Nichol's Mill, and there have not been seen any but a few stragglers there. The idea of the enemy passing from Sunday road to the Wilderness road by Nichol's Mill is simply absurd. There is hardly a trail there. If one, no army could possibly pass it that would startle a hare. I am compelled to stand here and fight as long as I can endure and ammunition lasts. All is at stake with my command, and it shall be sold dearly.

I am, very respectively,
(signed) Henry A. Wise

September 23, 1861

Major General R.E. Lee, Commanding, &c.

General: I am directed by General Wise to say that the enemy in very heavy columns has occupied the top of Sewell Mountain. Infantry, artillery, and cavalry are all plainly visible from our camp, about 1 mile distant. They have not as yet opened fire, and are reported by some of our cavalry as fortifying. When my last letter of to-day was written, I had just returned from a mission of truce, and the enemy came as fast as I did.

With great respect,
(signed) Nat Tyler
Lieutenant-Colonel, Infantry, C.S. Army

General Wise wrote:

"By this time the enemy had received more reenforcements swelling their number probably to more than 6,000, and their scouts pushed close to our lines, occasioning frequent sharp skirmishes, in all of which our men and officers acquitted themselves to my entire satisfaction."

On the afternoon of the 25th Wise, on the field of battle, received an order from the President directing him to transfer his command to Floyd and report to Richmond. He set out the following morning, arriving two days later.

Barton H. Wise, in his *The Life of Henry A. Wise*, makes this pertinent comment upon the campaign in Western Virgina and upon General Wise:

"The campaign in that section had not been a successful one and Wise failed to meet the expectations of his admirers. More than one circumstance had made against Confederate success beyond the Alleghanies, and General Lee himself was destined to return to Richmond later on with greatly diminished reputation. It can hardly be said that the assignment of either Floyd or Wise to command the Kanawha region was dictated by the soundest judgement, and political motives doubtless largely controlled their selection. Wise had been too long in public life to divest himself of his former habits at once, and his letters during this period often suggest characteristics begotten by campaigning of another sort. His excitable temper and apparent lack of appreciation of the prompt obedience required of a soldier by his superiors in command were, doubtless, a source of frequent annoyance and embarrassment to both Generals Lee and Floyd; yet it is idle to endeavor as some southern writers have attempted, to fasten the failure of the Western Virginia expeditions upon him. The true reasons for this failure are to be found in a variety of unfavorable conditions, rather than in the faults of any one officer. The Federals had been much more prompt than the Confederates in occupying this territory, which was far more accessible to them; and after the defeat of Garnett by McClellan, the real key to the Kanawha Valley was lost to the South. Had the force under the last named officer been held at bay, the Confederates could without much difficulty have retained control of that valley as far westward as the Ohio; and it is probable that considerable number of inhabitants would have enlisted in the Southern army.

Throughout the campaign, Wise had retained unabated the confidence of the troops under his command, and if he was deficient in military training, he did not lack true courage, or the faculty of inspiring his men with zeal for the cause in which they were engaged, under circumstances most trying. One other quality of a military leader he possessed more than in ordinary degree. He had an excellent topographical knowledge and the faculty which enables some men to know instinctively the course of mountains, rivers, and streams; while his thorough understanding of the various roads, in the sections where he was operating, enabled him correctly to determine beforehand the route that would be taken by the enemy."

Colonel Walter H. Taylor, in his *General Lee, His Campaigns in Virginia 1861-1865*, says of General Wise:

"He was a grand old man, heroic in his courage and of inflexible will, knowing little of subordination, but ever ready to fight, and steadfast to the last."

Let us now follow the movements of the Company as they appear from the Record Book:

Monday, September 23rd. General Lee arrived in camp which is about 2 miles from the top of the mountains. We were called out in the evening for review, and after waiting several hours, Gen.Wise rode up and informed us that quite contrary to his expectations, the enemy were on informed us that quite contrary to his expectations, the enemy were on Big Sewell Mountain, and that we should be ready for an attack immediately, and soon after firing was heard from the Pickets, but night coming on nothing could be done, and at night we lay on our arms in sight of the enemy's camp fires. We expected by day light of the coming day the attack would commence.

Tuesday, September 24th. Day dawned and no fight, nor was there any during the day.

Wednesday, September 25th. We were re-enforced today by Brig. Genl. Floyd's command and all under the command of General Lee; Genl. Wise being today ordered to report himself at Richmond, left the next day. We remained in sight of the Yankee Army for ten days awaiting an attack. On one occasion we were without food for two days, and during most of the time, without tents although it was very cold and disagreeable, but the men bore it patiently and with resignation.

Sunday, October 6th, 1861. Early this morning to our surprise we found that the enemy had left and we were again "knocked out" of a fight. We remained on Sewell's Mountain until the 20th of October, nothing having occurred worthy of note during the interval.

Sunday, October 20th, 1861. We were awakened at 4 A.M. and received the pleasing order to be ready for marching eastward. After a severe march up to our knees in mud and in a drenching rain for two days and nights, we arrived at Meadow Bluff on the 22nd inst. Lt. Fred Carter being on furlough and Lt. C. P. Bigger on a recruiting service Capt O. Jennings Wise had gone to see about our removal eastward. We remained encamped at Meadow Bluff without anything occurring beyond regular camp duty worthy of record, until about the 15th November. We were anxiously awaiting day by day for an order to take us to Richmond. During the time the weather has been quite severe, it having snowed several times. Our company are still in tents and we have made them tolerably comfortable by building fireplaces in them.

Friday, November 22nd, 1861. Lieuts. Carter and Bigger arrived here today and to our great joy report that the Blues are certainly going East.

December 10, 1861. Received orders this morning to strike tents and be in readiness to march by 6 o'clock. Never were tents struck with more pleasure or a march begun with lighter hearts than did our corps, and we were on our way eastward. Arriving that night at Lewisburg, although we came through mud knee deep, slept in the Presbyterian Church.

Wednesday, 11 December, 1861. Marched over to Dry Creek and remained two days.

Friday, 13th Dec. 1861. Went to Red Sweet Springs and remained two days.

Sunday, 15th Dec. 1861. Left this morning for Salem, arriving there the 17th of December. Took the cars for Lynchburg and on Sunday evening , the 22nd, started for Richmond, and on Monday morning, the 23rd, we arrived home where we were met by the Armory Band and marched out to the Reservoir and were there dismissed until Tuesday, 24th December, when we had a dress parade in our new uniforms presented by the city. We have to report every day at four o'clock for dress parade.

Thus the members of the Company had the good luck to spend this first Christmas after the war in their native city, remaining in Richmond until the 14th of January, 1862, when the journey which was to end so disasterously at Roanoke Island was begun.

The Richmond Light Infantry Bules had participated in a very difficult campaign in the Kanawha Valley region of western Virginia, but worse was soon to happen. They were once again placed under the command of General Wise, the Company commander's father, and marched off to the south. They were ordered to defend the North Carolina coast from Federal invasion, but the approaching amphibious force under General Burnside was far too large to check effectively. The next chapter's heading gives an idea of the result:

The Battle of Roanoke Island - The Company Practically Annihilated - Captain Wise Killed in Action

The Richmond Light Infantry Blues were not going to be "knocked out of a fight" as they had been on Sewell Mountain when Rosecrans ordered the Federal army to retreat, but their first real combat would be the last for many of them. Their captain was to die and nine others were wounded (two were to die) and fifty-one of the survivors were captured. This was a devastating blow to General Wise, the company, and to the people of Richmond.

The young men of the 22nd Virginia Volunteer Infantry Regiment came from the Kanawha Valley region and adjacent areas in the new Unionist state of West Virginia. Most of the men recruited into the Confederate regiment remained with their friends in their regiments until the end of the war. True to the oath they had taken to both Virginia and the Confederacy, most of these young men remained true to their cause until the war was over for them -- one way or the other. Their homes were deep within enemy-controlled country and they were unable to visit their families while on their infrequent furloughs. If they were to be able to come home for a short visit, they had to slip undetected through the hostile lines on both their outgoing trip and during their return.

An interesting episode ocurred in early 1864 when a small group of these Confederates were given a furlough and permitted to depart for their homes in the Union-controlled area of the new state. In order to visit their friends and family, the men had to infiltrate through the Federal lines. This was to be an interesting journey. The story was recorded in the West Virginia Historical Magazine *(Vol.1, No.1, January 1901) and was written by Joseph Ruffner.*

THE TABLES TURNED
A True Incident of the Civil War

In the month of January, 1864, a small army of Confederates was encamped near Kates Mountain in Greenbrier County, West Virginia. The winter was a severe one, and the snow covered the ground to a depth of about a foot. Active operations being suspended a party of soldiers whose homes were in the Kanawha Valley obtained a furlough with the design of visiting their relatives and friends from whom they had been long absent. This party was composed of Sergeant Henry W. Rand, and privates Sam Young, Andrew V. Donnally, Andrew M. Donnally, James Van Bibber and John Duling, all belonging to the 22nd Virginia Regiment.

It was a long and difficult journey which lay before them. There were high and rugged mountains to climb, deep and rocky gorges to journey through, cold and hunger to be endured, and the danger of capture and death to be confronted. But they were dauntless men, and inured by soldiers' experience to all the difficulties which were before them.

After three or four days' toilsome marching they reached a mountain cabin near the head of Big Sycamore Creek, in Clay County. Hungry and fatigued they sought food and rest for the night under its roof.

Hospitality was accorded them and soon such a meal as the scanty means of their host afforded was set before them. The two Donnallys having finished their supper before the others, with a view of discovering if all was safe, made a reconoisance of the outside surroundings and quickly discovered that a force of the enemy was quietly surrounding the house. They returned immediately to their companions with the unwelcome information and at once it was agreed that they should claim to be deserters from the Confederate Army on their way to the Federal lines at the mouth of Gauley. So when the leader of the Guerillas with some of his men appeared in the doorway with the demand to surrender, no fear was manifested, but instead, an expression of pleasure from the johnnies greeted him. He was welcomed as a friend in need. Their story was soon told, and the play so well maintained that the enemy was more than half convinced that they were indeed deserters. They yielded their arms at the suggestion of the chief of their captors, that they were deserters they would not have further use for them. Rand, however, retained upon his person a revolver which afterward played a part in this episode.

The next morning accompanied by a guard of six men they started for the enemies lines. The guard wanted to take them down to Charleston, but they insisted that as one or two of them were acquainted with the colonel commanding the Federal post at or near the mouth of Gauley, they would prefer to be taken before him. They had good reasons for wishing to avoid Charleston, as they were well known there. The good-natured guard willing to oblige "repenting rebels," yielded to their preference and started for the Gauley post. After marching all day they came at last close to and within sight of the fires of the Federal pickets, near the mouth of Bell Creek. The guards were for taking them at once into camp, but Van Donnally objected on the ground that the pickets would detain them overnight, and they would have to sit around the fire in the cold all night and get no rest. As there was a house belonging to one McGraw, whom Donnally knew, near at hand, he proposed that they seek shelter there for the night. This reasonable proposition was assented to and they repaired to the house. As they went in Rand turned the key of the door, to keep out intruders as he said, and quietly pocketed the key.

The disposition of affairs after entering the room was about as follows: To the right was the fireplace in which a fire was burning; to the left in a corner farthest from the door was a bed upon which the guard deposited their guns and accoutrements. Seated nearst the door were the prisoners, Andrew Van Donnally nearest the fire and Rand next to him. Opposite the guard were seated and directly opposite Van Donnally was the man in charge of the guard. He was a large man and wore at his side a navy revolver, and was the only man on his side so armed. It became necessary that he should be put out of the fight at once. Rand in a low tone told Van Donnally, when the signal was given, to spring for him and as he rose from his seat to strike him and knock him down, and then jump upon him and disarm him. Very shortly afterwards the signal was given, Donnally sprang toward his man and struck him with all his might as he rose from his seat, flooring him. Before he could rise Donnally was upon him and the struggle for the revolver commenced. Donnally reached for it and his opponent foiled his efforts to obtain it. Finally Van Bibber came to Donnally's help with a captured gun, and presented it at the prostrate but struggling guard, pulled the trigger. The only report was the snapping of the cap, where upon Donnally told him to use the butt of the gun, which Van Bibber proceeding to do, the enemy threw up his hands and surrendered and Donnally got the much prized revolver.

While this struggle was in progress events had declared themselves in favor of the Whilom captives. They were first at the guns and the guards finding themselves disarmed broke for the door with the design of alarming the pickets near by, but Rand's foresight had availed to prevent that very thing being done.

In the meantime one of the guards had floored Duling and was endeavoring to throttle him, while Sam Young was wielding the blade of his pocket knife with considerable damage to Duling's adversary who refused to abate his efforts until Rand shot him through the shoulder with the pistol he carried upon his person. This was the only shot fired in the struggle, and it brought Mrs. McGraw from an adjoining room upon the scene who begged them to "shoot easy" or the pickets would come in upon them.

She then began to scream with all the force of her lungs until reminded that unless she became quiet the pickets would come and there would be more shooting.

Immediately after the reversal of the *status quo,* the Confederates started with their prisoners back towards their camp, which they reached after a hard journey of four or five days. Once they narrowly escaped a disaster. The weather was freezing cold, and one night they were at a loss for shelter, and were also bewildered as to their way. Fortunately they met a mountaineer who knew one or two of them and was in sympathy with their cause. He told tham that if they pursued their course they were on they would have to camp in the mountains and probably freeze to death, and he offered to take them to a friendly house where they could be sheltered. Just before this fortunate intervention the party had been seen by some Confederate bushwhackers armed with long rifles of the mountaineers, and as the prisoners all wore federal uniforms and several of the Confederates had on Federal overcoats, the mountaineers took them to be a party of Federal scouts, and went ahead to a place favorable for bushwhacking them. They would have accomplished their purpose but for the fortunate meeting referred to. This fact they were informed of by the owner of the house where they took refuge, who afterwards went out and called in the bushwhackers. The next day the party reached Lewisburg.

They left the scene of their struggle with the belief that the man shot by Rand was mortally wounded, by in 1871 the writer learned from a brother of the victm that though seriously wounded, he had recovered.

One singular circumstance connected with the affair was that none of the rifles of the guards were loaded. The guns were capped, and the cartridge boxes were full, but the guns were empty. Had it been otherwise this narrative would have had more tragic features. Of the Confederates who participated in this drama four are living. Rand and Duling are dead.

Joseph Ruffner

Incidents such as this one were not rare as the young soldiers tried to go home for short visits with their families. Their families and friends were residing deep inside Federally-controlled territory and while many were obviously Confederate sympathizers, they couldn't express their true feelings openly without fear of retaliation. It was probably during these infrequent infiltrations that the "unofficial" mail was hand-carried through the lines for other families.

The "escapees" did not remain free after they returned to Lewisburg. Henry Rand was captured following the Confederate defeat at the third battle of Winchester in September, 1864, when Colonel Patton, the 22nd Virginia's commander, was killed. Rand was held at Fort Delaware.

There is little information available about Sam Young, but he apparently survived the war.

Andrew V. (Van) Donnally was captured at Gaines Mill in June, 1864. He was in prison at Pt. Lookout and Elmira, New York, but survived captivity and was paroled near the end of the war.

Andrew M. (Mat) Donnally was also captured at Gaines Mill and was imprisoned at both of the Federal prisons with Van. He also survived prison.

James Van Bibber was not re-captured and survived the war.

John R. Duling was captured again in late May, 1864.

These young men were typical of the Confederate soldiers from Virginia's western counties during the war. All that was required of them to end their personal war was a short oath which was sworn and they could return to their homes and families. For reasons known only to themselves, they remained true to their original oath and endured severe deprivations, hardships, and physical danger for the remainder of the war.

The gentleman who communicated these facts ... is a grandson of the famous F.R. Hassler, organizer and first Superintendent of the United States Coast Survey ... The grandson was in West Virginia when the Rebellion broke out, looking after the property of his family in that region. Like many other men of Union sentiments, he was forced into Rebel service, in which he was compelled to remain, until the victories of Sheridan and demoralization of Early's Command, enabled him to escape.

The Regiment (22nd Virginia Volunteer Militia) in which he was forced to carry a musket and uphold principles which he detested and predicted must eventually fall, was commanded by Christopher Tompkins, a graduate (in 1836) of West Point. This gentleman assumed his command with reluctance (so says Hassler) in obedience to a mistaken view of the rights of his native state; but retired into private life, as soon as he could do so consistently with soldierly honor.

Hassler, in partnership with his brother, opened a factory in the new state and the brother was a member of the State Legislature.

This letter was published in the Historical Magazine *in volume* VI. *There was no date on the copy used to recover this material on the early part of the war in the Kanawha Valley.*

A Military View of Passing Events From Inside the Confederacy, No. 1, THE CAMPAIGN IN WEST VIRGINIA, 1861 AND 1862 By Frederick W.B. Hassler, of the XXII REGIMENT, VIRGINIA VOLUNTEER MILITIA

My first engagement was on Scarey Creek, and a few days before the battle of Beverly. We were opposed to the Thirteenth Ohio, under General Cox, with a Battery of Artillery. After an engagement of three hours, Cox retreated. Colonel Norton, of the Thirteenth Ohio, was wounded and taken prisoner. That night, two Union Colonels, de Villiers and Neff, rode up into the Rebel lines, supposing that their side had been successful; patted the Southern troops on the back, and said: "Well done, you brave Ohio boys; you have whipped the Rebs;" when they were captured.

When Cox again advanced, with superior forces, on Charleston, Wise fell back to Gauley-bridge; burnt the bridge; and retreated to Lewisburg, at the White Sulphur Springs, to re-organize his forces for the Fall campaign.

Wise next made a stand at Meadow-river, in Greenbrier-county, where he was joined by Floyd, the two hoping to overpower Cox and re-take the Kanawha valley. Floyd took a portion ofthese troops and crossed the Gauley River, at Carnifex-ferry, and attacked the Seventh Ohio Regiment, at Cross-lanes.

This Regiment, out on a reconnoisance, fell back on General Cox. At Carnifex-ferry, the river forms a horse-shoe. The banks are very high, except where a road crosses the stream, which is rough water, not fordable. Floyd fortified the short line between the heels, or bluff, and built a trestle bridge at the toe, so that he could retreat, in case Cox forced his position.

Rosecrans, who had been opposing Lee on Cheat-mountain, made a complete fool of General Lee, deluded him and got away so adroitly that Lee was not aware that he was gone from his front, until Rosecrans had actually whipped Floyd, at Carnifex-ferry. We heard that this move of Rosecrans, and its complete success, came near upsetting Lee, in whom we lost all confidence.

Rosecrans attacked Floyd at the Ferry; and after a fight which lasted until dark, Floyd, finding he could not maintain his position, retreated in the night. Had it not been for the trestle-bridge which Floyd had built for the very purpose of getting away on, Rosecrans would have bagged him.

Meanwhile, Wise and Floyd fell out. Floyd retreated back again to Meadow-river; but Wise remained in position, on Little Sewell Mountain. I was with Floyd.

Lee, after Rosecrans had slipped away from him, came down, round, by a short cut, and reinforced Wise and Floyd, at Little Sewell Mountain. Rosecrans was in camp, on the other crest of the same ridge, known as Big Sewell Mountain.

Wise and Floyd quarreled about a wagon, which the former accused Floyd of having stolen from him. Moreover, Wise wanted to fight on the Mountain; whereas Floyd preferred his position on the Meadow-river.

Lee now ordered Floyd up, to reinforce Wise, and stop the further progress of Rosecrans, who had crossed the Gauley, at Carnifex-ferry, and effected a junction with Cox, on the Lewisburg and Charleston turnpike. We heard that Cox had not come up to time. He was to have attacked Wise at the same time that Rosecrans was to have attacked Floyd. At all events, we now found ourselves opposed to the united Union forces on Little Sewell Mountain. Lee was in chief command of the Rebels, as I said, on Little Sewell Mountain. The two armies skirmished for about ten days, in the depression between the crests which were not more than a mile apart. We could make out the Union lines, very plainly; and there was some cannonading.

Rosecrans, soon after, fell back to Gauley-bridge. We did not think that we forced him to retreat, but supposed it was on account of the horrible condition of the roads, in consequence of extremely hard rains, which rendered the transportation of supplies very difficult.

No one can conceive how bad these roads become when soaked with water. They are rough and difficult, at the best of times; and storms soom make them almost impassable for heavy wagons.

After the Union forces fell back, Floyd took a portion of Lee's army; crossed the New-river, at Pax-ferry; went down to Cotton Hill-mountain, on the Kanawha-river; posted his artillery on the mountain; and cannonaded Rosecrans's forces, at the crossing, in hopes of cutting off the Union communications with the Kanawha-valley. This waste of ammunition was kept up for almost a week. After this, Rosecrans sent a Brigade or Division, under Benham, up Loup-creek, in hopes of getting in the rear of Floyd, at Fayette-courthouse, and cutting off his retreat.

Rosecrans did drive Floyd out of his position at Cotton Hill-mountain. My Regiment was on the top of the mountain and saw the whole movement. We perceived the Union forces gaining ground, all day. When night came on, Floyd, knowing he could not maintain himself there, burnt his supplies and stores of clothing, and fell back so precipitately that, by daylight, he was at Fayette-courthouse. I think it was twelve to fifteen miles, from Cotton Hill-mountain to the Courthouse; but I know that we cooked our breakfast at the latter place, and ate our supper at the former.

We thought that General Benham disgraced himself here. We heard from the country people, that General Benham was in the woods, with four thousand men. He occupied such a position, they said, right along the road along which we were retreating, that if he had only "gone in," upon our flank, we could not have formed so as to make any resistance; so that by a little ability or energy, he could have bagged the whole of our crowd. Floyd was so glad to get off, that he never stopped retreating until he got to Dublin station, on the Virginia and Tennessee-railroad, one hundred miles from Cotton Hill and the Gauley.

The weather was so infamous and the roads almost impassable, so that the troops had to push the trains and artillery along. We heard that the Union troops pursued us about twenty-five miles, and then had to stop, on account of the mud. The roads in this part of the country are never good in wet weather. The best are what we term "mud turnpikes." The country is rolling, rather than mountainous, but is very rough, and rendered as difficult as it is possible for a country to be by rain and snow, both of which fell at this time. On the retreat, our rear was pressed by the Union Cavalry. I was in none of the fights; but I saw and heard the firing, and I know that Floyd was in a great hurry to get out of the way.

I forgot to say that the whole country is very little cleared and densely wooded with evergreens, especially pine, hemlock, and laurel. The streams are numerous, but not difficult, running into New-river, which, united with the Gauley, at the falls of the Kanawha, form, thenceforth, the river of that name.

We got to Dublin-station about the first of December. Here I was made glad with a furlough from General Floyd, in order to go go to Richmond and eat my Christmas dinner.

While I was in that city, Floyd received orders to go to Bowling-green, Kentucky, and thence to Tennessee, with all his command, except my Regiment, the Twenty-second Virginia. It appears that my Colonel, Christopher Q. Tompkins, had had a quarrel with Floyd at Cotton Hill-mountain. Rosecrans occupied the Colonel's house, at Gauley-bridge, and sent the family through the lines, to Richmond. When Colonel Tompkins asked General Floyd for a leave to go and see his family, the latter accused the Colonel of being a disloyal man, on account of his intimacy with Rosecrans.

It appears that Tompkins had either served with Rosecrans or was friendly with him. I knew Tompkins well; for he was a Cadet when my grandfather, F.R.

Hassler, was a professor at West Point. We often talked together; and the Colonel said "that he did not believe in the Re'bellion." He always told the rebels that "The Yankees would fight as well as they would." They disliked him for this; and so he resigned, and never would have anything more to do with the War.

After my furlough was out, I returned to my Regiment, and met it at Lynchburg, on its way to Lewisburg, to take up Winter-quarters. In the Spring, we went into camp, on the Charleston-turnpike, and remained there for about a month, doing little else but drilling. This was about March, 1862. Then we went to White Sulphur-springs, and were re-organized, under the Act which conscripted every able-bodied man, between eighteen and thirty-five.

Here the officers elected a new Colonel, Patten, a graduate of the Lexington Virginia Military Institute, in the place of Jackson, a Militia Colonel, whom Floyd had appointed to succeed Tompkins. This Jackson we liked about as little as we liked Floyd.

Patten took the Regiment, now one thousand, one hundred strong -- originally six hundred to eight hundred -- back to Dublin-station; and soon after, we had a fight at Gile's-courthouse, where we surprised two Union Companies, but did not "gobble them." Then we encamped on the "Narrows" of the New-river.

Here we were joined by the Forty-fifth Virginia, by Edgar's Battallion of Virginia Troops, and by two Batteries of Artillery. General Heth, who was a graduate of West Point, and had been Colonel of the Forty-fifth Virginia, had been promoted to Brigadiership, and taken command. He advanced upon Lewisburg, which was held by two Ohio Regiments, the Thirty-fourth and Thirty-sixth, under Colonel Crooke. An engagement ensued on the twenty-third of May, 1862; when Crooke gave us a tremendous licking, capturing four pieces of artillery and nearly the whole of Heth's command. Those who escaped got back to the old camp, at the "Narrows" of the New-river.

Major-general Loring then came on with re-inforcements, and took command of us. He had his headquarters at Salt Sulphur-springs, where he re-organized his little Army, received re-inforcements, and advanced, by Pax-ferry, on Charleston. At Fayette Court-house, we had a fight with the Union forces entrenched at that place, drove them out, pursued them down the Kanawha-valley, and captured Charleston. We remained in this District for about six weeks, gathering up all the cattle and salt, for the beenfit of the Confederacy. Then, as the Union troops had been largely re-inforced, Loring got off with his plunder and went to Lewisburg. Here he took up his Winter-quarters, on the Greenbrier-river.

The Brigade to which my Regiment belonged, was commanded by Brigadier-general Eccles, and laid at this point until Spring, (I think it was April) 1863.

Fred. W.B. Hassler,
Ripley, Jackson County,
West Virginia

Hassler was able to "escape" from the Confederate army in 1864 during the demoralizing defeats experienced by the 22nd Virginia that began with the death of Colonel Patton at Winchester in 1864. The remainder of Early's retreat through the Shenandoah Valley in the face of Sheridan's frequent attacks had only one brief bright point -- the initial phase of the battle of Cedar Creek when the retreating Confederates turned and attacked the Federal camp. Sheridan was able to restore order to the near-rout and regain the initiative against the retreating rebels.

It was probably at this time that Hassler was either captured or deserted from the 22nd Virginia to gain safety amoung his friends, the Federals.

Joel Abbott was working on a large cotton plantation in Louisiana with his future brother-in-law, William Bahlmann, during the spring of 1861. Both decided to return to Fayette County, Virginia, where they soon enlisted in the Fayetteville Rifles, shortly afterward to become a company in the First Kanawha Volunteer Infantry Regiment and later re-designated as the Twenty-second Virginia Volunteers Infantry Regiment.

Abbott and the Fayetteville Rifles were to see a great deal of action during the war. Bahlmann, Abbott's brother-in-law, was captured and exchanged. Abbott was transferred to the Eighth Virginia Cavalry where he served for the rest of the war. He observed a great deal of history as it was being made, but unfortunately he did not keep a diary or write extensively about his wartime experiences.

Long after the war, Abbott wrote (or dictated) this story about his experiences in the area of the upper Kanawha valley. It was originally published in a Charleston area newspaper and later re-appeared in Fayette County History.

A CIVIL WAR NARRATIVE
As told by Captain J.H. Abbott

From memory, I will try and give you a statement of what occurred in Fayette county during the Civil War, commencing with the battle of Cross Lanes, Nicholas county, which was fought September 11, 1861.

I was then second sergeant of Company K, 22nd Regiment, Fayetteville Rifles. I volunteered to carry a dispatch to General Chapman, commanding the militia of Monroe, Raleigh, and Fayette counties, at Fayetteville, and was detailed to help organize and drill his troops which were stationed at Fayetteville and Cotton Hill.

About ten days after my arrival at General Chapman's headquarters, we received information that General Cox was marching up the valley and that his advance guard had reached Kanawha Falls. Captain Herndon's company of the 8th Virginia Cavalry, acting as our scouts, was ordered over Cotton Hill. Nine of his men were killed from ambush on Falls Branch and were hauled over Cotton Hill on sleds drawn by oxen and buried on a knoll at the foot of Cotton Hill on the farm of T.S. Robson.

Two days later three companies of the militia were ordered on a scouting trip over the mountain to Kanawha Falls. I commanded one company, Lieutenant Loughborough, adjutant for General Beckley's brigade, commanded the second, and Captain Richards had charge of the third. We met the advance guard of the Federal troops on Falls Branch, near where Captain Herndon's men were killed. Captain Hunt, who was in charge of the federals, surrendered to Lieutenant Loughborough when ordered to do so; but he picked his chance, drew a revolver, fired and killed our officer and then made his escape with his men. We brought the lieutenant over the mountain and buried him with the others. The Cox army crossed Cotton Hill and a fight ensued. We retreated to Fayetteville.

There being no field officer for the Fayette Regiment, I was appointed lieutenant colonel and was in command until we disbanded at Beckley.

The first Union officer that came into Fayetteville rode to the court house square and down to the old well in the corner, where he was shot and killed by one of our own men.

Late in the fall the militia was disbanded at Raleigh court house. I then reported to General Heath[25], who made me a member of his staff with the rank of captain. We wintered in the narrows of New river. At the re-organization of the army in April 1862, I was elected second lieutenant of Company H, 8th Regiment, Virginia Cavalry, known as the Tazewell Troopers, but remained with General Heath until after the battle of Lewisburg, May 23, 1862.

General Loring, about September 9th, moved down on General Cox's army then located at Fayetteville, where he built fortifications. I was ordered to pilot a detachment of cavalry through the woods to Cotton Hill, then went up the road until forced away. We got axes from David Harshbarger and cut the poles and wires to the top of Cotton Hill, then went up the road to the red bank on George Tyree's place where we could see the road leading down to Miller's Ferry. All day they went down the Hawks Nest road, crossed the river at Miller's Ferry, and went down the other side of the river to Gauley Bridge. Cox's men made no effort to dislodge us. And all day the battle at Fayetteville raged.

Late in the evening of September 10th, a regiment of Federal infantry crossed Cotton Hill and came up in our rear, cutting off our escape up Laurel Creek. We had but one way to retreat, and that through the woods back to our army, which we did with great difficulty. The fighting was still going on and continued till long after dark when all

---

25 Henry Heth pronounced his name "Heath."

became quiet. Some of the men laid on their arms and slept.

The next morning, September 11th, General Cox's army was gone, and our army followed as quickly as possible. At the top of Cotton Hill, General Loring ordered a brass cannon to be taken down a long ridge to the top of the cliffs overlooking Gauley Bridge. We planted the gun and knocked down the temporary bridge across Gauley and blew up the magazine in the mouth of Zoll's Hollow, and then trying to get the gun back and finding it a difficult job, we hid it in a deep ravine, and it is there yet. General Loring continued his pursuit of General Cox and fought the battle of Charleston, September 13th. The army retreated back through Fayetteville about November 15th, in a continual fall of rain, and many of the soldiers died from exposure. Several died of pneumonia and measles.

During the summer of 1863, General J.B. McCausland made a raid on Fayetteville with three regiments of Infantry, the 22nd. 36th, and 45th, and three companies of Cavalry. We advanced into Fayette county without any trouble until we were about two miles below Mount Hope, where we met a scouting party. We fired on them and fell back to Mount Hope, where we dismounted and sent our horses to the rear. We formed behind a rail fence running up the ridge by a large chestnut tree standing on a knoll above the Warner log house. We did not have long to wait. They came up, jumped their horses over the fence, and wound their way up the hill. When they got within close range, we fired, and seven or eight of them fell from their horses and rolled down the hill. These men were buried under or near the large chestnut tree.

That evening Captain Phil Thurmond dropped into our camp and said that his men were on Arbuckle Creek and that he would throw the planks off the bridge above Rook Huddleston's mill, if we would run the cavalry into it. The next morning we came on the pickets at the Hickman place, and one man was killed. We next met them in force on top of the hill above Oak Hill and charged them into the bridge. The first horses went in on the sills and stuck fast. Some ran over the cliffs below the mill and were killed. We rescued sixteen live horses wedged in the bridge, and about fifty revolvers and as many carbines were captured. About twenty-five men were killed on both sides. We arrived near the town that evening and went into camp. I was ordered to take a few good men to Cotton Hill and cut wires, which we accomplished. We captured three fine teams and returned safe. The firing continued on the fortifications until late in the evening, when our retreat commenced.

About the first of November our cavalry was left in Raleigh to guard the road and to use some forage on the Ferguson and other neighboring farms. Captain Irvin Lewis with part of his three companies made a raid down lower Loop Creek to its mouth, surprised and captured sixty-five men and seventy-five horses and equipment. We retreated out up Armstrong creek, crossed Payne's mountain, where we rested and ate up everything we had. We went down a ridge to Paint creek and then to Raleigh court house. The prisoners were sent to Dublin depot.

In 1864, I was stationed at Princeton, and on July 4th, I raided Fayetteville and captured four sutler wagons and a large quantity of all kinds of goods, and carried the goods out on our horses. These wagons were placed outside of the lines for the purpose of trading with the people on that day.

I wish to add that I became captain of my company by the promotion of Captain Henry Brown to the rank of major.

Joel Abbot was a witness to several events that didn't find their way into the Official Records, *but there is no reason to doubt most of his account. He gave the interview from memory when he was quite old and a few accounts may have been confused. First, the story of the cannon being successful in destroying the bridge across Gauley*

River is not consistent with military practices. The same is true for the destruction of the "magazine at the mouth of Zoll's Hollow". There was no reason to destroy those two targets as the successful Confederates were only minutes away from capturing both. The Federal rear guard tried unsuccessfully to burn the suspension bridge and had to chop the cables and drop it into the river in order to slow the Confederate advance.

The story of the cannon lead to the development of a legend that still is told at Gauley Bridge. There are letters of participants in the shelling of the Federal camp at Gauley Bridge which describe the removal of the cannon, but skeptics must remind themselves that the town was shelled on three different occasions. The first was during the early part of the Federal invasion (September, 1861) when the Confederates had General Cox under a great deal of pressure. General Chapman's militia placed a cannon on Cotton Hill and fired on the Federals without doing any significant amount of damage.

The second shelling of the town and camp occurred in November, 1861, when General Floyd's regiments occupied Cotton Hill and behind a screen of high water were able to keep the Federal garrison under the command of General Rosecrans under seige for over ten days. Several cannon were involved and were placed in at least three locations along the ridge overlooking the New River gorge. These cannon were successfully extracted when the Union troops of the Eleventh Ohio and the Second Kentucky were able to cross the upper Kanawha River and scale the mountain to engage the Confederate infantry screen located in front of the artillery batteries.

The third shelling of the town and Federal camp occurred in September, 1862, during the Confederate invasion of the Kanawha Valley which successfully forced the understrength Union army out of the area for a short period. It was during this period that Abbott described the abandoned cannon. It is entirely plausible that a cannon was left on Cotton Hill and is there today.

Colonel L.S. Mayre was an officer in General Loring's command when the Confederates invaded western Virginia in 1862 with the goal of regaining the Kanawha Valley. Mayre was from Charlottesville, Virginia, and wrote this interesting history after the war was over. It appears in Fayette County History.

THE BATTLE AT FAYETTEVILLE

In the summer of 1862, General Loring, with a command of some 5,000 men, was encamped at the Narrows of New river. This river divides Giles county from Monroe. Pearisburg, the county seat of Giles, is five miles from the Narrows. A village has since sprung up at the Narrows, but at that time there were no houses there except a grist mill, and the miller's dwelling house. Loring lingered at this pleasant encampment six months, instead of marching forward in pursuit of the enemy, as was the expectation of the Confederate authorities at Richmond, and for this delay incurred the displeasure and censure of the Confederate Secretatry of War, George W. Randolph.

Loring had been a dashing cavalry colonel in the Mexican war, where he lost an arm at Capultepec, and afterwards in the department of the west, which included the state of Texas. He had been made a brigadier general in the Confederate service, and because of his experience in the mountainous campaigns was considered a suitable officer for the service to which he was assigned in the summer of 1862, the second year of the "war between the states"; and indeed was in the service to which he had been assigned the first year of the war, at Valley mountain, in Randolph county. While at the Narrows, he being an old bachelor, made frequent visits with parts of his staff, to the hospitable home of Mr. Oliver Bierne, a distance of some twenty-five miles, near Sweet Springs. The attraction of this Bierne home was the beautiful daughter of the prominent and wealthy gentleman.

At last, however, the forward movement commenced, the objective point being Charleston on the Kanawha river, now the capital of West Virginia. Between the Narrows of New river and the Kanawha, a Federal force of some three thousand men were stationed at Fayetteville. the county seat of Fayette county. Fayetteville is, in a direct line, but little more than fifty miles from the Narrows; but by the only practicable country road (for there were then no railroads in that region) some seventy-five or eighty miles; and it may be even more. The route lay through the southern part of Monroe county, through Summers, and the eastern part of Raleigh, into Fayette. When we arrived within a mile and a half of Fayetteville, Loring, with his command, halted and sent forward two companies of artillery under the command of Major Floyd King, with an infantry supprt to shell the enemy out of their entrenchments at Fayetteville. For hours Loring impatiently waited to hear Major King open his guns. After two or three hours of impatient waiting, Major King was seen approaching us, walking alone. On coming up to Loring he said he had come to recover his sword which he had carelessly left under a tree, up which he had climbed to reconnoitre the situation. Loring flew into a temptestuous passion, saying, "Major King, consider yourself under arrest; Captain Mayre, go take command of the guns and open on the enemy." King was, of course, greatly mortified; and sympathizing with him, I whispered to him to accompany me. This he did, and as we walked along together I told him that I would permit him to seem to be in command , and to direct the bombardment of the enemy, so that it would not be known that he was in temporary disgrace. This he greatly appreciated and after the war cordially thanked me for it. It was merely a piece of thoughtlessness and imprudence on his part, for he was a gallant noble fellow.

We opened on the works of the enemy, and soon drove

them from their position, and in rapid flight down towards the Kanawha Falls, some ten or twelve miles distant, at the junction of the New and Gauley rivers, which here form the Kanawha. Loring pursued the fugitive Federals to Kanawha and down the river forty miles to Charleston. The Kanawha throughout this portion of its course is a wide direct, beautiful stream, and its banks are dotted with the cottages of the primitive people who formed the inhabitants of that region. In the backyards of their cottages and within 50 yards of their back doors, dwellers in these humble homes would dig down a few feet and find the cannel coal that burns light a lightwood knot upon the application of a match, thus affording an abundance of fuel in their very back yards. From the oil of this cannel coal is made the beautiful and varied cannel candles that decorate the parlors of so many mansions on festive occasions.

In consideration of my part in driving the enemy out of Fayetteville. and as a vidette on his march down the Kanawha, Loring wrote a letter to the Confederate Secretary of War, recommending my promotion to the rank of lieutenant colonel, and sent it by messenger to Richmond. But on arriving there, the secretary, General Randolph, informed me that Loring had been relieved of his command in the Kanawha department, and assigned to duty elsewhere. The secretary of war had never forgotten his long delay at the Narrows of New river.

Loring had also ignored or disregarded his orders following his successful occupation of the Kanawha Valley. He chose to leave without placing any defensive garrison to hold the area for the Confederacy and the Federal regiments under General Cox simply marched back into the valley without meeting any significant resistance. This, more than the long delay at the Narrows of New River, was the reason Loring was sacked by George Randolph -- but the long courtship period while the Union troops were unopposed was also enough to anger the Confederate Secretary of War.

This is the very interesting story of the conflict which developed between two of the officers of the Eleventh Regiment, Ohio Volunteer Infantry. Most of the trouble between the two developed while they were in the area of Gauley Bridge during the battle of Cotton Hill. This material has been compiled from several sources, primarily General Cox's Military Reminiscences of the Civil War *and William Forse Scott's* Philander P. Lane, Colonel of Volunteers in the Civil War. *Some background material has been selected from several additional minor sources, such as Horton and Teverbaugh's* History of the Eleventh Regiment, Ohio Volunteer Infantry, *Levi Welch's* Battle of Scary Creek, *James Sedinger's* Border Rangers, *and the* Diary of William Clark Reynolds, *most of which appear in this book.*

General Cox describes De Villiers initially, and the remainder of the story is told by Lane's biographer and the other participants and witnesses.

THE STRUGGLE BETWEEN THE COLONEL AND THE CAPTAIN

In the Seventh Ohio was a company recruited in Cleveland, of which the nucleus was an organization of Zouaves, existing for some time before the war. It was made up of young men who had been stimulated by the popularity of Ellsworth's Zouaves in Chicago to form a similar body. They had as their drillmaster a Frenchman named De Villiers. His profession was that of a teacher of fencing; but he had been an officer in Ellsworth's company, and was familar with fancy manoevers for street parade, and with a special drill and bayonet exercise. Small, swarthy, with angular features, and a brusque, military manner, in a showy uniform and jaunty *kepi* of scarlet cloth, covered with gold lace, he created quite a sensation among us. His assumption of knowledge and experience was accepted as true. He claimed to have been a surgeon in the French army in Algiers, though we afterward learned to doubt if his rank had been higher than that of a barber-surgeon of a cavalry troop. From the testimonials he brought with him, I thought I was doing a good thing in making him my brigade-major, as the officer was then called whom we afterward knew as inspector-general. He was a most indefatigable fellow, and went at his work with an enthusiasm that made him very useful for a time. It was worth something to see a man who worked with a kind of dash, -- with a prompt, staccato movement that infused spirit and energy into all around him. He would drill all day, and then spend half the night trying to catch sentinels and officers of the guard at fault in their duty. My first impression was that I had got hold of a most valuable man, and others were so much of the same mind that in the reorganization of regiments he was successively elected major of the Eighth, and then colonel of the Eleventh. We shall see more of him as we go on; but it turned out that his sharp discipline was not steady or just; his knowledge was only skin-deep, and he had neither the education nor the character for so responsible a situation as he was placed in. He nearly plagued the life out of the officers of his regiment before they got rid of him, and was a most brilliant example of the way we were imposed upon by military charlatans at the beginning. He was, however, good proof also of the speed with which real service weeds out the undesirable material which seemed so splendid in the days of common inexperience and at a distance from danger.

The choice of De villiers for colonel proved to be a terrible misfortune for the regiment. If it was not ruined by his year of command, it was only because there was among the inferior officers and men enough of sterling qualities, with zeal for the cause and endurance of continuing neglect and bad administration, to bear their disgracing incubus until it could be thrown off.

De Villiers was an example -- a rather extreme one -- of a peculiar class of officers who appeared in the volunteer service early in the war, under the anxious search for men experienced in the instruction and drill of new soldiers. The instant, pressing need of training led to an eager acceptance of the help of any one who had or professed to have any knowledge of such work. Tho the regular army was depleted of its younger officers, to serve as instructors and field-officers in the volunteers, the number so used was very far from supplying the hundreds of new regiments called out. Any one who had been an officer or soldier in the army or in the volunteers in the Mexican war was now sure of a respected position, tho in that short war the most of the volunteers saw no important service. But there were in the country many foreigners who had been minor officers or soldiers in the armies of Europe, and others came over as military adventurers when our war broke out. These were looked up to with a kind of awe by the credulous American militia, and, with surprising ease, with little or no inquiry as to their history or real capacity, and without trial, they obtained many important military positions. Germans were the most numerous, but there were English, French, Austrians, and Poles.

When the new Eleventh Ohio was assembling in this rendezvous-camp the Eighth Ohio was already in adjoining quarters. The parade-ground employments of that regiment were much enlivened by the activities of a small, dapper, very alert man as drill-master. He was conspicuously "foreign" in appearance, of very dark complexion and sharp features, wore a smart red and gold cap, bright blue tight coat and red trousers, and was highly conceited in his manner and talk (he spoke English fluently, tho with bad pronunciation); and he appeared to be acting as a "sort of Inspector-General" of the camp, tho it does not appear that he had any real official position. The soldiers commonly spoke of him as "the Major" and supposed him to be Major of the Eighth Ohio, but he was not. He was always active and conspicuous, and he made the green soldiers gape with astonishment at his brilliant sword-play and bayonet-gymnastics on the Eighth parade-ground. He was the wonder of the camps and, in the ignorance of the time, was believed to possess all the military science and arts. He was, or was believed to be, a Frenchman. If so, he had probably been a minor officer in the French army or a fencing-master; but his former career was unknown and no care was taken to inquire into it. When his true character came out he was believed to be a disreputable adventurer, -- probably a good guess. This was Colonel De Villiers.

When the colonelcy of the Eleventh became vacant by the resignation of Colonel Harrison, who commanded in the three-months service, there was an "election" in the regiment for his successor. De Villiers was easily a candidate, was elected, and the Governor gave him the commission, probably influenced not alone by the election, but also by the reports of the rare qualifications of the candidate. Afterward his enemies said that his candidacy and election were due to intrigue. Very likely they were due to a concealed plan, for a much abler man would have been found in either the lieutenant-colonel or major, or indeed in almost any one of the captains. But this knowledge and understanding came too late. When De Villiers was chosen the Eleventh Ohio was thought to be rarely fortunate in getting such a paragon of military ability for their instructor and commander. But he proved to be almost wholly unfit for the place; and, so far from developing the capacity of his regiment, his persistent failure in duty and misconduct prevented that development as far as it could be prevented. If he was not a mere charlatan, his regiment was at least never benefitted by his supposed knowledge and skill. It had never any effective drilling or manuevering by him in either the rendezvous-camp or the field. His inefficiency in actual service in the field was so frequently shown that he lost all confidence and respect of the regiment ...

When Cox first moved up the Kanawha, Wise moved down from Charleston and destroyed the Pocotaligo bridge; and when Cox established himself at Pocotaligo, Wise was only a few miles in front, in observation. A few days later (July 16) Cox sent Colonel Norton, with part of the Twenty-first Ohio (his own regiment) and of the Twelfth Ohio, 1,200 men and one gun in all, up the west side of the river for a reconnoisance. Norton was not to bring on an engagement, but when, within a few miles, he came to Scarey creek, a stream flowing into the Kanawha from the west, thro a deep and rocky ravine, he was fired upon from the other side by an enemy concealed, but evidently of considerable number, with two or three guns. Being only on a reconnoisance, he should have fallen back, out of fire, and tried to learn the strength and purpose of the enemy; but, being inexperienced and a brave man, he considered himself in a battle and undertook to hold his ground and return the fire. The "battle" was thus fought across the ravine, which Norton could not, or did not, reach: probably he could not have found a passage across it if he had reached it. Wise seems to have had the greater part of his forces there and was himself in command.

Norton soon fell, wounded, as well as several of his men, and his command, unable to advance and not ordered to retire, became confused, fell back in disorder, and retreated to the camp at Pocotaligo, having lost two killed, six wounded, and six officers and a few men captured. Wise, in a delirium of joy, crossed the ravine by a circuit and followed almost to the camp.

But this was not all the disaster. Colonel De Villiers, who had just joined the little army, with part of the Eleventh Ohio, left the camp with two or three other officers (one a colonel) and rode up the east side of the river, to observe Norton's movement, for entertainment. Hearing the firing, and the view being obstructed, they rode down to the river, and finding a "flat" at hand were ferried over, and immediately rode into the enemy's lines. They said afterward that they were betrayed by the display of a United States flag. So Wise had as prisoners three colonels and three minor officers (Norton's wound being so severe that he could not move and one of his staff remaining to care for him), with a few men.

This was the "Battle of Scarey Creek", of little more consequence in military view than if Wise had driven in a picket; but it at once became in the excitable imagination of the time a "great Victory" on one side and a great disaster on the other. Morally it did have, temporarily, a good effect on the rebel side and a bad one on ours....

Meantime, in July, while McClellan was still lying in camp at Beverly, exulting over his success at Rich Mountain, General Cox, meanly ill-treated and practically abandoned by him...tho still expected to force his way up the narrow and easily defended valley of the Kanawha against an enemy superior in numbers and guns, was steadily doing his duty, without complaining and without the advertisement of repeating reports, learning by experience in daily action how to meet and oppose his enemy, and winning the ground by untiring care and persistence....

He was not disheartened by Colonel Norton's repulse,

nor did it in the least alter his movements, tho it must have had temporarily a demoralizing effect upon his command. With his practically isolated brigade he simply kept at work, feeling sure it would redeem itself from the false imputation it had had to bear. Fortunately, he did not then know of McClellan's injustice to him. He had been directed to get Charleston and Gauley Bridge, and to that job he applied all the abilities he had until results should prove whether or not it was possible to do it with the means allowed him.

The first step must be to cross the Pocotaligo, and to do that he must replace the long bridge destroyed by the enemy. In the arrival of Captain Lane and his company, the night of July 18, he had the means. Captain Lane was full of mechanical resources, his company was largely composed of mechanics used to heavy work, and another regiment of the regiment supplied more. For some reason Company K was not landed till the night of the 19th; but, beginning early on the 20th, the zealous Captain and his men took only seventeen hours for the construction, from improvised materials, of a rude, but substantial, floating bridge by the side of the destroyed one; and on the 21st the troops and guns were moving over.

This compelled Wise to retire to his fortifications a little below Charleston. He had now 4000 men in three fortified positions, with 10 guns. Cox had five regiments, two nearly full and three small, and four guns, about 3000 men in all. But the Eleventh Ohio was increased by the arrival of a new company (G) from Ohio, adding 80 or 90. Cox pushed forward, with the Eleventh Ohio in advance, now (since the capture of its Colonel) commanded by Lieutenant-Colonel Frizell, a good and capable officer. Wise imagined Cox receiving heavy reinforcement and hastily abandoned the position and the town (July 24), retreating toward Gauley Bridge, forty miles above, closely pressed by Cox. On the 29th, without fighting, he left the very strong Gauley position, burning the big bridge over the Gauley, and retreated up the mountain to Lewisburg, thirty miles further. Thus, within two weeks after "Scarey Creek", the little brigade forced its way fifty miles up the river and possessed all the Kanawha.

Wise merited the scornful comments of his rival, General Floyd, upon this retreat. He could have held back such a force as Cox's almost indefinitely if he had been a soldier and of cool judgement. Half a dozen streams falling into the Kanawha and passable only by bridges offered fine positions for defense, his left flank always protected by the Kanawha and his right by continuous rocky hills. As Cox had not enough men for safe flanking operations, he could only drive ahead on the one narrow road to the front.

This road lay close along the river, crossing a number of streams at their mouths, the smaller ones fordable, but seven or eight requiring bridges, to replace those Wise had destroyed. Captain Lane's success with the Pocotaligo bridge threw all this work upon him; and he won the respect and admiration of the whole command by his untiring labors of himself and his men. Within ten days he built five important bridges and as many lesser ones.

It being impossible to get and ship bridge timber and tools in time and there being no saw-mill within reach, he did all this work with axes and hand-saws, augers, spikes and trees felled near, except that for the Elk river bridge, near Charleston, he found some milled timber in the town. This bridge was the largest, but it was a "wire" bridge (that is, suspension), and Wise's men had got only one span (about forty feet) effectively destroyed. Captain Lane put a span of timber in its place and made the other repairs required, all between four o'clock p.m. and two a.m. On the 28th, between Charleston and Gauley, the zealous engineer noted, "Built four bridges within the last three days." But he and his company were doing more than bridge-building on this march. They had a part in driving the enemy. In the march upon Charleston, after crossing the Pocotaligo, the Eleventh Ohio had the advance, at least on the day the town was taken, and Company K was in front. There was some exchange of shots, -- not much, but it made the first definite engagement of the regiment with the rebels. Lieutenant Johnson, with part of the company, in his eagerness got separated from and ahead of the remainder, led by Captain Lane on the other side of the road, and, as it happened, was the first to enter the enemy's intrenchments.

In view of the bad condition of the roads and the absence of bridges above Charleston, General Cox gained time by moving the main body of the troops on boats up to the falls (about half way to the Gauley) where they landed and marched on as rapidly as the road permitted. But Wise had destroyed the long bridge over the mouth of Gauley, and the whole army halted. The energy of Captain Lane and his pioneers had, however, completed the bridges from Charleston up, and they reached the Gauley little behind the main column. Here was the most serious problem the new "Chief-Engineer" had met, tho there were others to come. General Cox left it to his discretion. The one important thing was, to get the men and artillery across at the earliest hour possible. The bridge destroyed was five hundred feet long, the abutments one hundred and fifty feet apart. The stream was three hundred feet wide at ordinary water, swift and turbulent, interspersed with large rocks which rose above the water at a low stage and were buried at a high stage, and there were deep holes between them. To rebuild on the old abutments would certainly take too much time. To build a lower, and therefore shorter, bridge would probably take no less time, and its approaches would be steep and difficult for wheels. The currents and the rocks made a floating bridge impossible.

Captain Lane had decided upon a ferry as the only means practicable under the circumstances; but the swift and irregular currents presented special difficulties and compelled great caution. There were some flat-boats below the falls, but they could not be got up. The Gauley above the bridge was so shallow and so filled with rocks that timber could not be floated down. He sent back for a steamboat hawser, to be used as a cable, and set about building a boat with such planking and timbers as could be found or cut near by with axes. On the fourth day he finished a boat sixty feet long, eighteen wide, with a capacity of two hundred men or four loaded army wagons and their animals, or two guns and their caissons. Of course it had to be built and caulked bottom up and on the shore, and its great weight made it very difficult to turn it over and into the water safely without a derrick, but this was accomplished successfully by a simple mechanical means. The hawser was dragged across and secured at both ends, a "walk" was built along the outer side of it, on which the men could pass to work the boat, which was secured to the cable by guide-ropes at stem and stern. Six men on the "walk," pulling on the cable, could then easily propel the boat with full loads. On the 4th of August, the fifth day after beginning, the ferry was in regular operation, carrying over the troops and trains.

This kind of employment of Company K (it was aided more or less by details from other companies, usually B and G, which contained many mechanics) must have had a salutary influence upon the development and health of the men, being done, as it was, for an obviously important purpose and under the immediate observation of the officers and men of the brigade. Captain Lane writes at this time, "Our position as a company is very desirable one and is the only one so far as I know in the volunteer service. We have less sick, better food, better order, and retain more of our self-respect than any company in the brigade." About the same time he wrote that he had 83 men present (i.e., of Company K) and not a man sick....

In the Kanawha Brigade at this time they were looking daily and anxiously for news of the approach of Rosecrans from the north, with more men and guns. Already his march had taken more time than he had set for it. Floyd was strong enough, with good management, to defeat Cox east of Gauley Bridge, or below if he could safely cross the Gauley; but, not withstanding his "biggity" announcement to Wise ... his resolution failed when he had made half the distance, and he turned off to the north, to occupy Summersville, a town twenty-five miles northeast of Gauley Bridge. He may have had an idea that this movement would flank Cox out of Gauley Bridge and compel him to retreat to Charleston; but he seems ignorant of Rosecrans' march, which was directy toward Summersville. Floyd's cavalry advance reached Cross-Lanes, near Summersville, September 8th, and caught a small detachment (part of a company)[26] of the Seventh Ohio infantry (not of the Kanawha Brigade), whose proper guard duty had been neglected, and killed or captured the greater part of it. Floyd lost no time in reporting this "battle", in extravagant language, to Richmond, and the officials there celebrated "another crushing defeat of the enemy on the Kanawha." If he had waited a bit and skilfully questioned his prisoners, his report would have been sobered. He had hardly settled himself in Summersville with his pleasing reflections when he was surprised to learn of an enemy near at hand, coming from the north.

To reach Summersville he had to cross the Gauley, at Carnifex Ferry, about thirty miles above Gauley Bridge. He immediately abandoned Summersville and fell back to Carnifex Ferry, taking a very good defensive position in a bend of the river, sheltered by a thick wood and covering the ferry crossing. Rosecrans found him there a day later, on the 10th. The two forces were about equal in numbers and guns, tho Rosecrans's guns were probably much better; but Floyd's peculiarly strong position for defense put any attack upon him at great risk. Rosecrans finally advanced, however, late in the afternoon, and there was a hot battle, with varying hopes, until night put an end to it. Rosecrans had gained ground, but had severe losses, due to the necessity of open frontal attack. But Floyd was not equal

---

[26] This is incorrect. The entire Seventh Ohio Infantry Regiment was defeated at Cross Lanes by Floyd's regiments.

to the occasion, was unnecessarily alarmed, and thought only of getting away. He spent all night moving his army back across the river; and in the early morning Rosecrans's reconnoitring parties found the position abandoned and Floyd's rear guard on the left bank.

As Floyd obviously must be retreating to Lewisburg, and probably in haste, to avoid an attack by Cox on his right, Rosecrans ought to have vigorously pushed a crossing and pursuit. But he was dilatory and ineffective, and it was more than a whole day before he moved over even a detachment. Yet he was very anxious about Cox, fearing that Floyd would strike him with his larger forces above Gauley Bridge; and he sent several messages to Cox during the day.

But he did not understand Floyd. That general was not at all seeking another fight. Cox was in fact twenty miles above Gauley Bridge, with a considerable part of his brigade, but he had not heard of Carnifix, nor even of Rosecrans' arrival. Floyd could easily have given him serious trouble, but he was thinking only of Lewisburg, and hurried by Cox's ground, so near that his movement was easily observed; and Cox was perplexed as to what his great haste could mean. But, feeling sure that it was caused by Rosecrans' advance, he concentrated and followed up the retreat, sending back a courier to get a report to Rosecrans. The next day, the 12th, he had his first news of the battle at Carnifix, in a letter from Rosecrans; but did not yet know that Rosecrans had that morning got one brigade across the Gauley, with orders to reinforce him...

But, if Rosecrans was not then very zealous against Floyd, Cox's brigade kept at least part of his men busy on and near the Lewisburg road. The Eleventh Ohio in particular, under the active and courageous Lieutenant-Colonel Frizell, pressed closely upon his rear or western front, with sharp fighting at times. But Rosecrans had lagged so much in following up his advantage gained at Carnifix that any further movement against Floyd would not be a pursuit, but only a renewal of the effort to drive him back into the mountains. He did finally take the field himself, and, with a force now much stronger than Floyd's, slowly pushed him back toward Lewisburg. So slow, indeed, it was that he did not reach Big Sewell Mountain, thirty miles from Gauley Bridge, until September 23. His advance finally reached the top of the mountain and found the enemy holding it in a fortified camp; but he did not venture an attack. He seems to have been much mistaked in estimating Floyd's strength and in his belief that another force, under Lee, was waiting its opportunity to strike down the Huttonville road on the northeast. Lee had come down from the north of the state on hearing of Floyd's defeat, and remained about Lewisburg and Big Sewell until early in November, directing affairs generally, but not taking command of troops in active operations. By his unvarying patience and courtesy he had gained the confidence of both Floyd and Wise, but he could not reconcile them: nobody could. All the troops were finally called the "Army of the Kanawha", however, and Floyd was placed in command. This clipped Wise's wings, but had no other effect upon him; and he was at last ordered to Richmond and sent with a brigade of Confederate troops into North Carolina, while Lee, in November, was sent to Charleston, S.C., to command a Confederate department.

For two days after reaching Big Sewell Rosecrans manuevered in a desultory way, with a few unimportant skirmishes, and then withdrew and slowly fell back to Gauley Bridge. He reported he did this because of lack of force enough, want of transportation, and almost impassable roads; but his forces already exceeded Floyd's and the War Department was ordering six more regiments from Pittsburg to re-inforce him. While the difficulty of transportation and bad roads was but temporary, the latter being due to rains, which were usually, at this season, followed by fine weather. Continuous bad weather could not be expected until late in November.

Tho the most of the Eleventh Ohio was with its brigade on the Big Sewell movement, Captain Lane, with his company, was retained at Gauley Bridge, to make sure of the protection and operation of the ferry, since the supply of the army above depended upon it. There was a sudden great rise in the Gauley, from a phenomenally heavy rain, and it was with great anxiety that he saw the big torrent rushing down and rapidly rising in height. In spite of the unceasing care and labors of himself and all his men, the swift flood at last carried away the cable, all the boats but one, and the lumber and timbers collected and prepared for reserve. It was said to be the greatest flood the country had known.

It was not impossible for the army to cross the Gauley, if compelled to retreat, and at the same time impossible to supply it with food and ammunition where it was. Captain Lane keenly felt the weight of the disaster and the urgency of action. He wrote in a private letter "I felt as if I had the whole army on my back." There would have to be some fall of the flood before a new cable could be carried over and secured, and it would take time to get a new one anyhow. Meantime he had every man and axe he could find hard at work, geting out new materials, to be ready for the first hour when reconstruction could possibly begin. Tho he does not say so, he must have worked, in reliefs, by night as well as by day.

On the 2nd of October, only four days after seeing nearly all the product of his former labors swept down the flood, he sent the first wagons, loaded with supplies, over the new ferry. In respect to time this was a remarkable performance, against the great obstacle of the high water, which was still running at flood.

But neither the restoration of his communications nor the fine October weather nor the coming of reinforcements induced Rosecrans to proceed with the campaign. He had said, in a report, that the country he was yielding could be "retaken when we require" and that "the troops would move nearer to the Gauley, to get their pay and clothing." Of course they could get pay and clothing just as well at Big Sewell, by only bringing the paymaster and quartermaster up there; but he really had also the idea of going into winter-quarters, tho the winter was yet some time ahead. Whether due to him or not, this idea got among the men, and they were to some extent demoralized by the fixed belief that they were now to lie for four of five months in comfortable camps, perhaps back on the Ohio.

So, by the middle of October, all the troops were back on and behind the Gauley, but were not paid. The paymaster had not come, and did not come until near the end of the month. Lying thus idle in the camp the men were much discomfited by the failure of what they considered a promise of their pay (but few had received any pay since entering the service, from four to five months before) and by the lack of definite news of winter-quarters.

One incident is of special interest. A small force was kept at Summersville, already mentioned, as a kind of outpost of the Kanawha army. Captain Lane "had occasion" (he does not say what) to go there personally. The distance is twenty-five miles and the road hilly, very rough, and often thro woods and narrow ravines. Guerrillas were much on the roads, in hope of getting one or several Union men or soldiers; and some of the citizens who professed to be Union men were more than suspected of treachery, really belonging to guerrilla gangs, or at least harboring them and giving them information of any Union movement. Captain Lane decided to go by night, and, for some reason not given, went alone. He rode thro the night without stopping, cautious in passing any house or other possible lurking place, and keeping his arms always ready for instant use. Nothing happened, but he writes "It was a lonely ride." He does not speak of his return to Gauley, from which it is assumed that he returned with troops.

One of the greviances of the soldiers at Gauley was removed by the appearance in camp of the paymaster, who arriver near the end of October, and immediately had many of the officers and sergeants busy on the preparation of the "muster-and-pay-rolls" required for his use. For the Eleventh Ohio, however, this agreeable experience was marred by a disaster. Its Colonel returned from his three months captivity, and of course resumed command of the regiment. He had notified the brigade commander that he was coming, and the regiment was turned out, on formal parade, to "welcome" him, tho to nearly all the officers and men the occasion was anything but welcome. At the best there was in his regiment but little respect for him or confidence in him, and what there was had been diminished by the circumstances of his capture. As there was little or no evidence of his adventures after his capture beyond his own story, and, as that story contained many fearful and hairbreadth perils and deeds of daring, he found few believers. He may have been in one of the escapes of officer prisoners from Libby Prison, but also may have been merely one of those exchanged: no one seems to have taken the trouble to make an inquiry, and his loquacious boasting was left to free play. He had little or none of the personal dignity that induces respect for an officer, and some of his tales of dangers and daring were openly rediculed as being only lying inventions.

During his absence the regiment had been finely developed under the Lieutenant-Colonel and Major, and had become at least the equal in discipline and efficiency of any regiment in its army. Now, under the new regime, it fell rapidly into a bad condition of discouragement among officers and men. By his erratic performance of his own duties, his rash orders, violent language and many threats of punishments that were never attempted, he broke down discipline instead of strengthening it; and, with this and his obvious lack of a real knowledge of drill and maneuvers, he hampered and irritated the officers; frequently during the winter got into a quarrel with one or another of them, indulging in the most vulgar and insulting language. During the next four months after his return he made his camp the scene of unhappy turmoil, involving both officers and men. The Lieutenant-Colonel and one of the captains resigned in disgust, seeing no other way to escape their share of the trouble. The Major (Coleman) accepted the place of Lieutenant-Colonel, hoping to see soon the natural end of such a condition; and the end did soon come. But it was to Captain Lane, much more than any other man that the regiment owed its release from the dreadful handicap. It was he who took the risks and responsibilities of action, endured the disgrace of arrest and court-martial and a long period of conspicuous deprivation of his command, with constant anxiety as to the rsult for the regiment and for himself. But his final exoneration and success were complete. It is not too much to say that, by risking the sacrifice of himself, he saved his regiment from ruin.

1861: November - December

Early on the morning of November 1, 1861, when the paymaster was ready to begin paying the Eleventh Ohio at Gauley, a gun was heard, fired from the south side of New river, opposite the mouth of the Gauley, and a shell struck in the camp of the regiment. Naturally, all other considerations were suspended. While the excited wonder was still on another shell struck. No damage was done. The paymaster moved himself and his money to a safer place, and, tho the shelling continued during the day, he resumed his work after a time; and by night had paid off all that regiment. Floyd had crossed the New river from Big Sewell, moved down the south side, and planted a battery of two guns on the front of a high and very steep hill having a bold face rising almost directly from the waters edge, directly opposite the mouth of the Gauley. He meant to annoy and disorder Rosecrans's camp and destroy the ferry. One of his guns got the direct range of the ferry, and his sharpshooters, concealed by rocks and trees along the shore, stopped the use of a piece of the road which lay open and exposed just east of (above) the ferry.

Captain Lane had been relieved of duty at the ferry (as there was no movement of troops now, the operation of it was only routine work for a small party) and was in camp with his regiment at some distance. When the shells began to strike near the ferry, some one there sent a messenger in a rush to tell him. He could answer only that he had no authority and that the message should have gone to Colonel DeVilliers. The messenger ran to find the Colonel. He had taken no action in the emergency, and did nothing now but send the man to Captain Lane with authority to do what he thought best. Angered by this cowardly shuffling off of responsibility, but seeing the importance of instant action, the Captain at once ran down to the ferry. He found thirty or forty men there, sheltered, but in a helpless state of mind, while the ferry-boat was at the other side of the river, clearly in sight from the rebel battery. A shell had just struck dangerously near it. He called for four men to go over with him and move the boat out of range. Three did volunteer, and with these he crossed on the "walk" attached to the cable, which, like the boat, was fully seen from the battery, and, with strenuously rapid labor, they released the boat and hauled it up stream and behind a projecting point of rocks. The movement took time enough, however, to enable the rebels to get in three more shells, which he describes as "two very close and one wild."

Tho the Captain was muched vexed by the manner in which this affair was thrust upon him, it added to the reputation he had already gained for ready resource and unshirking behavior in danger. The promptness, courage and success of his action were quite in line of what had already been seen in his service.

But the ferry was put out of use while that battery remained there, except under the cover of night, a condition that proved very awkward. For Rosecrans was not able to dislodge Floyd's guns for seven days, and every day the camps at Gauley and just below were teased by the shelling, tho no serious injury was done by it. The sharpshooters, however, having a shorter range, wounded a few men and killed or wounded a number of horses and mules.

Whether Rosecrans knew of Floyd's movement down the New river does not appear. He probably did know, but yet, if he did, it is curious that he did not occupy this hill opposite his ferry and camp. The road on that side of the river ran close behind the hill (curved around it, in fact), and the nature of the ground was such as that one brigade could have held both hill and road against the whole of Floyd's force; and Rosecrans had three brigades at hand.

Floyd was engaged in what he considered a momentous campaign. The authorities would not, or could not, increase his army to 10,000, as he had repeatedly urged, to enable him to plant himself firmly on the Ohio, but he could show that he deserved it. When Rosecrans retired from Big Sewell to Gauley, Floyd was satisfied that it was a defeat, and he proposed to Lee a joint movement with an ambitious goal. He was to cross the New river, move down the left bank, by Fayetteville, and take Cotton Hill (the hill opposite Gauley, on the river-front of which his guns were now planted), while Lee should advance on the Lewisburg road and make a determined attack on the Gauley position. By co-operation Rosecrans would be decisively defeated, or at the least driven down and out of the valley. Floyd would then occupy and easily hold all that part of the State south and west of the Kanawha, if not also a portion north and east. Lee was not so hopeful; in fact he disapproved of the scheme as quite impractical -- as indeed it was, from lack of force, lack of transportation, bad roads constantly getting worse and the peculiar great strength of Rosecrans' position behind two rivers. One cannot but wonder that Lee had the patience to treat Floyd's plan respectfully, but he listened to it and finally consented to the trial of one feature of it, -- an attempt to take and hold Cotton Hill.

Floyd accordingly crossed New river with the greater part of his "army" -- about 4000 -- and marched down the Fayetteville road. he wrote afterward, when he was accounting for his failure, but in cautious language, as if Lee had neglected to make the expected attack on the Lewisburg road on the north side, but there is nothing in Lee's reports or correspondence to give any color to such an expectation; and there are other instances in Floyd's career of disingenuousness. Floyd, indeed, knew that Lee had just been compelled to send his best or most experienced troops (Loring's Brigade) a hundred or more miles away, to reinforce "Stonewall" Jackson in the Shenandoah valley. It would have been a mere waste of effort, or worse, to throw his small remainder against Gauley Bridge. It ought to be said, however, that Lee did have a hope, if not more, that Floyd's movement would "cause the enemy to withdraw from the Gauley", but that is one of the rather many instances in which Lee's military judgement was poor.

Floyd left behind, at Big Sewell, the "Legion" of Wise, saying, in contempt, that it was "so insubordinate and ill-disciplined that it was unfit for military purposes"; but, privately, he would have been glad of any kind of a reason for keeping Wise out of the campaign.

If Rosecrans knew of Floyd's movement he took no steps to interfere with it. He must have known the disadvantage to him, or worse, of letting his enemy get possession of Cotton Hill. One of his brigades placed across the Fayetteville road, east of the hill, could have prevented it, and, with a couple of regiments in reserve, could have brought Floyd's enterprise to naught and put him out of account for months. But he did nothing about it; and, within a few days after crossing the New, Floyd's advance occupied Cotton Hill and he was encamped a short distance east of it. There he remained a week, undisturbed, while he planted the battery already mentioned on the river front of the hill.

The is no indication in Rosecrans' reports or correspondence that he had any knowledge of this until the shells began to fly on November 1. Then he busily set about dislodging Floyd, but he found it a long and awkward job. He sent General Benham, with his brigade, some eight miles down the Kanawha, to cross and get the Fayetteville road near the mouth of Loop creek, while General Schenk, with another brigade, made a persistent but futile effort to cross New river above Floyd's position. For seven days the only thing accomplished was the crossing of Benham's brigade. Schenk could not yet get over, without going too far up the river for safety, and Benham, slow and lacking in energy, failed to make the advance required. Meantime the two guns and the riflemen along the shore kept up the daily practice, to the great annoyance and mortification of the whole command.

Floyd knew what was being done against him. From the front of Cotton Hill, with a glass, he could see the greater part of Rosecrans's camps, and reconnoitring parties must have reported to him Benham's position and Schenk's efforts. On the 7th, having no stomach for another battle, tho superior in numbers to either of the two brigades, if not to both, he decided to withdraw, and did that night withdraw the two guns and the sharpshooters, but still occupied, with part of his command, the west or south end of the hill, which was higher than the river end and wooded.

As it happened, it was Captain Lane and his company, later supported by the remainder of his regiment, who brought the situation to a fighting crisis. He had been ordered to build two scows large enough to carry troops, and they were done on the 7th or 8th. What use they were intended does not appear. A fair guess is, that they were for Schenk's crossing above the Gauley, tho they may have been for crossing Cox's men at the mouth of the Gauley, in which service, apparently, they finally were used.

The shelling and sharpshooting having ceased late on the 7th and the two guns having apparently disappeared from the brow of the hill, a reconnoisance was ordered. Why it was not made from Benham's brigade, already on that side of the river, is not learned. Captain Lane was chosen for this service, probably by General Cox, because of his skill in the use of boats (both rivers being then high from the recent rains) and his proven courage. At night of the 9th he received an order to move at three a.m., with his company, cross the river by boat, and find out what the enemy had done on the hill. He was ready on time, but found only 37 men of his company fit for the duty (the regiment was much reduced at that time, from hard service, detachment &c, and mustered for duty much below 300), but with the 37 he set out in the two boats he had built. He was to run down the Gauley and pull with oars across the mouth of the New, but a heavy rain that day had raised the Gauley to a very swift current, the boats were caught in it and swept down the Kanawha toward the falls. This was great danger, and it was only with desperate efforts that the boats, after a mile or more, could be worked out of the flood of the channel and into the slower current at the side. They finally escaped the peril and reached the shore on the side they started from. But the Captain was not daunted: he was intent only on obeying his order. With great labor they hauled the boats up along the shore to the Gauley, up that river to a possible crossing place, pulled over to the left side, and again ran down, this time taking great care to keep in the shore current and to work up into the New river along its right shore with every energy. This brought them into comparatively easy water, and, with the strongest men at the oars, they got over the New without mishap, and landed at the upper side of the foot of Cotton Hill.

But several hours had been lost and dawn was now appearing. Captain Lane was very anxious to get to the top of the hill without being met or seen by the enemy. Leaving a small guard with the boats, with the remainder he climbed the hill as fast as possible, tho its steepness and roughness , -- small, difficult ravines, rocks and tangled thickets, -- made the work slow at best. The gun of one of his men was fired by accident. This halted him for an anxious minute or two, but no sound from an enemy following, he was reassured and hurried on to the top. Here, in the misty light of early day he found the field abandoned, the guns gone, and no enemy in sight.

Taking as position with prudent care for retreat, if compelled, he sent out small parties to scout in several directions; and, finding no sign of the enemy near, he advanced himself, and found him about a mile from the

Gauley front, at the interior or southeastern end of the hill (where it was the highest) and sheltered by a wood.

This took some hours and, seeing by Captain Lane's advance that the enemy had left the front of the hill, General Cox sent over the remainder of the Eleventh Ohio -- then little more than 200 for duty -- under Colonel DeVilliers, whose order was to "occupy and hold the crests if possible". At the same time he sent Lieutenant-Colonel Enyart, with 200 of his regiment (First Kentucky), to cross just below the hill, reach the Fayetteville road and the left of the battery position. Again appears the puzzling question, why was this latter movement not made by Benham's men? He was already on that road, a few miles below, with his whole brigade. If there was a strong force of the enemy between him and Cotton Hill, it would be far too strong for Enyart's 200. The only explanation suggested by reading the records lies in the marked inertia of General Benham, a charge which seems to be fully justified in the perfect hail of orders and messages sent to him by Rosecrans within a week with no effective results.

Whatever the reason was the whole affair was now left to Cox's brigade, tho still on the north side of the river. Seeing that DeVilliers had landed his contingent of the Eleventh Ohio and advanced beyond sight, General Cox, for some reason not found, sent over no more troops until night; and that regiment held the hill (that half nearest the river), with several skirmishing advances and retreats, throughout the day (Sunday, November 10). This was very creditable to the small command, tho also a proof Floyd had now no great force on the hill and expected to abandon it.

Captain Lane's share in this day was characteristically steady and self-reliant. He had no instruction for action beyond the stage he had reached, but he understood it to be his duty to remain in immediate observation of the enemy until relieved by orders or driven back by attack. Accordingly, after making sure of the position of the rebels by feeling their pickets, he disposed his men where they could best watch and yet quickly concentrate for defense or retreat if compelled. He then sent a man back to the river to report the situation. He had had skirmishing in fixing the rebel position, but as yet not loss.

His messenger saw Colonel DeVilliers[27] at the river,

---

27 Captain Lane tells of two incidents of this arrival of DeVilliers whch are very amusing, not only in themselves, but in Captain Lane's taking them so seriously. His indignation, however, was more than justified. The Colonel came over in a rowboat with three men, two at the oars and one steering. On landing he ordered these men to remain in their seats, then called off the sergeant commanding and one man from the guard Captain Lane had left in charge of his two large boats, directed the man to hold the bow of his rowboat to the bank, ready for instant use, and the sergeant to remain there in command of the four and shoot at once any of them who attempted to leave, while he provided for the sergeant himself by declaring his intention to cut his head off if he failed in any of these duties. This rediculous seems almost incredible, but tho it comes only from the men thus marked for sudden slaughter, and so must be taken with some allowance, there were so many such incidents in the career of this curious mountebank in office. The men directly concerned in the Colonel's careful provision at the boat account for it upon the simple tho harsh theory that he was thinking only of his personal safety. Perhaps they did not then know it is the duty of a commanding officer to avoid exposing himself unnecessarily, tho that rule is supposed to apply to the field of action in front rather than to a position in the rear!

The other incident was in an absurdly comical scene, tho both actors were hotly in earnest, one of them righteously angry enough to knock the other off the earth. The Colonel must have known of the misfortune by which the boats were carried down on the flood, inasmuch as they were hauled back along the front of the camps, and undoubtedly the Captain had reported it on the way; but, whether he knew it or not, he now worked himself into such a passion he would listen to nothing. In the coarse and profane language he was given to, he declared the Captain was unfit to command, and that he had failed to cross the river and get up the mountain from cowardice; and all the time he was flourishing in the air a cavalry sabre (he carried it constantly, instead of the proper infantry officer's sword) as "wildly as a madman." Captain Lane at first tried to speak, but seeing the uselessness of it and unwilling to lower his dignity in a quarrel, he was silent, only keeping his hand on his pistol "if the fellow came near me."

where he had landed, made the report, and was sent back with an order to him (Lane) to report in person at the landing at once. As I find no where any comment upon this astonishing order, I would make allowance for the possibility of circumstances not reported which might make it seem less unreasonable. What it did was to take away the commanding officer from a small party of troops in a dangerous position directly in front of the enemy, and take him so far away that he could not return, at the best, for nearly an hour, meantime not knowing what was happening at his post. If it was necessary to see the Captain, the Colonel should have gone at least as far as to the top of the hill before sending for him. If he had done that, he would have met him much sooner and kept him from his post less than half an hour.

As it was, the Captain hurried down to the river, and the Colonel, without asking for further report or information, at once began to berate him for not getting across the river earlier, and filled the air with violent and vulgar abuse and epithets, applied to the Captain and his men and all the regiment. Captain Lane, tho in a deep rage, commendably restrained himself and waited for the end, only keeping ready for action if he were struck or approached. When the truculent little Colonel's wind was spent, he was so far from ordering anyone to execution that he ordered the Captain to take that portion of the regiment now landed to the position of his company on the top of the hill and command the whole till further orders. It was barely in time, for the enemy was showing signs of activity. Closer skirmishing followed, soon afterward Major Coleman appeared -- an experienced soldier and very capable officer -- and took command;and finally Colonel DeVilliers came, as he ought to have done long before. There was a great deal of desultory fighting, with no definite gain that day.

As the battle here the next day had a decisive result (tho it was not improved) and was the most important one the Eleventh had up to this time, some account of it ought to be given. It was known as "Cotton-Hill" or "Blake's-Farm" in the Kanawha army, but is "Gauley-Bridge" in Phisterer's "Stastical Record".

Cotton Hill is a ridge or "hog-back", about one and a half miles long, lying northwest and southeast. The northwestern end rises to a head or promitory, several hundred feet high, overhanging the river, with a precipitous, rocky face, inaccessible except that at a few places footmen may climb up thro narrow gorges. Behind the head, on top, the land falls away into a "saddle", making a fairly workable tract large enough for a small farm, which was then occupied by a farmer named Blake. Southeast of this farm rose the true hill, higher than the river end and then covered with forest. The southwestern side of the ridge is deep and steep, but to the north and east of it the land is considerably higher, so that from there the hill is easily reached.

Floyd had a couple of regiments encamped at the foot of the southwestern side, on the Fayetteville road, which there curves southward to get around the base of the hill, but he withdrew them when he did the guns; and his whole force was now on the Fayetteville road, east of the hill. Thus there was nothing to prevent Benham's brigade from moving up the Fayetteville road to the southern end of the hill, a movement which would have induced Floyd to give it up at once; and there need have been none of the labor and cost to Cox's men of taking it by attack on the top.

When the Eleventh Ohio detachment arrived in support of Lane's company, it was posted, with that company, beyond Blake's farm, and finally, under Major Coleman, advanced to an attack. The rebels soon broke and fell back thro the wood on to the higher ground. Getting aid, however, they returned and, in a counterattack, drove the Eleventh men back to the edge of Blake's farm. Here, behind a ravine, a defense was undertaken and the rebels were held until another detachment of the regiment arrived. Then the advance was renewed and the rebels were driven farther than at first, -- beyond the farm and well up the wooded hill at the outer end of the ridge. Night coming on the command was posted in a good defensive position, its left holding the ground nearest the New river ferry, and remained there during the night.

If it were not Floyd in command it would be remarkable that this small force -- less than 250 -- was allowed to remain on the hill. With any boldness he could easily have destroyed it in a single movement. He does seem to have had an idea of his opportunity. In the night a feeble attempt upon it was made, under which its left wing, under Major Coleman, moved back a few hundred yards and lost six men captured (Lane's company was, as I gather, on the right), but just then two companies of the Second Kentucky, sent over by General Cox, arrived to re-inforce, and Coleman recovered his ground. Some firing then followed upon all parts of the line, but seemingly without any set purpose, and, after an hour or two, the enemy retired without having accomplished anything and without any spirited effort.

During the night four more companies of the Second Kentucky came over from Gauley, thus raising the command to about 600 men, but it was impractical to bring up even a small gun. General Cox too came over, to direct operations. At daybreak (the 11th) began an advance of the whole force, by General Cox's order but under immediate command of Colonel DeVilliers. The rebel pickets were soon uncovered and driven in, and the main body steadily pushed again onto the wooded hill, tho keeping up a constant fire. Judging the enemy's force there to be much superior to his, General Cox halted this movement; but it had gone far enough to bring the Fayetteville road into view to the southeast, and the enemy's baggage train was seen there, moving toward Fayetteville. Floyd was preparing for full retreat, as was further shown by the fact that Enyart's detachment of the First Kentucky (that first sent over) now moved up the Fayetteville road, by the southwest and south side of the ridge, and in the afternoon was on Laurel creek, at its southern-most point, where it remained until the next day.

General Cox did nothing more, not even "feeling" the enemy more than he had done with his contingent on the hill. He could now easily communicate with General Benham, a few miles down the road (as of course with Rosecrans across the river), and one would expect to hear that Benham was ordered to move at once up the road, at least so far as to determine what Floyd was doing or what his position was. And so he was ordered (as soon as Rosecrans learned from Cox that Floyd's wagons were moving) to move up immediately; but he says, in his report, that he received the order at 11 p.m., while Rosecrans says, officially, that his acknowledgement is dated 7 p.m. Whatever the hour was, Benham's idea of "immediate" was such that, as his report says, he began his march "next morning" (the 12th) and spent the day up to 4 p.m. in reaching, on the Fayetteville road, the right of Cox's position on the hill, a march of eight miles. Here his advance had a slight skirmish (probably with a small section of Floyd's rear guard. left in observation), and he bivouacked for the night. During the night his picket or scouts reported hearing wheels moving up the Fayetteville road, but it was not till "next morning" again that he sent a reconnoitring party to learn what it meant. He waited till after 4 p.m. of that day (the 13th) for this party to return, and then advanced. Of course he found no enemy; and he marched ten miles (to and beyond Fayetteville)without seeing one. Floyd had passed there the afternoon of the 12th, more than a whole day and night ahead of him.

Early in his operations Roescrans had sent General Schenk, with his brigade, a few miles up New river, to try to make a crossing at a long-abandoned ferrying place, in the hope of getting the Fayetteville road above Floyd's position, and six days of labor were spent there in making boats or floats and getting them down the bluff to the water. This was done when the river rose high and the crossing was declared impracticable. But Floyd was then (night of the 12th) known to be in retreat; and on the 13th Schenck's brigade was brought down across the Gauley and put over the Kanawha where the first detachment of the First Kentucky had crossed, thus placing it on the Fayetteville road, several miles in the rear of Benham's brigade. Schenck then followed up Benham, and was directed by Rosecrans to take command of both brigades.

On the 14th Benham moved on and that night was ten miles further toward Raleigh, tho he had been twenty-four hours or more in doing it. Under these persistently adverse conditions, disgusted with Benham and hopeless of recovering the prey he had believed surely in his hand, Rosecrans stopped the movement, and Schenck ordered Benham to return to Fayetteville, which he did promptly and within one-fourth the time he had used in marching the same distance in the other direction.

A certain hasty judgement, characteristic of Rosecrans, may well be said to have led to his failure in this campaign. There was, in fact, no good reason why he could not cross New river some miles above the place attempted by General Schenck. Without any certain information he believed that General Lee was on the Lewisburg road with a strong force, ready to attack him at Gauley Bridge, and, so, of course, able to prevent his sending a brigade any distance up New River. He could have learned, without any serious difficulty, that the force remaining after Floyd crossed was practically insignificant and that after November 5th Lee was not there. Schenck could easily have been over and in control of the Fayetteville road before the 10th, and then, cut off on his only road on both flanks, Floyd's command would have been taken, if only Schenck and Benham attacked and pressed him with energy.

On the 13th, when it was certain that Floyd was in full retreat and Benham was at Fayetteville, in pursuit, Cox's men were withdrawn from Cotton Hill to their camp at Gauley. They were in high spirits and proud of themselves. As they saw it, the fighting had been done by them, and Floyd's whole army was beaten. And when they learned that Benham and Schenck were in pursuit, taking wagons and picking up prisoners without a battle, they claimed that the hard work and dangers and conflict were theirs, while the other brigades reaped the credit. That is the way soldiers talk, because, usually, they know only what occurs immediately under their observation and do not know the causes or meanings of operations or movements as a whole. But they were really entitled to high credit. They had been two days and nights on the field, in immediate contact with the enemy, under constant excitement and probably with little or no sleep. Tho they had not fought any large part of Flyod's forces, as they, or some of them, seem to have imagined, they had finally beaten those they did meet, and in their several advances and retreats had been under fire a dozen times, several times quite hotly; and they had borne all the loss in men in the whole affair. They had, in short, successfully maintained the most important action in the field that had yet fallen to their brigade.

The Eleventh Ohio had, indeed, borne the hardest part. The most of the work and all the losses had been in that regiment. And Captain Lane and his company had done the most, or at least had been the longest on the field and most at risk. Their adventure in crossing the two flooded rivers in the night and climbing the high, steep hill, to meet an enemy of unknown strength, would make a thrilling story. The particular part taken by the Captain and his company in the various fights of the 10th and 11th as not known. What he wrote about the actions was but little and was all of a general character.

A day or two after Cox's men got back into camp Benham's brigade was brought back, while Schenck's was left at Fayettevile, where Rosecrans now intended to erect defenses, to be held indefinitely as the outpost of the army on that side of the river. But there were to be no more field operations until spring: indeed no more were practicable, the roads having become quite impassable and sure to be kept so by the winter storms.

That was Floyd's view too, and, partly for that reason,

partly because half his men were sick and all demoralized, at the end of November he moved thro the mountains southeastward and encamped on the Virginia & Tennessee railroad, near Newbern....

1862: January -- May

The year of the greatest trials of the Eleventh Ohio, of the hardest labors, of the most profitable experiences, and of its steady and rapid development as effective soldiers. But, for Captain Lane, it was all that and much more. As an engineer, he exceeded the achievements of 1861. As a recruiting officer in Ohio, he succeeded not only in replacing the losses of the regiment, but in filling it up to the maximum, -- a condition never reached before. As an officer burning with zeal in the great cause and with a mind single to the best development of the regiment and the good of the service, he planned and, at great personal risk and sacrifice, resolutely fought out to success the dismissal from the army of the unfit Colonel. No wonder that before the end of the year he was the foremost man of the regiment.

The very beginning of the year was marked by the undertaking, led by Captain Lane, to force Colonel DeVilliers out of the regiment. It was his greatest battle and greatest success of the war. It proved his courage and his capacity for self-sacrifice in the highest degree; and, so far from crushing him, as he keenly feared from the beginning of the attempt, it led, indirectly and wholly unforeseen, to his becoming the Colonel of the regiment himself.

In so large an army of volunteers as that in the Civil War, hastily assembled, containing, comparatively, very few men of military training, with no system or standard in the selection of officers, it was inevitable that many unfit men would be commissioned. The "line" (company) officers were, relatively, better than the "field" officers (majors, colonels and lieutenant-colonels), because, as a rule, they had proved at least their zeal in the cause and energy in action by "raising"their companies. But the field-officers were mostly commissioned thro the "influence" of political or social friends of conspicuous position; their possession of military capacity remained to be tested by trial. It is true, a number of the field-officers were men of former experience in the regular army or in the volunteers in the Mexican war; but another class was that of certain foreigners who had experience in the armies of European monarchies. Some of these were naturalized Americans, but many were still aliens and many came to America after the war began, confident of obtaining positions much higher than any they could hope for in their own countries. Some of these foreigners were very troublesome, from their lack of adaptability, and some were imposters or mere adventurers. Little or no care was taken to learn their antecedents and in some cases the only knowledge obtained of them was in their own tales.

The Eleventh Ohio had the great misfortune to get for its colonel one of these imposters. He was said to be French, but he spoke German fluently, his former career was unknown, and when he was dismissed in disgrace from the Eleventh Ohio he disappeared so completely that he was never heard from again. Whatever connection he may have had with a European army, he proved to be a man of low breeding, of no high purpose or sense of honor, and without personal honesty. He showed knowledge and skill as a drill-master in sword and bayonet exercise, tho his regiment profited little or nothing by them. It seems that the only thing he tried to do with any persistence was to bring his command under "discipline", but he was so conceited, mercurial and impatient that he could not wait upon the necessity (for green soldiers) of laying the proper ground by constant drilling and practice in the primary school of the soldier. So he tried to teach his end by erratic violence and harshness, personal redicule and insult, and wholly failed. He was, however, very alert mentally and physically, made a smart, soldierly appearance, had an ingratiating address toward superiors, and to them in his earlier service appeared to be a capable officer. Even General Cox wrote of him, on his return from prison, in a manner which, later, must have brought him mortification and regret. Colonel Frizell, of the Eleventh Ohio, was much better qualified to form a correct judgement, as appears by his letter to Mrs. Lane, written December 27, 1861.

Colonel DeVilliers had been in the field but two or three days, and on no important duty, when he was captured. He had hardly returned to his command (November 1, 1861) when his ability and courage were put to test (at the battle of Cotton Hill, as already described) and failed. His vicious and insulting abuse of Captain Lane and his company at that time was soon followed by similar instances in dealing with other officers of his regiment, while many of the non-commissioned officers and soldiers were subjected to his vituperation and silly threats of impossible punishments. Disrespect and contempt of him spread thro the regiment and was not carefully concealed by either officers or men. He lost hold of the regiment practically, while discontent, disorder and demoralization were only too apparent. To most of the officers the situation became intolerable. Privately nearly all wanted to get rid of him, but for any action there must publicly be a leader, tho the position must be one of serious risks, from which, naturally, most men of inferior rank would shrink. There were but few of the officers who could be reasonably be called upon to undertake it. Either of the two junion field-officers would fall under imputation for seeking his own advancement. A lieutenant would lack weight because of his inferior rank. So the leader must be a captain.

Captain Lane had been the first to suffer conspicuously, and in his case the Colonel had followed up his first offense by an exasperating petty persecution. The Captain had plenty of courage, braced up by righteous indignation at the injustice of his own treatment and that of others; but, in his simple-minded directness of speech, he had openly expressed his opinion of the Colonel personally and of the bad influence of his conduct upon the regiment, -- indiscreet, of course, to say the least, but also a breach of military discipline and law. An obvious handicap, too, this was in his heading the movement against the Colonel, but his mind was made up to accept any risks in the clear duty to himself and the regiment as he saw it. It is true, he exaggerated the possible evil results to himself, but that made his act in taking leadership all the more creditable to him. He reduced the whole case to the simple proposition that either DeVilliers or himself must be driven frm the army, and he would think of no compromise.

Soon after the army reached Point Pleasant, to go into winter-quarters (early in December, 1861), consultations of company officers were held and Captain Lane became their spokesman in requesting the Colonel to resign. Seeing that they had a set purpose, he finally said that, if the officers and men (i.e., the regiment generally) should ask it, he would resign. He fancied that they would not commit themselves to writing, but they did. Captain Lane soon had a petition signed by a number so large as to make it certain that the Colonel could not have many friends in the regiment. When he saw this he denied that he had given such a promise, but said that if all the officers, or a majority of them, should really demand it, he would resign. Then, curiously enough, he himself called a meeting of the officers. Perhaps he thought they would not dare to make the demand openly, for (apparently) he was himself present. There were then eighteen officers in camp (the other six or eight were absent sick or on furlough), and sixteen attended the meeting; and their vote was unanimous for the resignation. But his word was worth no more now than before. He refused, and in a passion declared he was the Colonel and would be the Colonel in spite of them.

Captain Lane immediately set to work in drawing up charges against him for court-martial, a step which he quite expected he would have to take. He finished them the same night and handed them in the next morning, December 27, 1861. He must have felt a sense of relief in reaching at last a definite, clear-cut issue; but yet his troubles were only just begun.

At that time an order for the court-martial required could be made only by the general commanding the Department, who was General Rosecrans. But the charges could reach him only thro the "regular military channel" (as it was commonly called), that is, the person making them must deliver them, in writing, to his immediate commander, and so on, each commander endorsing upon the paper his approval or disapproval or recommendation. Thus the first officer to see Captain Lane's charges was the one accused. It is not now known what he did with them nor what endorsement he wrote upon them, if any. But what he did on seeing them was clear and quick.

Captain Lane delivered the paper at the regimental headquarters and returned to his company with much relief of mind in the performance of a high duty. It was the regular hour for drill. He ordered out his company and was engaged in drilling on the parade-ground when an officer arrived with an order from Colonel DeVilliers, putting him under arrest and demanding his sword. The Colonel did not wait until the Captain was off duty, but put this humiliation upon him in the presence of his men and in a public place. No charge was made, no cause for the arrest was stated, and the Captain knew of no cause unless it was in the filing of the charges against the Colonel; but that he had the right to do, not only in the mere nature of things, but under the Articles of War. The fact was that the Colonel was in a reckless rage. Likely he had a vague idea that the filing of the charges could be punished as an act of insubordination. The effect of an arrest is to deprive the officer of his command and of regular service and "confine" him to his quarters, the next junior officer taking over his command. So a captain arrested must stay with his company while his lieutenant controls it.

When the Colonel's head cooled he saw that he had

gone too far, especially in depriving the Captain of his sword. Probably now, for the first time during the quarrel, he read the military law. The Articles of War require an officer under arrest to give up his sword only when a specific charge is made of criminal conduct; and the filing of charges against a superior officer, so far from being a crime, is a right expressly recognized by the Articles.

The Colonel within two days sought to repair the mischief he had done, but, instead of taking the reasonable and manly course of frankly admitting his blunder and apologizing, he only sent for the Captain (December 29) and offered his sword to him. The Captain demanded an explanation and a statement of the cause of his arrest, and refused to receive his sword without it. The mean-spirited Colonel would not comply. He sent for the Adjutant and ordered *him* to receive the sword; but he was still met with a refusal to receive it. Then he directed the Adjutant to take the sword to the Captain's quarters and, if he still refused it, to leave it there. At the same time he (the Colonel) ordered the Captain to return to duty and resume his command. The Captain declined to do either until he was told why he had been arrested, -- that is, he refused to be released from arrest! However, he seems to have then consulted someone, and to have been advised that he "could not make any point in refusing my sword and that my only redress was in preferring charges for false imprisonment." This was not correct advice as to the law, for the acts of the Colonel in the arrest and taking the sword were clearly usurpation of power and furnished ground for another charge against him, under one of the Articles of War. The Captain says, however, that he did prefer a charge of "false imprisonment", but he does not tell what was done about it, and such a charge does not appear among the papers nor in the proceedings of the court-martial. Perhaps it was thought good policy to drop it, to avoid as far as possible the appearance of a personal quarrel.

The war was now on. It could end only in total defeat of one side or the other; but, for the present, Captain Lane did nothing more in it than to prepare his evidence for the prosecution, tho he or some other officer at some time added further charges, based upon other tyrannical acts of the Colonel, committed while awaiting the creation and sitting of the court and while he (the Colonel) was under arrest.

The Colonel would have liked to placate the Captain, knowing that there were many witnesses against him and knowing also that there was ground for yet more serious charges if enemies should discover the evidence of them. But the Captain was perfectly implacable. He was quite settled in mind to risk his position and army career, and (as he then imagined) himself, in the cause of justice and the good of the service. He wrote to his wife at this time -- "I have come to the determination deliberately to follow the thing as long as there is a place to hang a hope on, and one or the other of us must be dismissed from the service in disgrace:.

"I have feared that I might have General Cox as my opponent in this matter, but I have strong hope that his good sense will dictate the proper course for him. I have right on my side and I will prevail against all that oppose; and if it is necessary for me to fight General Cox, I will do *that*. It will only prolong the struggle."

A few days later he wrote her -- "I promise you I will do my best to drive such a scoundrel from the American army and from a country of freemen." This "promise" was not due to her asking it: On the contrary she shrank from the contest, because of fear of the possible consequence to him and the family of a failure, naturally not fully understanding the affair, but feeling keenly the apparent disgrace of his public arrest and loss of his sword. It was probably this that led him to write, in this last letter -- "Do not let my children suppose that I am dishonored, but teach them it is better to die in defense of a right than to live in luxury and submit to a wrong".

Fortunately, he did not forsee the further sacrifice and humiliations he must endure to reach the decisive act in the struggle, tho his course would certainly have been just the same if he had foreseen. It was full ten weeks from the day he filed the charges when, at last, he heard the welcome call of the case for trial. This delay, in the dark and full of anxieties -- for he could get no news of action by the authorities, except that of the arrest of DeVilliers upon his charges, -- was heart-breaking and seemed almost intolerable. The bad news, morely, of the uncertain conflict upon the company and the regiment, the lack (real or fancied) of whole-hearted sympathy among his fellow officers, the natural (tho mistaken) apprehensions and doubts of his wife and personal friends at home as to the necessity or wisdom of his undertaking, and finally his fear (unreasonable tho it was) of a disasterous result to himself, even if DeVilliers were also destroyed, -- the situation must have been a constant distress to him, tho it could never shake his fixed purpose. He was penetrated by the conviction that he was right, and he did not permit himself to doubt his final triumph, however much the labor and pain might be. It was all a strikingly fine exhibition of his strong character. The authority to order a court-martial lay with the Department Commander, General Rosecrans, and he, or his Judge-Advocate-General (the prosecuting officer) did not consider the case as one for a special court. It was, therefore, left to await convenience of occasion for a general court to try accumulated cases. So the order was not issued until February 26, 1862, two months after Captain Lane's charges were filed. But he did not know -- could only surmise -- the causes of delay, and so was almost daily looking for news of action. It is quite possible that this delay was, in part, due to mere neglect or official indiference to the need of prompt action for the good of the service. The administration work of the Department must have been much influenced by the slip-shod, happy-go-lucky methods of its head.

Officer and men under charges are off duty and often under arrest, or even under guard, in disgrace in any event, tho a trial might prove them not guilty; the other officers and men see it all; and there is usually more or less demoralization. In common sense and common right, therefore, a military trial ought to be more speedy. The case of Captain Lane seemed to him of great importance, not merely to himself, but far-reaching (as indeed it was), and, not knowing why it dragged, looking every day vainly for some sign of progress, his anxious thoughts and feelings can well be imagined.

Colonel DeVilliers' character justified a suspicion that he would supress the charges against him or, at least, withhold them as long as possible from his brigade-commander; and Captain Lane was determined, in that event, to insist upon filing another set directly with General Cox. Accordingly, six days after he first filed his charges, he sent a duplicate set to General Cox, at Charleston, and at the same time asked leave to go up to see him. The leave was granted, and on January 8th he reached Charleston, saw General Cox, dined with him that day, and on the next returned to Point Pleasant.

His interview with the General must have been satisfactory. He does not tell what occurred, nor whether the duplicate set of charges was officially accepted and filed; but the General found occasion to constitute him a "bearer of dispatches" to General Rosecrans at Wheeling. Probably the chief reason for this mission was to enable him to see General Rosecrans, in the hope of assuring and expediting the court-martial. Incidentally, he was probably advised to ask at Rosecrans's headquarters for immediate approval of the application he had made in December for a leave of absence, and to make use of it at once. At any rate he stopped at Point Pleasant only long enough to get the next boat to Wheeling, took aboard at Marietta his wife and three children (Laura, Harry and Bertha), and landed at Wheeling on the 11th. Unluckily, General Rosecrans was absent, -- gone to Washington.

Whether he was able to do anything more than to deliver his dispatches does not appear, but he must have received his leave of absence; and he left the same day, by boat, landed with his family at Marietta, stopped there two days and, as appears in his diary, went to church on Sunday "(the first time in seven months)", "attending Lotta Bosworth's wedding at 6 a.m. on Monday", and on the 14th went to Cincinnati, beginning that day his twenty days leave of absence, the first he had had since he enlisted nine months before.

More than half this leave he spent in travelling to and from Cleveland and Streetsboro (Portage cunty), where certain of the Lane family affairs required his personal attention. Before and after this journey he spent a few days at Cincinnati with his family and in the affairs of his firm, which had suffered much by his absence. He was constantly anxious about the case of DeVilliers, however, and wanted to be on the ground. The day before his leave was up he was again at Point Pleasant. But he was to endure another whole month of delay in the case, with more troubles.

One thing occurred in his absence, however, which gratified him, as being an earnest of his progress toward the court-martial so much desired. When his charges were seen at Department Headquarters, Colonel DeVilliers was ordered under arrest. It does not appear whether he was deprived of his sword (probably he was, since some of the charges against him were of criminal character), but he remained under arrest and without command (Lieutenant-Colonel Coleman commanding the regiment) until he was tried and cashiered. Not withstanding his arrest the Colonel continued his plotting against Captain Lane, but, worse than that, the damage to the morale of the regiment, due to his lack of efficiency in command and now notorious antagonism between him and the most of the company officers, had reached a stage greatly discouraging to all. The position of the late Lieutenant-Colonel (Frizell) had become intolerable to him, thro the Colonel's conduct, and he had gone home and resigned in disgust. One of the best captains (Drury) followed his example. Others held on only in the hope of Captain Lane's success.

But even this condition of the regiment was not enough trouble for Captain Lane. During his absence his company had been put under the command of a lieutenant transferred from another company (B); and this officer, from either weakness of character or indifference to duty, had failed to get control of the company. The discontented and mutinous men in it (some are found in any company of volunteers), aided by the general bad spirit in the regiment, had nearly ruined its discipline and obedience.

Among other evils the whiskey-drinking in the camp was at its worst. There had never been any effective restraint upon it in the army, because up to that time the general public opinion was not really opposed to it; and the men and officers who were accustomed to drink regarded any attempt at restraint as an interference with personal rights. Yet probably every camp in the army was under orders absolutely forbidding the bringing in of liquors. But the devices of drinking men and their confederates outside, with lack of vigor and persistence in the officers in enforcing the orders, assured a means of supply, small in some commands it is true, but existing in all or nearly all.

Captain Lane saw little control of the evil in the regiment when he returned to Point Pleasant and less in his own company. He had set himself uncompromisingly against it from the beginning, and had tried repeatedly to get the other officers to join in efforts toward its real suppression, but he met small encouragement. This was, no doubt, one reason why the bad element in his company was hostile to him. They must have remembered, among other things, his conspicuous descent upon the keeper of the store on the wharf-boat at Point Pleasant soon after the regiment arrived there for winter-quarters. Suspecting that an increase in drinking was due a concealed trade carried on by this man, he went himself, with a file of soldiers, searched the boat, and found and dumped into the river nine barrels of whiskey. If this act added any to the number and strength of his friends, it must have increased more the number and hostility of his enemies. It was no doubt one of the causes of the peculiar personal obstruction he found in his company after returning from his leave, tho his determined cause in recovering control and discipline and resisting the attempt of the Colonel to appoint non-commissioned officers were causes enough. It reached such a pitch as that, at the end of some particularily trying day, he wrote in his private diary (February 23, 1862) "My men all hate me." But this pitiful entry was to be followed by another, seven months later, which shows that all the companies then joined in a vote (when he was absent from the regiment), by which they called unanimously, or practically so, for his promotion from Captain to Colonel.

To-day it seems singular that the officers of the regiment did not, as a body, share in a determined course to prevent the men from getting liquor, but they left Captain Lane practically alone in it. A letter written four or five months after the raid upon the wharf-boat shows he was still struggling unsuccessfully against the evil. He says he is glad the regiment is out in the field again, because "there will not be as much whiskey for a time. How it is to be checked is more that I can tell. If I had three of four to stand by me, I would hope for a reform, but as I am alone what can I do?"

It was with a heavy heart, then, that he resumed the company command the day after his arrival at Point Pleasant (February 3) and set himself to the work of recovering it from the low condition it had fallen into under the several demoralizing influences described.

The result of the Colonel's venture in the arrest of the Captain was far from satisfactory to him; he was further angered by it, indeed, and spurred on to another attempt. He found two soldiers in Company K -- a sergeant and a corporal -- who could be influencd by the flattery of his attention, and he descended to plotting with them against Captain Lane. He probably hoped to discredit him in his company and annoy him so far as to bring him to resign in disgust. And he undertook to reward the soldiers in advance. On the first of January, 1862, he issued a formal regimental order appointing the sergeant to be First-Sergeant of the company and the corporal to be sergeant. As he had, probably, not read the law when he ordered the Captain to surrender his sword, so, probably, he did not read the law when he made these appointments.

Under the Army Regulations the commanding officer of a regiment had the power to appoint the sergeants and corporals in a company, but only "upon the recommendation of the company commander". This is based, of course, upon the good sense and necessity of things, since no one can know as well as the captain the fitness of his men for the several positions and services required.

Captain Lane took this bull by the horns at once. He acknowledged the order in writing the same day it was issued, and added -- "I would refer you to paragraphs No. 73 and No. 80 of the Revised Army Regulations. I have not been advised with or consulted in regard to the promotions named in the order and shall disregard it as an illegal act". Number 73 was the one which required "the recommendation of the company commander" for the appointment of his sergeants and corporals, and Number 80 provided that "The first, or orderly, sergeant will be selected by the captain from the sergeants". Thus the Colonel had had no power in any event to appoint the First-Sergeant.

The ill-balanced Colonel, in his rage against the Captain actually used the Captain's refusal to recognize the "promotions" as the basis of one of the charges he made against him in the court-martial now appealed to both parties. The two misguided soldiers were disposed to insist upon their rights under the "promotions", but the Captain seized the first chance they gave him in refusal or neglect of duty in their old positions, and put them under arrest for disobedience of his orders. The sergeant appears to have yielded, but the corporal was, later, so troublesome that the Captain had him reduced to the ranks as soon as circumstances brought Lieutenant-Colonel Coleman into command of the regiment. Thereupon he too preferred charges against the Captain for court-martial. He got over his disorder, however, became a good soldier, and a year later was promoted to sergeant, and became First-Sergeant near the end of his term of service. But while the struggle between the Colonel and the Captain was in progress both of these soldiers tried secretly to help the Colonel by finding matter for charges against the Captain, tho nothing was found.

The charges of the reduced corporal against Captain Lane appear to have been filed directly after he was reduced. What they were is not now known, but the time and circumstances indicate, pretty surely, that they were instigated by the Colonel and were based upon the Captain's refusal to recognize the promotions. A court to try them was appointed and assembled with remarkable speed. It tried the case only ten days after the corporal was reduced, and apparently at Point Pleasant. Captain Lane appears to have paid little attention to it. The only record or statement of any kind I can find relating to it is an entry in his diary on February 24, 1862: "Court-martial on McGowan's charges against me. Verdict not known yet." The Captain must have been promptly acquitted, as he never afterward refers to the matter; and he went next day to Charleston on the business of his own charges against DeVilliers.

But this affair was only an incident in the campaign of the truculent Colonel. A few days after Captain Lane resumed command of his company at Point Pleasant he received a message from General Cox, calling him to Charleston. He was then busy (whenever off regular duty) in the preparation of the testimony to support his charges against the Colonel, and he spent two days more in that work. Then he went to Charleston, arriving on February 9, but found that General Cox had gone away. He waited a couple of days, but the General was not heard from, and he had to return to Point Pleasant without seeing him. He learned then, however for the first time, that Colonel DeVilliers had, a month before (early in January), filed charges agaist him for a court-martial and had demanded his arrest. He could not then learn what the charges were, but he did learn that General Cox had not acted upon them and had not considered an arrest, from which he inferred that the General regarded the charges as trivial or founded in malice. Finally, however, they were forwarded to Department Headquarters, and Captain Lane was tried upon them (with additions, based upon later acts) by the same court which tried DeVilliers.

Then, for a month, he could only wait and hope for news of the court, in unceasing anxiety and yet eager for the trial any day, spending half that time at Point Pleasant and half going back and forth between there and Charleston under orders and notices relating to the sitting of the court, -- which was to be at Charleston.

What wounded him most of all at this time, perhaps, was that, from the time he filed the charges he had to endure the coldness of many of his fellow-officers, who hedged when it was seen that the struggle must damage some one (not willing to be identified with the losing side), and the constant disrespect and covert shirking of duty among the men who considered him to be in disgrace and likely soon to be out of the army. But yet, excepting that his comments on the character of the Colonel were usually unqualified and in vigorous words, the only bitter thing he is found saying during this period relates to these hedging officers. In a private letter to his partner at Cincinnati, written soon after the trials of DeVilliers and himself by the court-martial, but before the result was known in either case, speaking generally of the other officers in the regiment and their attitude toward the cases, he says they "are as an intelligent set of men as you would be likely to get together, but their vacillation and indecision and want of any fixedness of purpose in this matter surprised me. A majority of them were ready to jump into the boat that was likely to win, with no other compass than self-interest."

But the Captain was more or less diverted from his troubles, and much comforted, by the news of the war in February. His diary contains more about that than his own affairs. Foote's capture of Fort Henry, Grant's of Fort Donelson and Burnside's of Roanoke Island especially filled him with joy. He thinks Foote and Grant great heroes, says he has "read their reports twenty times and will continue read them until the next victory." He "thinks the rebellion virtually crushed and not much more to be done," tho in writing this optomistic opinion, he was trying to comfort his wife, who was much troubled by what appeared to her his great dangers and long absence.

At last the painful delays of the court-martial came to their end. On March 1, at Point Pleasant, he had notice that it would sit at Charleston on the 5th. He was there at one o'clock in the morning, but the members of the court were not all there until the 7th. His diary on the 8th reads: "My case called at 1 o'clock. Pleasant day." "My case" means, not the case against himself, but his case against DeVilliers: but it was postponed to the 10th. On the 9th his diary only says "Sunday. Went to church. Pleasant day."

Now, after more than ten weeks of keen anxieties and many struggles, tormenting him in a hundred ways, came the day which, to his simple, honest mind, appeared big with fate. But it was a very welcome day, and he was ready and confident.

Here ought to be told just what was to be tried, -- what the two cases were. They were both to be tried by this court. A court-martial must be composed of officers of whom at least some are of rank superior to that of the officer under trial. So the "President" of this court was a Brigadier-General -- Hugh Ewing, a son of the famous "Old Tom Ewing" of Ohio and a brother of the General "Tom" Ewing who was distinguished in the war in Missouri, as well as the brother-in-law of General Sherman.

The case against DeVilliers was called first, on the morning of March 10. The charges against him were, in form, but one charge, with many "specifications." This charge was "Violation of the 83rd Article of War," which was "Any commissioned officer convicted before a general court-martial of conduct unbecoming an officer and a gentleman shall be dismissed from the service."

Whoever aided Captain Lane in preparing the charge and specifications was little, if any, more skillful than himself in the work. They show lack of experience and good advice. The specifications disclose ground for making charges under two or three others of the Articles of War, as well as under the 83rd. In fact eight of the specifications do not come under Article 83 at all; but, as it happened, this defect did not prevent a conviction. We do not have a copy of the proceedings of the court -- only of the charges, specifications, conviction or acquittal and sentence, -- but we can assume that the court treated the charges against DeVilliers as if amended at the trial to conform with the evidence presented.

There were thirteen specifications under the charge against him. The first was upon a gross and vulgar insult to Lieutenant McAbee, of Company F of the regiment, the second, upon the insult to and personal abuse of Captain Lane and his company on the occasion of the action at Cotton Hill already mentioned; the eighth, upon an insult to and personal abuse of Lieutenant Alexander (afterward Adjutant and killed in action); the ninth, the general charge that he was "in the habit of insulting officers under his command and making use of unofficer-like and ungentlemanly language:" the third, that on November 11, 1861 (at the battle of Cotton Hill) he "made a speech" to officers and privates of the Second Kentucky Infantry, in German, in which he used the "reproachful and provoking language" -- "Gentlemen: I am glad you come; the officers and men of the Eleventh Regiment are cowards"; the fourth and fifth, that he had obtained a sum of money from the sutler of the regiment upon a false and fraudulent (written) statement; the sixth, that he had seized (without authority) certain cattle in the country near Gauley Bridge, sold them to the Quartermaster and kept the money; the seventh, that he had plundered the house of a citizen at Point Pleasant and had taken from it a sum of money, silver-ware and much other personal property, all of which he had appropriated to his own use; the tenth, that he had arrested a citizen of Mason County, Virginia, and two negroes, slaves of other citizens of that county, and refused to release them until he was paid a sum of money for each of them, and had appropriated the money to his own use; the eleventh, that he had brought two soldiers of Company K to his quarters, put them under oath and required them to give information upon which charges might be made against their Captain (Lane), and this after Captain Lane had files charges against him; the twelfth, that, while himself under arrest, under charges, he had advised a corporal of Company K not to obey an order issued by Lieutenant-Colonel Coleman, then in command of the regiment; and the thirteenth, that he had delivered to General Cox a letter which was addressed to General Rosecrans, containing charges against Lieutenant-Colonel Coleman, then in command of the regiment, made by two privates at his (DeVilliers') suggestion.

The thirteenth specification is not clearly drawn,and it must seem, to most readers, rather indefinite. It was, I think, intended to charge a violation of the army regulations in trying to reach Department Headquarters directly with charges against a regimental officer, instead of taking the required "military channel" thro the brigade-commander, and, at the same time, "conduct unbecoming an officer and a gentleman" in acting personally (being under arrest, he had no official command) for private soldiers in promoting their charges. It must have been well known to him that the soldiers could have filed charges against the regimental commander in the regular manner, thro their captain, and that they would be duly forwarded thro the brigade adjutant unless obviously trivial or false or malicious. The explanation is, naturally, that these charges were really to cover his own and that the soldiers were meanly used as a cover in an attempt to injure Colonel Coleman. The comment already made upon the lack of good sense in DeVilliers seems quite justified.

When the case was finally called and the trial begun Captain Lane found himself excluded from the court room, altho he was the accuser and had filed the charges. Whether this was due to a rule adopted by this particular court or by the Judge-Advocate-General of the army at that time I do not know. It was a serious disappointment and discouragement to Captain Lane, who thought it highly important that he should be present, to aid the Judge-Advocate with information and suggestions. The fact was, that he distrusted the Judge-Advocate, because he had heard that, on the boat on the way up to Charleston, he was "drinking more than was good for a judge-advocate," that he had got a favorable idea of Colonel DeVilliers and asumed that the charges against him were filed by a "sore-head," and because he could not get him to spend any time in conferring on the case before the trial. But, tho he could not be present in the room, he stood outside the door and wrote questions to be asked the witnesses, and must have been able to send them in so that the rule of exclusion seems to have been enforced in form only. DeVilliers must have been present, tho I do not find it said that he was, nor whether he had counsel, nor what defense he made. But to the charge and all specifications he pleaded "Not guilty."

Captain Lane must have had many witnesses ready, as he says one-third of them were examined, altho the trial occupied two days. One of his witnesses was the Lieutenant-Colonel commanding the regiment (Coleman), who told him, when he came out, "how things stood." So it was probably on Coleman's information that he wrote in his diary, at the end of the first day -- "Many of my charges thrown out." By "charges" here he means the specifications, for there was only one charge (as stated above) and on that DeVilliers was found "guilty," as he was on six of the specifications. In fact, as the limited record we have shows, none were "thrown out", as Captain Lane understood, but all were considered in the final verdict, tho as to seven the ultimate finding was "not guilty." Anyhow he learned enough on the second day to give him the satisfaction of writing in his diary -- "I think I have won. DeVilliers is proved a scoundrel."

But near the end of the second day a sensational event brought the Colonel's trial abruptly to an close and made it not necessary to call more of Captain Lane's witnesses. It had happened that a detective of the Cincinnati police was at Charleston, a man known to Captain Lane and probably to General Cox. Upon certain testimony given on the first day, this detective was sent by the court at once to Point Pleasant. The next day he telegraphed a report. He had searched DeVilliers quarters and found there "a lot of stolen property under lock, a trunk packed ready to ship, filled with stolen goods, a lot of money -- over $1000, probably stolen," and papers showing a preceding shipment. It also appeared that there was an accomplice at Charleston.

The court thereupon closed the trial (the civil courts would now take charge of the criminal acts, i.e., in addition to the action of the court-martial), ordered the accomplice arrested and sent under guard to Wheeling for trial, changed DeVilliers arrest to "close confinement" ("they have got him here in jail," writes Captain Lane on March 15), and, for the purposes of a final judgement on the trial. "took the case under advisement." That ancient phrase always sounds particularily wise, judicial and carefully considerate of the interested involved, but quite too often, as in this case, it only covers unnecessary and injurious delay.

When the work of the court was completed, it was necessary to send the proceedings to Washington for approval or disapproval, because only there was the power to order execution of the sentence in such a case; but in this case, as the evidence made a conviction and dismissal certain, "the good of the service" loudly demanded that the officials should not lose a day in reaching final action. The Colonel was in deep disgrace and in prison for crime the

Captain who had brought him to judgement was himself in disgrace by arrest and compelled to remain in camp, seen by all to be without authority, awaiting judgement on the charges against him, conditions only too favorable to the malcontents and demoralizing the whole body. But it was two months after the real decision of the case by the court (at the end of the trial) when the judgement was announced in the regiment! One could safely risk his salvation upon the proposition that there was no sufficient reason for all this delay.

Immediately after the trial of DeVilliers Captain Lane was put under arrest and called for trial on DeVilliers's charges. This arrest, tho really only formal, was necessary under the practice, because of the penalty, if he were convicted, would be dismissal. He had expected arrest long before; and the Colonel had tried to have him arrested, but had failed, probably because General Cox believed, as already said, that his charges were induced by malice.

There were three charges against Captain Lane, alleging violation of the 6th, 7th, and 9th Articles of War, and under each charge one specification. Article 6 provides that "Any officer or soldier who shall behave himself with contempt or disrespect toward his commanding officer, shall be punished according to the nature of his offense, by the judgement of a court-martial."

The specification was, that, "on sundry occations in December, 1861, in the presence of various members of his company, Captain Lane did behave himself with contempt and disrespect toward his commanding officer, Colonel Charles A. DeVilliers, aplying the term 'scoundrel' to his said commanding officer."

Article 7 provides, that "Any officer or soldier who shall begin, excite, cause or join in, any mutiny or sedition in any troop company in the service of the United States, or in any party, post, detachment or guard, shall suffer death or such other punishment as by court-martial shall be inflicted."

The specification was, "that between the 15th and 31st

days of December, 1861, the said Captain Lane did write or cause to be written a petition requesting Charles A. DeVilliers, Colonel of the 11th O.V. to resign his commission; and that in his efforts to procure signatures to the said petition that the said Captain Lane made such false statements as were calculated to create a feeling of hostility and prejudice against the said Colonel Charles A. DeVilliers and his lawful authority."

Article 9 provides, that "Any officer or soldier who shall strike his superior officer, or lift up any weapon, or offer any violence against him, being in the execution of his office, on any pretense whatsoever, or shall disobey any lawful command of his superior officer, shall suffer death, or such other punishment as shall, according to the nature of his offense, be inflicted upon him by the sentence of a court-martial."

The specification was, "that on the 1st day of January, 1862, by the order of Colonel Charles A. DeVilliers, commanding the 11th Regt. O.V., 2nd Sergt. John Girten of Co. K, 11th Regt. O.V. was promoted to 1st Sergeant of said Co. K, and Corporal Elliot McGowan of Co. K was promoted to Sergeant in said Co. K, and that the said Captain Lane refused to acknowledge said appointments and did place the said John Girten and Elliot McGowan under arrest, because of their having obeyed the orders of the said Colonel DeVilliers."

To all the charges and specifications Captain Lane pleaded "Not guilty."

Courts-martial take their methods and practice, substantially, from the civil courts, and "Not guilty" does not mean a denial of the facts alleged, but a denial of a violation of the law, even if the facts can be proved as alleged. In fact, all of the allegations in the specifications were substantially true, except the one that "false statements" were made in obtaining signatures. Captain Lane *had* spoken with contempt and disrespect of the Colonel and *had* characterized him as a "scoundrel," both directly and to others; he *had* written the petition requesting the Colonel to resign and obtained signatures to it (which, taken alone, was insubordination, tho hardly to be construed as "mutiny or sedition"); he *had* refused to recognize the Colonel's promotions in his company, and *had* put under arrest the two promoted, for disobedience of his own orders; so that, practically, the only question for the court was, whether these acts constituted violations of the law as charged.

Unfortunately, as in the other case, we know nothing of the proceedings of the court upon this trial, who the witnesses were (except one), what the evidence was, nor anything from which one could guess at the result. But the trial was short, not much evidence could have been required for the prosecution and the defense must have been proof that the statements made in obtaining signatures to the petition were not "false". The diary on that date (March 12) shows that Captain Lane was much relieved in mind, tho it says only "DeVilliers does not make much of a case". And the next day he was back at his quarters at Point Pleasant, under arrest, to begin that unhappy experience -- "waiting for the verdict," knowing that he would not be relieved of the arrest until the verdict was officially declared and having at least some fear in the possibility that the relief would be by dismissal from the army.

For, not withstanding his frequently expressed confidence in a favorable result, he was extremely uneasy. Tho he magnified the chances of disaster, they were real chances. Under strict construction his acts had made him liable to punishment under either or all of the Articles of War invoked against him. Under Article 6 it would come as some form of humiliation, and perhaps as a fine. Under Articles 7 and 9, it could be extreme, that is, either "death or such other punishment" as the court might decree (tho, if "death", it would be subject to the approval or disapproval of President Lincoln). While a death penalty was, practically, inconceivable under the circumstances, yet the alernative "such other punishment" might be of a character not much less painful to a man of high nature.

So Captain Lane evidently had the possible outcome often in mind during the three months between the filing of charges against him and the official news of the judgement, -- a period of infernal inward disturbance it would be to anyone. He felt compelled to tell his wife of it, and at last did so, tho not till after the trials were over and the probabilities could be judged; and then he took care to couple the statement with what he artlessly thought an artful device to overcome her fears, saying that the other officers were offering "to take his chances" of the penalties for different sums, "from 25 cents to 5 dollars." Looking on from the outside of these events, however, one sees that the only dread he could reasonably have -- tho that was enough -- would be the dread of the consequences of delay in the rendering of the judgement, the character of which was now a foregone conclusion.

To close the episode without the interruption of an account of other events during the two months between the trial and the official announcement of the judgement, it appears that during the period he remained at Point Pleasant, still under arrest and without position or duties. A significant disclosure of his state of mind at this time is found in his diary on March 24, when only two weeks of the two months were gone -- "The monotony of my life is intolerable".

On May 5 an officer (Captain West) from headquarters at Wheeling, casually stopping at Point Pleasant, "brought news of the cashiering of Colonel Devilliers", -- the first news to reach Captain Lane since the trial. To that statement in his dairy that day, he adds only the words "York evacuated" (meaning Yorktown, Virginia, in McClellan's campaign against Richmond), one of the many bits which show that his eager interest in the operations of the war gave him some relief of mind from his personal troubles. But Captain West's news was only "camp news", and it included nothing about the case against himself.

Three weeks before this the regiment was moved to Winfield on the lower Kanawha, for the beginning of the spring campaign in the Kanawha district. Captain Lane remained at Point Pleasant (deprived of service by his arrest), and must have found a certain comfort in being for a time out of the camp, where he had to feel his humiliating position every day; but the day after he heard Captain West's story he followed to the camp at Winfield, probably feeling sure that the end of his trials was now near.

In fact the end had already been reached, apparently a full month before, certainly more than two weeks before. It is a shameful proof of mismanagement of administration in the Department, that he was not informed and at once released from arrest when the judgement was finally approved as rendered by the court. Nothing but gross neglect of officials can explain this period of delay. In the "Horton & Teverbaugh" history of the regiment it is stated that the judgement of the court-martial was approved April 4, 1862. That date may not be correct (no authority is given), but the printed official record of the judgements, sentence and orders in both cases, issued from Department Headquarters at Wheeling and showing official approval, is dated April 23, 1862. The Department must, therefore, have had the approval at least some days before April 23 (for the official routine and copying and printing); so there could have been no reason why they were not communicated to General Cox and to Captain Lane on or before the 23rd, if not on the 4th, of April. Two days after Captain Lane arrived at Winfield the regiment was moved up the Kanawha, to its old ground at Gauley Bridge, and he went along. They reached Gauley on the 9th, and the same day he received his first certain news of the end of his long war, in an order releasing him from arrest and putting him in command of his company. His diary of that date reads only "Was released from arrest. Have been under arrest two months"; and after that nothing more appears in his diary at any time relating in any way to DeVilliers or either of the cases.

The judgements were as follows: In the case against DeVilliers, on the first, second and eighth specifications, charging gross insults to or personal abuse of certain officers, or both, he was found "guilty" on the first and "not guilty" on the second and eighth; on the ninth specification, charging a "habit of insulting officers under his command &c," he was found "guilty"; on the third, charging the use of "reproachful and provoking language", insulting to the officers and men of his regiment, in a speech he made in German to officers and men of another regiment, "not guilty"; on the fourth and fifth, charging the getting of money by fraud from the regimental sutler, "guilty" on the fourth and "not guilty" on the fifth; on the sixth, charging the seizing of cattle in the country, selling them to the Quartermaster and keeping the money for his own use, "guilty"; on the seventh, charging the plunder of a citizen's house and keeping the goods, "guilty"; on the tenth, charging the arrest by him of a citizen and two slaves of other citizens and taking their money for their release, "guilty"; on the eleventh,twelfth and thirteenth, charging an abuse of his position in requiring two soldiers of Company K, under oath administered by himself, to aid him in finding ground for accusing their Captain, advising a certain soldier in Company K not to obey a certain order issued by the Lieutenant-Colonel commanding the regiment, and making an improper attempt, thro two other soldiers, to get charges made against the commanding officer of the regiment, "not guilty". But the field of all the material specifications was substantially covered by the verdict "guilty" on the first, fourth, sixth, seventh, ninth and tenth specifications; so that, finally, "Of the Charge" (violation of the 83rd Article of War) it was "guilty".

And therefore he was sentenced "*To be dismissed from the service of the United States and forfeit all pay and allowances. And the Court orders his property to be seized by the commanding officer of his post and held, subject to future and legal disposition.*" (The italics are in the original.)

The judgement and sentence were approved except as to the order to seize property, that being "referred to the United States District-Attorney for action", -- i.e., for criminal proceeding in the civil courts.

Whether he was indicted or criminally prosecuted in a civil court we cannot now tell. There is no later reference to him of any kind in any of the papers I have seen, except one scrap, in a slip torn from a newspaper, showing no place or date or what paper contained it, tho I think there is evidence in the slip that the paper was printed during the war, probably toward the end. It reads -- "Charles DeVilliers has been arrested in Baltimore on a charge -- which he has admitted -- of passing a worthless check. He is the individual of whom Colonel Ellsworth learned the famous Zouave drill, and was at one time Colonel of the 11th Ohio Infantry."

Captain Lane ought to have had (no doubt he did have) unmeasured credit and graditude for this great service and achievement. By his unshakeable conviction of duty, his courage, tenacity and self-sacrifice, he had rendered a service of supreme value to his regiment, to the army, and to the country. The cost to him had been terrible, but it is sure that he felt amply repaid for all in his success, -- perhaps especially in having kept his "promise" to "drive such a scoundrel from the American army".

In the case of DeVilliers' charges against Lane: on the first charge, that of violation of the Sixth Article of War, and on the specification under it, that he had "behaved himself with contempt and disrespect toward his commanding officer", the Captain was found "not guilty"; on the second charge, that of violation of the seventh Article of War, and on the specification under it, that he had written and procured signatures to a petition requesting Colonel DeVilliers to resign, "not guilty"; and on the third charge, that of violation of the ninth Artice of War, and on the specification under it, that he had refused to acknowledge the appointment by the Colonel of two non-commissioned officers in his company and put these men under arrest for obeying the Colonel's orders, "guilty":" And the Court did *therefore honorably acquit the prisoner Philander P. Lane, Captain of Company K, 11th Regiment Ohio Volunteer Infantry"* * * * "Sentence approved. The Captain is ordered to duty with his company." (The italics are in the original.)

It will seem curious to one not experienced in courts and military affairs, that Captain Lane was found "not guilty" under the first and second charges and specifications when the facts alleged against him were notoriously true and were not denied, and that he was found "guilty" under the third charge and specification, and was then "honorable acquitted". The reasons must have been that the Court was satisfied that at least the first and second charges were made in malice, and that the Captain's provocation was great, if not, indeed, a justification; while, as to the third charge, that it was merely fatuous, since, under the Army Regulations, a colonel had no power at all to appoint a first-sergeant and could appoint sergeants and corporals only on the recommendation of the captain. That is, that the court used an underlying discretionary power to defeat a malicious prosecution.

Philander P. Lane was later elected Colonel of the regiment following the death of Colonel Coleman at the battle of Antietam in which the 11th Ohio participated following its transfer to the Army of the Potomac in 1862. The regiments under the command of General Cox had performed so well in the opening fighting at South Mountain that they were given the priviledge of opening the attack on the Confederates at the battle of Antietam. The men of the 11th Ohio were in the lead as the Union army attempted to cross at Burnside's Bridge.

Following the death of the gallant Augustus Coleman, Captain Lane was elected to command the regiment and he served as an honest, honorable officer in the Union army while DeVilliers disappeared into the shadows from which he did not re-emerge.

James Hamilton lived near Woodville (presently Ansted), Virginia, and the twenty-eight year old man worked as a surveyor, taught school, and was a good neighbor for those in the area. He frequently recorded that he had participated in stable raisings and barn raisings. He began his diary on January 1, 1858 and began with several resolutions. His resolutions were much like those of the present day:

1st RESOLUTION -- Esteeming the habit of using tobacco a useless and disagreeable habit, and the money consumed in this manner may be far more wisely used, I hereby renounce the use of tobacco in any and all forms.

2nd RESOLUTION -- Seeing that I have now been serving the Devil for 28 years -- and a good servant I have been -- I think it is time that I should change masters, and with this thought, I hereby resolve, or rather renew the resolution that I made some time ago, that God being my helper, I will more truly and faithfully serve "Him that hath made me."

3rd RESOLUTION -- That in the future I will more diligently try the rule "Do as you would be done by" and not let my passion and my tongue run off with my wits.

4th RESOLUTION -- That as Dr. Franklin says: "Early to bed and early to rise, makes a man healthy, wealthy and wise" is sound wisdom. As for health I have a good supply of that, and as for wealth I am not anxious about that, but for wisdom since I have only a small stock of that article and while I am afraid that I am getting too old to learn yet nevertheless Franklin's advice is good, therefore I will endeavor to profit by same, and resolve to rise at five o'clock every morning.

Hamilton was an intelligent, religious man who was

soon to feel the pressure of events occurring in the new country as the Civil War came closer to reality. He reported in his diary that he began to attend "muster," the monthly meeting of the area's militia. He reports nothing about politics, but there was a substantial change in the man's personality by the time he made his last entries in the diary.

The entries in the last pages of the reprinted section found in Fayette County History *are listed under the year 1863, but either Hamilton or the editors of the book made an error. The events described were in 1861. Hamilton wrote daily in his diary during 1858 and 1859, but reduced his entries in late 1859. His father died on May 30, 1859, and this may have had a strong effect on the young man. He wrote infrequently in June and didn't write again until November 14, 1859.*

He made two entries prior to the outbreak of the war; one on December 6, 1860, and the other on February 2, 1861. He wrote only when he was troubled and the entries were essentially prayers. He began to record some of the events of the war as the Confederates retreated past his farm and the Federals appeared in pursuit.

The Diary of James B. Hamilton

Sunday -- August 18th -- The Federal troops under Col. Frizell fell back from Mountain Cove to Woodville.

Monday -- August 19th -- The Federal troops were busy engaged putting up shelters and breastworks. The Confederate troops were in full view in the evening.

Tuesday -- August 20th -- Firing commenced about 8 o'clock on the morning between the pickets -- not much damage done. One of Frizell's men was killed, and two taken prisoners. No loss on the Southern side. About ten o'clock the Federal troops retreated from their position and fell back to Turkey Creek. About 2 o'clock the Southerners under Col. Croen[28] appeared in sight of here. They halted here a few minutes when they were advised not to proceed, as danger was apprehended below. Nevertheless they proceeded about 200 yards when they were fired upon by a body of the Federal troops concealed at the end of my lane. Four of the Southern men were wounded, one dangerously. And it is reported that one of the Federal troopers was killed. Our whole family with several neighbors who were here were in the fire from the road to the house.

Friday -- August 23rd -- A body of Federal troops marched up to Woodville and back, having seen nothing.

Saturday -- August 25th -- Federal troops went up again. About 10 o'clock the firing commenced again and continued three-quarters of an hour at Westlake's Creek. One of the Federal troops killed and one wounded. One Southerner killed and two prisoners taken, also a good many guns, pistols, & etc.

Hamilton's diary was not continued. As the war's violence developed more fully in the vicinity of his home, it was originally thought that he may have moved to safety as many others did. His name does not appear on the rosters of Confederate units recruited from the men in the area and he is not listed as a member of the primary Confederate partisan ranger unit in the region, Thurmond's Rangers. No record that Hamilton was imprisoned as a Confederate sympathizer was located in the available literature (even though it was probably Hamilton who warned the Confederates to wait at his house on the day of the fight at the end of his lane). The original hypothesis developed was

---

28 Colonel Croen was actually Lieutenant-colonel Croghan, later to become Floyd's cavalry commander. His name was frequently mispronounced and was spelled phoenetically.

was that he and his immediate family probably moved to safety rather than stay in the area where they were in danger from the fire from the guns of both sides.

The story of James B. Hamilton was completed by Fayette County, West Virginia, historian -- Shirley Donnelly -- in a newspaper article[29]*. The diary entry described was dated December 6, 1860, but Hamilton (or the original editors) made incorrect date entries. The entry was probably written in December, 1861, (or possibly 1862) and Donnelly described the mood of the writer:*

"Dec. 6, 1860, found James B. Hamilton in a pensive mood. That day he took his pen in hand and left this writing on the pages of his private journal:

'What shall I say or what shall I write? I have nothing good to write, only that I am alive and still where mercy may reach me, though I deserve it not. Since I have taken up my pen to write in here, how varied have been the scenes of life and how eventful our career. Friends and neighbors have come and gone and still I am spared, and for what?'

"Little did he know that Confederate Partisan Rangers were soon to size him up as being opposed to secession and states rights down in Dixie. That was his undoing and in about three years he was to languish unto death in Andersonville Confederate Prison."

---

29 Donnelly, Clarence Shirley, "Hamilton Diary Depicts Civil War Action", *Beckley-Post Herald*, Beckley, West Virginia, July 19, 1957

The violence of the Civil War was not limited to only the battlefield. There were fewer civil authorities such as sheriffs and deputies, particularily in the rural areas, at the time of the war. Unfortunately, the breakdown of legal authority occurred at a time when violence was an accepted fact and large numbers of men both in and out of uniform were heavily armed and highly mobile. Unionist settlers in the valleys and hollows of western Virginia were frequently the prey of Confederate bushwhackers settling scores due to the frequent burning of their homes and property by the Federal "arsonists."

In addition to the two-way reprisals that were occurring on parallel to the actions of the war, there was an increase in common criminal activity, especially in the rural areas where the disappearance of a victim could be effectively managed without fear of discovery and punishment.

One such crime was written about in The Pioneer, *an annual report prepared for the descendents of the French Creek pioneers. This particular story, "A Civil War Episode," tells about the killing of a man who was murdered and robbed after selling his cattle to the Confederates. It appeared in the seventh annual edition of* The Pioneer *in 1930.*

A Civil War Episode

Following is an account of the murder of a French Creek citizen during the heated days of the Civil War, the victim being Garland T. Ferrell, grandfather of Garland P. Ferrell, who is well known to many of our members. The account is taken from a volume, "Moccasin Tracks and Other Imprints," written by William Christian Dodrill ("Rattlesnake Bill") of Webster Springs. It might be noted that Garland P. Ferrell spells the name of his grandfather's murderer as "Hartsook" instead of "Hardsock," as Dodrill has it.

"One of the most atrocious deeds perpetrated in the country during the Civil war was the murder of a man named Ferrell at the mouth of Straight creek by Dr. Hardsock. Mr. Ferrell had taken a drove of cattle through the mountains within southern lines and had sold them, receiving a large portion of the selling price in gold. On his way back he met Hardsock, who proposed that they travel together. They arrived at the Gauley late in the evening of the first day's travel and camped on the bank of the river. Some time in the night while Ferrell was wrapped in slumber Hardsock cut his throat with a hatchet. Hardsock continued the journey very early the next morning. When he arrived at the first settler's cabin, he said that he and a comrade had been attacked in the night by the "Yankees" and that he and his companion had become separated in the night. He asked that someone be sent in search of the missing man. He seemed to be much agitated and very anxious to proceed on his way. But haste was useless because his guilty conscience would pursue him to the uttermost parts of the earth. The possession of the dead man's gold but augmented its excruciating pangs. The body was buried near the place where the murder was committed.

Hardsock was apprehended by the Confederates and was kept under the strictest surveillance. By an order from the general in command of the troops whose duty it was to guard him, he was put under the hottest fire of musketry in every battle in which they were engaged. His companions fell around him but he escaped unharmed. He sickened and died of a fever before he could be tried by civil authority. Some rude rock slabs and a small spruce tree planted by loving hands mark the place where Mr.Ferrell was buried. He was truly a victim of greed and avarice."

There were many other killings on both sides during the war which were committed by either side. The population found in the border states lying adjacent to the two warring sections consistedof essentially three groups: Those favoring the Union, the Confederates, and those who may have favored one side over the other, but decided to remain as noncombatants. The latter group was also divided into two groups: Southern sympathizers and Northern sympathizers. There were frequent episodes of violence committed by one group on the other during the war and of sudden reprisals of revenge against the original attacker or the attacker's family. It was a difficult time and most of the stories of the atrocities were never recorded.

One of the stories which has endured concerns the death of a young man from Nicholas County, West Virginia, a few days after the battle of Carnifex Ferry. The grave of Nicholas Ramsey lies a mile or so from the river crossing which was fought over by Rosecrans and Floyd in September, 1861. Few people know of its' existence, but few hikers or kiyakers who wander up the overgrown road that leads down the mountain to the ferry ever forget their discovery of the lonely grave. The word MURDERED appears to leap out of the stone.

The story of Nicholas H. Ramsey has been assembled from several obscure sources that include a 1930 article from The Fayette Tribune *of Fayetteville, West Virginia;* The History of Nicholas County, West Virginia, *by William G. Brown; and the* Ramsey Family History *by J. C. Ramsey which was written in 1933.*

It is an interesting story because it shows how easy it was to die during that violent period and the story reveals how long the memory of a Mountaineer can be and the lengths one will go in order to right a wrong.

The Death of Nicholas Ramsey

Nicholas H. Ramsey, the son of James Riley Ramsey, was shot from ambush and killed four days after the battle of Carnifax Ferry was fought in 1861. The lonely tombstone stands under a rock ledge beside a road leading from the historic ferry to Mount Lookout. It is a fairly tall, weathered stone monument which was erected by someone who felt strongly about the wrongful death and the anger seemed to leap out of the stone from the inscription:

Nicholas H. Ramsey
Born January, 1839
MURDERED
Sept. 14, 1861

The Murder of Nicholas H. Ramsey[30]

In the shadow of a great rock in a weary land, Nicholas H. Ramsey has been sleeping the long sleep since September 14, 1861. The lonesome sepulcher is just off the ancient road that formerly led to Carnifex Ferry in days long since joined to the ages.

It is a mile and a half from the historic ferry that the grave is to be found, marked by an humble stone that stands hard by a cliff whose overhanging rocks make the situation as eerie as man ever gazed upon. All of this is within the heart of a primeval forest of giant oaks, enormous poplars and hemlocks green and indistinct in the twilight that has prevailed in this remote region for years untold.

---

30 The story of the murder of Nicholas Ramsey was written by C. Shirley Donnelly in the *Fayette Tribune*, Fayetteville, West Virginia, in 1937.

Close to this immense rock, and through dense thickets of sugar trees and rhododendrons, fringed by the most beautiful wild ferns in never-ending variety that mortals ever saw, splashes a little mountain stream of water that is as clear as crystal and refreshingly cool. Over the towering tops of the trees that have maintained their silent sintinel over these weird surroundings so long, the winds of the mountains sweep like the breath of a mighty organ.

One is overcome by the majesty of this lonely spot. There thoughts fashion themselves into prose and prose, in turn, flows into poetry. Poetry blooms into music and misic fades away into the brooding silence that overhangs this place.

Then, as one strolls off along the trails that lead by pine and poplar and birch and beech, with sweet murmurs of the mountain stream lulling his soul into peace, one hears the voice of the Lord God walking in this garden of nature in the cool of the day, asking of the pilgrim, "Where art thou?" This is Nicholas County, West Virginia, land of Bible names and hospitable people who, in the sweat of their faces still eat their bread and, for the main part, deal justly, love mercy and walk humbly with their God.

It was while traversing this winding mountain byway on September 14, 1861 that Nicholas H. Ramsey was slain ... He was, therefore, not quite twenty-three years of age.

The Battle of Carnifex Ferry had ended less than seventy-two hours before a musket barked, and its minie ball crashed through the Union cap visor and forehead of the young mountaineer on his way home to his wife and three-month-old son, W.H. Ramsey. The Battle of Carnifex Ferry, between the Union army under Rosecrans and the Confederate forces under Floyd, was fought on September 10, 1861. It was in this battle that William McKinley, then but eighteen years of age, received his initial baptism of fire.

Citizens of this community were nerve-frazzled over the events of September 10, and the events prior thereto. The community was very strongly Southern in its sympathy, but Nicholas Ramsey was thought to be just as strongly for the Union. This made him a marked man and started a chain of events that led up to the tragedy on September 14, 1861.

...Nicholas had married a daughter of Alexander McClung, who was the only union man in the McClung settlement, that wasn't afraid to say which side he was on. He was so determined in his ways that when a boy around there showed signs of self assertions they said he got his "Aleck up."[31]

Well, because Nick Ramsey was a son of Riley Ramsey and a son-in-law of Aleck McClung it was said he must be killed. The persons who plotted his murder were not soldiers. So they got James Remley to act as leader and waylay the road and shoot him. When they were tried for his murder they made a scapegoat of the said James Remley. Remley left the neighborhood and went to Virginia where secession prevailed. While in Virginia boasting about what he had done, someone said something about a Ramsey being around there, and he left at once and went to Missouri, ostensibly for the purpose of joining Quantrell and his clique of robbers and murderers. I shall now let W.H. Ramsey the son of Nicholas Ramsey tell the story of his father's murder.

"Nicholas Hance Ramsey was killed by being shot in the breast and head on the 14th day of Sept. 1861. He with his wife and infant son were living with his father-in-law, Alexander McClung in Nicholas County, near Carnifix's Ferry. He was killed three days after the battle of Carnifix's Ferry between Gen. Floyd on the Confederate side and Gen. Rosencranz on the Union side. He had left a few days before this battle and was among his relatives in Fayette County. He with John Wiseman crossed Gauley River in a canoe near Wood's Ferry and were fired on from the cliffs when they were about midway in the river.

---

[31] This and the following four paragraphs are from the *Ramsey Family History.*

They swam out on the Nicholas side but lost their clothes except trousers and shirt. He went barefoot to his uncle Richard Ramsey's on Bell Creek and was there provided shoes, clothing, etc.

He was killed near a gate leading from the country road to home-place on his return, and remained where he was killed for three days. His wife with infant son in her arms made three trips on three successive evenings hoping to meet him at the gate. All this time he was lying dead only a few yards on the outside of the gate. He was discovered by his brother-in-law, L.P. McClung, and was buried on the spot where he lay, by a company of Union soldiers. After the war was over his father Riley Ramsey and his brother Addison Ramsey built around his grave a loose stone wall which remains there today."[32]

By a curious coincidence,[33] Abraham Lincoln was to be shot on this same day four years later, September 14, 1865. A still further coincidence is to be found in the fact that William McKinley was to die likewise on September 14, 1901, just forty years after Nicholas H. Ramsey died at the hands of an assassin. Thus Ramsey, Lincoln, and McKinley, all three Union men who were vitally interested in the outcome of the Carnifex battle, were to die or be mortally wounded on the same September day, but some four to forty years apart. And all three were shot!

Nicholas Ramsey may really have been a Southern sympathizer like his neighbors, but he "took no stock in the war" or "at least was neutral" according to Crosby McClung who has collected information on the murder. "He was against war in any form," said McClung. But because he was the son-in-law of a Union man in a largely pro-Southern community, some local characters who were not soldiers decided that Ramsey should be killed.

---

32 W.H. Ramsey, the son of the murdered man, later became a sheriff. He probably heard the story of the death of his father dozens of times as it was repeated by family members who helped the young widow raise the young boy.

33 Shirley Donnelley's article is now continued.

Among the plotters of Ramsey's death was James Remley who said, according to McClung, "That man won't fight on either side. He ought to be killed and I could do it."

Nicholas Ramsey was a hard worker who had toiled in other farmers' cornfields that fall. He was returning home from working in a garden in Nicholas County when he was murdered. In some way he had acquired and was wearing a Union army cap. He was shot in the breast and in the head, a bullet tearing through the visor of the cap and into the young man's skull.

Union soldiers found the body of Ramsey on a big, flat rock where it had lain for three days in the road, a few feet from where he had fallen. According to Crosby McClung, the buzzards had plucked out the eyes of the dead man. The soldiers buried Ramsey in a shallow grave, underneath a rock shelf on this little traveled road. They ripped a slab from an old tree and then, with another slab and bark from nearby trees, they improvised a coffin. They wrapped the body in a blanket and carefully cast the rich mother earth upon it. The soldiers filled the grave with rocks.

Later, Ramsey's young widow Margaret removed the rocks from the grave to see her dead husband. McClung said, "She didn't shed a tear but went her way stoically." Margaret sold eggs and butter and saved every cent she could until her infant son, W.H. Ramsey, was eighteen years old. Then she called her son "to take this money and avenge the man who killed your daddy."

Those accused of the murder had been rounded up and tried. But James Remley had taken off for parts unknown. In Virginia he boasted of his part in the Ramsey murder, but when he was told of a young man named Ramsey being seen there, he lit out for the West. According to McClung, W.H. Ramsey took up the trail of his father's alleged assassin. The trail stopped, McClung thought, in Montana. W.H. Ramsey never admitted that he had killed Remley, but only said that he had "seen him in his coffin."

The rancor and venom that took on such sectional

aspects after the war between the states has long since ended. It took the Spanish-American war to bark over this terrible feeling in the United States. However, I heard the last faint echo of it when Mrs. Virginia Ramsey, with evident feeling, spoke on the day of this service.[34]

Her father had been taken prisoner by the Confederate armies, and had died in prison. Added to this was the killing of her relative, Nicholas Ramsey. This was a double blow, and one that added acid to open wounds. The years for the past three-quarters of a century have served to mellow the feelings of the 82 year old lady. As she spoke and told of her own transformation by grace devine, Mrs. Ramsey added that she now could honestly pray, "Father forgive them for they know not what they do."

Mrs. Ramsey may have been able to forgive the murderers of Nicholas Ramsey, but the young, fatherless man, W.H. Ramsey, was far less forgiving. He lived with his mother until she re-married seven years later to William Aaron McClung, college-educated, a lawyer and prominent in the community. The young Ramsey benefitted greatly from the influence of the new father. He was able to attend schools - a three year course at Marshall College, West Virginia University for part of two years, and Grand River College in Missouri. He returned to West Virginia in 1887.

The question persists: Did he kill James Remley as the story seems to indicate? The real answer will not easily be located after such a long period of time, but there are a few clues to use in making up our individual minds as to the answer:

First, he was out of West Virginia and in Missouri for

---

34 Donnelly was asked by Nicholas Ramsey's seventy-five year old son to accompany him and the rest of the Ramsey family to the scene of the murder and conduct a funeral service after the monument was erected. Seventy-five years did not dim the memory of the murder.

a considerable period of time. Legend has it that Remley went to Missouri in order to join Quantrell's raiders after leaving Virginia. This does increase the possibility that he was searching for Remley. If he were able to pick up any signs of a "trail" that lead to Montana, he could have followed Remley and could also have "seen him in his grave."

Second, W.H. Ramsey felt sufficiently strong about the death of his father that he arranged for the funeral ceremony which was conducted by the Reverend Donnelly seventy-five years after the murder. He was obviously the person who paid for the large stone momument which was erected in the wilderness on the site of the killing and Ramsey was still angry enough to have the word MURDERED engraved on the stone marker. He was also obviously angry enough over the killing to keep the memory fresh in his mind for most of his life.

Third, Ramsey-McClung family was quite large and must have had a large part in the raising of the young, fatherless boy. They must have spent a great deal of time cursing the absent killer, Remley, in the presence of the boy and thoroughly convinced him that he should resent the killer of his father. Evidence of this long term anger in the extended family is indicated by the fact that many of these same people went down to the grave site at the time of the funeral ceremony -- including an 82 year old lady.

Fourth, a man who was a friend of W.H. Ramsey was asked in an interview if W.H. Ramsey ever admitted to killing Remley. He replied, "I once asked him about it. Willie Hance only looked at me and said, 'What do you think?'"

Ramsey certainly had the reason to look up Remley, he was absent from the state in a region where Remley had been, and he obviously had strong feelings about the death of his father. The answer may never be found, but the story is one more of the fascinating mysteries that developed in the hills of West Virginia -- where evil deeds done leave a long memory among a slow to anger, but vengeful people.

The partisans of each side formed into companies of "Home Guards" for the Union while many of the Confederate sympathizers joined "Partisan Ranger" units. While there were no major battles fought on West Virginia soil that were equivalent to those fought in the eastern theater, there was a near constant low intensity level of combat as the two sides guarded, raided, and counter-raided one another.

The following story is a history of a Confederate raid on a Union fort which was constructed at Cross Lanes near the site of Camp Gauley, the location of the battle of Carnifex Ferry, and the approach to the strategic ferry on Gauley River.

This fight is of special interest to the editor as his Great-Great Grandfather, William Jeffries, was a member of one of the Confederate Partisan Ranger companies which participated in this operation. The story appears in the Ramsey Family History *which was written by J.C. Ramsey in 1933.*

Union Captain J.R. Ramsey was the father of the unfortunate Nicholas H. Ramsey who was murdered by Confederate sympathizers early in the war.

Capt. Ramsey's Fight at Cross Lanes

Last August, A.A. Hamilton of Cross Lanes took quite an interest in showing me the site of Capt. J.R. Ramsey's fort that was captured and burned by Confederate soldiers in August 1864. The fort stood just above Zoar Baptist Church on the hill west of Kessler's Cross Lanes. It was about 100ft. by 110 ft., built of split timber about 1 to 2 feet in diameter. The logs were split in halves and planted four feet deep in the ground making a solid wall perhaps 12 feet high. The timber was cut out toward where Huston Dunbar now lives. There is little if anything to show where the fort stood. The site is now being used as a burying ground and I am told that in digging graves pieces of the lower end of the logs are found still in the ground. When the fort was attacked by the Confederates, Capt. J.R. Ramsey and a part of his men were away on a scout, perhaps in Fayette. There were in the fort at the time it was attacked about 22 men or more commanded by T. Addison Ramsey[35] who was First Lieutenant. The Confederates were under the command of Col. V.A. Witcher who was making a raid through Nicholas and Braxton Counties. In that raid he captured quite a number of Union soldiers and property, under Col. Witcher were Captains J.J. Halstead[36], Bill Thurmond and Phil Thurmond. I have been told that there were about 500 Confederate soldiers.

Some of the Union soldiers were pitching horseshoes

---

35 "Add" Ramsey was the son of Captain Ramsey and the brother of the murdered Nicholas. The Civil War in the mountains was much like a family feud as the extended Ramsey-McClung family and their friends formed a Federal unit as the Thurmonds from across New River and their extended family formed a Confederate group to oppose them.

36 The Halsteads were some of the Federal neighbors of the Ramsey-McClung family.

out on the west side of the fort when the rebels appeared on a rise perhaps less than 100 yds. from the fort. The rebels fired and the Union soldiers ran into the fort and shut the heavy gate. Tom Collison who had a sleepy disease was sitting perhaps on a barrel in front of the gate when the firing began, which awakened him and he ran into the fort going so fast he could not stop until he struck the wall on the opposite side.

I have been told that after the Union soldiers had fired a few rounds at the rebels that the rebels sent Lieutenant Ramsey a flag of truce demanding a surrender and threatening to shoot the fort to pieces with cannon. Tho' they had no cannon there at the time. Ramsey agreed to surrender but while he was arranging terms of surrender 5 or 6 of the yankees jumped out of the fort and ran away. Lieutenant Ramsey stopped this as soon as he found it out.

After the fort was taken Capt. Halstead went to John R. McCutchen's to get some harness and equipment to haul away the spoil and was fired on by some of Capt. Isaac Brown's men and maybe some of Capt. Ramsey's men. No one was killed in the affray. Capt. J.R. Ramsey and some other Union soldiers were keeping their clothes at Mr. Hamilton's where Andy Hamilton now lives. A.A. Hamilton who was then a boy 12 or 14 years of age took Capt. Ramsey's clothes and buried them in a cane patch and saved them. Some other of the family hid Hiram Pierson's clothes in a box of oats but the rebels found them and took them.

One of the prisoners taken was Abe Snedegar whom you remember played off on the rebels when Capt. Ramsey's house was shot into as I told in my last paper.[37]

---

37 Abe Snedegar was only about 16 years of age when he joined the Union home guard. He had not been issued a uniform when the Rebels attacked Captain Ramsey's house. J.C. Ramsey was in the house as the attack took place: "One of the Yankee soldiers was Abe Snedegar. He was only about 16 years of age and had not drawn his uniform. He was in the house with my brother Jake and myself. Jake was about 14 years of age and I was about 5. When the shooting began, Abe ran to the

After firing a few shots at the rebels he took a big chew of tobacco and made himself very sick. When the rebels came in the fort they found him in bed very pale and claiming he was not able to walk. They carried him down to John Vaughn's and left him. About as soon as the rebels were gone Abe left to find the rest of Capt. Ramsey's company as soon as he could.

I shall now let Mr. Wesley Chapman tell the story of the capture of the prisoners and their prison life or death as it fell to the lot of each.

"I, Wess Chapman, volunteered in Capt. Ramsey's company, also Joe Bryant and Bill Chapman February 4, 1864.

We were at Cross Lanes in the fort about 18 men. Capt. J.R. Ramsey and the rest of the men were in Fayette County on a scout trip. The men at the fort were surrounded by about 300 Rebels before we knew it and captured. Addison Ramsey was First Lieutenant and in charge of the fort when it was captured.

The fort was captured August 2, 1864, and we started on our trip to prison. We crossed the river at McVey's ferry (mouth of Meadow River) and reached the top of the cliffs and camped. (This was at the Kessler place near where the Clifty P.O. is now. The prisoners were shut in an old house that my father showed me after the War; J.C.R.)

The next day we went on through Greenbrier County past the White Sulphur Springs on to some small creek. I can't recall the name of the creek.

The names of the prisoners taken were Wess Chapman,

---

door but as the bullets were striking the house and whizzing past he was afraid to go out. So Jake took Abe's gun and put it under the stair steps in the closet. Abe sat on a chair and looked and felt as little as he could. The rebels came in and searched the house, but could not find Abe's gun and presuming him to be a neighbor boy went away and left him."

Bill Chapman, Addison Ramsey, John Dorsey, Austin Campbell, Jack Sanders, and a Martin, I can't recall his given name.

(I think it was Emannuel Martin; J.C.R.) As Mr. Chapman could not remember all the names of the men taken at the fort I here insert their names obtained by the help of A.A. Hamilton and others:

Hiram Pierson, Hiram Read, Ben Dorsey, Lewis Halfpenny, two Kincaids, John Campbell, Add Ford, Abe Snedegar, and Hosea Fitzwater; J.C.R.

"We went through Fayette and Greenbrier to a place called Floyd's Mountain, and here there was a battle.[38] The yankees drove the rebels out to a place called Daublin Depot[39] and we prisoners followed on. We came to Lynchburg and here spent two days. The bridges had been destroyed and we could not get over. Then we went on to Richmond, Va., and here we spent a few days. Then we were sent to Salisbury, N.C., to a prison camp.

I was in camp from August 1864 to March 1, 1865 or about seven months. When we first landed at camp there were about 300 men there and before we left there were about 12,000 men in camp. Some were there only about 2 or 3 months. When the exchange came there were only about 700 of the 12,000 men that could walk. The ones that could walk, did so to Richmond and the others were taken to a place of exchange by boat. On the way to exchange we spent a few days in Richmond. I had bone fever and was sent to Baltimore and there remained three months and the war was over before I got home.

We had very little to eat in prison. We had 6 or 7 bites of bread, tin of rice soup, and two bites of meat. We got this food twice a day. The rice soup was very thin and we

---

38 This was the battle of Cloyd's Mountain where General Albert Gallatin Jenkins was mortally wounded.

39 Dublin Depot

drank it. It often had the worst kind of meat and many times the meat had maggots in it and the maggots would be in the soup. We drank them. We were treated like dogs and shot down any time.

We had men among the prisoners that did not care for anything. I saw a man one day take a knife and walk up to a poor fellow standing leaning against a tree and when this bad man came up to him he cut him open from hip to hip and the man's bowels fell out on the ground. He stood there a few minutes and fell over dead.

I and three other men had a dry place to sleep. We four dug down in the red clay about 15 to 17 inches deep and just wide enough for the four men. We took sticks and poles such as we could find and covered this over the top. Then we took this red clay and covered over these sticks. When it rained we would take paddles and smooth this clay down and it would turn water like boards. When the sun came up the mud would crack then when it started to rain we would take paddles and plaster it over again. We had one old blanket we spread on the ground and slept on it. The ground under this kept perfectly dry."

All of the eighteen were taken to Salisbury. Ten of them died in prison. Mr. Martin died at Richmond on his way home after exchange. Mr. Chapman claims he always intended to come home. He said many men just gave up and died. He got so he could tell them by their looks. They would go out and build up a little gnat smoke and sit down with hands out to the fire and there die. Ben Dorsey died in Charleston, W.Va., on his way home.

John F. Dorsey, Jack Sanders and a Mr. Fuller and another man dug out of prison. Jack Sanders was shot just after he got out. (John F. Dorsey and Mr. Fuller traveled at night and laid up in day time obtaining a little food from Negroes. They got through to Cincinnati and went home; J.C.R.)

Mr. Chapman says "there were good men in prison. They would often sit down on one of these mud beds and hold meetings. Two thousand or more, would gather around and have greatest respect for worship."

Of the 18 who were taken prisoners, 9 or 10 died in prison, one was shot by guards, one or two died on their way home. The men who got back were as follows: Wesley Chapman, John F.Dorsey, Hiram Pierson, Addison Ramsey, Lewis Halfpenny, and I am not sure who the other one was. If any person knows, please let me know. Thomas Collison was one of the men in the fort but whether he jumped out and left or was taken prisoner I am not sure. If he was taken prisoner he got back.

Mid Brown was taken prisoner but he belonged to Capt. Isaac Brown's Company. Geo. McMillron and Isaac Nicholas were running away from the fort and the rebels after them when Isaac Nicholas fell into the brush and fern and the rebels failed to find him. The rebels said Nicholas would not throw down his knapsack. This was the Isaac Nicholas known as Humphy Ike.

The Ramsey family was probably representative of families living in western Virginia during the Civil War. All of the men in the family were affected by the fighting and the hatred that accompanied it. Even the young author of the family history was nearly killed by rebel bullets which were fired into his home. His next older brother, Jake, was taken by the rebels even though he was only twelve or thirteen because of their suspicions that he was carrying messages. The author asked his older brother, Wallace, to write about some of his war time experiences:

"... As to the skirmish I was in in Fayette County, a part of our Company had been to Gauley Bridge for rations. I was driving an ox team and Cousin Mary Legg (Uncle Bill Legg's daughter, who married Wesley Farr) met us out on the Saturday Road and told us there were sixty rebels watching for us. So we went on. Some of the boys wanted to leave the road and go some other way; but I told them I was going on until we were shot at. John F. Dorsey had command of the squad." (He was Lieutenant in Capt. J.R. Ramsey's Company.) "So we went on. Steve Eads was with us. He was not a soldier, so he said he would go on ahead of us. As he got to the top of the Dogwood Ridge, (this was not the main Dogwood Ridge, but a prong of the ridge, Osborne ridge) they shot at him, and that let us know where they were. So we stopped at the foot of the ridge, left the wagon there with Ward Wiseman and Uncle Bill Legg, and the rest of us went on around through the woods and came in behind them. But they saw us first and fired at us killing Austin Eads and cutting me on the left shoulder. Did not hurt much but tore a big hole in my shirt. So we skipped. In place of sixty there were only ten rebels there. The rest of them were over in the Wilderness. They were the ones that father and the other boys were fighting at the old shop and Collison's creek. The names of the ones at Collison Creek were father (J.R. Ramsey) Addison and Reed Ramsey, Allen Berry, and I think Hosea Fitzwater. There were 8 that fought at the shop but only 5 or 6 at the other place...

These were the same rebels that came in on Wesley Ramsey and shot him. All of these skirmishes included the 60 rebels on the scout. I do not know who the rebel commander was...

I don't know much about the surrender of the fort at Cross Lanes as I was not there. Addison Ramsey (First Lieutenant under Capt. Ramsey) was in command. He did not want to surrender, but the rest thought it best to give up. That was in August, 1864. There were 18 taken prisoners. I can't remember all the names, and only 6 got back alive. These were Add Ramsey, John Dorsey, Hiram Pierson, Louis Halfpenny, Wesly Chapman, Him (he) and ___Dorsey got out of prison at Salisbury, N.C., and came through most of the way in the night. (They hid through the day and at night would stop into negro shanties and beg for something to eat. I have heard John Dorsey say they had nothing to eat for four days but a few persimmons.

They came through Tennessee and Kentucky to Cincinnati, and came up the Ohio River on a steam-boat and walked on home. They were treated very cruelly while in prison, almost starved. Sickness, exposure and starvation caused most of them to die. They dug a hole under the floor of the prison and tunnelled out, coming up outside the prison wall; J.C.R.)

"That raid in Greenbrier, I was not along, but they got about 25 horses, but the rebs got after them and got most of the horses back. While I was in the company we made a scout up about Hominy Falls and we got 15 horses from Capt. Pollick. We caught them in pasture while the rebs were asleep. There were 11 of us, father and five of his boys." (Add, Cass, Reed, Wesley and Wallace) "The rest as far as I can remember were Bill Hawkins, Dave and Harve Crookshanks, I can't recall the other names now." (I think Sam Ramsey was along.) That was in the summer of 1863.

Those two men that were killed on Sewell were Andy Cavendish and a Crane boy. We were watching the road and they came along. We halted them and they stopped. We told them to throw down their arms and they should not be hurt. They threw down their guns and started to run and they were both killed before they went more than five steps. They were dead before we got to them." (They were carried into a school house and their friends notified.) "I can't say who was in command when father's property was taken...Well, the first time Add (Ramsey) was taken prisoner as a civilian was in August 1861. He was taken to Richmond and put in Libby Prison. He got back that winter following. When he (Add) was taken at the fort in Aug. 1864, he was in Salisbury awhile, then they moved him to Danville, Va. He was exchanged about March 1865.

"Well there were a few things I forgot. When the rebels surprised us at Leftridge Bail's on McKee's Creek and run us off, I ran 450 yards and them shooting at me every step but did not hit any of us, but about run the wind out of me. They caught Ward Wiseman and Henry Backus, but did not take them very far till they let them come back. That was in October, 1863.

In the fall of 1862, father, Ward Wiseman, Bill Hawkins and Hosea Fitzwater, and myself were over on Panther Mountain and we met this same Mary Legg that met us in Fayette. She told us there were 4 rebs at Old Betsey Grose's taking their horses. So we picked our place to watch for them. They soon came along and we fired on them, wounded two or three of them. The five of us gave them eight shots. That was my first shot at rebels. Then up at Old Gigal Church we shot at a gang of cavalry, but did not hurt any of them. I think that was Fall of 1862. So I think that is all."

The small fights at "the shop" and at Collison Creek were rather small affairs and probably didn't get recorded into the Official Records of the War of the Rebellion, *but were representative of the small-scale skirmishes that continued between the two sides during the war. Most of the large military units left western Virginia to fight in the larger campaigns that were being fought, but the Partisan Rangers and the Home Guards continued to fight.*

Long after the war, the rebel commander in the area and the arch-enemy of the Ramsey family responded to a letter sent to him by the author of the family history. He was willing to explain some of the unknown people and actions that took place in one of the fights.

...Yours of Dec. 1, rec'd and contents noted. Captain Sanders was in command at the fight at the shop. I was ordered to come up on the South East side of the shop, but looked over the ground and thought that Captain Dan Heifner would cover that part of the woods as he came down from White's place. I took my company and went straight to Captain Ramsey's shop and met Captain Sanders' Company at the shop. Just as I got to the shop Cap't. Ramsey and his men just across the fence on the East side in the woods opened fire on my men, and Cap't. Sanders' men give back behind the shop. But Capt. Sanders ordered up and we charged Capt. Ramsey and his men and they took to the woods.

How Capt. Ramsey missed me and Capt. Sanders I never could tell, the shop door was full of bullet holes; but you may bet we were not standing still.

Capt. Ramsey was guessing a little closer than I would like him to. The bullets were whistling around my head. When we routed him we started to the mouth of Meadow River.[40] We went down by the Collison Creek bridge. James Walker and I were in front of the command. Capt. Ramsey had flanked us and got up on the cliff and opened fire on us, they shot James Walker in the leg; (one other rebel was slightly wounded; JCR). We charged them and put them to the woods again.

Then we went on across Meadow River into Fayette and back to our command. I am in my 89 year since 29th day of October, 1925.

In October (1863) I was ordered to go on the Wilderness Road above the White House and not let any one pass, and was ordered by the Colonel of the 14th Cavalry. I had three men with me, George Halstead, William Gwinn, and William McClung. I held every one that come down the road until very late in the evening, he (I suppose the Colonel) got drunk and sent his men down on Hominy Creek. I turned all loose to go where they pleased. There was one colored woman in the crowd and she broke for Capt.Ramsey's Company (I suspect this was Jemima Williams).

I took my boys and went up Hominy Creek road to big John Amick's widow ... We put up there for the night. It was raining and the boys built a big fire and I lay down to take a nap. One of the women woke me up and I went to

---

40 This is near the spot where Nicholas Ramsey was murdered.

the window and saw the porch full of blue coats. Then I made for the outside door intending to shoot my way out. But as I opened the door Cap't.Ramsey was at the door and the room full of soldiers. So I handed my gun to Capt. Ramsey and surrendered to him. He took us to J.R. McCutcheon's and kept us till morning. (Capt. Ramsey took them to his own house the first night. I remember the next morning when my father, Capt. Ramsey, formed his men in line of march, Capt. Halstead picked up a stick for his gun and got in line with the Union soldiers; J.C.R.)

He, Capt. Ramsey appointed four soldiers to guard each of us to Charleston. When we came out of the house to start, Dan McCoy wanted Capt. Ramsey to let him shoot me. He told Dan that he would not hurt a hair on me. I asked the Captain to let me have a gun and let us try our hands.[41]

When Capt. Ramsey bid me "good bye" he wished me a safe trip to Charleston. I thanked him and told him if nothing happened I would see him in two weeks.

The night of Nov. 6, 1863, William Gwinn and I dug a hole under the prison wall. The plank was sunk 2 1/2 feet in the ground. We came out into the street. Gwinn went out first, I next, then George got fast in the hole, but I managed to pull him out, but made him leave his boots as they made too much fuss.

I know Cap't. Ramsey was as cunning as a red fox for I tried to pen him seven or eight times, but he would slip out and always got most of his men out with him. I know a good many things you will want in your history.

Your true friend,
J.J. Halstead."

---

41 Captain Ramsey apparently didn't hold Halstead responsible for the death of his son, Nicholas, or McCoy would probably have had his wish.

I have copied Capt. Halsteads' leter almost *ver batim.* I went to see him and he has to use two pairs of spectacles when he writes. I highly appreciate his writing this letter, for I know it cost him considerable effort. I hope to see him when I have time and have him tell me more about the war. As he says in his letter he is past 88 years of age; but I want to say that his mind seems clear as any young man's mind, especially on the war.

He has written an account of the fight at my father's blacksmith shop. I was an eye witness to the fight, standing in the kitchen and looking out the window. I was only 5 1/2 years of age, but it seems vivid to me now. In addition to what he has told I shall add a few items.

When my father's men fired on the rebels, they called over and said "Is that you Capt. Sanders?' "Yes. is that you, Capt. Heffner?" "Yes." "Well give us the countersign." Al Berry, one of Capt. Ramsey's men said, "Poke your head around that shop and I'll give you a countersign." Then the shooting began again. As well as I remember Capt. Ramsey had 6 men and there were 30 rebels. The Yankees had 3 or 4 revolving 6 shooters, rifles and Colts revolvers. The fight lasted long enough that Capt. Halstead came around to the old log smoke house and shot at my father three times, as he could see him from there where he was hid behind a tree from the shop.

Capt. Heffner was three quarters of a mile from them when the fight began. He had 20 men and they ran down from the fork of the road at Wm. Whites and got close to the Yankees before they saw them. Capt. Ramsey saw them just as they were squatting behind a large Chestnut log to shoot, and calling his men they dropped over a steep slope and ran off. They ran around to the South of our house and down to Collison Creek bridge,and waited for the rebels to come. Then occurred the fight as Capt.Halstead has related. As Capt. Ramsey's men were running to beat the rebels to Collison Creek they stopped at a Sulphur Spring to get a drink and Uncle Hiram Pierson being fleshy gave out and staid there. So, As I have it only

5 of the Yankees were at the bridge fight.

The names of the yankees at Collison Creek were Capt. J.R. Ramsey, Add Ramsey, J.Reed Ramsey, Allen Berry and Hosea Fitzwater.

In addition to the men who chose to remain at home and attempt to protect their homes and families from their neighbors having different political views, large numbers of western Virginians entered military service on both sides. While the Confederate Partisan Rangers and the Union Home Guards raided one another's homes, farms, swiped horses, and fought small and deadly skirmishes, those young men in their respective armies were involved in the large, deadly battles that are typically remembered by historians.

The following letter was sent to the family of Marshall Dorsey, a young man from western Virginia serving in the Union army as a member of the Ninth Virginia Vounteer Infantry. He had joined the army early in the war and apparently intended to to his duty to the last.

The letter begins on page 194 of the Ramsey Family History.

"Winchester, Frederick County, Va.
May 3rd, 1863
Company F 9th Regiment, Va. Volunteer Infantry.

Dear Parents;

I take this present opportunity to let you know that I am well and enjoying the best of health, hoping these few lines may find you all enjoying the same blessings when they come to hand.

I have not heard from you for some time. I would like to hear from you very well.

Well we were on a scout five days. We went to Lost River and made a bridge of wagons and planked across it, and carried our ammunition for our cannon across the river to the Moorefield Road and back around to Strausburg. There the Pennsylvania Cavalry and the Rebs went into a fight. Our battery and us came in the rear of the cavalry and planted the cannon. Our regiment was drawn in line of battle to support the battery, and gave the Rebs Hail Colombia, and away they went. We took nine prisoners and killed some. The cavalry lost six in killed and five wounded and several more missing. That is the amount of the battle.

The "grillers" have pitched in on the Baltimore and Ohio R.R. and tore up some bridges and stopped our mail for a week but we have it in repair and two brigades on the road. We have a strong force here at present.

So I must close. Write soon and let me know how you all are getting along. Take good care of yourselves until I get home. So Good by. I remain your son till death.

MARSHALL DORSEY

to Andrew Dorsey and family."

His family received several letters from their soldier in the Union army, but the last is most interesting. A letter written by Marshall Dorsey on April 24, 1864, contains a premonition of death:

"There will be a move before long and what will be the result is unknown. If this is my last thought, I shall fall in the defense of my country that I may fall in sight of Heaven with glory in full view and my prayer is that God may keep us all by his protecting power, and though we may never have the priviledge of meeting on earth, I bless God that we have the priviledge of meeting in Heaven where parting will be no more."

The young Union soldier did not return home to his parents.

Among the many Home Guard units,there was a company called the "Snake Hunters," a company which was commanded by "Captain Baggs". The colorful name was derived from their opposing Confederate equivalent, the "Moccasin Rangers," and the unionists compared their opponents to their reptile counterpart, the water moccasin. There are a few stories about these irregular troops from western Virginia and these were generally humorous as the press correspondents explained their colorful attire or language to their subscribers. The following article came from Reminiscences of the Blue and Gray, *by Frazar Kirkland and it was published by the Preston Publishing Co, Chicago, in 1895. This story appears on page 406.*

These were probably typical of the type of irregular troops which were raised in Virginia's western counties in support of both sides. They were primarily young men from the countryside who were long accustomed to the use of firearms and life in the forest. They were ideal counter-guerrilla units, but they were facing Confederate Partisan Ranger units which were raised from the same segment of Virginia's rural population. Their reasons for fighting for either side can only be guessed at as their lives would not be appreciably changed with the victory of either side.

This section includes several articles about these rural soldiers.

Snake Hunter's Style of Drill

Among the rebel guerrilla organizations, the most noted band was that known by the name of "Moccasin Rangers." They had a good time, too, until Captain Baggs got up his 'counter-irritant' in the shape of a company of "Snake Hunters," a delicate allusion to said venomous reptile -- the moccasin. As to their arms, these were of every variety; and as to toggery, no two were dressed alike. As to parades, their extraordinary system of tactics included no such dandyism.

But most peculiar was their drill. Every movement was accomplished on the double-quick, or in a run. They acknowledged no "common time", and if reduced to a dead march they would surely have mutinied. This, for instance, was Captain Baggs' very original style of dismissing his company:

"Put down them thar blasted old guns and be ____ to you!"

(Which being interpreted, is "Stack arms!")

"Now to your holes, you ugly rats, and don't let me see you till I want you!"

(Which, being reduced to Hardee vernacular, means, "Break ranks, march!")

Exeunt Snake Hunters on the run, with grand divertissement of whoops, yells and squeals, interspersed with life-like imitations of birds and beasts.

Once, when the Snake Hunters were detailed to guard some stores between Fairmont and Beverly, two elaborate gentlemen from Philadelphia, who were making a tour of that country, had the good fortune to witness their very original style of drill, and at the close of the performance invited Captain Baggs to take a drink in a neighboring rummery. As the tin cups were laid out, one of the aforesaid gents expressed his astonishment, not to say admiration, of this particular style of dismissing, "which looked to him very much like a stampede," and was curious to know where in the world they were all gone to, and how the Captain expected to get them back if he wanted them in a hurry. Baggs replied that the process was rather difficult to explain verbally, but "if they'd just let that 'ere rum wait a minute, he'd show 'em;" whereupon going to the door, he fired three barrels of his revolver. The echo of the third report was still lingering among the cliffs when every blessed Snake-Hunter burst into the bar-room with a whole menagerie of roars and screeches and hee-haws, and without question or apology called for tin cups. This demonstration of Captain Baggs' style of "falling in," cost the elaborate gentlemen from the Quaker City $5, the very thought of which almost turns their brains to this day.

The Moccasin rangers were quite active and the newspapers were often printing reports of their activities. The Wheeling Intelligencer *reported in early June, 1862, that:*

The town of Burning Springs, in West County, Western Virginia, was burned by a party of guerrillas known as the Moccasin Rangers.

In late July, 1862, there was concern in Parkersburg, a considerably larger town than Burning Springs, that the guerrillas were about to attack. The newspaper reported:

Great excitement pervaded the town of Parkersburg, Va., caused by the report that a band of guerrillas was about to attack the town. The report was without foundation, but the citizens were so terrified that they tore up the flooring of the bridge across the Little Kanawha, and planted a cannon at their end of it. The City Council held a meeting and appointed a committee to go out with a flag of truce, and prevail upon the marauders not to burn the town. The money in the bank was removed to Marietta, Ohio. Numbers of persons fled from the town, and crossed into Ohio.

The exploits of the Moccasin Rangers continued throughout 1862. Frank Moore reported one of their attempted raids in his Rebellion Record, *1862, Volume 3:*

November 19. Some men of Capt. Hill's Cavalry had a skirmish near Wirt Court House, Western Virginia, with a gang of rebels calling themselves the Moccasin Rangers. There was a corn husking at the house of a secessionist, about a mile from Wirt Court House, and some of Capt. Hill's men obtained leave of absence and attended the affair without arms. After the men had started, the balance of the company were advised that their companions were to be attacked and captured at the husking, by the Moccasin Rangers. Accordingly the company armed themselves, and proceeded as quietly as possible down to the husking. They had scarcely reached the house and formed themselves in position,when the Moccasin Rangers made a charge upon the house. Capt.Hill's men fired upon the Moccasins[42] before the later were aware of their presence in force, killing a lieutenant and wounding five or six others. The rangers retreated.

Captain Charles Leib, the Assistant Quartermaster in General Rosecrans' headquarters at Clarksburg, wrote a

---

42 The "Moccasins" were also known by their official name, the Virginia State Rangers.

humorous story of the expected attack on a town by the guerrillas. It appeared in his book, Twelve Months in the Quartermaster Corps, *and starts on page 100.*

The Night Attack

Hearing that a noted guerrilla chieftain, whose deeds of cruelty had made him the terror of Western Virginia, had threatened to attack the town, pickets, composed of the valorous Guard, were stationed at all the roads leading to it. It was a time of expectation. When citizens retired, they feared they would waken to witness scenes of blood, and to hear the death shrieks and dying groans of their neighbors, and to find their homes in flames. At sunset, the detail was made from the guard of those who were to stand picket for the night. They were well-armed with primitive weapons, and, to keep their courage up, a flask of the principal production of Western Virginia "apple whiskey."

One moonless, though starry night, as the shivering and alarmed pickets, marching to and fro upon the end of the bridge nearest town, fancying in every bush an armed man, and an enemy behind every tree, suddenly they were startled, with what appeared to them the uniform and heavy tread of approaching soldiery. To revive their fainting courage, which was oozing out at their finger's ends, they applied themselves to their flasks. Again they listened, and again they drank, for nearer, and yet nearer, came that solemn tread, each footfall of which seemed their death knell. And now it reaches the bridge, and, against the starlit sky, they see the gleam of innumerable bayonets.

"Who goes there?" one of the pickets in faltering accents cried, his hair standing on end and his voice sticking in his throat. No answer but the solemn tread! Firing their guns in a perfect paroxysm of terror, the pickets fled toward town, shouting at the top of their voices:

"The enemy are coming: the Secesh are upon us!"

Rushing to the Court House, the bell peals out its wild alarm. The town is roused; men rush frantically from their houses, half-dressed followed by women, with disheveled hair and scanty attire, moaning as if the day of judgement had come, begging their husbands and sons not to go to war.

That innumerable band, the "Home Guard," assembled tumultuously in front of the Court House, and the line having been hurredly formed, amid the tears, and against the entreaties of the women, take up their line of march to the bridge, resolved to do or die. They near the fated spot; and as they do, their pace decreases, and at last comes to a dead halt -- fear and anxiety depicted on every countenance.

What brave spirit dare lead the attack?

They listened. No sound was heard save the sighing of the wind among the trees, and the dashing of the waters of the Monongahela against the abutments of the bridge. Some masked battery or ambuscade, they were sure, will open upon them.

Who dare reconnoiter?

At last, an old man, of Falstaffian proportions, with fair round belly, with good cap on lined, like him of Shakespeare, dares the venture. A lantern is procured. He nears the bridge. He hears nothing save the heavy breathing of what appears to him, like one in agony.

Gathering fresh courage, he proceeds up on the bridge, followed by the "Guard," and finds, instead of the dreaded enemy thirsting for blood, an innocent cow, in the last agonies of death. She had been mortally wounded by the chance shots of the valiant pickets, before their precipitate retreat. Her horns, dimly seen in obscure light, they had taken for the bayonets of the foe, and her heavy tread for that of the approaching soldiery.

The "Guard" were crest fallen. and each swore a solemn oath never to divulge the secrets of that fearful night. But, alas! for human frailty. When under the influence of apple whisky, one of the parties related to us these facts.

There were some of the rebel guerrillas who were soon to stop spreading fear and destruction throughout sections of western Virginia. Their opponents -- the Snake Hunters-- were deployed as might modern counter-insurgents who searched the region where the Rangers formerly were able to move freely and captured many of them. The prisoners were marched to Wheeling and placed in prison in a converted carriage depot, the Athenaeum.

The story was told in the Wheeling Intelligencer *on January 2, 1862. It is also recorded in Frank Moore's* Rebellion Record, *1862, in volume 4 as:*

The Pet Lambs

Capt. Baggs ... arrived yesterday from Wirt County, having in charge some thirty-four prisoners, most if not all of whom belonged to the somewhat notorious Moccasin Rangers, who have been pillaging and murdering throughout Wirt, Roane, Gilmer, and adjoining counties, for some considerable length of time. The prisoners were captured by the men of the 11th Virginia Regiment of which Capt. Baggs and his company are now members. They were found at Big Bend, at West Fork and at their homes in different parts of the counties named. The cold weather of the past three or four days drove them into their homes. The music of their popular song, "Never Mind the Weather," froze in their throats and they had to seek shelter. They had eaten up everything in the woods, including hoop pole bark and were forced to come into a civilized neighborhood to get something to eat. We have no hesitation in saying that they are the hardest looking sets of vagabonds we ever saw. Some of them are lame, halt, and frosted, and there is scarcely a comfortable suit of clothes in the whole crowd. Among the number is the notorious Dan Dusky, who is said to have boasted that he had a little graveyard of his own in which he had buried a considerable number of Union men.

Coming up on the boat during Christmas day, Capt. Baggs got a pitcher of whiskey and gave the "Pet Lambs," as he calls them, a Christmas drink all around. When the prisoners were formed in line and started from the boat to the Atheneum, Capt. Baggs instructed his men to knock the first man down who insulted any of the lambs.

The acts of the Partisan Rangers continued in the western counties of western Virginia throughout the war. There was little actual strategic value gained for the Confederacy by these acts. The Union men were still able to organize into "Home Guard" units to defend themselves against the raiders and they were able to continue their meetings which resulted in the formation of a new state which was to enter the Union as West Virginia in 1863.

The Partisan Pangers felt much like the Union men. The Federal Army and the "Home Guard" were involved in attacks and burnings of Confederate sympathizer's property while they arrested suspected rebel sympathizers. John D. Imboden began recruiting for a Partisan Ranger regiment soon after these units were authorized by the Confederate Congress. He wrote some of the reasons for the need of these men in the recruiting posters used to attract potential recruits:

My purpose is to wage the most active warfare against our brutal invaders and their domestic allies; to hang about their camps and shoot down every sentinel, picket, courier and wagon driver we can find; to watch opportunities for attacking convoys and forage trains, and thus render the country so unsafe that they will not dare to move except in large bodies. Our own Virginia traitors -- men of the Pierpont and Carlile"[43] stamp will receive our special regards.

Our enemies are waging a war of unparalleled barbarity and ferocity upon us; murdering unarmed, peaceful citizens; outraging helpless women; burning the houses over the heads of innocent childhood; plundering the homes of widows and orphans; in short, laying waste the land wherever their armies have penetrated. Their hellish passions not satiated with these acts of fiendish brutality, are seeking further gratification by emancipating the slaves and putting arms into their hands to inaugurate a war of such atrocity as to make devils stand aghast at its horrors.

Such being our enemies, and such their purposes, I hold that by the laws of God and man, it is our duty to slay them by all the legitimate means in our power. We have conducted the war on the highest principles of christian nations. Our enemies have adopted the *Cammanche* code in all except scalping. There is but one mode of putting an end to such a contest and such a system. we must rise as one man and slay the invader wherever and whenever we find him. The honor of our wives and daughters, the sanctity of our homes, the liberty of our children MUST be defended by MEN of the South, or all is lost. We all desire peace, and yet there is but one mode by which it can be secured -- the destruction of the Yankee armies. We can have peace by this means, and that right speedily, if every men will do his duty. We are infinitely stronger as a nation today than we were one year ago. Our independence is as certain as any future event can be and the time for its recognition is a matter perfectly under our own control.

I therefore appeal to the men of the West to unite with

---

43 Pierpont was the governor of "loyal" Virginia; Carlisle was representing the state in the U.S. Senate.

me at once in the effort to deliver our native mountains from the pollution that has been brought upon them. It is only *men* that I want; men who are not afraid to be shot at in such a cause; men who will pull a trigger on a Yankee with as much alacrity as they would on a mad dog, men whose consciences won't be disturbed by the sight of a vandal carcass. I don't want nervous, squeamish individuals to join me -- they will be safer at home where the women can protect them and the children, and calm their nerves when alarming news is circulating...[44]

The fear of both sides and the inflammatory nature of the propaganda released by both Federal and Confederate commanders produced a situation in which each raid resulted in a reprisal which in turn caused another reprisal. When pre-emptive raids began, this became open guerrilla warfare in which civilians were at as much risk as were the combattants. The fear, and resulting hatred, continued for long after the war as the partisans from both sides continued to hate and fear one another. Some of that continues to the present day.

---

44 This is part of the text of a recruiting broadside that is currently in the West Virginia University Library. It appeared in "Bushwhacker's War: Insurgency and Counter-insurgency in West Virginia", edited by Richard O. Curry and F. Gerald Hamm; *Civil War History*, Vol. 10, No. 4, December, 1964, pg. 416-433.

There were tragedies that occurred which were not on the battlefield. Scavengers accompaning every army have always been less noble than most of their uniformed counterparts who remained in their regiments rather than straggle or desert. For the deserters from either army to survive, they frequently moved to crime in order to support themselves and were liable to arrest by either side as well as the civil authorities. Unfortunately, in a famous but now forgotted episode near Lewisburg, a straggler committing a crime was to set into motion a sequence of unstoppable events as an occupying army attempted to punish what they decided was a crime.

The story was told by perhaps the best and most prolific local historian in the southern portion of the state which emerged from the Civil War as West Virginia. This historian was Clarence Shirley Donnelly and the story of the tragedy was written in Oak Hill, West Virginia. He got most of his material from a story written by a Lewisburg resident, W.H. Syme, M.D., called "David S. Creigh, The West Virginia Martyr; or, The Crime of a Major-General," which appeared in Burhring Jone's The Sunny Land. *This book was published in 1868.*

His preface is excellent reading and sets the stage for the entire story:

"When an event makes an impression upon the mind of a mountaineer that impression is more than apt to linger a long time. The memory of it is kept alive by telling the story over and over to friends and relatives. One such event was the tragic happening in the life of David S. Creigh, Esq., of Lewisburg, Greenbier County, West Virginia, during the Civil War. All who had first hand information of that noted case have gone the way of all the earth but amid the limestone hills of Greenbrier County and the adjacent sections the details of the Creigh case are rehearsed to this day. Because of the perennial interest in the war episode which shocked all Greenbrier county, I am re-telling the story that those who run may read."

We will repeat it a third time.

David S. Creigh, the Greenbrier Martyr

It is probable that the execution of David S. Creigh at the hands of the Union army authorities during the Civil War stunned the Greenbrier country of West Virginia more than anything that ever happened to one of its citizens.

David S. Creigh -- pronounced C-r-e-e -- was born in Lewisburg, Greenbrier county, Virginia, on 1 May 1809; according to the inscription on his tombstone in the cemetary at the rear of the Old Stone Church (Presbyterian) at Lewisburg, West Virginia[45]. He was the fourth child of Thomas Creigh (January, 1766 - 2 December, 1847), native of County Antrim, Ulster, Ireland. In the year 1792 the north Ireland native settled in Lewisburg and became one of Greenbrier's most influential people. In 1801 Thomas Creigh married Miss Margaret Linn Williams, daughter of Captain Samuel Williams, himself a native of Ireland, and who had moved to Greenbrier county in 1795. Previous to his removal to Greenbrier, Captain Williams had married Mrs. Agatha Wilson, a widowed sister of Colonel John Stuart, prominent figure in the early annals of the Greenbrier region. Through his mother, David S. Creigh was related to some of the most prominent people who ever lived in the state of West Virginia. Thomas Creigh and his wife were blessed with a numerous family, David S. Creigh -- as stated above-- being their fourth child. The greater part of the time Thomas Creigh resided in Lewisburg he was

---

[45] Colonel Beuhring H. Jones, *The Sunny Land, or Prison Prose and Poetry*, Innes & Co., Baltimore, Md., 1868, pg. 402, lists the year of Creigh's birth as 1807. The year 1807 is there given by W.H. Syme, M.D., in his article "David S. Creigh, The West Virginia Martyr, or the Crime of a Major-General", in Col. Jones book. It is more likely that the date on the stone is the correct birth year of the ill-fated man.

engaged in the mercantile business at which he accumulated a sizeable fortune. He was a "blue stocking" Presbyterian and brought up his family in the faith of that church.

As a natural result of his father's teaching and example, David S. Creigh grew up to be a staunch Presbyterian, becoming an elder in the congregation of the historic church of that denomination at Lewisburg. However, it was not until the summer of 1857 -- when he was a man of at least fifty years of age that he made a public profession of religion. Even prior to the time of joining the church, David S. Creigh had been a man of spotless integrity and unbending rectitude. Like his father before him, Creigh devoted the years of his youth and early manhood to mercantile pursuits. In the year 1833 he was united in marriage to Miss Emily J. Arbuckle, daughter of Captain Charles Arbuckle. The Arbuckle family was one of Greenbrier county's oldest and most respected families. Soon after his marriage, Mr. Creigh quit the store business and devoted the rest of his life to general agriculture at which he was emminently successful.

Being a man of considerable prominence it was only natural that David S. Creigh would be singled out for political honors. Time and again he declined to accept posts of profit and honor. The only exception he made to this rule was his acceptance of the Magistracy, the only public office he ever held. The Governor of Virginia appointed Mr. Creigh to that office in 1838 upon the recommendation of the Greenbrier county court. After the adoption of the Constitution of 1850, Mr. Creigh continued to be elected by the people until the time of his lamentable death. For many years, as a stockholder in the bank at Lewisburg, he was elected to serve as a member of the Board of Directors of that institution. Following the death of his father in 1847, the settling of the estate was largely left up to the fourth child of the deceased parent. It was in this happy state of affairs blessed with wealth and surrounded by a devoted wife and eleven noble sons and daughters that David Creigh lived on his grand estate between Lewisburg and Ronceverte when the Civil War storm broke over the land.

Like most proprietors of his time, Creigh was conservative in his national feelings. He was a slave owner as were his friends and neighbors in the lush Greenbrier lands. As a man who loved peace and stood for the Union, Creigh opposed the revolutionary extremists of both South and North. He wanted nothing better than to see the country at peace and in the enjoyment of prosperity. When the war rumblings came nearer and nearer and fighting broke out, Mr. Creigh felt honor bound to champion the Southern cause. His was the general feeling in Greenbrier and through out that section of the Old Dominion. Lincoln's call for 75,000 volunteers served to emphasize the terrible fact that armies of aliens would soon be on their way to the sacred soil of the Southland -- a thing that was abhorrent to the country squire who felt his people would be wronged and oppressed by these invaders. Creigh's age precluded service with the Southern colors. There, too, there was the care and responsibility of his great family which devolved upon him. But in spirit and attitude his Irish soul was one with the Southern cause.

Lewisburg was in the path of the two armies. Columns in grey and armies in blue see-sawed back and forth through the fine little Southern city -- Southern to this day of 1950! Hardships and privations fell alike upon men in uniform and the people of old and cultured Greenbrier. In this state of affairs the Creigh family went along with the rest -- patient and long suffering under a ruthless and merciless invasion. When the smoke of battle had lifted from the scene at Lewisburg on 23 May 1862, David S. Creigh was among the first civilians to be found on that bloody field extending the hand of help and healing to friend and foe alike. His free-hearted Irish nature and his spirit of Southern hospitality would not allow him to withhold from even the enemy such fare as the Creigh table afforded. In David S. Creigh the spirit of good Samaritan and Christian charity generously blended.

During 1862, Major-General David Hunter was Federal Commander for the Military area of Western Virginia. Under Hunter were Brigadier-General George Crook, U.S. Army, Commanding the Second Infantry Division; Brigadier-General William W. Averell, U.S. Army, Commanding the Second Cavalry Division; and hordes of lesser commanders and fighting units of varying sizes. The Lynchburg Campaign was in process of unfolding and Union generals, Crook and Averell, were to approach the hill city from the west and fall upon it. While General Crook and his force were in the vicinity of Lewisburg in November, 1863, there occurred the tragedy which led to the trial and execution of David S. Creigh some seven months later.

CREIGH HOME DESECRATED

On or about 8 November, 1863, in the absence of Mr. Creigh a federal soldier came to the Creigh house in the afternoon. He was carrying a bridle in his hand. As soon as the Yankee entered the large brick mansion a couple of miles outside of Lewisburg he began to pillage and loot every room on the first floor. After plundering the rooms of the first floor the blue uniformed man went upstairs where one of Mr. Creigh's daughters lay sick of a fever. For days the life of the young woman had been despaired of, so violent had been the attack of the fever upon her. After using very insulting and abusive language at Mrs. Creigh and her daughters and flaunting some of her daughter's clothing in the face of the mother, the soldier started to break open a trunk of Miss Lewis, daughter of former Sheriff John E. Lewis of Greenbrier county. Miss Lewis had been employed as a teacher and governess in the Creigh family and the trunk held her personal belongings. At this juncture, Mr. Creigh came in and was told of the presence of the man in the sick room and the trouble he was causing. As Creigh entered the room the Yankee jumped up from the trunk, drew his pistol and aimed to shoot, but Mrs. Creigh, seeing her husband's life was in danger, caught the soldier's arm and held on to it until Mr. Creigh caught the man by the collar and forcibly ejected him from the sick chamber. When the upper hall was reached by the two struggling men a shot was fired. According to Dr. Syme's account of this encounter[46] when Mr.Creigh accosted the trouble maker the soldier "threw down his pistol, cocked it, and pointed it at Mr. C., exclaiming, 'Go out of this room! What are you doing here? Bring me the keys!' Mr. C. drew his pistol, snapped it at the fellow, he, at the same instant, firing his pistol, and the ball grazing Mr. Creigh's face, passed into the wall. He then seized the robber and in the scuffle which followed, was pushed out into the passage, and the soldier falling upon him. They rose together, and in the attempt to wrest the pistol from the Yankee's hands it was accidentally discharged, and the first discovery of its effects upon his person was from seeing the profuse flow of blood. He struggled into the portico where he again fired his pistol at Mr. C., the ball going into the upper part of the front door."

While the death struggle was going on between Mr. Creigh and the robber, black Sallie -- one of the Creigh Negroes -- came running with an axe in her hand. She begged Mr. Creigh to use the axe on the Yankee lest he get up and try to kill someone else. By this time the whole place was in an uproar and Mrs. James Arbuckle came upon the scene. She was on her way to assist in nursing the daughter who was ill and arrived in time to witness the fracas.

THE BODY HIDDEN AWAY

When it was apparent that the Yankee was dead

---

[46] Jones, Beuhring H., *The Sunny Land*, pg. 411

hurried efforts were made to dispose of the body. Mr. and Mrs. Creigh, Mrs. James Arbuckle and black Sallie carried the corpse out in the yard and covered it with straw.[47]

In a few minutes twenty Yankee cavalrymen rode up to the Creigh barn and searched for horses but, as luck would have it, they did not come near the house. As soon as the Yankee cavalry were gone, Mr. Creigh sent one of his servants across the way for neighbor John W. Dunn. As the Federal army was in the Greenbrier community it was not deemed wise to try to dig a grave and bury the body lest the matter come to light. Mr. Creigh well knew that it was impossible to carry the case before the civil court for judgement, the presence of the enemy preventing this action. After consultation and advice it was decided to dispose of the body in a private manner. A dry well was at hand and into this well the body was placed and covered with trash. It was thought this disposition of the matter might end the case until the general situation of the country had quieted down but in this all concerned were doomed to disappointment.

THE STORY GETS OUT

Stirred by the excitement and with the average human's weakness for telling exciting news, black Sallie told Cezar -- one of neighbor Edward's Negro men -- that she believed her master had killed the Yankee that had created such a commotion in the Creigh house. The story was given credence by the Negro man and he made haste to tell the mournful intelligence. While Hunter's cavalry were camped at Bunger's Mill during the last of May -- the first of June, 1863, four miles west of Lewisburg,[48] Cezar ran away from home and reported to the Yankees what Sallie

---

47 O.W. Kittinger, "Last Survivor of the David Creigh Trial," *The Fayette Tribune*, Fayetteville, W.Va., Wednesday, 16 May, 1928.

48 *Official Records of the War of the Rebellion*, Series I, Vol. V, pg. 152

had told him. A detail was sent to search the Creigh premises with the result that the dead body was discovered. Creigh was placed under arrest and brought to Bunger's Mill for trial.

John W. Dunn, Mrs. James Arbuckle, Mrs. Creigh and two of her daughters were brought to the place of trial. Mrs. Creigh and her daughters were taken from their home on a very dark night and placed on horseback behind their guards and taken to the military headquarters four miles away at Bunger's Mill. They were not asked a question, nor were they permitted to see Mr.Creigh. The three Creigh ladies were forced to walk the four miles back to their home. While John W. Dunn was sent for by the authorities as a witness for the accused man, Mr. Dunn was not permitted to answer a single question. The courts martial trial was held on 2 June 1864 upstairs in the home of former sheriff Wallace Robinson, the house being later owned by Charles W. Young. With a show of concern for the public interest the military commission which tried Mr. Creigh permitted a few civilians to attend the trial. The civilians who sat in on the trial were George L. Knapp, S.S. Hern, George W. Kittinger, and O.W.Kittinger, son of George W. Kittinger. O.W. Kittinger wrote his recollections of the celebrated trial when he was an old man and when he was the sole survivor of those who attended the military tribunal.

The indictment brought against Mr. Creigh ran as follows:[49]

"Charges and specifications against David S. Creigh.

"Charge Murder. Specification: That on or about the eighth of November, 1863, the same Creigh killed a soldier in his house, dressed in Federal uniform, name unknown.

"Signed,

A. Myers, Provost Marshall."

---

49 Jones, Beuhring H., *The Sunny Land*, pg. 421

The accused man made a clean breast of the whole unfortunate affair. He was careful to give all the details as they occured. Creigh was adjudged guilty as charged in the indictment and death by hanging was the sentence pronounced. O.W. Kittinger, an eyewitness, says:

"I shall never forget how this good man looked when he came down to tell us all goodby. He was very much agitated and great beads of perspiration stood out on every feature of his face. I was the last one he said 'goodby' to, and perhaps the last he spoke to in Greenbrier, for it was then twenty Yankee cavalrymen marched him up the hill towards Lewisburg and little did I think as a boy that it would be the last time I would see David S. Creigh until I meet him at the bar of God."[50]

CONDEMNED MAN TO VIRGINIA

When the Union army left Lewisburg for Virginia to play its part in the Lynchburg campaign -- a campaign that met with Federal defeat -- David Creigh was marched on foot to Staunton,Virginia, a distance of one hundred miles. Meanwhile the papers in the trial were forwarded to Major-General David Hunter, Department Commander, for study. The sentence was approved by Hunter and Creigh's execution order carried out. The day set for carrying out the Military Commission's sentence of death by hanging was 10 June 1864 on Friday. At that time the condemned man was at Brownsburg, Rockbridge county, Virginia. About dark that evening the Federal army chaplain, the Rev. A.G. Osborn of Uniontown, Pennsylvania, called at the home of the Rev. James Morrison, Pastor of New Providence Presbyterian Church of the Brownsburg

---

50 O.W. Kittinger, "Last Survivor of the David Creigh Trial," *The Fayette Tribune*, 16 May, 1928.

community. The Federal chaplain told Pastor Morrison of the plight of the condemned Creigh, adding that the man about to die besought the benefit of the pastor's prayers. The prisoner was not permitted visitors. He was kept in a Negro cabin close by, the Chaplain told the preacher -- kept under strict guard. The Chaplain retired from the manse that the minister might pray for the man who was soon to be hung by the neck until he was dead.

LAST HOURS ON EARTH

While the time pieces ticked off Creigh's last hours he wrote his beloved wife the following letter:

"June 10th, 1864

"Dear Emily: I arrived this morning at the Rev. James Morrison's, in Rockbridge county. After eating my supper I was taken into a house and the sentence pronounced that I was to be hung. I was not permitted any counsel in my case.

I wish you, my dear beloved wife, to bear up under this dreadful bereavement; you and all the children bear up under this as well as you can, and all try to meet me in heaven. I am meeting death with calmness, believing and trusting in the Lord Jesus Christ, the Savior of sinners. My sincere wish is that all my brothers and sisters meet me in heaven.

In my sentence it was read, that the house was to be burnt to the ground, but the gentleman who brought me this paper said that part of the sentence would not be carried out. I hoped that I would once more see you all on earth, but it is decreed otherwise, and I have to submit. I wish my remains to be removed and laid by the side of our father's and mother's, as soon as convenient. The Rev. A.G. Osborn has prayed for me before I commenced writing...

I sent for him this minute, and he and the Provost Marshall came in together, and the Provost Marshall was authorized to stay the execution, if I wished, should not take place until daylight, which I accepted; that much more time to offer up my prayers to God, for myself and dear beloved wife, and children to meet me in heaven.

My dear brother Louis, I know how this will affect you. You know all about my business ... I wish my beloved son Cyrus, if he is spared through this dreadful war, to manage my business with your assistance; as dutiful a son as ever lived, and I must say so for all my sons and daughters. I now leave you, Cyrus, Thomas, Charles, Rufus, David, Christopher, Lockhart, Egbert, Margaret, Mary and Elizabeth; leave you with your Christian mother. God be your stay and support, trusting God, and preparing to meet you in heaven.

David S. Creigh"

On the morning of 11 June, 1864, shortly after sunrise, Creigh was brought out under guard, put into a wagon, and conveyed up a little vale to a spot about a quarter of a mile to the north of the house and in plain view of the house. There upon a tree, close by a fountain of living water known as "the big spring," they hanged the man who dared to defend his home and family against an intruder. Chaplain Osborn returned to the Morrison manse to notify them that the awful sentence had been carried out. The body was left hanging and was taken down and buried in a blanket in a grave hard by the spot, the work being done by the minister's wife together with such help as she could muster. On the following Thursday -- six days later-- a coffin was procured, the remains disinterred, and temporarily buried in the graveyard of New Providence Church. This was done by one of the dead man's sons who was in General Breckinridge's army and had been permitted to come over and attend to the melancholy duty. From the Official Records it would seem that men of Averell's command were detailed to execute the Greenbrier man. In his report of July 1, 1864, Averell wrote:

"Hqrs., Second Cav. Div., Dept. of West Virginia
Charleston, W.Va., July 1, 1864.

...On the 2nd (June) Mr. David Creigh a citizen of Lewisburg, was tried by a military commission and found guilty of murdering a Union soldier in November last. The proceedings were subsequently approved and Mr. Creigh was hanged at Bellview on Friday, the 10th of June...

Wm. W. Averell

Lieut. Col. Charles G. Halpine
Ass't Adjt. Gen., Department of West Virginia."[51]

CREIGH HONORED AT LEWISBURG

On 4 July 1864 the Session of the Lewisburg Presbyterian Church, the old Stone Church passed resolutions of respect in appreciation of the Elder of the church who had been meted out such an ignominous death at Federal hands. On 25 July of the same year, the court of Greenbrier county passed a set of resolutions setting forth Creigh's virtues and deploring his untimely end. On 28 July 1864 Creigh's remains were brought from Rockbridge county, Virginia, to his home where they were watched over for three days by his devoted family. On Sunday, July 31st, a funeral cortege more than a mile long wound its way over a road of sorrow to the church in Lewisburg. In the old church the venerable Rev. Dr. John McElhenney, Pastor of the church portrayed the manly virtues of the dead elder. The funeral was preached by Rev. J.C. Barr, associate of the church. The Rev. Barr's subject for his funeral discourse was *The Christian Martyr*. Following the services the earthly remains of David S. Creigh were buried for a third time -- in the plot where his parents are sleeping the long, unbroken sleep. The inscription on his tombstone runs as follows:

SACRED TO THE MEMORY OF DAVID CREIGH
DIED AS A MARTYR IN DEFENSE OF HIS
RIGHTS AND IN PERFORMANCE OF HIS
DUTIES AS A HUSBAND AND FATHER
BORN MAY 1, 1809, AND YIELDED TO HIS
UNJUST FATE JUNE 11, 1864 NEAR
BROWNSBURG, VIRGINIA.

The death of David Creigh and the destruction done by the army of "Black Dave" Hunter's Union forces were to have a cruel result for the people of Chambersburg, Pennsylvania, when the troops of John McCausland were to arrive there and demand a ransom. General Early, McCausland's commander, had left him no room for interpretation of the orders that resulted from the cruelty of Hunter. Chambersburg was to pay $200,000 in gold or $500,000 in Yankee greenbacks to replace many of the destroyed homes in the Shenandoah Valley or the town was to be burned to the ground. The City Council decided not to pay...

Jubal Early remembered the story of the death of the Greenbrier County man who was hanged for defending his home from the Federal intruder when he gave the order to McCausland. He wrote in his memoirs:

"The scenes of Hunter's route from Lynchburg had been truly heart-rending. Houses had been burned, women and children left without shelter. The country had been stripped of provisions and many families left without a morsel to eat. Furniture and bedding had been cut to pieces, and old men and women and children robbed of all clothing except what they were wearing. Ladies' trunks had been rifled and their dresses torn to pieces in mere wantonness. Even negro girls had lost their little finery. We now had renewed evidences of outrages committed by the commanding general's orders in burning and

plundering private houses. We saw the ruins of a number of houses so destroyed. At Lexington, Hunter had burned the Military Institute, with all its contents, including its library and scientific apparatus; and Washington College had been plundered and the statue of Washington taken. The residence of Ex-Governor Letcher, at that place, had been burned, and but a few minutes given to Mrs. Letcher and her family, to leave the house. In the same county a Christian gentleman, Mr. Creigh, had been hung because he had killed a straggling and marauding Federal soldier while in the act of insulting and outraging the ladies of his family. The time consumed in the perpetration of those deeds was the salvation of Lynchburg, with its stores, foundries and factories, which were so necessary to our army at Richmond."

It was fortunate for Major-General David Hunter that he did not fall into the hands of Early's Confederates and the citizens of Pennsylvania were also lucky that the reprisals and burning that accompanied McCausland's raid to Chambersburg were not far worse. The destruction produced by Hunter's army and the death of David S. Creigh were partially avenged in the minds of the Confederates as Chambersburg burned.

Beuhring Jones was an attorney who was the organizer of a company of Confederate volunteers, the "Dixie Rifles," who were primarily from the vicinity of Fayetteville, West Virginia. He later was to become the commander of the 60th Virginia Volunteer Infantry Regiment and served as a Confederate officer until the battle of Piedmont in 1864 when he was captured while attempting to rally a rear guard. He was imprisoned at Johnson's Island and remained there until the end of the war.

Jones wrote about his experiences as a Federal prisoner at Johnson's Island and it is interesting that while a great deal of information has been written about the Confederate's prisoner of war system, little is known of the realities of life as a Confederate officer held in a Union prison. It was as miserable an experience as it was for the Federal soldiers who were held in the South. Jones' story appears in his book, The Sunny Land, *which was published in Baltimore in 1868.*

Twenty-four Hours of Federal Prison Life
By Col. B.H. Jones

Outsiders are curious to know how Prisoners of War pass their time. Should what I am about to write ever go beyond the hated steel-bristling walls, by which I am surrounded, this desire may, to some extent, be gratified. Reader, follow me from dawn to dawn again, and you will see what these three thousand Confederate prisoners are doing.

Awaking at the peep of day, we may, if we wish, get up and make our toilette; but we must be careful not to stir abroad, but confine ourselves to our room until *reveille*. For, should we go out to snuff the fresh breeze of morning that comes floating so softly across the placid bosom of Lake Erie, before we have heard that signal, we will certainly be ordered to our quarters by one of those blue-coated gentlemen promenading the parapet, and should we stand "upon the manner of our going," instead of going at once, the crack of a minie rifle, and the sharp whiz of a ball, will remind us that, here, at least, we are not the creatures of our own volition. After *reveille,* however, we are at liberty to go where we please within the prison, provided we do not please to essay a transit across the 'dead line', in which event, we should be carried back on a stretcher; so a due regard for the well-being of "mama's darling child" forbids a trial of that experiment.

Hark! the *reveille* is sounding, the sharp *rat tat too* of which goes rattling across the waters, and is lost in the forests of the circling shores. Now, there is a general uprising, though of a very peaceful character, throughout our community. The next task, a very light one, however, is to prepare our breakfast. By the way, have you ever studied that word, "breakfast"? It implies that we have been fasting, and that the fast is about to be broken *break-the-fast.* It is misapplied here, however, for we fast all the time: not because of our remarkable piety, for we are as bad as other people; nor from choice, but necessity.

Breakfast is over. Listen! The drum is sounding "roll call." Get ready to "fall in," for a surly, prying, peeping corporal will be around, and if we should be found in our room, our rations -- unless we are sick and having a written permit from our Block Surgeon to remain in -- will be stopped for full twenty-four hours; a serious matter for the consideration of starving men.

Now the gate opens, and a squad of tastefully attired Federal Lieutenants enter, and, separating just inside the "dead line," take their positions in front of the several blocks. The prisoners, divided into companies, swarm from their quarters, like bees from their hives, and fall in line. The roll is next called, and each man, as he answers to his name, steps two paces to the front, thus gradually forming a second line. This stepping to the front is a new regulation, the design of which is to prevent our "playing off" upon those loyal custodians of our persons. Formerly we remained stationary as we responded, and if a companion had escaped during the preceeding night, by previous arrangement a mess mate, after answering to his own name, would slip down in rear of the line, take the place of the fugitive, and when his name was called, answer to it. This "sharp practice" would be kept up for probably five or six mornings, the roll calling officer deceived all the while, and while reporting "all present or accounted for;" after which, the substitute would call out: "Well, Lieutenant, I reckon" Southerners always "*reckon*," Yankees "*guess*" "I reckon I have answered for John Smith long enough, and as he is, by this time, either in "Dixie" or Canada, you had as well scratch him off!" The blank look of the Lieutenant, upon the receipt of this startling piece of information, may be readily conceived. This game, however, is now "blocked;" when there is no response to a call, and no one steps to the front, the roll caller makes a peculiar mark opposite the name, and then, if the prying, rummaging Corporal, already alluded to, returns from his search through the quarters and reports the gentleman "not found," it is very reasonably "guessed" that he is somewhere on the Ohio shore, making a forced march, either for the dominions of Jefferson Davis or those of her Royal Majesty, Queen Victoria; and the agency of telegraph wires is promptly invoked to "head him off."

Roll call is over now, and what means the sudden rush of the "grey jackets" upon the heels of that little German Jew "Yank," who, having come in, is walking briskly towards the space in the rear of the Sutler's store? He is the most interesting personage on the Island, not even excepting the affable and dignified Col.Hill, Commandant of the Prison. He feels his importance, too, most hugely. His ascension in the scale of human greatness has far excelled the loftiest flights of his youthful ambition, when indulging in copious draughts of his favorite lager, on the banks of the crag-castled Rhine, he dreamed of the exalted position of a gentleman's lacquey. He is Express Agent for Confederate Prisoners, and the book in his hand contains the names of those for whom packages of nice clothing, and boxes of edibles, have just been landed from the Island steamer. He places himself as quickly as possible beyond the "dead Line," and faces to the "right about;" and well he may thus seek refuge from the thousand excited, eager, yelling prisoners. They follow him, however, to the very edge of the fatal line that marks the boundary between life and death, where, as if by a common impules, they come to a sudden and simultaneous halt. How the poor fellows crowd, and elbow, and jostle each other! No fear of pickpockets here -- empty pockets fear no picking. The money sent them is retained outside, the Sutler receiving checks on the Treasurer for bills made in his gouging establishment. True, there may be a five,ten, or even twenty dollar gold piece nailed up in that "Reb's" boot heel, as a sort of sure "stand by," should he ever escape, but what thief so sharp as to scent coin through an inch of sole leather, or unobserved, to steal the heel of a man's boot -- the boot on the foot, and the wearer standing in it? How they tip-toe! How eager and expecting their faces! How breathlessly they listen to each name as it is read out! How savagely they utter curses upon his semi-barbaric tongue that refuses to call the name intelligibly! How they torture the pronunciation of each name into a fancied resemblance to their own! With what a vim the lucky ones shout: "Here!" and what a grin defines itself from ear to ear as they do; and how suddenly a shadow of disappointment saddens a thousand eyes, just blazing with hope, as the last one on the list is called and the book is closed. How suggestive is this scene, of that, when the Book of Eternal Life shall be opened for the grand and final roll call of the Universe!

Who sends these packages and boxes of nice and good things to the prisoners? Their friends. Have they friends within the Federal lines? Yes, thousands of the kindest, the bravest, the truest, and the best. Where? Everywhere; in city, town and county; in New York, Philadelphia, Louisville, Cincinati, St.Louis, Alexandria, Washington, even in Southern-hating Puritanic Boston; and in glorious Baltimore, the fair queen of the Patapsco. Her daughters, famous as they have been for the witchery of their personal charms, are destined to be even more renowned for their inextinguishable patriotism, and their warm, active, full, free, and constantly flowing sympathy for the imprisoned and oppresed.

But the scene changes. "Here's your mail!" "here's your mail!" from a thousand throats, and Block postmasters rapidly wend their way to Block "One," where the prison mail, the arrival of which is so vociferously proclaimed, will be opened; and when they receive it, they will distribute it among the inmates of their respective Blocks. This distribution will be attended with the same excitement, the same manifestations of hope and disappointment, that marked the calling of the Express list. Then they wanted packages and boxes; now they want letters from the "loved ones at home." I shall not attempt to depict more minutely the phase of prison life presented on an occasion of this kind, but advise you, if you can lay your hand on it, to read a thrilling sketch of this scene, entitled "Here's Your Mail!" written by Lieutenant Howard C. Wright, of Louisana, an occupant of Block "Eleven."

What is that? "Come and draw your rations!" Well, let us go. The officer who is on that duty for our mess today will draw ours. You ask if one man can carry the rations for the eighty occupants of our room. Two can easily do so. They are not likely to be heavy; only a little baker's bread, some salt beef, or, in its stead, a few salt fish, too poor to fry themselves. Perhaps we shall draw cod fish, in which case I shall fast. Codfish would make a good fertilizer for worn out lands, but I cannot believe they were created for human food. It cannot be that the Creator, in his goodness and wisdom, ever invested anything intended for the human stomach, with a stench so intolerably putrescent as that of the codfish. A man may so torture and pervert his taste as to relish codfish, just as Chinamen relish the flesh of puppies, and California Indians that for skunks and grasshoppers; but naturally, nothing excepting birds and carrion-eating propensities, relish such abominations. Like many other odious things of the present age, the eating of codfish is of New England origin, and I have no doubt the first morsel that ever offended a human palate, was devoured by Miles Standish and his followers, on Plymouth Rock.

"Will we get any vegetables?" Oh no, we drew them yesterday -- one potato and an onion apiece, for eight days. "Sugar and coffee?" Why sir, I have been here ten months, and not an ounce, or a grain of either have I known to be issued to the prisoners. For three or four months of my imprisonment, we were not allowed to buy at the Sutler's, nor to receive boxes containing provisions forwarded by our friends, unless the "permit" of the Federal Surgeon, peevishly and stingily granted, were found inside. "How did we manage to live?" Well, you know that the Children of Israel were, at one period in their journey from Egypt to the Land of Canaan, supplied with showers of quails; we were scarcely less fortunate, in being supplied with droves of *rats*!

Well, as the rations have been distributed, this spot has lost its interest, so we will continue our stroll. Here is a Chair Factory. This man saves every tough and straight stick of wood that he can lay hold upon, and converts the same into the legs, backs and arms of chairs, which, when put together, he sells to the prisoners. The seats are made of strips of leather, bark, tough wood, or scraps of half-worn clothing.

Now let us cross to yon Block. Here is a tailor busily employed at his trade; and here, again, is a shoe-maker. He is allowed to receive leather, for it is Governmental economy, but he is not allowed to make boots, only shoes. Boots are contraband, and should a friend send you a pair, they would be carried outside. I can't undertake to say what would be done with them there. I suppose somebody might be found whom they would fit. Perhaps they would be sold for the benefit of the U.S. Government. I only know that hundreds of pairs have been thus taken from the prisoners here. Here is a law student: visions of an office crowded with clients, with plethoric purses, while bills, declarations, answers, &c., lie scattered thickly around, flit before his imagination. And there is a student of medicine, whose pills may be destined to kill more men than any battery of artillery now thundering around the beleagured cities of Richmond and Petersburg. Here is another of dentistry: and still another preparing himself for the most exalted of all stations -- the ministry. Here is a school of the "old field" pattern, where only the elementary branches are taught, and there goes a teacher of a class in the dead languages and the higher branches of mathematics.

We must be careful as we pass on, not to interrupt that game of baseball, nor yon cricket match, nor those quoit pitchers. Baseball, cricket, and quoits are not only amusements in whch the prisoners indulge themselves. We have a company of amateur actors, known as the "Rebellonians," who occasionally furnish entertainments of a dramatic character, which are sure to be liberally patronized. The pieces are original, the writers being prisoners with fine literary attainments, and the style of the "Rebellonian" performances would do no discredit to the boards of a first-class theatre.

In many of the stage plays, as well as at our dancing parties, the opposite sex is represented by the most youthful and femininely featured prisoners, disguised in appropriate toggery, for the introduction of which we are indebted to Yankee cupidity, which is ever ready to turn any thing to account that promises to yield a penny. It is surprising, as well as amusing, to observe how successfully the ladies are imitated, not only in the arrangement and completeness of their outfit, the grace with which it is worn, and the advantageous display of certain personal charms, but also in that coyness and diffidence which so powerfully attract our sex. It is easy for men who have not spoken to, nor heard the soft voice of a woman for eighteen months or two years, to work their imaginations to the point of faith in the actual feminity of an ideal Miss Florence Henderson, the brunette, or Miss Kate Hayward, the *blonde*, when so artfully disguised, and the result on one hand, is all the gallantry and difference, and on the other, all the amiability and condescension that mark the bearing of sexes toward each other, in the most aristocratic and refined society.

Here is a Confederate cap manufactory. Look at that article -- a neater and better one than you could buy in "Dixie" for twenty times the money asked for it here. He gets them up out of cast-off uniforms selecting a sound piect of cloth, here and there, until the garment only hangs together by strips. He makes a great many. You may see them all over the prison. The knife he is using in lieu of a pair of scissors, was made in Block "Twelve," by an ingenious and eccentric character from one of the border counties of Western Missouri, who goes into every block and room with the enquiry, shouted at the top of his voice: "Gentlemen, hev you any demned old files?" meaning files worn out by the manufacturers of prison jewelry, who are counted by hundreds. We see them everywhere, sawing, filing and polishing finger rings, necklaces, breast pins and bracelets, all made of gutta percha, and set with sea shell, pearl, silver or gold. Many of these trinkets are very beautiful, exhibiting both ingenuity and skill, of a high order; and few men can be found here who have not tried their hand upon one or another of the articles named. They are sent through out the United States, to the kind ladies who contributed so much to our comfort, and many are carefully preserved to be carried home to mothers, wives, sisters and sweethearts.

But who would dream of a photograph gallery being carried on in such a place as this? Nevertheless, there is one here, in full blast. In the gable end of Block "Three," you will perceive a small opening, made by removing a portion of the weather-boarding. The gallery is there, and the artist manufactured his own apparatus. His operations are unknown to the Federals, who, otherwise, might cause him to "shut up shop." An entrance to the gallery is effected by means of a hole in the ceiling of the upper story, the visitor pulling up the ladder after him. He always keeps some friend on the *qui vive* for the approach of "blue jackets." He gets off quite a creditable picture; and as almost every prisoner desires to take away a specimen of his work as a momento, and his charges are moderate, it is quite certain that he will soon have a plethoric purse; for, although we are searched before we were "turned in," and all the money that was found on our persons taken from us, and that sent us no letters by friends, is retained on the outside; still, many succeed in concealing their "Greenbacks" so effectually, as to elude even Yankee vigilance.

If you would rather have a portrait than a photograph, we will call on our old friend from St. Louis, who, with an ordinary lead pencil, will furnish you with a tolerably correct picture. He has been here a long time, has taken hundreds, and his price is only fifty cents.

Would you like to have the initials of your wife's name, or some motto or device engraved on the finger ring you purchased in Block "Five"? If so, we will go to Block "Two," where we will find a wealthy planter from Mississippi, who follows that business. He will charge two cents per letter, and his work will compare favorably with the best job that can be "turned off" in Baltimore.

The man has just passed us, carrying several old canteens, is our tinner. His shop is in Block "Thirteen." He is a very useful member of our community. Out of canteens, oyster and fruit cans, he manufactures tin cups, and various other cooking vessels, for which, even in prison vocabulary, no name has been found, and repairs coffee pots. I am getting together material for a prison work; uncertain when I shall be exchanged, and fearing that my manuscript may be pronounced contraband, and taken from me when I start, I have employed him to put a false bottom, which shall be waterprooof, in my canteen, where it, together with many small articles, such as needles, pins, silk thread, &c., so much needed in Dixie, will be concealed.

In the Block on our left, is a prisoner who manufactures chessmen. You may be curious to know how he turns them. There is a man in Block "Four," who has erected a turning lathe; he is patronized by the chessmen maker, the chair maker, and the can-maker.

What is the meaning of this: "IN MEMORY OF," &c.? These are boards intended to mark the graves of Confederate officers who may die in this prison. They are made and lettered by Confederates, and the work is neatly done. Our cemetery, containing about a fourth of an acre, enclosed with a neat and substantial plank fence, white-washed, and the graves neatly sodded, all the work of our own hands, is located at the eastern extremity of the Island. There reposes the dust of some three hundred of our country-men. We bury our own dead, and on such occasions, like our working parties, we are always attended by a sufficient guard. The idea of dying and being buried on this lone Island is especially distasetful to us all. The desire to breathe our last at home, surrounded by those we best love, and to be laid away by their tender and careful hands, and to have them plant flowers upon our graves, and bedew them with tears of affection, is as natural as it is universal.

"Grape!" "grape!!" "grape!!!" from a thousand tongues. What does it mean? I don't know the origin of the term "grape," as used in this connection. You perceive, however, that it throws the prison into excitement, and that scores of men are wildly rushing towards the prison bulletin-board, against which a "Yank," who has just come in, is tacking a piece of paper. It means, as used here, news from the outside. Perhaps this is an announcement of a great battle, or that in which all feel, if possible, a still deeper interest -- an exchange of prisoners. The probability is, however, it is nothing more than some unimportant prison order, regulation or requirement. Yes, it is the latter; for see, the crowd is already dispersing with disappointment plainly marked on upon the faces of all. The question is "Is there any grape?" or "Have you heard the latest grape?" is constantly going around. Like the curious Athenians, rebuked by Paul, we are always anxious to hear some "new thing." Nor is this singular, considering our lonely and isolated condition, and the stirring events daily transpiring in the outside world -- events which we are powerless to affect one way or another, but in which we have such deep personal interests.

But see, there is something of a *"row"* at Block "Eleven," and one man is receiving rough treatment. That is what we term a "kicking out." The recipient of the kicks has applied to Col. Hill for permission to take the oath of allegiance to the U.S. Government, or, in prison phraseology, he has "gone back on the Confederacy," and his mess mates having discovered his treachery, are summarily ejecting him from their quarters. He will be certain to complain to the authorities, when a file of soldiers will be marched in, and he will be reinstated; but as soon as the bayonets are withdrawn, he will be again "kicked out," till finally, sore from kicking, spit on and despised, as he deserves to be, his very life will become a burden, and he will plead to be placed in that little building, standing between the 'dead line' and the prison wall, where two poor fellows under sentence of death or imprisonment for life, as bushwhackers or spies, have been confined for more than eighteen months. From this time forward, he will not be recognized by any Confederate in this prison. His former friends will not speak to him, nor allow him to speak to them. Every hand will be against him; every tongue will hiss at him; every heart will loathe him. Even the Federals, whom he seeks to propitiate, will regard him with illy concealed scorn and contempt. And why is this? Not because, from principle, he has taken this step, for in that there would be something worthy of commendation rather than censure; but because, they have a reason to believe, it was the result of the absence of all principle. Because, they believed, he had not the manhood to endure imprisonment, with its privations and suffering, for a cause, that, in his heart, he believes is just; but chose rather to take a solemn oath -- an oath that he is too cowardly to perform -- to support a cause that he believes is wrong.

There are two men using a patent clothes washer and wringer: it belongs to them, and they are making it pay, not withstanding there are at least fifty washer-*men* in the prison. You would be astonished to see how neatly these men wash and do up, even the finest linen. There are gentlemen here, who, at home, have thousands of broad acres, and can command thousands of dollars, actually engaged in the menial drudgery of cooking, washing and wood-sawing for others, who, in Dixie, could with difficulty obtain credit for a trifling sum. The first class have no acquaintances within the Federal lines to whom they can apply for relief; the second class have, and hence they have plenty of funds.

That large building, about 200 feet in length, 40 feet in breadth, and two stories in height, is the Prison Hospital. It is divided into four wards, and is always crowded with patients. It is kept scrupulously neat, and is so free from the confusion and uproar incident to the other blocks, that it is almost a luxury to be sick enough to entitle you to admission. The patients are treated by none but Confederate physicians, of whom there are quite a goodly number in prison. These gentlemen are untiring in the discharge of their voluntarily assumed, and, so far as money is concerned, unrequited labors. Their conduct is worthy of the highest commendation. The medicines used, are supplied by the United States Government, but most of the delicacies used to tempt the appitites of the sick, by contributions from their fellow prisoners. In this Hospital we find a beautiful exemplification of the virtues of Free Masonry. There are many members of the Order in the prison. These are thoroughly organized, and not only supply the sick with many delicate and tempting articles of food, but furnish constant details for hospital service as nurses, &c., who are not to confine their ministrations to their brethren, but to extend them to others, whenever they can do so, without prejudicing the comfort of those who have no especial claim upon their attention.

That little building in the rear of the hospital, is the

"Prison Dead-House, where
Few mourners come to weep!"

It is seldom without a pale and pulseless inmate.

You have noticed, in passing, one or more little stands or tables, in each block, on which butter, flour, sugar, coffee and vegetables were exposed for sale. The men engaged in this business, are known as sub-sutlers. They are Confederates, and sell for the chief, or Yankee Sutler, on commission. And just here, I may remark, that the priviledge of acting as sutler to this prison is very profitable. His profits for one year must amount to a handsome fortune. Half a dozen assistants are constantly busy waiting on customers, and the percentage realized is enormous. Three or four prices are charged for every thing that is sold, and his money can be turned over every day. The amount of money forwarded to prisoners is enormous, averaging, probably, five thousand dollars per week. Nearly the whole of this goes into the pocket of the sutler, prison rations being not only sadly inadequate in quantity, but, with the exception of the bread, against which, as a general rule, no complaint can be made, highly objectionable in quality.

But I see our cook beckoning us to dinner. Having dined, we will now fill our pipes and indulge a whiff of the weed. The number of prisoners who abstain from the use of tobacco in some form, is very small. The soothing effects of the narcotic upon the mind, and the want of better employment, is the secret of this habit.

This morning your attention was drawn to the large proportion of prisoners engaged in writing. They were writing letters. Each prisoner may write two letters per week, being careful to confine himself to one page of common size letter paper. At one period since my arrival, we were allowed to write one letter daily, and as at least one-third of the prisoners wrote each day, from five to seven thousand letters were mailed per week. This number per week has not been materially diminished by the existing restriction, for almost every man writes two letters, and there are upwards of three thousand officers confined here. Some write as many letters as they wish, each mail. This is accomplished by changing chirography, and borrowing the names of such acquaintances as do not wish to write. You will be curious to know how those to whom such letters written in a strange hand, over a strange name, comprehend the actual author. This difficulty is readily overcome by some familar allusion which serves as a key to unlock the mystery of authorship.

"To whom do we write so many letters?" To homefolks in "Dixie," and to persons throughout the United States, especially to our female relatives. Since the promulgation of the order prohibiting "aid and comfort" from any but relatives, we have discovered that we are akin to all the ladies of rebellious proclivities, in the country. They are our "sisters," Aunts," "cousins," and grand-mothers," while we suddenly find ourselves the "brothers," "nephews," "cousins" and even "grandsires" of hundreds of the purest, lovliest and most kind-hearted beings in the "wide, wide world." It is remarkable, that prior to our imprisonment, we had entirely lost sight of so many of our kinsfolk, with whom, according to their story, and our suddenly revived recollections, we played "hide and go seek" in our childhood, or whose cradle lullabies soothed to peaceful slumber the fretfulness of infancy.

It is said that, a few weeks ago, an officer solicited an interview with the Commandant of the Prison. It was granted. "Well, sir," said that Federal official, "what can I do for you?"

"Why, Col. Hill, I feel that a change of diet would be of great benefit, and I desire permission to make some purchases in Sandusky; a little sugar, coffee, cheese, a box or two of sardines, some pickles, canned fruits, &c., you know."

"Why don't you get a permit to apply to a *relative* for those articles? You know it would be a violation of the existing order, to allow you to obtain them from any other source?"

"I am aware of that fact, Colonel, but you will understand that I have no relative within the Federal lines."

"No relatives within Federal lines! Why, how long have you been here?"

"About nine months, Colonel."

"What! Been here nine months and found no relative in all that time? Why, had I been in your place, Captain, I would have discovered at least a dozen in half the time. Go back and retrospect your boyhood, and I am confident you will find that you have a sister, or brother, or aunt, or uncle, or cousin, or grandfather, somewhere within our lines!"

It is needless to add that the Captain took the hint, and

that his larder was soon supplied with the desired luxuries. I will not vouch for the truth of this anecdote, but as the Commandant is, in my opinion, a gentleman of generous impulses, I am strongly inclined to give it full credit.

We do not feel that Heaven frowns upon a "pious fraud" like this; while the spirit of romance attending a correspondence of this character, is positively enchanting. Doubtless, through such a channel, tender and peculiar hopes have already been awakened, and the origin of many joyous bridal, "when this cruel war is over," may be traced to prison correspondence. Gratitude is closely allied to love; and no portion of a woman's life is so loveable as that devoted to the relief of human suffering. The voice that speaks of loved ones far away, is ever burdened with melody; the form that bends over the couch of the invalid, is ever graceful; the hand that bathes the throbbing temple is ever soft; the bosom that pillows the aching head is ever affectionate and true, and the tear of sympathy never fails to brighten, with an angelic radiance, even the dullest eye.

I ought to have taken you to our libraries. We have two -- one of these is a miscellaneous library, and is an individual enterprise; the other is composed of religious works exclusively, and belongs to the "Young Men's Christian Association". Each contains some five or six hundred volumes. Prisoners are in constant receipt of books, from their friends, which, having read, they take to the one or the other of these libraries, as the fitness of things may require, and trade them for the loan of other books which they have not read. Again, donations of books are occasionally made to the library of the "Young Men's Christian Association." In these and other ways, these libraries have been built up.

The prisoner who owns the Miscellaneous Library, is making money by letting out his books to his fellows. No charge is made for the use of books of the library of the Christian Association, except barely enough to defray some trivial incidental expenses.

There are many pious men among us, including some

learned and eloquent devines. In fair weather, these gentlemen preach in the open air, and never lack for large and attentive congregations. We never fail to have preaching on the Sabbath, and, generally, twice or thrice during the week. Beside, we have Union Prayer-meetings, Bible classes, and Sabbath schools. The spiritual interests of the sick are not neglected, for religious services are held twice a week, in the Hospital. Prisoners are frequently converted and received into the denomination of their choice. I am happy to say that denominational prejudices here, are not strong. We have a Federal chaplain, but his office is that of a sinecure. He seldom attempts to preach; and even when he does, few, very few, attend.

Your attention was attracted to the various squads of prisoners engaged at games of cards, dominoes, back-gammon, dice, chess, &c. Many of the prisoners devote all their time to gaming, hardly pausing to eat; and here, as in the outside world, gambling is attended with cheating and profanity. Large sums are lost and won; sometimes the stakes are "greenback," sometimes Confederate currency, and not unfrequently, written promises to pay at some future day when the parties return to the Southern Confederacy.

Drunkenness, however, is a vice almost unknown in prison. There are scores of men here who, though not often inebriated prior to their incarceration, have not tasted a drop of liquor since. Why? Because they can't get it. Many bottles of old bourbon, and cognac, and claret, and champagne are sent here by friends, but those for whom they were designed, are merely tantalized by the sight, and then, being numbered among "contraband" articles, they are sent out again. I don't know who drinks them, on the outside; in fact, don't know whether they are drank there, at all; but I *do* know they never come back again.

I am not a drinking man, never was, hope that I will never be; but still, I think I can imagine, somewhat, the torture endured by a man who, fond of a "smile" -- and not having indulged in that luxury, so much as once, for a period of eighteen weary months, or two years -- sees the bead-covered beverage, which by every rule of justice is his, taken away, while he pleads in most earnest and pathetic tones for *"just one taste,"* and that being denied, frantically implores the tantalizing boon of smelling the *"stopper,"* only to be denied again. It would be carrying the idea of human compassion very far to suppose that such a man, once exchanged and returned to the battlefield, would, under any conceivable state of things, spare a yankee.

The police regulations of the prison are complete. They are enforced by details, each day, from the different blocks. Each block has its regularily elected chief, whose orders are strictly obeyed; hence, the cleanliness of our quarters and the prison grounds, generally. Last Fall, one hundred Confederate privates were sent here from Camp Chase, to do our policing. As soon as they arrived, and we learned for what purpose, we assured them that it was without our seeking, and urged them to positively refuse to play so menial a part. They did refuse, though brought out several times by Federal Corporals, and finally, the project was abandoned.

Having finished our "smoke," we will walk out again. Do you observe that Confederate officer on the platform of the stairs of Block "One"? He is looking through a glass, very intently, at some object, just on the outside, and it is evident that he is laboring under strong excitement. We will go up. Ah! the thing is explained. There is a beautiful lady over there, some forty or fifty paces from the prison wall. She has a glass directed towards him. -- See, she removes the glass and applies her handkerchief to her eyes. She is weeping. Come away, there is something too sacred in this for third parties; and my own heart is aching, and my own eyes are filling. I too have a wife, "away down South" who, though she were to travel alone, a thousand miles to reach Johnson's Island, as that man's wife has, would not be allowed to exchange one poor little word with me, or even make one sign with her hand, though we had been separated twice twelve long and weary months, aye, though I lay on my hard bunk breathing my last, and she went down on her knees and prayed and implored to be allowed to come in, that she might give one last clasp to my wasted hand, and press one last kiss upon my fever-parched lips, and then return broken-hearted, widowed, and desolate, -- that petition, however moved by it the Commandant of the prison might and would be, could not be granted without the assent of a superior officer far away; -- perhaps asleep and unwilling to be disturbed; perhaps attending a Presidential levee, or a Senatorial ball, or an oyster supper, or a wine party given by some vulgar upstart Shoddycrat; and even when found, perhaps refusing to attend any business outside office hours, and then only such as might present itself attended by all the formal tomfooleries of "red-tape"!

I ought to take you to our Lyceum, but as the discussion is probably half gone through with ere this, and as the Island steamer is now nearing the landing, we will remain just here, and see whether there are any prisoners aboard. Ah! do you hear that cry of "Fresh fish, fresh fish!" from the men standing on the stairs of Blocks "One" and "Two," watching the approach of the boat? That cry always announces the coming of a new squad of our countrymen, whom the uncertain chances of war have doomed to a lingering captivity. See, the boat has touched the pier, and the "gray jackets," accompanied by a strong guard, are filing off, and marching up the lawn toward the residence of the prison commandant. Now they are halted and "fronted." Now their names, rank, State, regiment, place and date of capture, &c., are being recorded, after which they will be searched for weapons, money, &c., and then they will be marched in.

Observe how intense the excitement among the old *residenters.* Three-fourths of them have already arranged themselves in two long lines, facing inward, extending on each side of Main street, nearly three hundred yards.

Now the gate opens, and with clothes soiled, faded

and torn, covered with dust, and in many cases, stained with blood, they sweep inward and onward. Now the singular cry that announced their approach to the Island, swells in volume, until it rolls like a mighty billow of human voices over the vast and motley throng. The new-comers are sadly disappointed. Where they expected expressions of sympathy, they find, what seems to them, heartless redicule and derision. As soon, however, as they cross the "dead line" and enter the space between the long lines of faces, the strange and offensive cry is succeeded by such questions as, "Where were you captured?" "To what command did you belong?" "How many of you there?" while here and there mutual recognitions occur, succeeded by hearty shaking of hands, accompanied by exclamations of surprise and delight, the poor tired fellows are literally dragged, neck and heels, away to hospitable quarters, where new robes are brought forth, and rings -- gutta-percha -- put on their finger, and fatted calves slain, and where there is feasting and dancing.

Those, however, who do not have acquaintances among the old prisoners, do not fare well. The Federals do not assign them special quarters. Once inside, they are turned loose to shift for themselves. They feel very lonely, though in the midst of hundreds of their fellow countrymen. They soon begin to realize that they must look out for "number one." All are sorry for them -- few sorry enough to help them, for men are as selfish in prison, perhaps more than anywhere else. All the surroundings of prison life tend to develop and nourish this hateful principle, If there is a mean streak in a man, prison life will disclose it. They wander from block to block, from room to room, inquiring "Is this Block filled?" Is there a vacant bunk in this room?" almost everywhere receiving the answers: "Yes, this room will not hold any more!" "No, there is no vacant bunk here!" They look with dissatisfied countenances at the size of the rooms, and seem to be comparing that with the number of occupants. The cast their eyes along the walls on either side, and they discover that places where bunks once stood are now vacant, or nearly so. The scales begin to fall from their eyes; they begin to "see men as trees walking." They congregate in knots and compare notes, and the conclusion is, that the old prisoners are not disposed to do the fair thing. At this stage of the game, some good-hearted man steps up and assures them there is plenty of room; that bunks in certain blocks have been cut down, and burned by the prisoners, to keep others from coming in; and winds up, by counselling them to go and take possession of all places from which bunks have been removed, and call in the Yankee carpenter to replace them with new ones. This settles the matter. Their "metal" is now up. They walk in and assert their rights, which are surily admitted; and within the next forty-eight hours, new bunks are erected and they have a home; and within less than one month, the new-comers will be bawling "Fresh Fish" as loudly as any, and as readily and stoutly denying that there is room in their Blocks for such as another man.

Hark! the drum is beating to quarters, so we must go in; but first cast your eyes over the grounds and see how the vast multitude which for the last two hours has been promenading Main street, the cross streets and alleys, is scattering in all directions, each man making for his own Block.

Now all have disappeared. The grounds which a moment ago, resounded with a thousand foot-falls, and echoed to a thousand voices, is now as silent and lonely as an Arabian desert.

We must not attempt to pass from one Block to another until after *reville* to-morrow morning. It would be contrary to orders, and we might be shot. And if we were, we would deserve no sympathy; no man, who needlessly and wilfully encounters danger, knowing the probable consequences of his folly, is entitled to sympathy. So we will sit in our room and converse until we grow sleepy, but not beyond "*taps*" and the cry of "Lights out!" or a minie ball may come splintering through the wall. Indeed we are not always safe here, even when we strictly observe the rules of the Prison. In proof of this, I need only mention an occurrence that came immediately under my observation. Not long since, after the lights were extinguished and perfect quiet reigned in our room, in Block "Five," a ball entered, and broke a bone in the arm of Lieutenant Dillard, of Mississippi, who was passing along towards his bunk, while badly wounding Lieutenant Inman, of North Carolina, while he was sleeping soundly. This affair created some excitement, even among the Federal officers, and we supposed the offender would be punished, but, so far as we know, nothing was done.

"Taps"! There it is -- "Lights out!" be quick! the day is over, and you know something of prison life at Johnson's Island. You have learned that we are a community within ourselves; that we present an epitome of a great city, with its schools, libraries and theatres; its literary and religious associations; its professional men; its teachers; its ministers; its students; its merchants; its artisans; its mechanics; its gamblers; its loafers; its sanitary regulations; its charitable institutions; its virture and vices; its pleasures and pains; its joys and sorrows; its living and dead.

Now for sweet dreams of liberty, and love, and home. Good night!

Miss Louisa May Alcott served as a volunteer nurse in a Federal hospital in Washington, D.C., during the Civil War and the sights she saw were to influence her greatly. One of the more pathetic cases she nursed was a wounded West Virginian named John. She later wrote a small book, Hospital Sketches, *in which she described her patients and experiences as a volunteer nurse. None of the other stories could have been more interesting than her recording of the last days of John. This story appeared in* Spies, Scouts, and Heroes of the Great Civil War, *by Captain Joseph Powers Hazelton. It was published by the Star Publishing Company of Jersey City, New Jersey, in 1892.*

This episode of misery on the part of the wounded man and all who knew him shows clearly the horrible nature of the Civil War. West Virginians experienced a great deal of this misery, but little has survived the oral history tradition of the hills to get into modern history books. John was a representative victim of the fighting that occurred and is also a small sample of the fate that awaited most of the seriously wounded in the pre-antibiotic era.

The Death of John
The West Virginia Blacksmith

"John is going, ma'am, and wants to see if you can come."

"The moment this boy is asleep; tell him so, and let me know if I am in danger of being too late."

The messenger departed, and while I quieted poor Shaw, I thought of John. He came in a day or two after the others; and one evening, when I entered my "pathetic room," I found a lately emptied bed occupied by a large, fair man, with a fine face, and the serenest eyes I have ever met. One of the earlier comers had often spoken of a friend who had remained behind that those apparently worse wounded than himself might reach a shelter first. It seemed a David and Jonathan sort of friendship. The man fretted for his mate, and was never tired of praising John -- his courage, sobriety, self-denial, and unfailing kindness of heart; always winding up with: "He's an out an' out fine feller, ma'am; you see if he ain't."

I had some curiosity to behold this piece of excellence, and when he came, watched him for a night or two, before I made friends with him; for, to tell the truth, I was a little afraid of the stately looking man, whose bed had to be lengthened to accomodate his commanding stature; who seldom spoke, uttered no complaint, asked no sympathy, but tranquilly observed what went on about him; and, as he lay high upon his pillows, no picture of dying statesman or warrior was ever fuller of real dignity than this Virginia blacksmith. A most attractive face he had, framed in brown hair and beard, comely featured and full of vigor, as yet unsubdued by pain; thoughtful and often beautifully mild while watching the afflictions of others, as if entirely forgetful of his own. His mouth was grave and firm, with plenty of will and courage in its lines, but a smile could make it as sweet as any woman's; and his eyes were child's eyes, looking one fairly in the face with a clear, straight forward glance, which promised well for such as placed their faith in him. He seemed to cling to life as if it were rich in duties and delights, and he had learned the secret of content. The only time I saw his composure disturbed, was when my surgeon brought another to examine John, who scrutinized their faces with an anxious look, asking of the elder: "Do you think I shall pull through, sir?" "I hope so, my man." And, as the two passed on, John's eye still followed them, with an intentness which would have won a clearer answer from them, had they seen it. A momentary shadow flitted over his face; and then came the usual serenity, as if, in that brief eclipse, he had acknowledged the existence of some hard possibility, and, asking nothing yet hoping all things, left the issue in God's hands, with that submission which is true piety.

The next night, as I went my rounds with Dr. P., I happened to ask which man in the room probably suffered most; and, to my great surprise, he glanced at John:

"Every breath he draws is like a stab; for the ball pierced the left lung, broke a rib, and did no end of damage here and there; so the poor lad can find neither forgetfulness nor ease, because he must lie on his wounded back or suffocate. It will be a hard struggle, and a long one, for he possesses great vitality; but even his temperate life can't save him; I wish it could."

"You don't mean he must die, doctor?"

"Bless you, there's not the slightest hope for him; and you'd better tell him so before long; women have a way of doing such things comfortably, so I leave it to you. He won't last more than a day or two, at furtherest."

I could have sat down on the spot and cried heartily, if I had not learned the wisdom of bottling up one's tears for leisure moments. Such an end semed very hard for such a man, when half a dozen worn-out, worthless bodies round him, were gathering up the remnants of wasted lives, to linger on for years, perhaps, burdens to others, daily reproaches to themselves. The army needed men like John, earnest, brave, and faithful; fighting for liberty and justice with both heart and hand, true soldiers of the Lord. I could not give him up so soon, or to think with any patience of so excellent a nature robbed of its fulfilment, and blundered into eternity by the rashness or stupidity of those at whose hands so many lives may be required. It was an easy thing for Dr. P. to say: "Tell him he must die," but a cruelly hard thing to do, and by no means as "comfortable" as he politely suggested. I had not the heart to do it then, and privately indulged the hope that some change for the better might take place, in spite of gloomy prophecies, so rendering my task unnecessary. A few minutes later, as I came in again, with fresh rollers, I saw John sitting erect, with no one to support him, while the surgeon dressed his back. I had never hitherto seen it done; for, having simpler wounds to attend to, and knowing the fidelity of the attendent, I had left John to him, thinking it might be more agreeable and safe; for both strength and experience were needed in his case. I had forgotten that the strong man might long for the gentler tendance of a woman's presence, as well as the feebler souls about him. The doctor's words caused me to reproach myself with neglect, not of any real duty, perhaps, but of those little cares and kindnesses that solace homesick spirits, and make the heavy hours pass easier. John looked lonely and forsaken just then, as he sat with bent head, hands folded on his knee, and no outward sign of suffering, till, looking nearer, I saw great tears roll down and drop upon the floor. It was a new sight there; for, though I had seen many suffer, some swore, some groaned, most endured silently, but none wept. Yet it did not seem weak, only very touching, and straightaway my fear vanished, my heart opened wide and took him in, as gathering the bent head in my arms, as freely as if he had been a little child, I said, "Let me help you bear it, John."

Never, on any human countenance, have I seen so

swift and beautiful look of gratitude, surprise, and comfort, as that which answered me more eloquently than the whispered --

"Thank you, ma'am; this is right good! this is what I wanted!"

"Then why not ask for it before?"

"I didn't like to be a trouble; you seemed so busy, and I could manage to get on alone."

"You shall not want it any more, John."

Nor did he, for now I understood the wistful look that sometimes followed me, as I went out, after a brief pause beside his bed, or merely a passing nod, while busied with those who seemed more in need of me that he, because more urgent in their demands; now I knew that to him, and to many, I was the poor substitute for mother, wife, or sister, and in his eyes no stranger, but a friend who hitherto had seemed neglectful; for, in his modesty he had never guessed the truth. This was changed now; and, through the tedious operation of probing, bathing, and dressing his wounds, he leaned against me, holding my hand fast, and, if pain wrung further tears from him, no one saw them fall but me. When he was laid down again, I hovered about him, in a remorseful state of mind that would not let me rest, till I had bathed his face, brushed his "bonny brown hair," set all things smooth about him, and laid a knot of heath and heliotrope on his clean pillow. While doing this, he watched me with the satisfied expression I so liked to see; and when I offered the little nosegay held it carefully in his great hand, smoothed a ruffled leaf or two, surveyed and smelt it with an air of genuine delight, and lay contentedly regarding the glimmer of the sunshine on the green. Although the manliest man among my forty, he said, "Yes, Ma'am," like a little boy; received suggestions for his comfort with the quick smile that brightened his whole face; and now and then, as I stood tidying the table by his bed, I felt him softly touch my gown, as if to assure himself that I was there. Anything more natural and frank I never saw, and found this brave John as bashful as brave, yet full of excellencies and fine aspirations, which, having no power to express themselves in words, seemed to have bloomed into his character and made him what he was.

After that night, an hour of each evening that remained to him was devoted to his ease or pleasure. He could not talk much, for breath was precious, and he spoke in whispers; but from occasional conversations, I gleaned scraps of private history which only added to the affection and respect I felt for him. Once he asked me to write a letter, and as I settled pen and paper, I said, with an irrepressible glimmer of feminine curosity, "Shall it be addressed to wife or mother, John?"

"Neither, ma'am; I've got no wife, and will write to mother myself when I get better. Did you think I was married because of this?" he asked, touching a plain ring he wore, and often turned thoughtfully on his finger when he lay alone.

"Partly that, but more from a settled sort of look you have, a look which young men seldom get until they marry."

"I don't know that; but I'm not very young, ma'am, thirty in May, and have been what you might call settled this ten years; for mother's a widow, I'm the oldest child she has, and it wouldn't do for me to marry until Lizzy has a home of her own, and Laurie's learned his trade; for we're not rich, and I must be father to the children and husband to the dear old woman, if I can."

"No doubt but you were both, John; yet how came you to go to war, if you felt so? Wasn't enlisting as bad as marrying?"

"No, ma'am, not as I see it, for one is helping my neighbor, the other pleasing myself. I went because I couldn't help it. I didn't want the glory or the pay; I wanted the right thing done, and people kept saying the men who were in earnest ought to fight. I was in earnest, the Lord knows! but I held off as long as I could, not knowing which was my duty; mother saw the case, gave me her ring to keep me steady, and said 'Go:' so I went."

A short story and a simple one, but the man and the mother were portrayed better than pages of fine writing could have done it.

"Did you ever regret that you came, when you lie here suffering so much?"

"Never, ma'am; I haven't helped a great deal, but I've shown I was willing to give my life, and perhaps I've got to; but I don't blame anybody, and if it was to do over again, I'd do it. I'm a little sorry I wasn't wounded in the front; it looks cowardly to be hit in the back, but I obeyed orders, and it won't matter in the end, I know."

Poor John! it did not matter now, except that a shot in front might have spared the long agony in store for him. He seemed to read the thoughts that troubled me, as he spoke so hopefully when there was no hope, for he suddenly added:

"This is my first battle; do they think it's going to be my last?"

"I'm afraid they do, John."

It was the hardest question I had ever been called upon to answer; doubly hard with those clear eyes fixed on mine, forcing a truthful answer by their own truth. He seemed a little startled at first, pondered over the fateful fact a moment, then shook his head, with a glance at the broad chest and muscular limbs stretched out before him:

"I'm not afraid, but it's difficult to believe all at once. I am so strong it don't seem possible for such a small wound to kill me."

Merry Mercutio's dying words glanced through my memory as he spoke: "'Tis not so deep as a well, nor as wide as a church door, but 'tis enough." And John would have said the same could he have seen the ominous black holes between his shoulders; he never had; and, seeing the gastly sights about him, could not believe his own wound would be more fatal than these, for all the suffering it caused him.

"Shall I write your mother, now?" I asked, thinking that these sudden tidings might change all plans and purposes; but they did not; for the man received the order of the Devine Commander to march with the same unquestioning obedience with which the soldier had received that of the human one, doubtless remembering that the first had led him to life and the last to death.

"No, ma'am; to Laurie just the same; he'll break it to her best, and I'll add a line to her myself when you get done."

So I wrote the letter which he dictated, finding it better than any I had sent; for, though here and there a little ungrammatical or inelegant, each sentence came to me briefly worded, but most expressive; full of excellent counsel to the boy, tenderly bequeathing "mother and Lizzie" to his care, and bidding him good-by in words sadder for their simplicity. He added a few lines, with steady hand, and, as I sealed it, said, with a patient sort of sigh, "I hope the answer will come in time for me to see it;" then turning his face, laid the flowers against his lips, as if to hide some quiver of emotion at the thought of such a sundering of all the dear home ties.

Those things had happened two days before; now John was dying, and the letter had not come. I had been summoned to many death-beds in my life, but to none that made my heart ache as it did then, since my mother called me to watch the departure of a spirit akin to this in its gentleness and patient strength. As I went in, John stretched out both hands: "I knew you'd come! I guess I'm moving on, ma'am."

He was; and so rapidly that, even while he spoke, over his face I saw the gray veil falling that no human hand can lift. I sat down by him, wiped the drops from his forehead, stirred the air about him with the slow wave of a fan, and waited for him to die. He stood in sore need of help -- and I could do so little; for as the doctor had foretold, the strong body rebelled against death, and fought every inch of the way, forcing him to draw each breath with a spasm, and clench his hands with an imploring look, as if he asked, "How long must I endure this and be still?" For hours he suffered dumbly, without a moment's respite, or a moment's murmuring; his limbs grew cold, his face damp, his lips white, and again and again he tore the covering off his breast, as if the lightest weight added to his agony; yet through it all his eyes never lost their perfect serenity, and the man's soul seemed to sit therein, undaunted by the ills that vexed his flesh.

One by one the men woke, and round the room appeared a circle of pale faces and watchful eyes, full of awe and pity; for, though a stranger, John was beloved by all. Each man wondered at his patience, respected his piety, admired his fortitude, and now lamented his hard death; for the influence of an upright nature had made itself deeply felt, even in the little week. Presently, the Jonathan who so loved this comely David came creeping from his bed for a last look and word. The kind soul was full of trouble, as the choke in his voice, the grasp of his hand, betrayed; but there were no tears, and the farewell of friends was the more touching for its brevity.

"Old boy, how are you?" faltered the one.

"Most through, thank Heaven!" whispered the other.

"Can I say or do anything for you anywheres?"

"Take my things home, and tell them that I did my best."

"I will! I will!"

"Good-by, Ned."

"Good-by, John, good-by!"

They kissed each other, tenderly as women, and so parted, for poor Ned could not stay to see his comrade die. For a little while, there was no sound in the room but the drip of water from a stump or two and John's distressful gasps, as he slowly breathed his life away. I thought him nearly gone, and had just laid down the fan, believing its help to be no longer needed, when suddenly he rose up in his bed, cried out with a bitter cry that broke the silence, sharply startling every one with its agonized appeal:

"For God's sake, give me air!"

It was the only cry pain or death had wrung from him,

the only boon he had asked; and none of us could grant it, for all the airs that blew were useless now. Dan flung up the window. The first red streak of dawn was warming the gray east, a herald of the coming sun; John saw it, and with the love of light which lingers in us to the end, seemed to read in it a sign of hope of help, for over his whole face there was that mysterious expression, brighter than any smile, which often comes to eyes that look their last. He laid himself gently down, and stretching out his strong right arm, as if to grasp and bring the blessed air to his lips in a fuller flow, lapsed into a merciful unconsciousness, which assured us that for him suffering was forever past. He died then; for, though the heavy breaths still tore their way up for a little longer, they were but the waves of of an ebbing tide that beat unfelt against the wreck, which an immortal voyager had deserted with a smile. He never spoke again, but to the end held my hand close, so close that when he was asleep at last, I could not draw it away. Dan helped me, warning me, as he did so, that it was unsafe for dead and living flesh to lie so long together; but though my hand was strangely cold and stiff, and four white marks remained across its back, even when warmth and color had returned elsewhere, I could not but be glad that through its touch, the presence of human sympathy, perhaps, had lightened that hard hour.

When they made him ready for the grave, John lay in state for half an hour, a thing which seldom happened in that busy place; but a universal sentiment of reverence and affection seemed to fill the hearts of all who had know or heard of him; and when the rumor of his death went through the house, always astir, many came to see him, and I felt a tender sort of pride in my lost patient; for he looked a most heroic figure, lying there stately and still as the the statue of some young knight asleep upon his tomb. The lovely expression which so often beautifies dead faces, soon replaced the marks of pain, and I longed for those who loved him best to see him when half an hour's acquaintance with death had made them friends. As we stood looking at him, the ward master handed me a letter, saying it had been forgotten the night before. It was John's letter, come just an hour too late to gladden the eyes that had longed and looked for it so eagerly; yet he had it; for, after I had cut some brown locks for his mother, and taken off the ring to send her, telling how well the talisman had done its work, I kissed this son for her sake, and laid the letter in his hand, still folded as when I drew my own away, feeling that its place was there, and making myself happy with the thought, that even in his solitary place in the "Government Lot," he would not be without some token of the love which makes life beautiful and outlives death. Then I left him, glad to have known so genuine a man, and carrying with me an enduring memory of the brave Virginia blacksmith, as he lay serenely waiting for the dawn of that long day which knows no night.

Conclusion

West Virginia had a very important early role in the development of the Civil War. Virginia adopted the Ordinance of Secession on April 17, 1861, and the following night State troops occupied the Federal arsenal at Harper's Ferry. Maneuvering and counter-maneuvering by both sides concluded in the first land battle of the war at the West Virginia town of Philippi on June 3, 1861. This was followed shortly by the first sustained military campaign as the Federal regiments under General McClellan began to force the Confederates away from the route of the Baltimore and Ohio Railroad. Laurel Hill, Rich Mountain, and Corrick's Ford were a few of the names of remote places which began to appear in the newspapers of both sides as battles were fought on West Virginia soil.

Simultaneously, Federal forces invaded the Kanawha Valley to the south of the initial Union invasion from Ohio and Scary Creek, Charleston, Gauley Bridge, Sewell Mountain, and Cotton Hill became familar names to readers of both northern and southern newspapers. The Confederates were routed from the valley, returned in strength, and were mismanaged once again into a retreat. They re-occupied the region briefly in 1862, but lost the area once again to the stronger forces from Ohio.

West Virginia, The Child of the Storm, was born out of the Civil War. It was a state with a population having divided loyalties -- as was found in most of the other "border states"-- as divided families supported the national government or fought to ensure that Virginia remained intact. It became one of the worst types of conflict, a family feud in which both sides believed firmly that their view of the war was the correct and proper one and they fought one another and their supporters in order to sustain their side.

As the Union regiments began to gain the upper hand in Virginia's western counties, the local Confederate supporters found themselves in an militarily unsupportable position. Their strength -- relative to that available to their opponents -- was insignificant and they began to resort to guerrilla tactics. They were determined to avenge the wave of burnings of homes and property which was being done by the invaders and lone sentries were to pay a high price as these local guerrilla bands began to raid in retaliation for Union arson.

The new state was to experience many ruthless events as raiders were counter-raided and killings were avenged. Many of these are explained in the stories and diaries of the people who wrote the various sections of this book as the region begame a battleground for the two sides. West Virginia was a "no man's land" which became a buffer region between the easily defended Alleghenies and the Ohio River into which troops marched and counter-marched to deny any advantage to their opponents. It was an active military region throughout the war and 632 military "actions" of one type or another occurred on West Virginia's soil during the four years of the war.

Large numbers of men entered military service from Virginia's western counties. This included Thomas J. (Stonewall) Jackson and approximately 8000 other soldiers who entered the Confederate service. It has been an unfortunate fact of historical neglect that the service of many of these men has been overlooked in modern histories. Numerous men served with distinction in Confederate regiments which were designated as "Virginia Volunteer Regiments" and they seldom were acknowledged as West Virginians, but they served the cause of their "Native State" as well as any of their eastern cousins. Entire regiments were raised for Confederate service from the western counties and the Twenty-second, Thirty-sixth, and Sixtieth Virginia Volunteer Infantry Regiments served along with the men of the Eighth Virginia Cavalry Regiment -- nearly all of whom were western Virginians. The artillery batteries of Lowry, Bryan, and Chapman were filled with westerners and at least ten companies of western

Virginians served in the famous "Stonewall Brigade". These men and their contributions have not been included in modern histories and the entire state was largely ignored by a recent Public Broadcasting System series on the Civil War. The single mention of the state was the opening fight at Philippi.

Equally ignored was the contribution of West Virginia's Union soldiers. Over 30,000 served in the Federal Army during the war and they were not simply recruited for duty as "Home Guards" -- these men served in the active regiments of the Federal army and fought in nearly every active campaign of the war. Three West Virginia regiments of cavalry served with distinction in Custer's Division until the end of the war. Many of these Federal Virginians volunteered for service as scouts and frequently infiltrated Confederate lines in Rebel uniform to collect information and prisoners to interrogate. These "Jessie Scouts" hunted Moseby and lead the retaliation attack on John McCausland and Bradley Johnson's cavalry brigades at Morefield following their raid into Pennsylvania during which Chambersburg was burned. Unfortunately, their contributions to the war effort have been largely forgotten.

Did West Virginia make any real difference in the war? That question is difficult to answer, but it must be addressed if the contributions of the veterans of both sides are to be seriously considered.

The early campaigns in Virginia's western counties were valuable training experiences for several key officers who were to have a substantial impact on the course of the war. George McClellan managed the initial Union incursions in to the area along the Baltimore and Ohio Railroad and emerged from the initial fighting -- with the help of inflated reporting -- as a "second Napoleon" and was soon in command of the Army of the Potomac.

Robert E. Lee gained his first Civil War command experience in western Virginia as he attemped to manage the conflicting generals, Wise and Floyd. He also had the egotistical W.W. Loring under his nominal command. Lee emerged from the western campaigns with a severly tarnished reputation -- he was "Granny Lee" and "Evacuating Lee" in the southern newspapers at the conclusion of the Sewell Mountain expedition.

William Rosecrans and Jacob Cox gained their early military experience in the mountains of western Virginia. Rosecrans commanded large Federal elements until a severe defeat at Chicamauga caused him to be replaced. Cox continued to serve as a Federal major-general until the end of the war.

Territory and population were as important in the strategic equation as were the men who lead the armies. Western Virginia had a large population, rich agricultural areas, one of the largest salt manufacturing sites in the South, and its importance as a buffer region between the two industrial areas -- Ohio and Virginia -- can't be understated. The broad region left ample locations for the maneuvering armies to block one another as they sought to defend the industrial areas of their individual "heartlands."

If Virginia had been able to retain the loyalty of the entire western region, the Confederacy would have had a relatively easily defended western border on the Ohio River -- well within striking range of the industrial and agricultural centers of the North, Ohio and western Pennsylvania. Raids and campaigns could have been conducted on Union territory rather than in the South and the lukewarm northern democrats may have demanded peace rather than endure combat on their territory.

With the western counties under their control, the Confederacy would have also controlled the primary railroad from the the North's western states that ran to Washington, D.C., and the eastern theater of operations. There were few other communication routes from the west and the Federal supply lines would have been stretched -- perhaps to the breaking point.

The loss of Virginia's western counties had a tremendous impact on the South. The strategic advantages just explained became advantages to the North and there was an equally serious political defeat as the Confederacy's most important state split over the issue of secession. Large numbers of relatively uncommitted young men began to enlist into Federal regiments, men who would under slightly different circumstances have entered the Confederate army with an equal willingness. This political defeat -- the creation of a new state which supported the Federal Government -- produced morale problems for the new Confederate government at a time when it needed to place all of its energy into forming a strong defense.

The loss of West Virginia to the North may not have had a decisive impact on the conduct and the outcome of the Civil War, but this was a very important factor. Politically and strategically significant advantages fell into the lap of Federal planners as Virginia split into two warring segments.

Many of the people who contributed to this book made contributions to their particular war effort that were probably of a small significance -- especially when the activities of the great commanders are considered. These small contributors did, however, see a great deal of the war as it developed and their observations are important to those seeking to understand the impact of the Civil War on the average citizen of the time. Frequently, we find that our ancestors were better educated and far more eloquent than we had given them credit and their stories, letters, and diaries are far more informative than anyone would have anticipated. These are a constant source of interesting observations on the great commanders and the events that they sought to control around them and their narratives frequently explain many previously unknown or misunderstood events that tease the historian as he begins to wish for more.

One of these "teasings" is contained in Sedinger's *Border Rangers* when he tells of the "colored boy" who was serving in an unknown capacity in the Eighth Virginia Cavalry and his courageous swimming of a Tennessee river while under fire to capture a Yankee soldier. Sedinger calls him "one of the colored boys" -- alluding to the presence of more black americans serving in the cavalry regiment. Many historians would be willing to spend a great deal of time in an effort scanning the records of the Eighth Virginia Cavalry for more information on this group of former (or current) slaves who were serving the Confederacy as combat soldiers -- apparently willingly.

The letters of Andrew Barbee mention a diary that he was faithfully keeping. This soldier-physician was an excellent observer and his letters describing the treatment of wounds among the wounded in his care lead us to believe that the missing diary would be a tremendous source of information on the Civil War in the Alleghenies and Confederate hospitals. The recovery of this diary would reveal much about the life of the ordinary soldier that has barely been touched on by other writers.

Another missing diary that would be valuable to historical researchers would be the records kept by Milton W. Humphries. He was an intelligent man who made detailed observations of the events occurring around him during the war. Fortunately, this diary has been recently located in the holdings of the University of Virginia where there is also a typed autobiography of this former Confederate soldier who later became the chairman of the ancient language department at the university.

The brief writings of all these soldiers contain little known information and all of it is associated with the Civil War as it was fought in West Virginia or was fought by West Virginians in other areas. It was an especially cruel war, but it should be remembered. We should also remind ourselves that West Virginians served proudly on **both** sides of the question throughout the four years of the war -- frequently giving their lives for the cause in which they believed.

Index

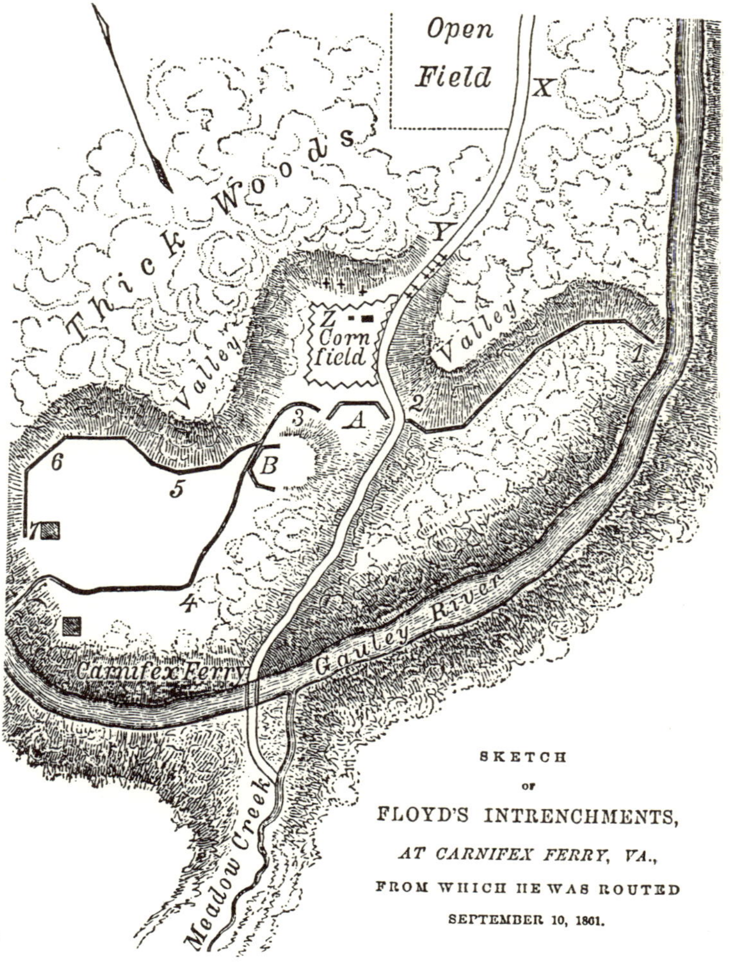

SKETCH

OF

FLOYD'S INTRENCHMENTS,

AT CARNIFEX FERRY, VA.,

FROM WHICH HE WAS ROUTED

SEPTEMBER 10, 1861.

1, 2, 3, 4, Inner Rebel Line.

5, 6, 7, Outer " " on crest of hill, protecting rebel right flank.

A B, Rebel batteries.

A, Rebel main battery, commanding the road.

X Y, Road to Carnifex Ferry.

Y, First position of our guns, consisting of two rifled 6-pounders and four mountain howitzers, against Rebel left.

Z, Second position of our artillery, half of the guns against Rebel main battery.

A, Rebels' strong point, defended by main battery and by flank fire from their right.

1, Rebels' weak point, attacked by Col. Smith with 13th Ohio regiment.

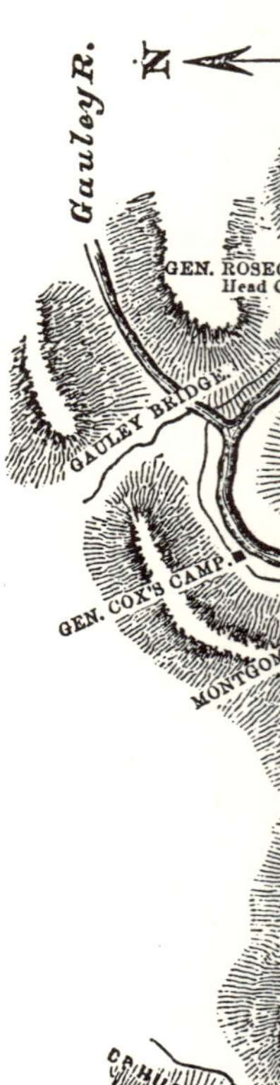